RETHINKING DISPUTES:
THE MEDIATION ALTERNATIVE

Cavendish
Publishing
Limited

RETHINKING DISPUTES:
THE MEDIATION ALTERNATIVE

EDITOR
Julie Macfarlane
Associate Professor of Law
University of Windsor

Cavendish
Publishing
Limited

First published in Great Britain 1997 by Cavendish Publishing Limited, The Glass House, Wharton Street, London WC1X 9PX.

Telephone: 0171-278 8000 Facsimile: 0171-278 8080

Coventry University

Rethinking disputes: the mediation alternative

1. Dispute resolution (Law) – England 2. Mediation – Law and legislation – England

I. Macfarlane, Julie

344.2'079

ISBN 1-85941-151-7

25/3/99

25/3/99

Printed and bound in Great Britain by Biddles Ltd, Guildford and King's Lynn

To the students of the
University of Windsor Mediation Clinic

CONTRIBUTORS

Genevieve Chornenki is the founder of Mediated Solutions Inc, a Canadian dispute resolution company. She was formerly a commercial litigator and is now Chair of the Canadian Bar Association's ADR Section.

Lisa Feld is a partner in the firm of Stitt, Feld, Handy, Houston in Toronto, Canada, which specialises in ADR services and training. She is an active mediator and researcher on ADR policy issues.

Peter Fenn is a lecturer at the University of Manchester Institute of Science and Technology and a chartered surveyor in private practice. He is an experienced mediator and arbitrator in the construction field (for the Royal Institution of Chartered Surveyors and CEDR).

Janine Higgins is a former litigator from London, Ontario, Canada. She now carries on a practice restricted to alternative dispute resolution and is an active mediator and trainer.

Gordon Husk is a mediator and consultant on criminal justice issues. He has worked in the criminal justice system – as a youth worker, prison advocate, counsellor and a family support worker – for the past 20 years. He lives in Waterloo, Ontario, Canada.

Stan Lanyon was formerly Chair of the Labour Relations Board of British Columbia.

Marian Liebmann is currently Projects Advisor with Mediation UK. She is an active mediator and trainer and liaises with government at both a local and national level on mediation issues.

Dr Julie Macfarlane is a law professor at the Faculty of Law, University of Windsor, Ontario, Canada. She teaches, researches and writes in the area of ADR and in particular on mediation. She is also an active mediator.

Professor Karl Mackie is Chief Executive of the Centre for Dispute Resolution (CEDR) in London, England and Special Professor of ADR at the University of Birmingham.

Judith McCormack was formerly Chair of the Ontario Labour Relations Board.

Catherine Morris is the Executive Director of the University of Victoria Institute for Dispute Resolution and a professor in the Faculty of Law.

Michael Noone practises law in Sydney, Australia where he also teaches at Macquarie University. He is an active mediator, particularly in the area of personal injury disputes.

Dianne Saxe heads a Toronto law firm specialising in environmental law. She is an active mediator and researcher.

Alan Sharp is Director of the Coverdale Organisation and an independent training consultant specialising in conflict resolution.

Peter Simm was formerly a Research Associate with the law firm Stitt, Feld, Handy, Houston (Toronto), which specialises in ADR services and training.

Barry Stuart is a criminal court judge in the Territorial Court of the Yukon, Canada. He has pioneered the development of sentencing circles in aboriginal communities.

Janet Walker is Professor of Family Policy and Director of the Relate Centre for Family Studies at the University of Newcastle upon Tyne. She is an active mediator, mediation trainer, and training consultant. She is a member of the Academy of Family Mediators, and the US Association of Family and Conciliation Courts.

PREFACE

Mediation is experiencing phenomenal growth as a dispute resolution mechanism, both inside and outside the court system. The 15 papers in this collection represent the many and varied faces of mediation in the UK, Canada and Australia.

As a consequence of my own links to mediation research and practice in both Canada and the UK, I was eager that the book reflect the burgeoning use of mediation on both sides of the Atlantic and the many common themes, interests and experiences. My goal from the outset was that the papers should reflect the experiences of mediation practitioners – rather than the detached observations of more traditional academic scholarship. I invited leading mediators to write reflectively about their experiences and in particular to describe how mediation was being used to resolve conflicts in their area of practice – whether family, labour, commercial, construction, community, environmental or other. I believed that the most interesting and insightful scholarship on mediation would be firmly rooted in the practice experiences of those entering the field from a wide variety of disciplines and professional backgrounds – academic, therapeutic, legal, community activist and so on.

The resulting collection of papers offers a rich and diverse introduction to the practice of mediation in both familiar, and less familiar, contexts. The core of the book is composed of 10 papers on the practice of mediation in specific areas of conflict. This core is framed by a number of papers that address broader questions and issues in mediation practice. The first paper in the book introduces the reader to the concept and practice of mediation as an alternative to more traditional methods of dispute resolution. Another paper examines emerging ethical issues in mediation practice. Two papers discuss the training of future mediators. The concluding paper considers the future of mediation practice and research.

One of the most rewarding aspects of my task as co-ordinator of this collection has been the opportunity to work with such a diverse group of authors. As a group they represent the many professional and academic backgrounds entering the field of dispute resolution. They include a surveyor, a former probation officer, a family therapist, an educational consultant, a judge, legal practitioners, community workers, and academics. This diversity is reflected in the different approaches taken by the authors to the task of describing their work in conflict resolution. Some of the papers take a highly functional and pragmatic look at mediation in a particular area of practice, while others are more rooted in the theoretical literature. The common ground is that each contributor is not simply talking about mediation – as increasingly, more and more people on both sides of the Atlantic are doing – but describing and evaluating the mediation alternative in light of his or her own experience as a mediator.

There is diversity also in the many models of mediation process described in these papers. Mediation practice varies between the different contexts included in the collection – family conflicts, building construction disputes, personal injury suits, complaints against medical professionals, and even the facing off of victim and offender in criminal proceedings. Each is differentiated by the substantive (legal and non-legal) norms of that area, the needs of the parties, and the manner of referral into mediation, among other variables. The diversity and the flexibility of the processes described is in sharp contrast to the rigorous – and often stultifying – uniformity of the adjudicative process. Peter Fenn, writing about construction disputes, describes the flexibility of mediation and related processes to respond to the circumstances of conflict in each case – which in the construction industry frequently include the need for a speedy resolution and the continuation of highly dependent, on-site relationships. Judith McCormack and Stan Lanyon make a similar point in their account of the development of consensual settlement processes in labour disputes, and demonstrate the adaptability of negotiation, facilitation and mediation principles in resolving workplace conflicts. The flexibility of resolution processes designed, and sometimes redesigned, by the parties themselves allows respect to be paid to important cultural differences and needs; differences that the adjudicative process often overrides in the interests of formal equality. Catherine Morris's paper on ethics and Judge Barry Stuart's paper on sentencing circles draw a clear relationship between the efficacy and legitimacy of dispute resolution processes and their capacity to respect different cultural identities and values.

Consistent with their belief that dispute resolution processes should be responsive to the conditions of conflict, mediators reject the assumption of the litigation model that all cases require the same 'treatment'. Differentiation of dispute type is critical to debates over the use of mediation. Nowhere in this collection is mediation proposed as a panacea. Within each area of conflict, the characteristics of a particular case – including the relationship between the parties, their relative power, what is 'at stake' in the dispute, and the alternatives to a mediated settlement – are relevant in determining whether this particular dispute is suitable for mediation. Michael Noone's discussion of the use of mediation in resolving personal injury disputes describes some of the case-based characteristics that might make mediation an appropriate litigation alternative. Two papers – Dianne Saxe, writing on environmental disputes and dispute resolution and Lisa Feld and Peter Simm's account of the use of mediation to resolve complaints made against physicians in Ontario – specifically address the question of the public interest in an accountable system of dispute resolution, and consider when mediation (essentially a private process) may be an appropriate option for disputes which also have a public interest dimension.

Given the diversity and adaptability of mediation processes, how does the public understand mediation? Janet Walker considers the growing public profile of mediation in the resolution of family disputes – and in particular those involving custody and access issues – and suggests that the proliferation of services, as well as 'turf wars' between professional groups over the provision of mediation services, may cause confusion among a public accustomed to the traditional role played by lawyers. She and others – including Karl Mackie and Catherine Morris – refer to the importance of the upcoming debate over regulatory frameworks for mediation practice. Walker and Mackie also make the point that a critical dimension of the transformation of ad hoc services into effective and credible conflict resolution services will be the development of a more rigorous relationship between theory and practice, in which research and evaluation of existing programs and models can be used to build the 'next stage' of mediation models and processes.

The current emphasis placed on the use of litigation to resolve conflicts in Western societies reflects the dominance of a 'rights culture', seen in both the justice system and public attitudes towards conflict and reconciliation. What are the broader, long-term implications of moving formal responsibility for conflict resolution away from public officials and judges, and into the hands of the disputants themselves? What would be the effect, for example, of supplementing – replacing even – the regulatory structures of public nuisance laws with intervention and mediation by other community members? (described in Marian Liebmann's account of the work of community mediation services in the United Kingdom); or allowing for consensual decision-making between the offender, victim, their families and communities, the Crown and the judge in circle sentencing procedures? (discussed in Barry Stuart's paper on circle sentencing).

All the papers in this collection speculate on the transformative potential of interests-based conflict resolution strategies whether at the level of the community (in Gordon Husk's paper on community mediation and changing values), in the boardroom (in Genevieve Chornenki's paper on business mediation and the substitution of 'power with' for 'power over'), or on the traditional practice of dispute resolution (in Alan Sharpe and Janine Higgins' models for mediation training). Although there are many different visions of what this 'transformation' might mean, a common thread is that in a mediation model 'satisfaction' in the resolution of conflict is more complex than simply the delivering up of a formal verdict which presumes to end the dispute. Instead, 'satisfaction' would be measured by the extent to which the parties can see their needs and interests recognised in the final outcome of the dispute, whether these are financial, emotional, social, relational or something else. The consequences of a mediation alternative are not simply procedural; they imply a transformation in how parties feel about the outcome of their conflict as well as how they may think about the next dispute they face in their personal or professional lives.

I would like to thank all the authors for their patience as we pulled the many strands of this collection together from across the world. I would also like to thank Cathy West, Jo Reddy and Sonny Leong at Cavendish Publishing and Nora Rock and Paul Emond at Emond Montgomery Publishing for their willingness to embrace this somewhat unusual cross-Atlantic project. Finally, thanks to my ever tolerant family who support me in everything I do.

Julie Macfarlane
Windsor
October 1996

CONTENTS

1 THE MEDIATION ALTERNATIVE

Dr JULIE MACFARLANE*

AN ALTERNATIVE TO WHAT?

The legal profession has been extremely successful in creating widespread public reliance on their services to resolve disputes. This success is largely based on an assumption that where a conflict arises between two or more individuals or organisations, the party with the strongest (or best argued) legal claim will emerge as the 'winner' (where 'winner takes all'). So-called 'rights talk' has entered the public culture in Europe and North America in a way unimaginable 100 years ago, and still unknown in parts of the world where there is little access to legal services for ordinary people. Whether it is the legal profession which has spawned the 'rights culture', or whether the growth of professional legal services is in response to it is not is not clear. What is clear is that in the West we are now habituated to evaluate both our position and our prospects in a dispute according to what we imagine, or know, to be our 'rights'. Even in the majority of cases where the conflict is resolved without recourse to either lawyers or the courtroom, dispute resolution strategies are characterised by the language of rights talk, whether moral, legal, political, or economic, or asserting some other basis of 'right'.

Assessing the impact of a rights culture is highly contentious. Civil rights advocates in the 1960s (for example, in the United States, in Northern Ireland) argued passionately for the enshrinement in law of positive rights that would prevent discrimination and end oppression for marginalised groups. In the 1990s, lobbies and interest groups continue to press for changes to the law to protect individual and group rights, and to campaign for change using test cases in the courts. A focus on rights has played a significant part in the transformation of Western political culture from the 'harmony ideology'[1] of feudal societies into 20th century participatory democracies. The creation and assertion of legal rights provide a brake on the arbitrary 'tyranny of the majority' and (although this point is more controversial) have achieved some important advances in the social and political status of those outside the dominant group. However, 30 years on from the birth of the civil rights movement in the United States, there are those who now express scepticism over the achievements of a rights-oriented public culture.

Some of these voices cast doubt on whether a reliance on the framework of legal rights to fight injustice has resulted in the hoped-for advances in public and

*   Associate Professor, Faculty of Law, University of Windsor. With thanks to Christine Chinkin, Richard Moon and Catherine Morris for their comments on earlier drafts of this paper.

1   In which conflict is regarded as a negative force which weakens social structures. See Nader, L, 'Harmony Models and Constructions of Law' in Avurch, K, Black, P and Scimacca, J (eds), *Conflict Resolution: Cross-Cultural Perspectives*, 1991, Greenwood Press; and 'The ADR Explosion: the Implications of Rhetoric in Legal Reform' (1988) 8 *Windsor Yearbook of Access to Justice* 260.

private consciousness and attitudes.[2] While landmark legal standards – in public housing, in immigration rights, in freedoms of speech, association and religion, and protections against discrimination and harassment – have been the consequence of the development of social and political rights, there is an increasing recognition that legal standards cannot in themselves ensure an end to systemic inequalities, or a change in attitudes. Furthermore, legal standards do not guarantee access to realistic solutions that meet the needs of individuals whose lives are ruptured by legal disputes. They may even obstruct access as dispute resolution through the courts becomes increasingly stylised, complex and expensive.

As a consequence, some now propose a rethinking of rights ideology, as both a method of dispute resolution and a definition of social relations, and the development of alternative processes for dealing with conflicts and claims traditionally characterised as being over 'rights'. Such strategies are generally described as offering 'alternatives' since adjudication according to rights remains the dominant (formal) approach to dispute resolution in the West. One such alternative which is now attracting widespread interest is mediation. In mediation it is the needs and interests of the disputing parties, rather than their legal rights alone, which are the focus of the conflict resolution process.[3]

WHAT DO WE UNDERSTAND BY 'MEDIATION'?

The process of mediation aims to facilitate the development of consensual solutions by the disputing parties. The mediation process is overseen by a non-partisan third party, the mediator, whose authority rests on the consent of the parties that she facilitate their negotiations. The mediator has no independent decision-making power, or legitimacy, beyond what the parties voluntarily afford her. In contrast, the adjudicative system looks to an authoritative third party decision-maker, whose appraisal of the rights of each party is binding on the parties. While mediators use many strategies and techniques to encourage the parties to reach an agreement, for example helping to generate so-called 'objective criteria' which both parties recognise as valid,[4] and in some cases assisting them with specific provisions of any settlement arrangement, the final result of a mediated agreement must be legitimised by the informed consent of the parties themselves. The essence of mediation is in

---

2   See for example, Bell, D, *And We Are Not Saved,* 1987, Basic Books; and *Faces at the Bottom of the Well,* 1992, Basic Books.

3   It should not be assumed, however, that mediation is the recent creation of Western culture. It draws on principles of dispute resolution that have long characterised many cultures and societies.

4   'Objective criteria' are standards for determining fairness which are recognised and agreed by the parties to the dispute. These may or may not be the same as legal standards; for example, objective criteria may include recognised 'industry practices'. See also Fisher, R, Ury, W, and Patton, B, *Getting to Yes,* 2nd edn, 1991, Penguin.

effect to be able to create the conditions under which the parties (or on occasion their representatives) will conclude a successful negotiation.[5]

The mediation process can be used in a wide range of conflicts, from family matters to major commercial disputes, which have been traditionally either been adjudicated (by the rich) or unresolved (or 'avoided' in dispute resolution parlance[6]) by the poor. Mediation is being used in disputes of both a private nature (for example, family disputes, business and commercial conflicts, personal injury suits, employment matters, medical care disputes) and also some with a public dimension (for example, environmental disputes, criminal prosecutions, professional disciplinary proceedings). Mediation is sought by parties on a voluntary basis who want to try an alternative to litigation; and sometimes ordered by courts as a result of changing policy in case management procedures.[7]

Mediation is not monolithic. Both mediation processes, and experiences within those processes, differ widely.[8] In theory at least, what is common to mediation as it is used in many different contexts is that the outcome is consensual rather than imposed and the solution fashioned by the parties themselves rather than by a third party.[9] In many cases the consensual nature of the mediation process may be diminished by the reality that a third party (a court) may be asked to impose a decision unless the parties can agree upon one; sometimes described as 'bargaining in the shadow of the law'.[10] Sometimes court-annexed mediation programmes mandate mediation, which for some writers also undermines the consensual character of the process.[11]

Nonetheless, the bargain, if one is reached in mediation, is representative of the agreement of the disputants in a manner which clearly sets mediation apart from traditional adjudicative processes. In some contexts (for example in some family matters) an agreement reached in mediation may be subject to review by a judge. An especially clear example of the retention of institutional authority is in the use of 'circle sentencing' in criminal trials,[12] where any solution proposed by

---

5   For a classic text on the mediation process, see Moore, C, *The Mediation Process: Practical Strategies for Resolving Conflict*, 2nd edn, 1996, Jossey-Bass.

6   See Felstiner, W, 'Avoidance as Dispute Processing: an Elaboration' (1975) 9 *Journal of Law & Society* 695.

7   For example, the court-annexed mediation pilot in the Ontario General Division (16 OR (1994) 3d 481); and the mediation provisions of the Family Law Reform Act 1996 (England and Wales).

8   See McEwen, C, Rogers, N and Mainman, R, 'Bring in the Lawyers: Challenging the Dominant Approaches to Ensuring Fairness in Divorce Mediation' (1995) 79 *Minnesota Law Review* 1317, at 1362.

9   Although in some mediation processes a recommendation may be made by the mediator which can be either accepted or rejected by the parties. A 'pure' model of mediation might nonetheless regard this as overly interventionist.

10   When predictions of legal outcome can both focus and coerce the bargaining process. See Mnookin, R and Kornhauser, C, *Bargaining in the Shadow of the Law: the Case of Divorce* (1979) 88 *Yale Law Journal* 950.

11   See Roberts, S, 'Mediation and the Civil Courts: an Unresolved Relationship' (1993) 56 *Modern Law Review*. Others have observed that mediator 'styles' can sometimes coerce settlement; see Alfini, J 'Trashing, Bashing, and Hashing it Out: Is this the end of "Good Mediation"?' (1991) 19 *Florida State University Law Review* 47.

12   See Stuart, B, 'Making Real Differences' in this collection.

the participants must be endorsed by the judge. However, in other contexts (for example, commercial and business mediations), any agreement reached is entirely a private matter for the parties themselves. Outcomes are not reviewed by any judge or public official and, contractual remedies aside, rely on the goodwill of the parties for their enforcement. Whatever the particular context in which a mediation process is used, however, the design of solutions in mediation is the result of the direct negotiation and input of the parties themselves. As such they reflect consensus and reconciliation rather than a game with winners and losers.

Mediation practitioners are emerging from a range of professional backgrounds including law, social work, psychology and labour relations. As the interest in using mediation grows, so does pressure for the development of formalised systems of training and accreditation for those entering the field as mediators. The diversification of mediation services available into a wide range of delivery models (including private, community and court-annexed), raises many questions about how best to formalise mediation as a dispute resolution mechanism in a manner which ensures that it is genuinely accessible and voluntary.

PUBLIC DISSATISFACTION WITH THE ADJUDICATIVE MODEL

While these and other questions remain about the practice and delivery of mediation services, pressure to explore and develop alternatives to the adjudicative rights model continues to grow. The search for alternatives to courtroom litigation is fed by growing consumer dissatisfaction with traditional legal services. In a recent study in Ontario, almost 60% of the client survey group said that they were either partly or very dissatisfied with the progress and outcome of their case through the civil litigation system. Of their lawyers, 5% said that they thought that clients 'never' received value for money in litigation; even more telling, only a slim majority said that they thought that the client 'usually' received value for money in pursuing litigation.[13] Recent reports indicate that the costs of civil justice in a court administered system have risen sharply over the past two decades, and that lengthy delays are now the norm in civil litigation.[14] Rising levels of litigation and court overload are among the consequence of a rights-orientated public culture.[15] Many legal clients complain of long delays in processing and resolving their dispute and high fee levels. As one client put it,

---

13 Macfarlane, J, *Court-Based Mediation for Civil Cases: an Evaluation of the Ontario Court (General Division) ADR Centre*, 1995, Ontario Ministry of the Attorney-General.

14 See, for example, the work of the *Civil Justice Review: First Report* (1995) (Ontario Court of Justice, Ontario Ministry of the Attorney-General) and *Access to Justice: Final Report to the Lord Chancellor on the Civil Justice System in England and Wales* (1996) (the 'Woolf Report').

15 See Galanter, M, 'Reading the Landscape of Disputes' (1983) 31 *UCLA L Rev* 4.

It's taken so long and we're still waiting. Its taken its toll on myself and my family. Nothing could have prepared us for this.[16]

There are other complaints which add to the pressure to explore alternatives to the traditional model of legal services. Clients often feel left out of the decision-making process by their lawyer.[17] They experience a loss of control when they turn their claim over to a lawyer. It is assumed that the lawyer will provide an authoritative interpretation not only of the law but also of the clients' needs and goals and the appropriate behaviour to achieve these.[18] Many clients are intimidated by the formality of the adjudicative process and feel that they cannot or should not participate. Somehow the burning issue which originally belonged to the disputants, both intellectually and emotionally, becomes detached from them on both levels once it is placed in the hands of the legal system. At this point the client may feel that she has become part of what William Simon describes as 'ritualist advocacy' in which 'the litigants are not the subject of the ceremony, but rather the pretext for it'.[19] Such detachment may be a symptom of the tendency, in a rights-based culture, for the focus of litigation to be transformed from 'an act of wrongdoing' into 'a structural suit'.[20] In the process the original, personal, facts of the case are reconstructed in order that they might 'fit' within the relevant legal rules.

The current interest in mediation is stimulated in part by its potential to facilitate early settlement of a dispute without recourse to the courts. Of course lawyers spend a great deal of their time engaged in efforts to settle cases. However, there is some evidence to suggest that the way in which lawyers characteristically approach the settlement of cases is inefficient, when measured in terms of overall client gains. Settlement is often only seriously addressed at a late stage, resulting in resolution only 'on the courtroom steps'. Although research suggests that most lawyers recognise the expediency of settlement and many (at least in family practice) are effective and 'reasonable' negotiators,[21] there is a tendency to delay negotiation until a court date is approaching and then to negotiate at 'arms-length' and on the basis of legal positions only. As Wayne Brazil puts it, 'the route to resolution can be tortuously indirect and travel over it can be obstructed by emotion, posturing and interpersonal friction'.[22] Brazil is referring not only

---

16 See Macfarlane, J, above at note 13.

17 Simon, W, 'The Ideology of Advocacy: Procedural Justice and Professional Ethics' (1978) *Wisconsin Law Review* 29, at 54 (hereinafter 'Ideology of Advocacy').

18 Silbey, S and Sarat, A, 'Dispute Processing in Law and Legal Scholarship: from Institutional Critique to the Reconstruction of the Juridical Subject' (1989) 66 *Denver University Law Review* 437 at 487 (hereinafter 'Dispute Processing').

19 Simon, W, 'The Ideology of Advocacy' above note 17 at 96.

20 Fiss, O, 'The Forms of Justice' (1979) 93 *Harvard Law Review* 1 at 18.

21 See, for example, Menkel-Meadow, C, 'Lawyer Negotiations: Theories and Realities – What We Learn from Mediators' (1993) 56 *Modern Law Review* 361; and Kressel, K, *The Process of Divorce: How Professionals and Couples Negotiate Settlements*, 1985, Basic Books.

22 Brazil, W, *Settling Civil Suits: Litigators' Views about Appropriate Roles and Effective Techniques for Federal Judges*, 1985, American Bar Association at 44.

to client hostilities; feuding and posturing between lawyers can also and sometimes does impede settlement.

Legal costs mean that in many civil cases[23] legal fees outweigh possible awards of damages by the time the case comes to trial. Early settlement can be both financially and emotionally advantageous to the client. It may also mean that an important relationship can be repaired and maintained, rather than finally ruptured by the trauma of litigation. However, there is little in the conventions of contemporary legal practice to indicate that early settlement of cases assumes the priority for lawyers that it may be for their clients. It has already been noted that lawyers traditionally negotiate with the other side at arms-length (often by correspondence), which means that any negotiation tends to be structured around a series of offers.[24] There is little or no opportunity to 'feel out' the other side and to explore options together. Negotiation often does not take place at all until the lawyer feels that the case has been fully developed with legal research and argument, sometimes six months or more into the file. Unlike mediation (where the parties are almost always required to be present) clients (unless they are experienced business clients) are rarely directly involved in negotiations. Instead they are required to instruct their lawyer regarding the level of settlement that would be acceptable to them. This process inevitably introduces an element of inflexibility and often works to exclude other options which have not been thought about in advance. The client may feel some dissonance between the optimistic advice her lawyer originally gave her regarding 'minimum' acceptable offers, and what she is now being asked to consider following negotiation. She may be unwilling to give up that initial, rosier picture. And most lawyers would usually have to agree that there would be a 'chance' that a trial might produce a better outcome. And so the process continues.[25]

Although between 92% and 98% of legal suits commenced appear to settle before a trial,[26] what is striking is just how long settlement takes in many cases.[27] This may be in part the consequence of the pressure game of litigation, when one side or the other refuses to make a move until the last possible minute. Sometimes it may be the result of inadequate attention to the file by an overstretched lawyer. However, late settlement is also due at least in part to a

---

23   The Civil Litigation Evaluation project (CLEPR) estimated that 22% of plaintiffs who paid their lawyers on an hourly – rather than a contingent – basis paid more in legal fees that they recovered in litigation. See Trubeck, D, Sarat, A, Felstiner, W, Kritzer, H and Grossman, J, 'The Costs of Ordinary Litigation' (1983) 31 *UCLA L Rev* 72, at 112 (hereinafter 'The Costs').

24   Clarke SE, E and McCormick, K, See *Court-Ordered Civil Case Mediation in North Carolina: Court Efficiency and Litigant Satisfaction,* 1995, Institute of Government, University of North Carolina.

25   See also Edwards, H, 'ADR: Panacea or Anathema?' (1986) 99 *HLR* 668, at 670; and Brazil, W, above note 22.

26   'The Costs' above note 23, at 89.

27   See Macfarlane, J, above note 13 especially at part one para 3. This study found that in a control group of 1460 cases proceeding through the Ontario General Division in 1995, cases that settled before trial did so in an average of slightly more than 200 days. Settlement on or just before the day of trial is a commonly recognised phenomenon in many jurisdictions.

preoccupation among lawyers with the development of a 'watertight' legal case based on rights. This assumes that a successful negotiation will depend entirely on the strength of the legal rights–based arguments which can only be fully developed following expensive and time-consuming processes such as discovery. This approach to negotiation, characterised by Fisher and Ury as 'positional bargaining',[28] overlooks other avenues of settlement opportunity, including alternatives to legal remedies which may address underlying client interests and needs (for example, offering an apology; providing a respectable letter of reference to an employee who has been 'let go'; offering the victim in a medical negligence case the opportunity to meet and talk with the doctor concerned).

Because mediation does not depend on the making of a full-blown legal 'case', discussions towards settlement may take place at an earlier stage in the disputing process than rights–based negotiations conventionally occur. This does not mean that expectations based on rights (both moral and legal) do not play a role. Such discussions often (some would say 'usually') take place 'in the shadow of the law' as the parties appraise the types of outcome likely to be imposed by a court; and develop criteria which both sides can accept as fair for reaching an agreement. The important difference is that other types of information – about interests and needs – are disclosed and discussed, and other types of solution – beyond win/lose in a legal framework – are considered. Some interests, for example, the plaintiff's need for the other side to acknowledge his injury in a personal injuries case, are bound in to feelings of 'right'. Determining the parties' interests, *why* they want what they say they want, inevitably includes addressing their perceptions of their rights (both legal and moral), and *why they believe* they should get what they want. Exploring the other sides's interests enables each party to better understand the other's answers to both these questions, and can lead to an agreement which acknowledges 'rights' at some level.

There is however an important distinction here between justifications (in the form of rights–based arguments) and motivations (in the form of disclosures over interests). The focus on interests in mediation changes the way in which a dispute is characterised, analysed and processed. An agreement is unlikely to emerge from a consensual process (in which there is no-one to decide which party is most 'right') unless the discussion can be moved beyond positions stated in rights–based terms, and explore how the conflict arose, the expectations of either side and how these were confounded, and uncover (by disengaging 'rights' from 'remedy') what is critical to each side in seeking a resolution.

Interests are the essence of a mediation alternative to dispute resolution. A focus on interests reflects a complex set of values about how we understand disputes and how best to resolve them. These values can be contrasted with the assumptions underpinning the adjudicative rights model of dispute resolution which dominates formal dispute resolution in North America and Europe. Instead of assuming that conflict must have arisen over incompatible ethical

---

28   Fisher, R, Ury, W and Patton, B, *Getting to Yes*, 2nd edn, 1991, Penguin.

positions, an interests-based approach to dispute resolution challenges the parties to consider whether their conflict is really over the sharing of resources in which they have a common interest; for example money (in fixing the price of goods or services or the amount of compensation), access to markets, or even, more broadly, the sharing of power, authority or control.[29] What may present, at first glance, as conflicts over absolute values or assertions of 'principle', may in fact include or disguise conflicts in which there are a range of acceptable solutions which meet the parties interests in full or in part. Mediation is much more than simply the introduction of a non-partisan third party into disputing contexts; it represents a paradigm shift in how disputants think about the resolution of their conflict. The following case studies explore these differences further.

HOW THE ADJUDICATIVE MODEL RESPONDS TO CONFLICT: A CASE STUDY

A homeowner lives with her partner and their three young children in a small town in the south of England. Her elderly mother, who is widowed, is moving into their home in order that her daughter can better care for her. The family home presently has only one bathroom and the homeowner considers it essential that a second bathroom should be built and installed before her mother moves in. She contracts with a local builder to build on a bathroom extension. This will involve building on to the side of the house and flat roofing the new addition. It is agreed that the work shall be completed by 20 December, to allow her mother to move in before Christmas. Payment is by instalments, with the final payment due on completion.

Work has not progressed as quickly as either the homeowner or the builder had hoped or expected. Bad weather has hampered building work and a supplier was late with some materials. As a consequence the work will not be completed by 20 December. The builder feels that he has made all possible efforts and hopes to be paid at least the instalments now due before Christmas (he needs the cashflow to pay his crew their Christmas bonuses). He is also concerned about future custom if word gets around that this job is not going to be completed on time. The homeowner has some sympathy with the builder – the weather has been appalling this year and the problems with the supplier appear genuine – but she is frustrated and upset that the work is so behind schedule. She does not see why she should be held responsible for the crew's bonuses when they haven't finished her job. Meantime her mother is determined to move in and spend Christmas with her family.

In an adjudicative, rights-based model, any legal advice provided to either the homeowner or the builder would focus on their contractual rights and

---

29   The distinction between conflicts over values and conflicts over resources is made by Aubert, V, 'Competition and Dissensus: two types of conflict and conflict resolution' (1963) 7 *Journal of Conflict Resolution* 26.

responsibilities. For example, is there a penalty clause in the contract which gives the homeowner a right to compensation (or a deduction from the agreed price) in the event of late completion? How extreme, foreseeable, unusual, was the poor weather that delayed building? Could it have been said to 'frustrate' the builder's intention to carry out his contractual responsibilities, thereby relieving him from liability? Does he have a right to demand payment for work done to date? Does the homeowner have the right to fire the builder and hire a new builder who has the resources to complete the job on time?

If this dispute reaches the courts, the case would be decided according to which party has the best legal argument. Is the homeowner's 'right' to have her bathroom constructed as she wished it, when she wished it, and as expressed in the contract between them, stronger than the builder's 'right' not to have to take responsibility for the vagaries of the weather and unreliable suppliers? The court would consider previous cases which might provide precedents. In assessing the 'relevant' facts the judge may throw in a measure of personal bias (which party does she feel most sympathetic towards?) and an intuitive sense of 'justice'. Eventually there would be a winner and a loser, determined by the decision of the judge. In an adjudicative culture, the losing side is not only told that their claims are subordinate to those asserted by the other side; they are told, in effect, that they are invalid.[30] Whatever the outcome, it seems unlikely that the bathroom would be completed either by 20 December or very probably for many months to come. An on-going conflict is unlikely to result in much work in progress.

What then are the arguments for this approach to dispute resolution? The first is the importance for a political democracy of an appeal to rights. Whether viewed as emanating from God,[31] as part of a natural moral order given form by the judiciary,[32] or developed as a consequence of an ongoing process of community dialogue,[33] rights are the articulation of a public and collective consciousness (albeit with varying degrees of participation envisaged for the 'ordinary' person). Such public consciousness is essential to the creation of social justice in which principles of 'right', as articulated by the courts in a common law system, can be asserted by one and all. Similarly the statutory principles developed in the legislature and applied by the courts are said to reflect the public will expressed via their representatives. Thus whether the homeowner or the builder succeeds in winning their dispute will depend (in theory at least) on whose rights are considered preminent in the collective consciousness, as articulated in the law.[34]

---

30 See Eisenberg, M, 'Private Ordering through Negotiation: Dispute-Settlement and Rulemaking' (1976) 89 *HLR* 637, at 644. Exceptions to this are common law principles such as contributory negligence and judicial discretion exercised in the award of costs.

31 The so-called 'natural law' model in which rights are immutable, universal and eternal.

32 A perspective epitomised by Dworkin, R, *Taking Rights Seriously,* 1977, Duckworth.

33 This perspective has been articulated, amongst others, by Martha Minow. See, for example, Minow, M, 'Interpreting Rights: an Essay for Robert Cover' (1987) 90 *Yale LR* 1860.

34 Similarly, any pre-trial negotiations are likely to focus on the assertion of rights-based arguments between their lawyers.

Earlier caselaw can help their argument where a direct or at least close parallel may be drawn between their situation and the 'facts' of another case. The legitimacy of the adjudicative system to which the homeowner and the builder might turn for a resolution of their dispute rests on the assumption that the 'right' identified as preminent by the judge in her decision will reflect previous decisions in similar circumstances, which were themselves an earlier articulation of who had the best claim to 'right'.

In reality, of course, the public may feel that they have little or nothing to do with how judges decide cases (or even how Parliament legislates). But the enforcement of a rights–based model by the courts assumes legitimacy from a mandate to reflect public consciousness. This may flow directly from legislation or from earlier judicial decisions. Both are understood as setting a standard for future decision-making which represents an expression of collective values and in which the public implicitly acquiesces.[35] It is also true that where a court makes an unpopular or controversial decision over 'rights' there will be an ensuing public debate and possibly the redefining of subsequent argument and outcomes.[36] The standards by which a court would decide the dispute between this homeowner and her builder are part of this same tacit agreement between the public and the legal system, however far removed they may appear.

Another important rationalisation for a rights–based adjudicative process is that such a resolution ensures the importance of consistency and equal treatment for all persons. This operates both internally, since the highly formalised rules of civil procedure establish a procedural equality between litigants (leaving aside the matter of the quality of legal advice and representation that can be afforded by the individual litigant); and externally, in the application of precedent cases. If the homeowner is to be able to assert a legal 'right' with any degree of certainty, there needs to be consistency in the outcome of decision–making in similar situations. In this way the homeowner may feel confident that she will be treated no differently, either as a litigant or in asserting the basis of her claim, from any other individual bringing the 'same' or a 'similar' claim. The rule-based model of precedent in a common law system assumes the responsibility for evaluating the degree of likeness between disputes and their history.[37] The principle of consistency is regarded as critical in a democratic society because it requires judges and other adjudicators to be able to justify their positions in the light of

---

35 See Fiss, O, 'Against Settlement' (1984) *Yale LJ* 93.

36 One example is the debate that has followed controversial decisions handing down life sentences to women who have killed their violent partners in the United States, Canada and the UK, and the gradual development in each of these jurisdictions of 'battered women's syndrome' to take account of the circumstances in which these women kill. Note also, the debate that attends controversial jury acquittals such as those in the UK of Clive Ponting (1985), Pat Pottle and Michael Randall (1991) and Ian and Kevin Maxwell (1996).

37 Note the critical and feminist critique of the criteria of 'relevance' for undertaking such an evaluation. See, for example, Mossman, MJ, 'Feminism and Legal Method: the Difference it Makes' (1986) 36 *Australian Journal of Law and Society* 30 especially at 44–45.

legal principles, rather than to assume personal discretion.[38] It is intrinsic to the theory of the rule of law which constrains the arbitrary use of authority.

In the rationalisation and justification of an adjudicative system, the process itself comes to assume a symbolic importance. It is representative of stability and social cohesion. The mystique surrounding the judiciary in an adjudicative system, with judges widely regarded as figures of great social stature and Solomonic wisdom, helps to sustain not only the legitimacy of the common law system on a day-to-day basis but also the continued, often awestruck participation of the public. It is tempting to suggest that the authority of the adjudicative system may in part be sustained by the circularity of the argument that 'they' (judges, lawyers) 'know best'. The trial itself is a ritual of quasi-religious character which provides a public declaration of principle and 'right'. When asked why a case has not settled earlier, an explanation regularly offered by lawyers is that their client 'wanted his/her day in court'. Where this claim is substantively true (and sometimes it may be little more than a rationalisation suggested by the lawyer), it is interesting to ask just why the client might want 'a day in court' when a significant proportion of the proceedings will in fact be either irrelevant to his or her central concerns, or simply incomprehensible. What the client really wants is more likely to be just the very end of the 'day (or days) in court', to hear a judge pronounce authoritatively and with appropriate gravitas that he is the winner.[39] In an adjudicative, rights-based, system a favourable decision by a judge ends the debate; it is a vindication of both the moral and the technical position of the winning side (even if the legal costs cancel out much of the award).

Is this what the homeowner or the builder need or want as the outcome of their dispute? Or does the homeowner simply want her bathroom completed as quickly as possible, while the builder needs a negotiated part-payment to get him through Christmas in funds and with his professional reputation intact?

HOW A MEDIATION MODEL RESPONDS TO CONFLICT: A SECOND LOOK AT THE CASE STUDY

Having considered the cost of legal action in an adjudicative system, the potential for lengthy delays, and the likely loss of personal control, some prospective clients reject the possibility of litigation and instead choose avoidance as their dispute resolution strategy.[40] Others may decide to avoid legalising their conflict in the absence of any legal advice, simply assuming that litigation will be too expensive and generally burdensome, for minimal return. For the homeowner, an avoidance strategy in this case would probably involve making some payment to the builder and making it clear that she expects work to

---

38   Dworkin, R, *Taking Rights Seriously*, 1977, Duckworth.

39   Eisenberg describes this as the 'binary character of adjudication', in which there is always a winner and a loser. Eisenberg above note 30, at 654.

40   See Felstiner, W, 'Avoidance as Dispute Processing: an Elaboration' (1975) 9 *Journal of Law & Society* 695.

resume immediately after Christmas. Somehow they will accommodate her mother in the meantime. For the builder, avoidance may mean being satisfied with no payment until after work restarts following the holiday period; the crew's bonuses will have to be financed by some other means. He must hope that having not insisted on payment that this client will not make her dissatisfaction known to other potential customers.

How would this dispute be processed, and what might the outcome be if, instead of pursuing either a strategy to avoid conflict or a rights-based claim through the courts, the parties decided to try mediation? The parties would first have to agree upon a non-partisan third party, possibly someone with experience of the building industry (but without a current vested interest in either the consumer or the vendor's position), or a lawyer with experience in commercial contracts. As a mediator, the third party is not there to offer a legal opinion. Arguably, she does not need to be legally trained or have legal expertise in the particular area which is the subject of the dispute.[41] However, some familiarity with the alternatives to a negotiated agreement[42] if the case were ultimately to be litigated may help the parties to more realistically assess their settlement options. The third party's first responsibility would be to convene a meeting which would include the parties themselves and their legal representatives (if any).

The next step would be for the parties to agree upon a process that will be followed in mediation. Sometimes mediators require that the parties agree to accept their particular version of the process and 'rules of mediation'. In other cases the parties will be encouraged to determine, or at least acquiesce in, the steps that will follow in the mediation process; for example, how long will the mediation run for, is a follow-up session possible, will private 'caucusing' between the mediator and one or other of the parties take place, what will the confidentiality rules be for caucusing, will the mediator intervene if she feels that the proposed settlement is unfair to one side or the other, will there be access to a judge or legal umpire if dispute over a legal issue threatens to mire the mediation, and so on.

Mediation will generally commence with a face-to-face meeting between the parties, but may proceed making occasional or even frequent use of separate caucus. As a general rule, mediation will only take place in the presence of the individual complainants, who may or may not be accompanied by their legal representatives. Some mediators may be willing to mediate with representatives

---

41 A debate continues over this question which will not be described here. For a range of views and arguments on the question of mediator qualification, see for example, Morris, C and Pirie, A (eds), *Qualifications for Dispute Resolution: Perspectives on the Debate,* 1994, UVic Institute of Dispute Resolution.

42 Sometimes described as the parties' 'BATNA' ('Best Alternative to a Negotiated Agreement') and 'WATNA' ('Worst Alternative to a Negotiated Agreement'). See Fisher, R, Ury, W and Patton, B, *Getting to Yes,* above note 4.

only, but recent practice (for example, in court-annexed programmes[43]) has discouraged this. Thorough exploration of needs and interests is rarely possible without the parties themselves being present. In the absence of the actual disputants, information is inevitably filtered through their representatives' experiences and perceptions[44] and flexibility in regard to settlement options will be diminished.

Beyond the basic requirement that the parties themselves be present, there are many variations in mediation practice. These diverse practices reflect different strands of rationale and justification (and possibly different contexts) for the use of mediation. Bush and Folger[45] describe three distinctive themes to mediation practice: the 'satisfaction story' where the emphasis is on settlement itself; the 'transformative story' where the emphasis is on personal responsibility and empowerment, whether or not settlement is achieved; and the 'social justice story' which considers the primary objective of the mediation process to be the construction of new models of community-based justice. Bush and Folger recognise that most mediation practice is dominated by the objectives of the 'satisfaction story', which produces a practice model centred on the making of agreements which appear fair and balanced. Alternatively, where the mediator is more concerned with the transformative potential of the process itself, there may be less pressure to conclude an actual agreement; and less likelihood of intervention by the mediator if the proposed settlement appears unfair, assuming the informed consent of the parties whose personal evaluation of the settlement is the overriding consideration. Most mediators would recognise their emphasis in one or other of these three models but diversity in practice (and adaptation to contexts and needs) abounds.

Whatever their 'school', it is commonplace for a mediator to begin a session by explaining her role to the parties and saying something about the purpose of mediation, which is to assist the parties in developing their own solutions to their problem. Most mediations then proceed by inviting each party in turn to explain from their own perspective how the conflict that has arisen, without interruption by the other party but possibly with some questions for clarification from the mediator. Often mediators will encourage this narrative account to be presented by the individual complainant him or herself; sometimes it will be presented by the legal representative who has accompanied the party to the mediation. Once both, or if there are more than two, all parties have had an opportunity to put their side of the case, the mediator will begin work on the essence of the mediation process; unravelling the interests and needs of the parties.

---

43 See, for example, the second of two Practice Directions ((1995) 24 OR (3d) 161) which determine procedure at the Ontario Court (General Division) ADR Centre, a court-annexed mediation programme in Ontario. This requires the parties themselves (ie the clients) to be present and even goes so far as to impose fines if they are absent without good reason.

44 See Simon, W, 'Ideology of Advocacy' above note 17, at 53.

45 Baruch Bush, R and Folger, J, *The Promise of Mediation*, 1994, Jossey-Bass, pp 15–28.

HOW DOES MEDIATION CHALLENGE THE ASSUMPTIONS OF THE ADJUDICATIVE MODEL?

In trying to refocus the homeowner and the builder on their needs and interests, and away from the rights each asserts, the mediator would ask each to say more not only about what they hope to achieve as a consequence of mediation, but also *why*. The simple question '*why* do you want that?' is a critical step towards unlocking the needs and motivations which lie behind the outward manifestations of the dispute. A focus on interests, using the question 'why', is a fundamental reframing of the causes of conflict. 'Wants and interests constitute the real motivation for claims while rights are merely justifications'.[46] For example, we would expect that someone who makes us a promise would keep her word. This is our legitimate expectation, both our moral (and possibly legal) right and also what we want. The further question however is why do we want someone to keep their promise to us? Because we need what they promised us? Because it is important to our sense of personal security that we can trust others? Because we want to be able to calculate our reciprocal obligation? These three possible interests all reflect a moral/legal rights analysis but tell us much more (and open up far more possibilities for resolution of the dispute) than simply the objective justification in rights–terms of a claim of hurt feelings.

Such is our absorption of a rights orientation that sometimes the response to the question of 'why?' is simply another, slightly different, assertion of rights. For example:

Mediator (to the homeowner): 'Could you say some more about why you consider it so important for the bathroom to be ready before Christmas?'

Homeowner: 'Well, it's obvious that when I made the arrangement I did with this builder I clearly specified that the bathroom had to be ready before Christmas.'

Experienced mediators are accustomed to this type of response. It asserts the importance, morally as well as legally, of keeping promises. But it still doesn't answer why it was important to the homeowner to have the bathroom constructed in time for Christmas. The mediator will need to continue to ask 'why', going behind the next likely response, 'so that my mother could move in with us', in order to discover what made the Christmas date significant for this family. What are the needs of the elderly parent, what are the needs of the homeowner and her young family, and what is the relationship between the homeowner and her mother, in particular the scope and basis of the homeowner's feelings of responsibility towards her elderly parent? In relation to the builders' interests, the mediator needs to determine his expectations of payment at this stage, what these expectations are based on, what are his particular

---

46   Silbey, S and Sarat, A, 'Dispute Processing' above note 18, at 483.

needs *vis-à-vis* payment (ie his immediate financial obligations, and to whom these are owed), whether there are issues of professional pride at stake here ('I always pay my workers on time' or 'I always get the job done'), how important it is to him to maintain good customer relations with this client and with others in the immediate community to whom she may complain, and so on.

It is critical to the mediation process not only to draw out this information from each of the parties but also for each party to hear the other describe their underlying interests and needs. In a case such as this one, interests and needs may lie close to the surface and may even be relatively uncomplicated. However, even in an apparently uncomplicated case, detailing and clarifying interests and checking any and all assumptions remain important steps in refocusing the parties away from rights, and towards interests.

Other cases will suggest a more complex range of potential interests. Take for example the following case of a landlord/tenant dispute. The tenant is in arrears of rent and the landlord (represented by a management company) is bringing proceedings to evict him. The tenant is alleging (in a counter-claim) that the landlord is in breach of statutory obligations to maintain the property. The relationship between the landlord and the tenant has become increasingly acrimonious over the past few months. The tenant has been organising a tenants group in the building (owned by this landlord) in which he rents his apartment. The management company has been instructed to evict this tenant whom they now regard as a 'trouble maker' (although until six weeks ago he had paid his rent in full and on time).

In the absence of an effort to clarify interests, a number of different assumptions might be made about the interests of the parties in such a dispute, all of them potentially erroneous and thus misleading in analysing and responding to this dispute. A history of tension and friction, as there appears to have been in this case, often further complicates the determination (and communication) of party interests. The tenant may be simply 'playing for time' because he is having financial difficulties and cannot afford to pay rent arrears. These financial difficulties may take many forms (he has lost his job, he has to provide support to a dependent, he has just made a major expenditure which has drained his resources and so on). The tenant may or may not wish to remain in the property. He may be planning to move to another apartment or house and needs the outstanding rent to put down a deposit on that property. Alternatively (or as well), the tenant's grievance over the landlord's failure to maintain the property may be genuine rather than strategic and may reflect expectations about the standard of the property that are different from, or possibly shared by, the landlord. Without clarifying what these expectations might be, it is not possible to know whether there might be any shared or mutual interests. The tenant may be motivated by a desire to publicly shame the landlord in order to vindicate his own failure to pay rent. Alternatively, his motivation may be less personally interested and arise from a conviction that this landlord deserves to be publicly reprimanded for failing to comply with a legal standard. Again, the tenant's interest in counter-claiming for failure to maintain may be to discharge a felt responsibility towards other tenants in the block who are experiencing similar difficulties with maintenance.

The landlord may have any one or more of a range of possible interests in resolving this dispute. The management company may have adopted a policy of pursuing rent arrears at an early stage to ensure that matters do not get 'out of hand'. Either the management company or the landlord may have cash flow problems which have necessitated this policy. The management company may have adopted a general strategy of earlier notification of court action in order to pressurise tenants into contacting them directly and making an arrangement to pay back arrears in instalments; the action can then be dropped. The company does not want to encourage other tenants to fall behind with rent by being 'soft' on arrears. Alternatively or as well, a shortage of rental accommodation would mean that the management would be able to replace tenants easily and will therefore not hesitate to evict for arrears. Again, the landlord may have other plans for this tenant's flat; refurbishment and a rent rise, selling it off, moving in a friend or relative.

How much of this information would have emerged in the course of each side instructing counsel? Some, possibly, but there may be some reluctance on the part of each side to go beyond a description of the 'facts' as they see them. They may simply not be invited by their legal representatives to describe and explain their interests. The lawyer for the management company will probably assume that she 'knows' what their (sole and uncomplicated) goal is (profit maximisation). Where a matter is seen as relatively straightforward in terms of law and procedure (an action to evict for arrears of rent, a counter-claim for failure to maintain the property) the focus is likely to shift rapidly to the legal merits of each side's argument. Where the relationship between the parties has become strained and antagonistic, it is even less likely that information about motivations and interests will be shared with the other side. There is an assumption in the adjudicative model that any disclosure of information, no matter what its nature, will inevitably 'weaken' that side's position.

Lawyers and para-legals working in this area of law rarely ask these types of questions. Where they represent landlords they are often instructed simply to pursue the claims being made through litigation, and even where such information is available it may be afforded little attention unless it is seen as bolstering the legal case (for example, this tenant's case might be strengthened if the landlord could be shown to have plans for the redevelopment of the property). Even where each side does have access to accurate information about the other's interests, the nature of imposed decision-making in the adjudicative system means that this will have no effect on the final outcome, which is placed in the hands of a third party and depends upon a weighing of their respective rights. Addressing interests is unlikely to be a factor in determining outcome, which for practical purposes is limited by the orders available to the judge within the statutory framework. At this point the conflict between landlord and tenant becomes necessarily objectified by the norms of the legal system and as a consequence, 'the needs of the parties, their wishes for the future, cease to be relevant to the solution'.[47]

In contrast, not only uncovering but also disclosing interests and relating them to outcome is the focus of the mediation process. Once information about needs and interests is uncovered and disclosed, the mediator and the parties can begin to explore possible options for settlement. Option generation is a litmus test for settlement; if options are not being generated by the parties themselves, most mediators would assume that further work needs to be done on unravelling interests. If one party is unwilling to explore his needs and interests or to listen to what the other side has to say about her own interests, private caucus between each party and the mediator may be helpful in encouraging further disclosure (at least to the mediator in private) and better listening (often by reminding each party of their WATNA, or 'worst alternative to a negotiated agreement'[48]). The point at which each party is prepared to acknowledge, not sympathise with, the other's needs and interests is characteristically the point at which the mediation moves forward, and options begin to be generated.

Rationalisation and justification of the adjudicative system, for example by tenant advocates fighting for better housing and tenants' rights, is often predicated on the need for standards which can be relied upon to prevent oppressive treatment of weaker parties by the economically powerful. Mediators themselves have raised concerns that the weaker party in mediation may be dominated and coerced into settlement.[49] The retention, development and strengthening of legal standards to protect the weak and the marginalised is critical to a fair and just society. However, not all disputes require the application of such standards in order to meet party needs and address their underlying interests. The law is a blunt instrument which is unable to respond other than in a highly generalised way to the facts of any particular dispute and inevitably characterises it, sometimes inaccurately or incompletely, as a conflict over values or principles rather than, more simply, a dispute over resources: for example, the relationship between rental payments and expenditures on proper maintenance. Legal standards often disguise the complexities and particularities of the conflict, and rest on generalised assumptions about the motivations and needs of the parties.

One final example may serve to illustrate the complexity and diversity of interests that may be present in any one dispute. The managing director of a small manufacturing workshop has recently become subject to new affirmative action laws which require him to develop an employment plan for the next five years that aims to hire at least 5% disabled workers and 15% women and visible minorities. Shortly after the new legislation comes into effect, the managing

---

47   Aubert, V, 'Competition and Dissensus: two types of conflict and conflict resolution' above note 29.

48   See above note 42.

49   See, for example, Alfini, J, 'Trashing, Bashing and Hashing it Out: Is this the End of "Good Mediation"?' (1991) 19 *Florida State University Law Review* 47.

director hires a machine operator who is in a wheelchair. The new employee is a competent worker and discharges his duties effectively. One day the managing director introduces the employee to a visitor he is showing around the plant as 'the fellow we had to hire because of that new equity rubbish the government is forcing down our throats'. The employee has complained about this incident to his union who advises him to bring a discrimination action against his employer.

If the managing director's offensive statement is scrutinised more closely, what possible interests and motivations does it expose? He may be expressing a straightforward bigotry against disabled persons. He may believe that such individuals are not equal to able bodied persons in the workforce. He may believe that the disabled employee cannot be as efficient a worker as an able bodied person (he may believe this even though it is incorrect). Alternatively or as well, he may be motivated by a resentment against government for forcing him to accept intervention in his recruitment practices. This may in turn stem from a dislike for this particular government and its policies. Again, this employer may place a priority on independence and freedom from outside interference, and it is this interest in personal and professional autonomy that fuels his feelings on the matter of employment equity. Alternatively or as well, he may feel a moral indignation that he does not 'need' government to tell him how to hire fairly, and that this regulation is personally insulting.

Whatever the interests lying behind the employer's statement, identifying what these actually are (rather than assuming what they might be) is critical to creating the conditions under which this dispute could be resolved by mutual agreement, rather than by adjudication. The employee may feel that on principle this dispute should be litigated to ensure that any such statement, whatever the reasons which lie behind it, should be proscribed. Statements such as the one made by the managing director arguably raise public imperatives.[50] Cases such as this one, in a similar but more explicit form than the landlord and tenant example, raise the question of whether or not private interest–based resolution is in the public interest where important public standards are compromised. Such an analysis assumes that the conflict rests on a conflict of values (over the worth of one employee over another), and not simply a conflict over resources (who to hire and what priorities to set). In this case, the answer to this question may in turn depend on an examination of the actual factors that led to this statement being made, what motivated it, and its intended effect. If these elements of the conflict can be drawn out in mediation, it will reveal whether there is, or is not, a conflict of values between the employer and the employee. The process may, or may not, enable the parties to understand one another better, for an apology to be made and for the relationship to continue.

---

50   Fiss, O, 'Against Settlement' above note 35.

HOW SHOULD WE EVALUATE 'SUCCESS' IN DISPUTE RESOLUTION PROCESSES?

This chapter has suggested a number of ways in which a mediation model challenges the assumptions of the traditional adjudicative model. Mediation offers an alternative dispute resolution process which differs from adjudication not only in form – who participates, how it is organised and conducted, and so on – but also in orientation and ultimately in substance. Mediation seeks different types of outcome to those available through litigation. These are win/win outcomes rather than win/lose, tailor-made solutions rather than choice between a range of legal orders, and agreements which are complied with as pragmatic solutions rather than because they are necessarily legally binding. It would be naive to assume that 'settlement' is always preferable to adjudication; comparing 'success' between mediation and adjudication is a little like comparing apples and oranges. There are, furthermore, significant methodological difficulties with making comparative judgments between outcomes in cases which are adjudicated versus those that are settled (by mediation or negotiation) since 'matching' cases for the purposes of comparison is beset by so many variables in context and dispute character.[51] This evaluation is further complicated by the wide range of practices within the mediation field itself. Nonetheless, questions about the relative 'value' of mediated settlements inevitably crowd in when alternatives to adjudication are being considered.[52]

The 'success' of the adjudicative model is generally evaluated according to so-called objective criteria which emphasise, variously, cost–efficiency, time–efficiency and the achievement of social justice (sometimes understood somewhat narrowly as stability and order). As a public system, it is held up to public scrutiny via the application of recognisable, valid and reliable indicators of 'success', low cost, speedy resolution, the development of consistent and authoritative jurisprudence (how long is too long to wait for a trial? what is the appropriate balance between legal costs and compensation? has the court developed a consistent line of authority on discrimination issues? tenants rights? tardy builders?). The same types of criteria can and are applied to mediation (how long did it take to resolve the dispute? what did it cost the parties?). Much more complex and elusive are evaluations of the 'quality' of the process and its outcome (was the process 'fair'? was the outcome a 'fair' one?). In relation to mediation these questions are not only conceptually and methodologically complex, but also fit uneasily within the self-determination ethos of mediation. In an interests-based dispute resolution process it is difficult to impose external criteria of quality, especially in relation to outcome, on the disputants.[53] Since participants in mediation do not buy into a

---

51 See Galanter, M and Cahill, M, 'Most Cases Settle: Judicial Promotion and Regulation of Settlement' (1994) 46 *Standford Law Review* 1339 at 1346–50.

52 In England and Wales, see the Woolf Report, above note 14; and in 'Systems of Civil Justice: Taskforce Report' Canadian Bar Association, August 1996.

53 Baruch Bush, R, 'Defining Quality in Dispute Resolution' (1989) 66 *Denver Law Review* 335.

public process claiming to represent collective standards, judgments about whether the outcome was worth the time and effort, or if the result was acceptable and 'fair' (in the light of either legal standards or objective criteria developed by the parties themselves), seem to be for them alone.[54] There are other trade-offs too which become significant if 'success' is evaluated from an individual perspective; for example, is the agreement reached in mediation a long-term solution or is it just a 'quick fix', but one that buys time and some much-needed emotional distance for the parties? (adjudicated outcomes of course often fall short of a final cessation of hostilities or the actual redressing of grievances).

There have been efforts to evaluate the adjudicative system on the basis of client satisfaction rather than the application of external standards.[55] This approach to evaluation comes closer to the types of methodology that are implied by a interests-based model. However, it is important to note that clients asked about their assessment of the adjudicative process are inevitably working within a frame of reference in which they see little or no alternative to either rights-based argument, or avoidance. The win/lose ideology of the 'binary model' is likely to be firmly established in their analysis of their dispute and its appropriate processing and resolution. It is inevitable that our understanding of 'success' in disputing is to some extent predetermined by the assumptions and the values of the dominant dispute resolution system.

This suggests that a broader, more systemic definition of 'success' in dispute resolution would include the impact of our dispute resolution mechanisms on our normative orientation to dealing with conflict, including both the impact of the dispute process on the parties themselves and beyond them on the culture of disputing within society. We can already recognise the reflection of adjudicative values in our habitual characterisation of disputes as arguments over rights, in a reliance upon 'tough' positional bargaining and a fear of disclosure (even of interests) as a sign of weakness in bargaining. Advocates for mediation argue that its greatest potential for 'success' lives in its educative and even transformative character, as it enables people to resolve their conflicts using interests-based bargaining and subsequently to enhance their 'compassionate strength' (strength of self and compassion towards others).[56] Transformation on a personal level, it is argued, can translate into transformation on a societal, or relational level, where social institutions facilitate and support this approach to conflict resolution. If this is true, just how important is it? Is it more or less important than ensuring a system that is publicly accountable to collective standards of social justice?

Questions about how we understand 'success' in conflict resolution are challenging and perplexing even if confined to the context of judicial

---

54   A further practical difficulty lies in gaining access to the substance of privately mediated agreements.

55   See, for example, Lind, A, MacCoun, R, Ebener, P, Felstiner, W, Hensler, D, Resnik, J and Tyler, T, 'In the Eye of the Beholder: Tort Litigants' Evaluation of Their Experiences in the Civil Justice System' (1990) 24 *Law and Society Review* 953.

56   Baruch Bush, R, and Folger, J, *The Promise of Mediation,* above note 45.

adjudication. The evaluation of dispute resolution mechanisms which aim for consensual solutions and take into account interests as well as rights introduces further levels of complexity, diversity and ambiguity into appraising both processes and outcomes. Mediation represents a paradigm shift in the values of disputing process and outcomes and as its use becomes more commonplace in a range of domestic and commercial contexts, the effect on our disputing orientation and values cannot be ignored or overlooked. The emergence of a mediation alternative demands that when conflict occurs we think harder not only about what we want, and why we should have it; but also about what we need to resolve our dispute, and why.

2 MEDIATING PERSONAL INJURIES DISPUTES

MICHAEL NOONE*

THE DAMAGES REMEDY FOR PERSONAL INJURY

In order to be able to assess opportunities for the application of mediation to the resolution of personal injury cases, it is necessary to understand how the common law has defined the remedy for injury and how these claims have been traditionally processed up to and during trial. It is also essential to be aware of important contemporary changes occurring in this area throughout the common law world.

Conventional lawyer's wisdom avers that in all personal injury claims the basic objectives of each side are clear:

*   The *claimant's* ultimate goal in settlement is to have in her hands the largest amount of money possible, whilst conceding the smallest number of deductions from this sum. Claimants are usually forced to accept deductions in recognition of various negative vicissitudes affecting their individual claims. Two important factors tending to reduce the size of lump sums are the accelerated receipt of compensation for a continuing disability, and the fact that a claimant might be shown to have failed to reasonably mitigate his loss. Another factor always bearing upon the size of the settlement figure, is the relative degree of certainty of ultimate success, should the claim be pursued to trial.

*   The *defendant's* and his or her *insurer's* goals are always to minimise the final compensation pay-out and also to ensure, before the file is closed, that the sum paid out, in all the circumstances of the claim, can be justified to the insurance company's directors and shareholders.

At common law, the remedy for personal injury aims high. In theory, damages are intended to fully restore the injured person to his or her pre-accident circumstances, as far as money can achieve this end. Of course, this is an impossible objective. Mere cash in the victim's hand cannot undo the pain and suffering and tragic loss of amenities of life resulting from a serious injury. In many cases, the restoration of lost physical and mental capacities and full psychological health is simply beyond the reach of contemporary medical science. All therapies, surgical interventions and drugs have their limits. Injured persons, unlike damaged goods, cannot always be repaired and in any humane society, it is certainly not acceptable to consign seriously injured accident victims, like badly smashed-up motor vehicles, into the oblivion of a 'written-off' or 'constructive total loss' pigeonhole.

*   Deputy Head of School, School of Law, Macquarie University, Sydney, Australia.

In practical terms, what the common law money remedy of compensatory damages can and does provide of greatest value to the victim, solace in the form of financial security for the term of the disability, which may be the rest of the victim's life. Secondly, it gives access to a range of alternative medical and rehabilitative services. Thirdly, it makes possible the chance of experiencing some more or less costly substitute 'pleasures', to alleviate the general post-accident diminution in enjoyment of life.

Compensation for personal injury at common law is not measured simply by the severity of the injury. Rather, it is the foreseeable consequences of the injury to the particular victim in each case which must be evaluated. It is this insistence upon a full valuing of all aspects of the claimant's loss, both pecuniary and non-pecuniary, on an individual, personal basis, and the consequent need for both sides to consider, and argue about, the combination of positive and negative contingencies uniquely affecting each claim which has made the torts litigation system such a costly and lengthy process. So insistent is the common law upon this elaborate individual assessment of each claim, that what might seem to be a common sense practice of making use of comparable verdicts – that is, of taking into account awards made by other courts in similar cases – is officially frowned upon.[1] Yet, it must be added (and is universally acknowledged amongst personal injury practitioners) that whatever the appeal courts may rule, trial courts will continue to informally inform themselves of relevant comparable verdicts. Despite this practice, it is also frankly acknowledged that awards made in similar cases often appear to lack consistency.

At common law, compensation can only be given in the form of an unconditional, once and for all, lump sum award.[2] This traditional focus upon the final pay-out figure in dollars or pounds, to be received by the claimant as a lump sum, has evoked much criticism. Many law reform reports have castigated the torts system for failing to provide either real financial security to accident victims or any sure entitlement to long-term rehabilitative care.[3] Two Law Lords have also made trenchant criticisms. In *Lim Poh Choo v Camden & Islington Area Health Authority* [1980] AC 174 at 183, Lord Scarman observed:

---

1   In Australia, the appellate courts have firmly placed a ban on trial judges using comparable verdicts: *Planet Fisheries Pty Ltd v La Rosa* (1968) 119 CLR 118; *Moran v McMahon* (1985) 3 NSWLR 700. Past damages awards remain a key reference resource for all pre-trial settlements of claims whether through the mediation process or by other means. A data base of reliable awards is central to the successful reality testing of claims. In England, the Judicial Studies Board has published *Guidelines for the Assessment of General Damages in Personal Injuries Cases* (1992), which gives compensation 'brackets of damages' awarded for different injuries. Commercial publishers in all jurisdictions produce monthly digests of classified personal injury 'comparable verdicts' and some services are now available, continuously updated, via modem 'on line'. For an interesting comparison of the level of personal compensation in different countries, see McIntosh, D and Holmes, M, *Personal Injuries Awards in the EU and EFTA*, 2nd edn, 1994, London: Lloyd's of London Press.

2   *Fitter v Veal* (1701) 12 Mod Rep 542; 88 ER 1506; *Fournier v Canadian National Rly Co* [1927] AC 167; *Todorovic v Waller* (1981) 150 CLR 402, at 412.

3   For example, Woodhouse Report New Zealand, 1967; Gair Report, New Zealand, 1970; Arnold Report, Victoria, 1972; Woodhouse Report Australian, 1974; Minogue Report, Victoria, 1978; Pearson Report, UK, 1978; Bradley Report, Northern Territory, 1979; Sackville Report, New South Wales, 1984; Accident Compensation Scheme Report, New Zealand, 1987.

The course of ... litigation illustrates, with devastating clarity, the insuperable problems implicit in a system of compensation for personal injuries which (unless the parties agree otherwise) can yield only a lump sum assessed by the court at the time of judgment. Sooner or later, and too often later rather than sooner, if the parties do not settle, a court (once liability is admitted or proved) has to make an award of damages. The award, which covers past, present and future injury and loss, must, under our law, be of a lump sum assessed at the conclusion of the legal process. The award is final; it is not susceptible to review as the future unfolds, substituting fact for estimate. Knowledge of the future being denied to mankind, so much of the award as is to be attributed to future loss and suffering (in many cases the major part of the award) will almost surely be wrong. There is really only one certainty: the future will prove the award to be either too high or too low.

In *Paul v Rendall* (1981) 34 ALR 569 at 571–72, in an appeal to the Privy Council from South Australia, Lord Diplock frankly stated that:

The assessment of damages in actions for personal injuries is not a science. A judgment as to what constitutes proper compensation in money terms for pain and suffering or deprivation of amenities of life, can only be intuitive, and the assessment of future economic loss involves a double exercise in the art of prophesying not only what the future holds for the injured plaintiff but also what the future would have held for him if he had not been injured.[4]

Nevertheless, for all this judicial animadversion and the multitude of reform proposals over the past thirty years, plus the patchwork of no-fault statutory schemes and provisions for early or interim payments, periodic payments and 'structured settlements' schemes which now exist,[5] the torts system of damages as the remedy for personal injury has not only survived but continues to prevail throughout most of the common law world.

---

4   The context of this statement, made in the last personal injury appeal from Australia to the Privy Council is interesting. The Australian court had allowed the admission of actuarial evidence to assist a hopefully more realistic, albeit certainly not completely scientific assessment of future loss (note that Canadian and United States courts also routinely admit actuarial evidence). The English courts remain wary of actuarial evidence and continue to assess future economic loss by simply working out a figure (the multiplier) which represented the claimant's present loss of earnings and then taking all the contingencies affecting the particular case into account, find a more or less, intuitive choice of a figure (the multiplier), which is the number of years of expected disability, less an appropriate number, to take account of all contingencies; see *Auty v National Coal Board* [1985] 1 ER 930, but *contra* this attitude, see *Hunt v Severs* [1993] 4 All ER 180 and the Law Reform Commission Report No 224 which has been incorporated into draft legislation in the Damages Bill 1996 (England and Wales). Whether or not actuarial and other economic evidence can be introduced at trial will obviously have a substantial impact on what may be up for discussion at a mediation conference.

5   Compare the Transport Accident Act 1986 (Victoria) a scheme which preserves limited access to the common law, with the Motor Accidents (Compensation) Act 1979 (Northern Territory) a purely non-fault scheme for transport related accidents. In New Zealand, a universal no-fault scheme has replaced the common law action in: Accident Compensation Act 1974 (NZ). *Early or interim payment schemes*. For examples see s 30B Supreme Court Act 1935 (South Australia); s 32A Supreme Court Act 1981 (UK). For examples of schemes for Periodic payments and structured settlements see, s 30B Supreme Court Act 1935 (South Australia); s 16(4) Motor Vehicle (Third Party) Insurance Act 1943 (Western Australia) and s 81 Motor Accidents Act 1988 (NSW).

ALTERNATIVES TO THE LUMP SUM DAMAGES REMEDY

Any discussion of the future prospects for mediation of personal injury disputes must mention the extensive range of alternative personal injury remedial provisions which now exist worldwide in a great number of statutes. The political imperatives informing most of these developments have been overwhelmingly the result of expedient and pragmatic balancing acts. The legislators have been concerned neither to deprive the voters of their cherished right to bring a tort action for recovery of compensation for personal injury, nor to set off a sudden and politically embarrassing rise in the premiums for compulsory third party liability insurance. At the same time it was usually agreed to be absolutely necessary to placate the interests of influential lawyers' groups and the insurance industry lobby in maintaining the status quo of a comfortably profitable personal injury litigation business.

Especially in the areas of transport and work related injury claims, the resulting legislation now greatly modifies the law as it applies throughout the common law world. These statutes generally adopt one of the following strategies. They either bar common law claims outright or impose an election between a statutory or a common law claim; limit the right to sue for damages to cases of 'significant' or 'serious' injury; limit access to particular heads of loss; place a ceiling on recovery of general damages; *and/or* offer a range of alternative remedies and alternative dispute resolution processes.

The most important alternative remedy to the traditional lump sum award is that of periodical payments. Parties in litigation have always been free to agree to a settlement on terms that the defendant will make periodical payments to the claimant, as and when required, for expenses and rehabilitation. These payments are usually made in addition to an initial lump sum payment. As an alternative remedy to the once and for all lump sum, periodical payments make a great deal of sense. An entitlement to such payments answers worries about whether the lump sum will in fact last the distance and cover all the future needs of the victim, and also survive the ravages of inflation.

In *Lim Poh Choo v Camden and Islington Area Health Authority* [1979] 1 QB 352 at 355, Lord Denning MR expressed the view that the interim awards machinery provisions in the rules of court enabled a trial court to award a lump sum on an interim basis and thus might permit the plaintiff to come back for an additional award. However on appeal, the House of Lords held that this was unsound and that such a radical reform would require legislation.[6] However, the English courts have been granted power to award provisional damages when these are sought by the plaintiff and when there is a substantial uncertainty about forecasting the full consequences of the plaintiff's injury.[7]

---

6   [1980] AC 174, at 183.

7   Section 32A Supreme Court Act 1981 (UK), as inserted by s 6 Administration of Justice Act 1982 (UK).

In a mediation conference the possible option of periodical payments as a part of a settlement package might be raised, for example, in a case where an injured child has suffered disfiguring injuries but plastic surgery must be delayed for years; or where the medical reports on both sides agree that the seriousness and disabling effect of an injury is subject to serious doubts which can only be resolved in several years time; or where medical evidence is substantially conflicting about the extent of reduction of the claimant's life expectancy.[8]

The term 'structured settlement' is used to describe agreements reached between the parties about compensation for loss of earning capacity and other future economic loss, whereby, the claimant agrees to accept periodic payments from the defendant for those aspects of loss as actually incurred. In some statutory compensation schemes such structured settlements can be imposed by a court without the consent of the claimant.[9]

Voluntary agreements for periodical payments and structured settlements have not proved popular with claimants. The main reason for this is that in most countries, the taxation laws and social security structures have favoured the acceptance of a lump sum. The lump sum transforms the injured party into an investor. In so far as periodical payments replace lost income, they inevitably attract tax, whereas the lump sum pay out gives the recipient both the opportunity and wherewithal to invest in such a way as to minimise future tax liability on the income coming from the investment of the lump sum.

THE TRADITIONAL PRE-TRIAL SETTLEMENT PROCESS CONTRASTED WITH A MEDIATION ALTERNATIVE

Whatever the major differences are which now exist between the substantive and procedural law of personal injury throughout the Australian states, the United States, the Canadian provinces and the United Kingdom, there is one consistent trend: in all these jurisdictions many personal injury claims are now being brought to pre-trial settlement through the application of mediation. Subject to any statutory prohibitions of alternative dispute resolution, or requirements of official administrative or judicial approval of settlement terms, there is no reason why disputes about entitlement to compensation benefits under the various statutory compensation schemes should not be as amenable to mediation as common law torts claims. In some instances the introduction of statute modified common law compensation systems have already opened up

---

8   Examples of the application of periodical payments schemes to such cases are *Cirjak v Todd* (1977) 17 SASR 316; *Grabowski v Marjchowski* (1978) 19 SASR 290; *Walker v Tugend* (1981) 28 SASR 194.

9   See for example, s 151Q Workers Compensation Act 1987 (NSW). More commonly, such court approved settlements require the consent of the parties; for example, s 81 Motor Accidents Act 1988 (NSW). For a thorough analysis of structured settlements, see, Goldrein, IS and de Haas, MR, *Structured Settlement – A Practical Guide*, 1993, London: Butterworths.

new opportunities for mediation where statutory authorities have supported mediation.[10]

In the torts system, surveys have consistently shown that over 90% of all personal injury claims settle before trial.[11] Prior to the availability of a mediation option, this multitude of pre-trial settlements usually resulted from negotiations between the parties' legal representatives conducted in the shadow of the dominant adversarial litigation culture. The style of negotiation employed was (and is) usually quite adversarial and position based. Such 'arms-length' negotiations are normally conducted solely between the claimant's solicitor and the claims manager of the tortfeasor's insurer and are often completed entirely through correspondence and on the telephone. The injured claimant and the tortfeasor are usually given no invitation or opportunity to take any active, personal role in the negotiations.

Furthermore, in a traditional negotiation process an obvious power imbalance exists, both in economic and psychological terms, between the claimant and the claimant's legal representative's bargaining position, and that of the defendant and his or her insurer. In economic terms, there is an obvious and dramatic contrast between, on the one hand, the claimant, injured and often in debt, frequently unemployed or in sheltered employment as a result of the accident, unable to spread his or her risk and exposed to the danger of financial ruin by way of an adverse decision on liability and costs. The 'payment into court' procedure means that if the defendant makes a payment into court, and at trial the damages awarded do not reach this figure, the claimant will have to pay the costs of both sides from the date of the payment into court.

From a psychological aspect, the claimant is in an even weaker position. Injured, often depressed and facing the dire prospect of a rigorous cross examination should the case proceed to court, claimants are also frequently very fearful of the risky long-term personal and domestic consequences of them not reaching an early negotiated settlement. Broken marriages and litigation neurosis are well established by-products of serious injury. This inherent inequality of bargaining power explains why historically, the typical result of settlement agreements to victims of wrongfully inflicted injury has been under-compensation.

On the other hand, the real defendant in the case, the defendant's insurer, usually a substantial institution, which through its claims officers, loss adjusters, and large data bases is a specialist in dealing with numerous personal injury claims in a detached and objective manner. It is also in the fortunate position of being able to average its risks over all its claims.

---

10   For example, the Motor Accidents Authority and insurers in New South Wales co-operated in setting up a compulsory third party mediation programme with the Australian Commercial Disputes Centre. In the United States and Australia, insurers have co-operated with Law Societies, Bar Associations and court registries in the success of court settlement weeks, where large numbers of personal injury claims are sent to voluntary mediation.

11   Atiyah, PS, *Accidents, Compensation & the Law*, 4th edn, 1987, Peter Cane, pp 256–57; Harris, D, McLean, M, Genn, H, Lloyd-Bostock, S, Fenn, P, Corfield, P and Brittan, Y, *Compensation and Support for Illness and Injury*, 1984, Oxford: Clarendon Press. The Pearson Committee found that 86% of claims were settled without even the need to issue legal proceedings.

This traditional negotiation model has been aptly described as 'zero sum', that is, if the negotiations do achieve settlement, they result in the total winnings for one party minus the total losses of the other party equalling the figure zero. The underlying assumption is of a finite resource, in this case a sum of money, being divided so that one bargainer will emerge as the winner and the other as the loser. The fundamental win/loss ethos represented by the traditional personal injury negotiation model is, of course, quite inimical to the alternative win/win approach presented by mediation model which promotes itself as a collaborative, problem solving process, working towards to a mutually acceptable solution which will satisfy the real needs of all the participants.

Mediation stresses the avoidance of a 'winner takes all' mentality and the advantages to both sides of abandoning adversarial positions in the search for creative solutions. As sometimes advertised, mediation might justly be accused of appearing to be 'too good to be true', raising the expectations to the parties far too high in the context of personal injury negotiations. However, it must be remembered that, in the real world, mediation of personal injury claims is almost always conducted in the context of a litigation in progress, with the remedial options already set by the development of well established heads of loss and the lump sum money remedy. Mediation is a continuation of the parties' negotiations by other means, the other means being the intervention of a third party mediator. By the time a personal injury mediation takes place, there has generally already been some very hard-nosed, confrontational bargaining between the parties. The claimant also has generally been well primed to expect a lump sum settlement and wants this remedy and no other. And, as mentioned above, taxation laws also generally bolster the attractiveness of the lump sum remedy over the alternative of periodical payments.

The phase of transition of a case from traditional adversarial negotiations into a mediation may sometimes prove difficult. One might ask as defendant: 'What are the benefits, if any, to the defence side in participating in mediation when it already enjoys a significant strategic advantage in traditional arms-length, position-based, negotiations?' The answer to this question is, of course, that unassisted, confrontational, negotiations often quickly run into deadlock when defensive positions on each side are not breached by the other side's bluffs or intimidatory tactics. Both sides reach the end of the line. It is either mediation or trial. Of course, with growing knowledge and experience amongst lawyers and insurers about the efficacy of mediation to resolve personal injury disputes which are ready for an intensive session, both sides may willingly attend to thrash out a settlement with the assistance of a trusted mediator, *before* they reach stalemate. However, whatever the state of the pre-mediation negotiations, money in the hand now, rather than long-term rehabilitation needs, can reliably be predicted to be the typical frame of mind of many claimants and their legal team when they emerge from earlier negotiations into the mediation arena. This means, that in practice, at the beginning of a mediation of a personal injury dispute, the parties are often overwhelmingly caught up with concern about the issue of 'how much', what the final settlement figure will be, rather than being focused on a meaningful discussion of the whole case afresh.

The challenge for the mediator is always to reopen the whole case to mutual reappraisal and encourage, from both sides, willingness to permit the emergence of new information. In personal injury mediation, the most important skill for a mediator to develop is the skill of breaking impasses, an ability to turn both sides away from a negative 'digging in' to their pre-mediation negotiating positions.

HOW APPROPRIATE IS MEDIATION FOR PERSONAL INJURY CLAIMS?

WHAT IS IN DISPUTE?

In many personal injury disputes, such as where a pedestrian has been knocked over by a drunken driver on a pedestrian crossing in broad daylight, before witnesses, there will be no active liability issues such as the fault of the tortfeasor or the contributory negligence of the accident victim. The dispute will be solely about quantum. How much compensation should the injured plaintiff receive?

The fact is that although quantum disputes might appear, at first sight, to be about a single issue of the final dollars or pounds figure, in practice this is rarely the case. In nearly all instances, the dispute is mostly about prospective loss rather than past loss and this will inevitably raise numbers of pecuniary and non-pecuniary heads of loss which will have to be disentangled in the mediation process.

In pure 'quantum only' disputes, the 'general damages' component of compensation often emerges as the real problem preventing settlement. There may be difficult problems of possible overlap between the heads of loss, for example future care expenses and future wage loss and diminution in earning capacity. In such cases, the mediator must assist the parties to systematically isolate the issues, to develop options for settlement, which usually involves concessions from both sides, so that they can reach an agreement, which may not be perfect, but which accommodates the interests and needs of both.

SUITABILITY OF CLAIMS FOR MEDIATION

Personal injury claims have often been targeted as being pre-eminently suitable for mediation. This has resulted, in a number of jurisdictions, in different forms of 'court-annexed' mediation procedures being introduced to expedite settlement of cases. Once a personal injury claim is in the court list, the disputants may routinely be referred by the judge of the court directly to the mediator's table. In most jurisdictions, the consent of the parties is required to commence the mediation, but in others, participation is mandatory.[12] This seems to be based upon a belief that while it may be impossible to make the parties agree, it is desirable to push them towards, or even through the mediation process. Whether this is just intended to be for the good of their souls or in the hope of straightening out at least some of the issues for the trial court, is difficult to surmise. It can be strongly argued that underlying these procedural 'reforms' there has been a far too easy assumption of the suitability of the mediation process to all personal injury claims, without any appropriate qualifications or exceptions.

This tendency towards wholesale, indeed sometimes automatic, reference of cases to mediation should be questioned. The advantages and disadvantages of the mediation process to a variety of personal injury disputes should be tested from three viewpoints: the material, the procedural and the psychological.

Mediation proponents stress the safe, 'no risk' characteristics of the mediation process in such statements as, 'it is an entirely voluntary and without prejudice process from start to finish' and, 'either party can withdraw from the mediation table at any time'. Although it is true that parties can never be forced to settle, once a mediation is under way a momentum builds which can place significant pressure upon all the parties to stay with the process all the way through to settlement. Therefore, it must be asked, are there circumstances when persons involved in personal injury disputes should be advised not to permit themselves to be pushed and pressured into mediation or to rush headlong into accepting a proposal from the other side for a mediation conference?

Personal injury claims range from minor abrasions causing merely temporary pain and inconvenience to the permanent loss of a part of the body such as an eye or limb, or the permanent loss of bodily function through paralysis caused by injury to the spinal cord. The injury may temporarily or permanently affect the victim's ability to continue her or his ordinary physical activities and may shorten his or her life expectancy. In some jurisdictions, personal injury has been greatly extended by statute and the courts beyond immediate physical traumas to claims for psychological injury and to illnesses or diseases precipitated by the defendant's failure to provide a safe working environment. Caution in entering mediation should be exercised in the following cases.

Where the injuries have not yet stabilised

It should be remembered that while early settlement is generally desirable, many disabilities take a long time to stabilise before the long-term effects of the injury on the claimant's health and employment is known. Personal injury claimants

---

12 For examples see, Courts Legislation (Mediation and Evaluation) Amendment Act 1994 (New South Wales), which provides that NSW courts may by order refer matters to mediation if the court considers the circumstances appropriate, but only with the parties consent. The courts maintain a panel of independent mediators for this purpose, but the parties may choose to appoint a mediator not on this list. The Courts Legislation Amendment Act 1995 (Queensland), provides for court annexed mediation at the discretion of the Supreme, District and magistrates' courts. When ordered, mediation can be made mandatory and parties are required to attend in person.

only have one opportunity to recover compensation. Once a case is settled in mediation the claimant has no further rights. If the available medical reports are still greatly at variance about the claimant's future prospects, then the case may not yet be ripe for settlement.

Whether or not and how far an injury has stabilised is always a relative question. For many injuries, such as lower back and brain injuries, and in cases of successive injuries, prognosis and causation issues may be very difficult. Doctors on either side may differ markedly (by 10 years or more) on the expectation of life issue. These often remain the key issues still in dispute between the parties some years after the accident. This does not *necessarily* mean that such cases should never go to mediation. Fresh medical reports may cast sufficient new light for a settlement to be achieved or the parties may prefer to attempt through mediation to come up with their own formula for dealing with the vagaries and inconsistencies in the medical reports, rather than leave this difficult decision to a judge or jury.

Another alternative is for the parties to agree to search for agreement on all the other aspects of the claim and refer the issue of further long-term deterioration or amelioration of the injury to a truly independent third party specialist, who is by general repute neither a 'claimant's' nor 'defendant's' witness, and agree to abide by the conclusions of his or her report.

Where further major surgery will be required

If it is clear that at some uncertain point in the future the claimant is probably going to have to risk surgery which might either greatly improve or worsen the disability. As with the issue of injuries not yet having 'settled down', there may be a real lack of guidance about the risk involved in the medical reports and no truly comparable verdicts to consult. Also, the facts may raise the legal question of choice of issue. Is this really a problem of certainty of loss, is it about remoteness of loss, or is it just a simple causation problem? Again, the parties may prefer to work out their own solution through mediation than risk leaving it to a judge to apply what must inevitably be a more or less intuitively arrived at percentage discount for what, in most cases, is rightly characterised as an issue of uncertainty of loss.

Where there is a dispute about the proper treatment for the injury

Difficult issues sometimes arise about whether a certain treatment might or might not greatly improve the claimant's post-accident condition. For example, it may be argued by the defendant that an operation might wholly restore a claimant's earning capacity destroyed by the accident, but the claimant refuses to undergo the surgery. At common law, the claimant has a duty to take reasonable steps to mitigate his or her loss. The defendant's medical specialists might all strongly recommend an operation but the claimant's doctors remain ambivalent. This is an example of an area where different standards have been set by different courts and both sides might prefer the case to go trial.[13] The reason for this is that failure to fulfil the duty to mitigate can have a very dramatic effect on compensation. On the facts just mentioned, a claim for tens of thousands of dollars for loss of earning capacity might be reduced to one of just a few hundred, being the cost of the treatment which should have been undergone by the claimant.

Where the injury is of a catastrophic kind

It must be questioned whether truly catastrophic cases should ever be referred to mediation. 'Catastrophic', here means claims involving very severe disability, such as serious brain damage or quadriplegia. Typically these are cases which result in a total loss of future earning capacity, where the victim nevertheless retains a substantial post accident life expectancy, during which he or she will require constant nursing care. These are the cases which produce record, multi-million dollar awards. In whatever context, when very large amounts of money are involved, it is always wise to consider very carefully the pros and cons of mediation.

A recent case in the New South Wales Supreme Court illustrates problems which might result from too easily sending catastrophic cases for settlement through mediation.[14] David Mundy was three and a half years old when he survived a car accident in October 1986, in which both his mother and sister were killed. David's injuries were severe and included quadriplegia and profound intellectual disablement. When his case eventually came on for trial in 1995 (nine years after the accident), the medical reports indicated that David still had a life expectancy of over 40 years. He could not speak and communicated only by inarticulate sounds. There was no prospect of improvement in his condition, except of a most marginal kind. He attended a special school accompanied by a nurse. The total award in this case was over A$6 million. This included $275,000 for general damages, $677,222 for out of pocket expenses and $140,000 for medical and therapy expenses.

The largest component in the *Mundy* award was for future care ($5,000 per week) over several decades. The most speculative aspect to the award was the valuation of the loss of the future earning capacity of a three and a half year old child. Referring to this component, the trial judge Acting Justice Spender frankly stated:

> How can I assess how David would have developed intellectually, how well he would have done at school, whether he would have gone to university, what kind of career he might have pursued, what interests he might have developed,

---

13   On the issue of mitigation in personal injury claims, the English courts have maintained a more objective 'reasonable person' standard in cases such as *McAuley v London Transport Executive* [1957] 2 Lloyds Rep 500, and *Selvanayagam v University of West Indies* [1983] 1 All ER 824, basing their decision on the consensus of medical opinion. In Australia, a more sympathetic allowance for subjective factors is allowed and such matters as the plaintiff's mental condition, poor education, ethnic background, command of English and prior medical history are taken into account: see *Glavonji v Foster* [1979] VR 536; *Karabatso v Plastex Industries Pty Ltd* [1981] VR 675; *Lorca v Holt's Corrosion Control Pty Ltd* [1981] Qd R 261.

14   *Mundy v Government Insurance Office of New South Wales* (Number 14795 of 1987), Decision given 21 June 1995, unreported.

how well or poorly motivated he might have been, whether he would have pursued a professional career ... or any career at all. Yet, the court must proceed on the judicial fiction that it is capable of assessing a loss of earning capacity to the age of 65 or so, for this young boy. This is task that no man or woman on this planet could wisely discharge.' Noting that David would probably survive into the sixth decade of the 21st century, the judge continued: 'How is the court to look so far ahead into the future with any possibility of understanding the social conditions which will exist, the means of care available for someone such as the plaintiff in 20 or 30 or 40 years time, or the costs of such care? It cannot ... [The court is] ... required to assess the unassessable, to pronounce the unpronounceable, to judge the unjudgable. But that is what I am required by law to do, and what, to the best of my abilities, I will do.

One should ask whether mediation is ever appropriate in cases like *Mundy*. The case shows just how speculative, unscientific and above all, unpredictable is the assessment of damages in such cases. In Australia over the past six years, record damages awards for personal injury jumped ever upwards from A$3 million plus to A$7 million plus figures. These large lump sums have now been surpassed by the astonishing award of A$31.8 million handed down by the NSW Supreme Court on 11 December 1995. The plaintiff was Jon Blake, an actor, who at the age of 23 was rendered quadriplegic and brain damaged in a motor vehicle accident. At the time of the award he was 36 years old with a limited degree of awareness but a life expectancy of at least 20 years. By far the largest component of the award was for the loss of Mr Blake's future earning capacity as a probable international film superstar. Mr Justice Hulme found that at the time of the accident, Mr Blake had a 15% chance of achieving super-stardom and a 35% chance of considerable success.

In *Todorovic v Waller* (1981) 150 CLR 402 at 454, Mr Justice Murphy observed from the Australian High Court Bench that he had detected a pervasive judicial policy of depressing personal injury damages awards. He cited a number of judicial methods of depressing damages awards as a means of keeping personal injuries insurance premiums within tolerable limits.[15] If there ever was such a policy as described by Murphy J, then many courts over the past twenty years, at least in Australia, Canada and the United States, have departed from it and greatly ameliorated the prospects of accident victims achieving reasonable compensation in court, especially in the more serious cases of injury.

What are the reasons for this rapid escalation in lump sum awards at a time of relatively low general levels of inflation? First, the courts have boosted awards by showing much more sensitivity to the needs of individual victims.[16] The judicial

---

15 They were: (a) applying unjustifiably high discount rates; (b) ignoring general increases in wages due not to inflation but to increases in productivity; (c) by miserable awards for pain and suffering for catastrophic injuries; and (d) by declining to implement the direction in compensation to relatives legislation [Lord Campbell's Act] to award damages proportioned to the injury.

16 In Australia, this approach dates back to *Teubner v Humble* (1963) 108 CLR 491, at 507, *per* Windeyer J. 'Any requirement which arises as a consequence, and a not too remote consequence, of the injury can I think be considered ...'.

acknowledgment of the need to allow compensation for the voluntary and gratuitous services provided to the victim by relatives and friends[17] was the real breakthrough in this new approach to personal injury compensation, which has been followed by the recognition of many other novel 'needs' of accident victims. For example, rather than routinely assessing damages on the basis of inevitable, long-term economical institutional care, many courts now acknowledge the advantages of independent living by victims and their reintegration back into society and the legitimacy of claims on the basis of 'live at home' or in shared 'half-way house' accommodation. Thus, expenses incurred in converting the claimant's residence by the installation of ramps, bathroom facilities and air-conditioning are now readily allowed. A further example of this tendency is provided by the Mundy case, just discussed, where the trial judge allowed $30,000 for special music therapy, on evidence that this might assist in developing the victim's awareness and communication skills. Another need now routinely recognised is for ongoing expert advice about investing the lump sum award.[18]

A second reason for common law awards in some jurisdictions now providing much more realistic and fair compensation than in the past has been the ready reception of actuarial evidence.[19] The admission of actuarial evidence permits the best available assessment of the present value of the notional earnings of the claimant to the end of her or his working life.

A third reason for recent jumps in the size of personal injury awards in some jurisdictions is the direct and indirect recognition of the effect of inflation on the award after it reaches the victim's hands. Courts have developed various ways of directly and indirectly addressing the problem of inflation.[20]

This escalation in the size of awards in catastrophic cases might lead well advised claimants in such cases to be doubtful about submitting their claims to mediation. Mediation is most appropriate in a context where it is possible for both parties and the mediator to be in the position to make a fair and objective assessment of the claim as a basis for discussing settlement. Such an objective

---

17 *Donnelly v Joyce* [1974] 1 QB 455; *Griffiths v Kerkemeyer* (1977) 139 CLR 161; *Thornton v Prince George School Board* [1978] 2 SCR 267; *Van Gervan v Fenton* (1992) 175 CLR 327.

18 See for example, *Burford v Allen* (1992) Aust Torts Rep at 81–184 and (1993) Aust Torts Rep at 81–266 (seven year old female – quadriplegia – award of $7.5 million, which included $230,000 for the professional management of the award by two accountants. The award was made on the basis that the victim would live at home until the age of 18 and then in shared accommodation). But see *The Nominal Defendant v Gardikiotis* (1996) Aust Torts Reports at 81–379, where the High Court of Australia held that the cost of fund management is not recoverable as damages unless it is necessitated by disabilities resulting from the defendant's negligence.

19 See above note 4.

20 Inflation is an economic condition in which the volume of purchasing power is constantly running ahead of the output of goods and services, with the result that as incomes and prices rise, the value of money falls. In England the courts indirectly acknowledge inflation in the choice of multipliers based upon rates of interest related to a stable currency. In Australia they use the techniques of taking inflation into account in setting the discount rate and in fixing the date for assessment of damages and in exercising the discretion to award interest. Some North American courts are willing to admit direct evidence of future economic trends.

assessment might be well nigh impossible when past comparative verdicts offer only very limited guidance as to what might be the jump to the next record high award. Also, the positive and negative contingencies applying to the future aspects of economic loss in cases involving child victims like David Mundy are so diverse, that forecasts become close to being wholly speculative.

Where the dispute involves behaviour meriting punishment

Courts have been divided on the question of whether personal injury claims should always be solely about compensation or whether in certain cases, punishment enters the equation in the form of an additional award of exemplary damages. Apart from England, where the House of Lords in *Rookes v Barnard* [1964] AC 1129 greatly restricted the availability of exemplary damages, the trend elsewhere has been towards an extension of exemplary damages to actions involving personal injury, even in situations where the exemplary damages (or civil fine) would not ultimately be paid by the wrongdoer personally but by the compulsory third party insurer[21] and to cases of mere negligence.[22] Exemplary damages have a social purpose, which is to censure and deter anti-social acts. In the context of personal injuries, this may include extreme disregard for another's health or safety. Imposing punishment in the form of a civil fine is essentially a task entrusted by society to the judiciary. Therefore, where the possibility of punishment in the form of a large exemplary award is in issue, the case may not be suitable for mediation.

Despite the reservations expressed above, most personal injury cases are suitable for mediation. It is in the interests of the parties, their solicitors and insurers for claims to be resolved quickly, particularly smaller claims. The results of early settlement are a reduction in emotional trauma for the claimant and a saving of substantial legal costs on both sides. Many times cases are ready and capable of being settled and yet wait in the court list for another two or three years while more expensive medical assessments and experts reports are generated, only for the case to then to be hastily settled outside the court. Far better would be a system for reference of all suitable cases to mediation, backed up by legislation which encouraged early notification to the defendant and insurer of the claim, an efficient assessment of all claims and a positive duty on insurers to attempt by all means, including mediation, to resolve personal injury claims as early as

---

21   *Lamb v Cotogno* (1987) 164 CLR 1 (using a motor vehicle as a weapon to injure the plaintiff – $5,000 exemplary damages). See also the discussion of exemplary damages in *Vorvis v Insurance Corporatio of British Columbia* [1989] 1 SCR 1085 (a claim for breach of contract for damages, *inter alia*, for mental distress, including a claim for exemplary damages).

22   See for example, *Midalco Pty Ltd v Rabenalt* [1989] VR 461 (defendant company employer negligent in not protecting plaintiff employee from high levels of asbestos dust – $250,000 exemplary damages) and *Coloca v BP Aust Ltd* [1992] ACL Rep 135 VIC 4; [1992] 2 VR 441; (1992) Aust Torts Reports at 81–153.

possible. Such legislation should not be overly coercive in setting strict time limits or imposing penalties and must also recognise that some cases do require much more investigation than others.

There is a definite advantage to insurers in settling most claims as early as possible. Interest and investment return on premiums will not, on average, balance out the expense of taking many claims to the courthouse steps. The argument that many insurers deliberately put off settlements in personal injury cases until the last possible moment (in the hope that the condition of injured claimant might improve) is not persuasive. For the large proportion of small and medium sized claims, such a policy would, on any objective assessment, be financially quite counter-productive. The longer a claim remains on an insurer's books, the more expensive it will be to the company in its ultimate resolution.

TWO UNUSUAL CHARACTERISTICS OF PERSONAL INJURY CLAIMS

Personal injury cases share two unusual characteristics, one of which suggests that mediation is indeed a most suitable process: and a second which raises special problems for the process, the parties and sometimes also for the mediator.

The essentially *personal* nature of all personal injury claims

In most societies the possession of physical and mental wholeness is viewed as a personal treasure of inestimable value. The primary characteristic of all personal injury claims is their essentially personal nature. Nothing affects a person so immediately and so much as suffering serious injury. The intensely personal nature of personal injury claims when compared with other legal actions does not diminish their suitability for mediation. On the contrary, it is one of the principal advantages of the application of mediation to personal injury claims that it provides a forum in which the injured claimant may freely express his or her full feelings about the accident and its aftermath. The presence of the claimant, playing an active role in the proceedings and taking advantage of the opportunity to fully ventilate his or her feelings in this way, and informally and directly communicate these deep feelings to the other party, can have a cathartic effect for the claimant and also often clears the air of an emotional overlay which may have hitherto blocked negotiations.

In the rhetoric of mediation, much is made of the positive benefits of the process in empowering persons by allowing them to manage there own disputes and fully participate in the process. In the context of personal injury claims, one must be cautious about such propaganda. This is an area where the claimant is much in need of expert advice at all stages of the negotiations. Yet, as long as the claimant is supported by competent legal advisers and protected by an able mediator from inappropriate cross-examination by defence lawyers, then the procedural and psychological benefits of the claimant's participation in mediation can be quite substantial, without in any way exacerbating any problem of power imbalance between the parties.

Apart from procedural and psychological benefits flowing from the personal participation of the victim, the families of victims of serious injury often have their own economic circumstances, personal lives and relationships deeply affected by the accident. It is one of the chief advantages of the mediation process that it provides an opportunity for parents and spouses of victims to be directly involved. In many cases it is essential for certain members of the victim's family to agree to settlement terms. In such cases they should be present throughout, not just as observers, but as active participants in the mediation.

The absence of the tortfeasor from the mediation table and the insurer's role

Mediation is by definition a process involving face to face interaction between the actors in a drama, yet usually the actual perpetrator (for example, the negligent driver or the employer) will not be present at a personal injury mediation. Nearly all personal injury claims will brought in the context of a compulsory third party motor accident or employee insurance schemes or because of the existence of a personal liability insurance policy, and the defendant's insurer will be the real defendant in attendance, either by the right of subrogation or by express statutory provision. Of course, the attendance of the alleged tortfeasor can be requested by the mediator, but in most instances that person will not volunteer to attend.

The fact that on one side there is a usually inexperienced and personally involved lay claimant, a one time player, facing across the table, a more or less detached insurance company claims manager, who assesses and negotiates personal injury claims for a living, raises obvious problems about inequality of bargaining power in the process. The mediator must be aware of and sensitive to this problem.

The interests of an institutional insurer defendant are clearly not the same as a typical tortfeasor. The insurer views the whole matter in business terms. She or he will be more concerned about averaging the outcome of this claim with many others than with feelings of personal financial ruin, judgment and appeasement which assail flesh and blood defendants. From the point of view of the insurer, perhaps the greatest attraction of mediation is the opportunity it gives to meet the claimant and make a close personal assessment of his or her credibility, what would be the effect of this claimant's evidence if the matter should the case go to trial? Different use of legal representatives is made by claimants and insurers in mediation. The claimant is usually very dependent upon her or his lawyers for advice about offers in settlement. The insurer will be completely *au fait* with personal injury law, language and procedure and although usually employing legal counsel for making the opening statement, will then often join in the negotiating process on an equal standing with the legal representatives.

AN OPTIMUM MEDIATION PROCESS FOR PERSONAL INJURY DISPUTES

Mediation is a voluntary process in which the mediator acts as a catalyst to assist the parties to identify mutually compatible interests and reach settlement in a confidential forum. We must ask: what is most likely to influence the willingness of personal injury disputants and their representatives to participate in such a process? The answer is twofold:

- the availability a good mediation process, which has been specifically developed for the requirements of personal injury disputants; and

- the availability of a trained and impartial mediator, knowledgeable and experienced in the area of personal injury law and the assessment of damages.

Good process is the key to successful mediation. This section describes an optimum mediation process for personal injury disputes. What follows is based directly upon the writer's seven years experience as a mediator and what has been gleaned from participation in debriefing sessions with other mediators. It is intended as a guideline only since it is not possible to be exhaustive on this topic. The mediation process must always remain flexible. The mediator must be ready to adapt the process to what is happening between the parties, on the day, and as the mediation proceeds.

THE MEDIATION PROCESS

In all mediations the parties' main concern is that they be fairly treated both during the mediation session and in the final outcome, whether that is settlement or reference elsewhere. They must feel that they are in a safe and fair environment. This is particularly so of the claimant in a personal injury mediation. She or he must not be made to feel, at any stage or for any reason, excluded or side-lined by the mediator or by the whole professional coterie of mediator, solicitors, barristers and insurer's representatives. In personal injury mediations the claimant will generally be the sole lay person in attendance in an atmosphere of legal exchanges with an inevitable use of the specialist jargon which is prevalent in this area of legal practice.

The mediator should generally resist requests by the lawyers on both sides for a joint 'lawyers only' session. In a very real sense the mediation takes the place of the claimant's 'day in court' and he or she will quickly become alienated if they are excluded from conferences. The mediator shall not easily permit the legal representatives to have private mediator-free sessions. The danger here is of the mediator losing control over the process and getting out of touch with how the mediation is evolving. As the mediation proceeds it takes on a life of its own. To be effective, the mediator must keep track of the changing dynamics and vibrations passing between all the participants from start to finish.

In co-mediation, two mediators are always present in all the sessions, joint and private. This style of mediation is rarely applied outside the area of community and family disputes, although there is no reason why it should not work very well in the context of personal injury claims if both co-mediators are experienced in personal injury law and practice, and have carefully planned the division of labour between them in the various stages of the mediation. There is wisdom in the adage that two heads are better than one, particularly in opportunities taken during the mediation for a brief private discussions between the mediators as to where each of the parties now are in the process, and during the final stages in working on options for settlement. Of course, co-mediation ought not to be attempted unless the co-mediators have a similar approach and style and know each other well enough to feel comfortable in sharing the mediation and creating a positive atmosphere.

THE MEDIATOR

The mediator must inspire the trust and confidence of all the other participants. Above all, this means remaining impartial and neutral from the first contact with the parties right through to the end of the mediation. Maintaining equal treatment of the parties in every respect is essential. This must not only be done but be seen to be done. If one party is contacted before the mediation, then the other party should be contacted at the same time. A party can become particularly aggrieved if the mediator spends a longer time in private conference with another party. Therefore, it is important that the mediator always explains that the need to spend more time with one party than the other is a normal aspect of mediation and in no way affects the mediator's impartiality and neutrality. In practical terms, it is hardly possible to give both sides completely equal treatment.

The mediator must have a good understanding of all the issues which can be involved in personal injury claims. This is not to say either that a very good mediator ignorant of personal injury law is necessarily incapable of conducting a successful mediation nor that all personal injury mediators must be lawyers. However, the common law of personal injury compensation is a complex area, made even more so by the interplay of law and policy in the large number of statutory modifications to the law in some jurisdictions. Of course, the mediator does not act as a judge. She or he never imposes a solution, and nor should the mediator ever offer legal advice to the parties. The need for depth of knowledge in personal injury law is for reasons of effective communication and translation of the discussion to the non-lawyers present, and in order to effectively 'reality test' the claim in the private sessions.

Finally, the mediator must have an ability to maintain control of the process. The mediator must intervene pro-actively to be effective in personal injuries mediation. This type of mediation is rarely a passive experience.

DURATION

Experienced mediators agree that all participants, including the mediator, need to focus upon a realistic but definite time-frame in which to work. The allocated time agreed between the parties for most personal injury mediations which the writer has been involved with has been a one hour preliminary conference, followed within six weeks by an unbroken mediation session of three hours duration. This allocation of time seems, in most instances, to have achieved the desired effect of allowing adequate time for preparation and concentrating all of the participants on the task at hand, without either wholly exhausting or seriously discomforting them. It should be noted that although some of the straightforward personal injury mediations conducted have taken less than one hour for a typical case involving multiple issues, three hours is a minimum advisable time frame.

OPTIMUM VENUE

It must be stressed that in mediation it can be a fatal error to treat the physical venue and logistics as merely incidental and unimportant. Successful mediation depends upon attention to many mundane details. The design of an optimum venue depends upon the subject matter of the dispute, whether it be a community, commercial, family, labour or personal injury matter and how many will be participating at the session. Attention must be given to such matters as the furniture and seating arrangements, who will face whom and at what distances and what angles to each other. Some personal injury mediators always insist on the Arthurian round table to reduce the image of confrontation which comes from parties sitting directly facing each other. However from personal experience and after various experiments, for personal injury mediation (where there will almost always be legal representatives on both sides) it works well to have the parties and their lawyers sitting at a table facing each other, with the mediator at the head of the table.

Figure 1

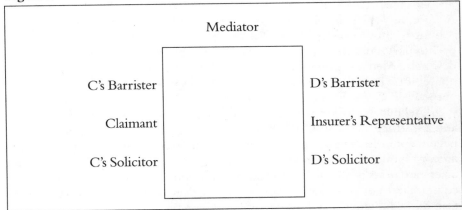

A good arrangement for personal injury mediations

During the initial phases of the mediation, the interactions will mostly be directed up and down the table with the mediator being the focus; gradually, as the parties move further into their negotiations the majority of interactions will shift to being between the parties and their representatives across the table. The mediator needs to learn when to be self-effacing and draw back from the naturally dominant position given by the above arrangement.

Apart from the mediation room, a second soundproof room where private discussions can be held without any fear of being overheard by the other side is an absolute requirement for successful personal injury mediation. Seating arrangements and furniture are not so important here, but for this caucus room, a round table for everyone to sit around would be appropriate. An informal room, with lounge chairs in which to retire for a short coffee or tea break is also helpful. One of the insights of mediation practice is that the physical set-up of rooms and the act of moving from one room to another, changing the environment, can play a positive part in the proceedings. It is surprising how many breakthroughs in the negotiations occur after a short 'recreational' break away from the mediation table. Also, ready access to telephones and a facsimile machine has been known to rescue settlements that needed to be further authorised by persons not present.

STRATEGIES FOR PERSONAL INJURIES MEDIATORS

What follows does not pretend to cover all the permutations presented in a typical personal injuries mediation. The aim is simply to give one mediator's perspective on some practical strategies which might assist an optimum outcome in this context. It is counter-productive to insist upon any series of actions or stages as the only right way. The first and only rule of mediation is flexibility. Good mediation must always seek to retain an element of *extempore* performance.

Preparation

Should the mediator hold a preliminary conference?

As soon as the mediator is approached to intervene in a dispute, the parties' solicitors should be contacted in order to decide whether in this case a preliminary conference, to be held before the main mediation session, is desirable. Mediators should normally advocate holding a short preliminary conference in personal injury disputes as it serves a number of important purposes. Personal injury cases seem prone to settle at or shortly after holding such preliminary conferences. After the opening rounds of demands, pleadings and interlocutory applications, it is a well-established phenomenon that negotiations often wither and the matter becomes moribund until the trial date approaches. Pre-mediation settlement prospects are optimised if the mediator takes care from his or her first contacts with both sides to encourage renewed communications between the legal representatives, and to ensure that both the plaintiff and the defendant insurer attend the preliminary conference in person. If barristers have been briefed they will usually not attend the preliminary conference unless the mediator stresses the importance of attendance by all participants. Preliminary conferences in personal injuries mediation are not merely about procedural matters.

Uses of a preliminary conference

First, a preliminary conference can be invaluable as a means of all the participants meeting each other before the intensive mediation session. It also gives the mediator the opportunity to observe the interpersonal and group dynamics of all the participants. Body language must be closely observed. Such observations will affect the way the mediator sets up the mediation room and where participants will be seated.

In the preliminary conference, the mediator can give an explanation of the mediation process. It is especially important for the claimant to understand from the beginning that mediation is the process of all the participants, including the claimants, and that they should be prepared to contribute personally and not just through their legal representatives. The mediator should explain to all those present what to expect at the mediation and who will attend. Personal injury victims often have a psychological need to confront the tortfeasor and expect to see her or him in person. The mediators should explain why the tortfeasor will usually not be attending the mediation.

The preliminary conference is also helpful for working out with the parties what needs to be done before the mediation session. Often new and up-to-date medical evaluations of the plaintiff's condition by both sides are essential. Sometimes other experts reports are needed, such as an engineer's view of the accident site. Without going too deeply into each side's case, it can be very helpful to get the claimant's solicitor to work on producing figures for the mediation about some aspects of the claim, such as the claimant's future care expenses. The parties may agree to supply the mediator with a jointly prepared summary of issues *not* in dispute. The parties should be asked to exchange all reports and documents with each other before the mediation session. How much time is needed for the preliminary work should also be worked out.

The question of authority to settle also needs to be discussed. Insurers may come to mediations with only a limited authority to settle. Sometimes the interest of a reinsurer in the matter is not disclosed until the parties are drafting a settlement agreement. The claimant may need a close relative to be present at the mediation to agree to any settlement proposal.

If there are formal terms setting out the 'agreement to mediate', this should have been delivered to the parties before the preliminary conference. It should be amended as necessary, and executed by the parties and the mediator.

The mediator's own preparation for the mediation session

The mediator must thoroughly read the medical reports and other materials sent by the parties and attempt to place all the information in a framework for analysis. Working on alternative scenarios for the mediation session, the mediator should try to identify and weight all the possible goals and interests on both sides which may need to be satisfied in any settlement, and consider possible avenues for bargaining and trade-offs which are suggested by the information. This preparatory work is useful to get the mediator's mind working on the case; naturally the mediator must remain at all times disinterested and open-minded about possible outcomes.

At the mediation

How to commence?

The main emphasis at the beginning of a mediation is to continue to build the trust of the parties in the mediator and in the process. Create a positive tone. Tell the parties about the high settlement success rates achieved in personal injury mediation.[23] Remind the participants again what mediation is all about, that it is not just an issues conference or a 'without prejudice' exchange of information and views on the case, but a voluntary and confidential forum for negotiation of a final settlement with the assistance of an impartial mediator. Remind them also that they must respect the fact that the mediator is in control of the process, but that the parties always control the exchanges of information, the style of negotiation (within certain agreed behavioural guidelines) and the ultimate outcome which hopefully will be achievement of their shared, specific objective in coming to mediation, that is, achieving a satisfactory agreement which will settle their dispute once and for all.

Go over the ground rules of behaviour – common courtesy and respect for all – which will apply during the mediation. It is also always helpful before beginning a session to ask the parties to express their commitment to the objectives of working together for settlement, and to acknowledge each others good faith participation in the process.

The parties' opening statements

Generally the claimant's legal representatives will open with a brief account of the circumstances of the accident and the claim, followed by a reply from the defendant. The mediator should always encourage the claimant to make her or his personal contribution at this stage. Personal injury cases are about personal tragedy, the destruction of hopes and enjoyment of an active pain free life. Statements from the injured party often meander and become emotional. However there is great value in allowing the claimant to let off steam. A great deal of the power of mediation to achieve settlements in personal injury claims is the unique opportunity the mediation process provides for the defendant insurer and their legal representatives to appreciate, close-up, just what the impact the

---

23   For example, 70–86% success rates of settlement for personal injury disputes recorded for mediations in NSW, Victorian and Queensland Supreme Court Settlement Weeks.

evidence of the plaintiff will be if the case goes to trial. One mediation, conducted by the writer, concerned an accident in the work-place, and involved complex facts and multiple reports from experts about how the accident might or might not have happened. However, the whole façade of the defence case about causation and contributory negligence collapsed at once in the face of a simple re-enactment of the event by the claimant.

Issue identification & agenda setting

The aim here is to locate and define all the contentious issues so that they can be worked on jointly by all participants. It is the writer's experience that it is usually most important that the mediator take fairly firm control of the proceedings at this stage and assist the parties in isolating the issues in dispute and starting to set an agenda for the rest of the mediation.

During this stage it is particularly important to keep the process moving along. The aim is to help each side get a clear view and appreciation of their own and the other side's overall view of the case. The parties need to be assisted in identifying all the information they will require in order to fully formulate a view about their own and the other side's needs in any final settlement. Therefore, the discussion needs to be kept on track. The mediator should not permit the parties to digress too far and avoid dodging the major issues. A useful tactic to employ is that of diversion to minor issues and then return to the key issues in dispute.

Mediators should listen very closely for underlying causes of conflict and help the parties to understand each others interests and needs by 'reframing' issues in a problem solving format. The mediator's neutral reframing in different words of one party's confrontational statements can often remove much of the pejorative tone or negative content which has prevented the other party from hearing the real issue which must be discussed if a settlement is to be achieved. For example, in a personal injury mediation this might concern the claimant's behaviour at the time of the accident. The defendant's statement might emphasise general lack of credibility in the claimant's prior statement that she or he had ' ... definitely not been drinking prior to the event'. The mediator may need to restate the issue objectively as one of the contributory negligence which both parties coolly need to discuss. The mediator must also always be on the lookout for any emerging common ground in the parties' statements, which needs to be highlighted by appropriate restatement. And, if the parties keep referring to past events, the mediator must redirect the emphasis, by reframing, to how a discussion of these past events must enter into working out a lasting settlement for the future. Reframing is an essential ability which all mediators must develop – its aim being to constantly nudge the parties towards mutual understanding and settlement.

First joint negotiating session

This first joint negotiation session evolves out of the issue identification and agenda setting phase and is aimed at thinking about the range of viable options for settlement.

Once negotiations begin, the main danger to avoid is the legal representatives slipping into their habitual positional bargaining mode. As we have noted, lawyers and insurers in the personal injury litigation business have developed a negotiating culture of tough position based bargaining characterised by an opening demand by the claimant which is optimistically large, accompanied by a minimum level of disclosure of information. The defendant replies with a very pessimistic valuation of the claim. The game then may continue with several incremental concessions, sometimes accompanied by threats to withdraw by the defendant, and bluffing about the strengths of the claimant's case. If this happens then the whole process may quickly descend to a game of offers and counter-offers of lump sums of money. This danger is particularly acute with legal representatives on both sides who are new to mediation but well practised in position based bargaining. Of course position based bargaining can produce settlements – but to continue this confrontationist and polarising style of negotiation into the mediation conference is inimical to the essential consensus building process of working together towards a solution. Holding positions often ends in entrenchment and deadlock. Therefore, the mediator should discourage the parties talking money, in terms of 'global figures', too early on in the mediation process.

It is often helpful to assist the parties at this juncture by providing an overview and even to suggest disclosure of certain obviously key pieces of information. By encouraging such disclosures there can be a gradual development of understanding and increased sharing of interests and issues. Hear both parties' views on the medical evidence, care expenses and positive and negative contingencies. Keep moving from one facet of the claim to another. The main objective to keep in mind in the opening joint negotiation session in a personal injury mediation is simply to keep the negotiation open and moving and getting the parties to really hear each other. How is this assisted? By many means, including, a mix of slow and fast tracking, reframing, the use of silence, and watching and interpreting the participants' body language.

During this phase the mediator must concentrate on obtaining a grasp of all mutually compatible interests and start formulating, in her or his mind, some high and low compensation scenarios on the facts for use in the private sessions.

First private (or caucus) sessions with each side

Occasionally, there is no need for any private or 'caucus' sessions. If the negotiations are making good progress in joint session do not intervene. Mediators need to know when to step back and let the parties get on with it. But mediators must also learn to distinguish between real progress and obfuscation, a skill which develops gradually with experience.

Most personal injury mediations go through several joint and private sessions. The importance of the private sessions in the process cannot be overstated. They permit the mediator to obtain the big picture, a map of the whole dispute, which can then provide the path to settlement. Therefore at the commencement of the first private sessions the mediator should reassure the parties about absolute confidentiality. It is completely safe to give the mediator access to this information and it will not be disclosed to the other side without permission.

It is important for the mediator to be aware of the need for a different approach and response in the private session with each team. In personal injuries disputes the defendant team is likely to be fairly detached, analytical and matter of fact. They are all specialists in the personal injuries industry. The mediator might therefore find it appropriate to mirror this matter of fact attitude when in private session with this team. In contrast, the claimant's team tends to be more emotive and may be genuinely upset about the apparent failure of the other side to hear and appreciate the claimant's plea for adequate compensation. The claimant's legal representatives may also be less experienced and not specialists in personal injury law. Reassurance and empathy from the mediator is therefore quite in place, so long as neutrality is preserved. Building a rapport with both sides is part of the mediator's trade and can lead to the emergence of the real issues and any hidden agendas.

Private sessions are about the mediator simultaneously obtaining new information and at the same time probing the various layers of the dispute in a way not possible in joint sessions. Often both sides will, without any prompting, immediately reveal their range of settlement figures to the mediator at the commencement of the first private sessions. This disclosure of positions and other information to the mediator which cannot (yet) be disclosed to the other side, places the mediator in a powerful position. He or she then knows where the parties truly stand in relation to each other and how wide the gap really is between them.

In private sessions, the mediator should be uninhibited about seeking more information. There is nothing wrong with asking each side such questions as : 'Well, what did you think about what has happened so far in the joint session?' 'This is how I see it ... what do you think? ... have I missed anything?'. 'How do you value the claim?' 'What do you really want?' The mediator might also put questions to test settlement options in the form of 'what if ...' statements, raising possible settlement options. The aim is to let more information, views and perspectives come out. The mediator should feel free to comment objectively on each side's presentations but never in an opinionated or judgmental way; impartiality and neutrality must be preserved.

In this or later private sessions, tougher questions from the mediator might probe and 'reality test' the strengths and weaknesses of each side's case and seek out hidden agendas; issues that have not yet surfaced but which may be crucial to settlement, such as, what are the damages really intended to be used for?

If there has been any hint of animosity between the legal representatives in the joint session these should also be probed by questioning in private sessions. It is not unknown for professional rivalries of the legal representatives to be an underlying current obstructing progress in the negotiations. As the parties move closer to settlement, the private sessions can be used for working on concessions from one side and reciprocal concessions from the other side.

Second joint session & further private and joint sessions (as needed)

This is the time for lateral thinking to assist the parties in generating viable options for settlement. In searching for ways around impasses remember that the self-interest in both parties in achieving settlement is central. Concentrate on any common ground, any progress towards agreement already achieved and the need for further concessions from both sides. Discuss with each side their best and worst alternatives to a negotiated settlement, reminding the parties of all the uncertainties in litigation and in personal injury litigation in particular.

Sometimes the mediator may find it helpful to speak to the participants individually in an attempt to resolve deadlocks or obtain more information which has not been forthcoming in the joint sessions or in the first private 'team' sessions.

Make use of a whiteboard to summarise what has happened to the present. Some people see arguments set out in this way more clearly than they can hear them. The whiteboard is particularly good for opening up multi-issues for discussion and for moving around the issues quickly with a brainstorming session. The following is an example of the use of a whiteboard in the final stage of a mediation. It shows how a summary of all the pecuniary and non-pecuniary aspects of a claim can be summarised. Points of agreement and disagreement and possible options for settlement can be written on the board. The parties can then be invited to write in their estimates.

Often when the whole matter is presented visually in this way, the participants will start attacking the problems preventing settlement This may lead them to suggest trade-offs between, say, the contributory negligence or mitigation issue and the amount claimed for future economic loss. Problems about interest on past and future components of the claim can also be brought into the bargaining arena. Provisional figures can be put up to see how they effect other components in the claim. By expanding the issues being discussed, there is more room given for the parties to manoeuvre and to create their own co-operative solutions.

Figure 2

Example of the use of a whiteboard in personal injuries mediation

	Claimant's estimates			Defendant's estimates		
General damages	$	to	$	$	to	$ .....
Less for contingencies	$	to	$	$	to	$ .....
Balance	$	to	$	$	to	$ ....
Out of pocket expenses	$	to	$	$	to	$ .....
Past loss of earnings	$	to	$	$	to	$ .....
Past receipt of voluntary services	$	to	$	$	to	$ .....
Future receipt of voluntary services	$	to	$	$	to	$ .....
Future medicals & pharmaceuticals	$	to	$	$	to	$ .....
Future economic loss	$	to	$	$	to	$ .....
Past costs	$	to	$	$	to	$ .....
Total	$	to	$	$	to	$ .....
Any discount for 'other factors'?	% to %			% to %		
Any additions for 'other factors?	$ ..... to $			$ ..... to $		
GROSS COMPENSATION FIGURE	$			$		

Amounts to be deducted

Unpaid medical expenses $ ....

Social security and workers' compensation paybacks $ ....

Solicitor's professional costs & disbursements $ ....

Unpaid specialists and experts reports $ ....

To give NET [clear to Claimant] the sum of : $ ....

Other factors: Causation   Interest?

Assumption of risk?   Costs?

Contributory negligence?

Mitigation of loss?

Remoteness of loss?

Certainty of loss?

Special needs of claimant?

As the parties move closer to settlement, private sessions can be used for working on further concessions from each side. Eventually there is usually a series of exchanges of offers which leads either to the parties working out a formula for agreement, or finally agreeing to disagree. Even where agreement is not reached (the so called 'failed mediation'), this does not mean that the mediation has been unsuccessful. It will at the very least almost certainly have achieved a better understanding on both sides of the real concerns and needs of the other side. It will also almost certainly have achieved a narrowing of the issues in dispute, and this will save time and costs if the case eventually goes on to trial.

In other cases short of final settlement it may be possible for the parties, with the help of the mediator, to negotiate a partial admission of liability and on this basis obtain an undertaking from the insurer to commence making payments for the continuing medical and rehabilitation expenses of the claimant as they occur.

Working out the details of settlement

After the parties reach a final formula for settlement, it is important that the claimant is clear about what this will produce as net amount in her or his hands at the end of the day. Costs issues, the difference between solicitor/party and party/party costs as part of the settlement agreement, often need to be explained to the claimant.

The memorandum of agreement

One of the principal maxims of mediation is, 'if the parties agree, get the agreement down on paper and get them to sign it before they leave the room'. In most personal injury cases a very simple memorandum usually suffices. For example:

Figure 3

Memorandum of Agreement

In the matter: $X v Y$

- Settled for : $ or £ .... inclusive of costs [or not inclusive of costs].
- Plaintiff to forthwith file Notice of Discontinuance at the [COURT REGISTRY].
- Parties on or before [DATE] to execute a Deed of Release with confidentiality clause.
- Note of any special term(s) agreed about the payment of particular outstanding accounts.
- Note of any special term(s) agreed about the waiver of outstanding costs.

Signed ....

      Plaintiff or Plaintiff's Solicitor   Defendant or Defendant's Solicitor

---

It is usually best for the mediator to ask the lawyers on both sides to work out the actual wording of the memorandum themselves. However in the interests of finality, if the lawyers do not include the terms about filing the notice of discontinuance and set a definite time limit for the execution of a formal deed of release, then it is appropriate for the mediator to suggest the addition of these provisions in the memorandum.

CONCLUSIONS AND RECOMMENDATIONS

CONCLUSIONS

Mediation is an appropriate process for the efficient and economic resolution of most personal injury disputes.

Personal injury mediation works fairly and well when the injury has settled down, when both parties have up to date medical reports and provided all the necessary preliminary work has been put in by both sides on all the economic and non-economic heads of loss. Statistics show success rates of above 70% as typical for personal injuries mediation. An especially effective method for personal injury claims is the use in mediation of a private session or caucus to 'reality test' both sides' lump sum 'range of settlement' assumptions and expectations. Parties are free in a mediation to mould their own remedy in terms, such as periodical payments, which cannot be obtained from a court.

Inequality of bargaining power and structural imbalances still exist between victims and insurers but in mediation this problem is redressed greatly by the protection provided by the mediator. The mediator can control and moderate the negotiations and reduce the opportunity and temptation on the part of the stronger party to indulge in opportunistic behaviour to the detriment of the weaker party.

There should be frank recognition that not all personal injury claims are necessarily appropriate for mediation. Some cases should be permitted and encouraged to go to trial. In particular, this applies to those catastrophic cases which involve very large general damages and future economic loss aspects.

From the insurer's point of view, mediation gives a chance for the insurer to appreciate what the impact of the plaintiff's evidence is likely to be and how the claimant will appear to the judge if the matter goes on to trial. The insurer also benefits from the chance to discuss the matter on a personal, one to one, basis with the claimant. Insurer's representatives are also human and can sometimes be influenced to rethink their pre-mediation view of the claim by the experience of hearing the claimant. There is no convincing evidence to suggest that insurers prefer to drag-out claims in order to obtain investment income from premiums on the short term money market. Both claimants and insurers can achieve big savings in costs, time and emotional stress in seeking settlement through mediation.

RECOMMENDATIONS

- Mediation should play a key role as a specialist process in a fully integrated system of compensation for personal injury. Mediation sometimes appeals to government because it seems to offer a cheap and quick fix for serious intractable problems such as exist in the excessive costs and delays involved in litigating. Mediation also fits in well with much existing policy encouraging the out-of-court settlement of disputes. It is important that personal injury mediation services are properly funded and mediators properly trained.

- Mediation of personal injury claims should be a voluntary option. Although one can argue that 'coercion into mediation' is distinct from 'coercion in mediation', any hint of coercion changes the whole complexion of the process. For the parties, mandatory mediation is likely to be seen either as unfair pressure to settle or simply as a hurdle to overcome on the way to trial. This does not mean that it is inappropriate for courts and legislatures to provide positive incentives to parties, particularly insurers, to go to mediation, but mandatory mediation of personal injury claims is inappropriate.

- Personal injuries mediation should remain non-institutionalised. This is an option best provided by independent, private mediators and mediation service organisations and not as a part of official court administrative structures.

- Mediation may not test some personal injury claims as well as the other alternative methods such as expert appraisal, mini-trial or arbitration. Other options to both litigation and mediation should remain available.

- Mediation of personal injury claims would work better if there were more real remedial options to consider, particularly if periodic payments and structured settlements were more attractive options to claimants. This could be achieved by legislation modifying the taxation disincentives which presently influence claimants towards the lump sum.

Some issues in personal injury law deserve and need exposure in the courts and should not always be resolved in a privatised, confidential process providing individualised settlements. Mediation, particularly quasi-mandatory mediation, has a great potential for defusing and de-politicising a range of economic and social issues which arise from the use of injury and death-causing motor vehicles and industrial plant. Should the law of personal injury have any preventative role? Have the public any interest in the outcome of these essentially private disputes? What about cases involving behaviour going beyond the issue of compensation to the need to deter anti-social activities? These are some of the larger issues which should be kept in mind in developing mediation alternatives.

3 FAMILY MEDIATION

JANET WALKER*

> As a judge, I have presided over a great many cases and I have seen how people
> tear themselves apart, wasting their resources, their money and their time,
> breaking their hearts fighting over things that really need not be fought over.
> (Mr Justice Allen Linden: President of the Law Reform Commission of Canada
> 1990).[1]

The relative merits of family mediation, typically contrasted with 'traditional'
adversarial approaches to the resolution of matrimonial disputes, have been
variously exalted, embraced and challenged in many countries since the mid
1970s. There has been particularly vigorous debate in England and Wales,
characterised by high levels of enthusiasm from some, and equally high levels of
scepticism from others. These discordant positions have been sharpened
considerably in the past two to three years following the government's decision
to put mediation at the heart of its proposals for divorce reform, enshrined in the
Family Law Bill 1995[2] and now the Family Law Act 1996. For the first time in
England and Wales, family mediation has found favour with policymakers, but
the struggle for universal acceptance and wider professional respect is far from
played out despite considerable recognition of mediation within the divorce
process in other jurisdictions, including Canada. In part, this is due to the
somewhat chequered history of family mediation in England, and the
consequent variations in practices and processes; and also to deep and pervasive
concerns about the increase in the numbers of couples divorcing, and widely
conflicting views as to the appropriate role of law in responding to them.

An understanding of the contemporary issues surrounding the practice of family
mediation in England must be informed by both sets of factors. In exploring
them, and contrasting them wherever possible with experience elsewhere,
particularly in Canada, some of the challenges and opportunities for the future
of mediation in resolving family disputes in a wide variety of jurisdictions are
highlighted. There is little doubt that the ongoing programme of reforms in the
family justice system in England heralds new approaches to family matters, and
that the future of family mediation here and elsewhere is likely to be determined
by its ability to dislodge and disarm its critics, and to realise the claims made for
it by its advocates.

*   Professor of Family Policy and Director of the Relate Centre for Family Studies at the University of
     Newcastle upon Tyne.
1   Linden, A, 'The Broader Issues: ADR and the Legal System', in Tannis, M (ed), *A Tribute to Conflict
     Resolution Day of Ottawa-Carleton*, 1990, North York, Ontario: Captus Press.
2   Lord Chancellor's Department, *Looking to the Future: Mediation and the Ground for Divorce: The
     Government's Proposals*, 1995, London: HMSO.

A DIVORCE REVOLUTION

Unlike any other area of dispute to which mediation has been applied, discussion about the resolution of matrimonial disputes requires us to address an issue which is imbued with personal, moral and religious values. While disputes within industry, commerce and the community are regarded as an almost inevitable fact of life, those which arise within families, and particularly those which emerge during the process of divorce, are viewed as an indication of 'failure' in interpersonal relationships which it ought to be possible to avoid. Thus dispute resolution mechanisms are frequently expected to address the underlying social issues as well as settle the emergent disputes. Even the language used – marriage *breakdown* – symbolises the sense of disaster and disappointment surrounding the dissolution of the marriage contract. Not surprisingly, then, debates about marriage, divorce and family mediation evoke emotionally-charged responses, fuelled by statistics which many regard as worrying, if not shocking.

Although the majority of people get married some time during their lives, the numbers have been falling steadily for the past 20 years. In both England and Canada marriage rates peaked in the early 1970s and then decreased by about 50% between 1971 and 1993. Falling marriage rates have been accompanied by rising divorce rates. The rather rapid increase began in most Western societies in the early 1960s. Over the following two decades, the rates of divorce doubled in Canada and in England, and new legislation in these countries and in other Western post-industrial nations was introduced in response to these dramatic shifts in patterns of marriage formation and dissolution.[3] The provisions within the reforms vary widely, but underpinning most of them have been two primary objectives: firstly, to buttress marriage, and to save 'saveable' marriages wherever possible; and secondly, to dissolve those marriages which have irretrievably broken down with the minimum of humiliation, bitterness and conflict. Some jurisdictions, notably those in Australia, New Zealand and many states in the USA, have embraced family mediation as central to achieving these objectives, while others, including Canada and the United Kingdom, have been more cautious. Nevertheless, the 1985 Divorce Act in Canada placed a duty on every lawyer acting in a divorce case to inform the client of 'mediation facilities known to him or her that might be able to assist the spouses in negotiating matters that may be the subject of a support order or custody order'. In this respect, the United Kingdom finds itself trailing much further behind in the legislative embrace of mediation.

The pace of change in contemporary society has had unparalleled impact on family life. The shift from a marriage relationship based primarily on women's economic dependence on men and the procreation of children, to one in which mutual fulfilment and companionship are essential ingredients has significantly shaped the expectations of young people and extended the options available to

---

3   Walker, J and Hornick, J, *Communication in Marriage and Divorce*, 1996, London: BT Forum.

them. Although there appear to be greater freedoms in the ways in which personal relationships are conducted, nevertheless in 'England's green and pleasant land' 'traditional' views of marriage abound and divorce continues to be perceived as an undesirable blot on the landscape.[4] Little public sympathy is accorded to divorcing families, but rather they are held responsible for the breakdown of family life and for rocking the very foundations of society. Concerns that the social fabric is disintegrating have boosted claims from moral reformers that we must call a halt to the apparent widespread disregard of marriage vows and invest more in saving marriages than in assisting couples to separate. Indeed, there are those who believe that divorce legislation itself is largely responsible for the increasing incidence of marriage breakdown, so that the remedy, for them at least, is to be found in making divorce legally 'harder'. Mediation is seen as inimical to such an objective and its credentials are, therefore, further challenged.

Since the 16th century, family life in England has centred on the marriage relationship: progressively, the family became the symbol of stability and societal well-being. So called 'traditional' family values have extensive currency still, but the far reaching changes in family life in the second half of the 20th century have made it impossible to ignore the deep unhappiness experienced by growing numbers of couples and the fact that some 25% of children under 16 now experience their parents' divorce. Since most divorced people enter new relationships, often fairly quickly, a third of all marriages each year are remarriages for one or both partners: sadly these marriages have an even lower chance of survival. While such trends indicate to some social commentators that marriage is being increasingly viewed as a disposable commodity, part of a throw-away society, experts are in considerable agreement that explanations for these apparent 'failures' in modern marriage are to be found in broader social, structural and cultural factors which include the greater participation of women in the workforce, smaller family size, growing secularisation, and a greater tolerance of a variety of living arrangements. Whatever the reasons for the changes we are experiencing, however, there is little doubt that divorce has become uncomfortably central to the daily lives of many people, and it has been all too easy to associate it with some of our more pressing social problems including juvenile delinquency, child abuse, family violence, poverty and unemployment. These problems are not new, of course, the links are far from straightforward, and causal connections are problematic. Nevertheless, the social and economic consequences of marriage breakdown are worrisome and have served to encourage the search for alternative ways of managing the divorce process, and, if possible, reversing it.

---

4   Walker, J, 'Family Mediation in England: Strategies for Gaining Acceptance' (1991) *Mediation Quarterly* Vol 8, No 4, at 253–65.

BREAKING NEW GROUND

It is widely recognised amongst professionals and researchers that marriage breakdown is rarely easy, and almost always painful and distressing. However well managed, divorce normally results in intense feelings of grief, sadness, rejection, anger, bitterness, hostility and an overwhelming sense of loss. It has been described as the second most stressful life event for adults after the death of a spouse.[5] As personal and social networks disintegrate and financial pressures bite, resentment increases, communication is further strained, and conflict flourishes.[6] These are just the kinds of conditions which undermine parenting abilities and cause the greatest difficulties for children. Of course, the main concern in most countries is, almost certainly, the potentially detrimental impact of divorce on children. There is widespread agreement that the breakdown of a human relationship can never be an intrinsically good thing (The Lord Bishop of Birmingham, *Hansard*, 30 November 1995).

A growing body of research has shown that the separation and divorce of parents, far from being a single, discrete event in the lives of children, is a process which usually begins years before the divorce, and has repercussions that reverberate into adulthood.[7] In high conflict families, when communication is at its poorest, more prolonged disturbance may develop,[8] although the majority of children whose families are disrupted by divorce show no adverse signs several years later.[9] The key issues in longer-term adjustment appear to be the quality of the relationships between children and their parents and economic factors, together with any residual effects of disturbance and upset experienced during the time of the separation. Stable post-divorce arrangements and the maintenance of good relationships with their mother, father and wider kin give children the best chance of recovering from the impacts of divorce.

In this respect, there has been growing concern that marriage breakdown for so many children results in them losing contact with one of their parents, usually their father. Our recent research on post-divorce relationships between non-residential fathers and their children[10] shows clearly the tremendous difficulties faced by fathers who struggle to maintain contact with their children, and to meet their

---

5   Holmes, TH and Rahe, RH, 'Holmes-Rahe Social Adjustment Rating Scale' (1967) *Journal of Psychosomatic Research*, Vol 11.

6   McCarthy, P, Simpson, R, Walker, J and Corlyon, J, *Longitudinal Study of the Impact of Different Dispute Resolution Process on Post-divorce Relationships between Parents and Children. Report to the Fund for Research on Dispute Resolution,* 1991, Newcastle upon Tyne: Family and Community Dispute Research Centre, Newcastle University.

7   Kiernan, KE, 'What About the Children?', December 1991, *Family Policy Bulletin*, London: Family Policy Studies Centre.

8   Cummings, EM and Davies, P, *Children and Marital Conflict: The Impact of Family Dispute and Resolution,* 1994, New York: The Guilford Press.

9   Morrison, DR and Cherlin, AJ, 'The Divorce Process and Young Children's Well-being: A Prospective Analysis', (1992) *Journal of Marriage and the Family*, Vol 57, at 800–12.

10 Simpson, B, McCarthy, P and Walker, J, *Being There: Fathers After Divorce,* 1995, Newcastle upon Tyne: Relate Centre for Family Studies, Newcastle University.

parental responsibilities. When they fail to do so, it is usually not because they no longer care, nor that they fail to take parental obligations seriously. Mostly, it is because communication has broken down between ex-spouses, and within the family as a whole. Our follow-up study of divorced parents revealed that four years on, there was little contact between many parents and that children had an unenviable role in acting as go-betweens in painfully divided worlds.[11] Such stark realities place a heavy responsibility on those seeking to settle the disputes which can so easily arise in the intense emotional contexts which exist during separation and divorce. To ignore them, or to perceive family disputes as no different to any others, is to seriously lessen the potential benefits of mediation.

The special characteristics of family disputes were cogently detailed by Sander[12] who believed that mediation can only be effective if they are taken into account. Firstly, family disputes usually involve those with continuing and interdependent relationships; secondly, family disputes arise, and have to be settled in the context of a range of distressing emotions and feelings; and thirdly, disputes which result from marriage breakdown frequently impact on other family members, notably children, but also grandparents, who are not usually included in the dispute resolution process, but whose interests should be protected. These characteristics, in Sander's view, render a simple transfer of an industrial bargaining model, or that used in settling environmental disputes somewhat problematic. Fuller[13] observed that interventions in matrimonial disputes should be person-oriented rather than act-oriented, suggesting that mediation is far better suited than more formal mechanisms to the sensitive, emotional issues surrounding family matters. Since families spend much of their time resolving disputes which arise in the normal course of events in daily living, most have some competencies in the practice of 'private ordering'. During the trials and tribulations of marriage breakdown conflict resolution skills are in high demand, but while some couples maintain a problem-solving approach, others find it difficult to do so unaided. It has been argued that using lawyers and the courts to provide such help is not always sensible since the law is a blunt instrument with which to deal with personal problems. Mediation, on the other hand, appears to offer a much more appropriate level of support, and is relatively cost-effective judged against four criteria for evaluating methods of conflict resolution: their ability to settle the dispute; the cost of the process; the justice of both process and outcome; and the promotion of social goals.[14]

11 McCarthy, P, Simpson, R, Walker, J and Corlyon, J, *Longitudinal Study of the Impact of Different Dispute Resolution Process on Post-divorce Relationships between Parents and Children*. Report to the Fund for Research on Dispute Resolution, 1991, Newcastle upon Tyne: Family and Community Dispute Research Centre, Newcastle University. Simpson, B, McCarthy, P and Walker, J, *Being There: Fathers After Divorce*, 1995, Newcastle upon Tyne: Relate Centre for Family Studies, Newcastle University.

12 Sander, FEA, 'Towards a Functional Analysis of Family Process', in Eekelaar, J and Katz, SN (eds), *The Resolution of Family Conflict: Comparative Legal Perspectives*, 1984, Toronto: Butterworths.

13 Fuller, L, 'Mediation – Its Forms and Functions' (1971) *Southern California Law Review* 44, at 301–28.

14 MacDougall, DJ, 'Negotiated Settlement of Family Disputes', in Eekelaar, J and Katz, SN (eds), *The Resolution of Family Conflict: Comparative Legal Perspectives*, 1984, Toronto: Butterworths.

The case for family mediation in most countries has rested on two claims: firstly, that it provides a more cost-effective way of settling disputes; and secondly, that it reduces conflict, improves communication, and so positively impacts on the quality of life for those experiencing family breakdown. During its formative years these claims were largely unchallenged. Concern about a rapidly rising divorce rate throughout the 1970s, and a belief that bitter exchanges between couples were seriously detrimental to children, merely served to substantiate calls for a 'more civilised' process. By contrast, the traditional adversarial system has been accused of escalating conflict thus incurring substantial costs in legal fees, the use of courts and the preparation of welfare reports. In reality, the pioneers of family mediation have been most concerned to promote those benefits which improve the quality of life both during and after divorce, viewing the potential cost-savings as a bonus. Indeed, most would advocate the use of mediation even if it cannot be shown to reduce public and private expenditure, on the basis of its overall contribution to the social good.

Governments, nevertheless, are driven in part by financial considerations. The introduction of new procedures within legal and welfare services are frequently required to be cost-neutral. In other words, savings have to accrue elsewhere in the system. This was one of the fundamental principles within the recent proposals for divorce reform in England, and almost certainly the one giving the most cause for alarm. Mediation will be financed from the legal aid fund, and in order to do this, there will have to be a reduction in the amount spent on legal advice and representation. Concerns that this will result in unjust and unfair processes, denial of legal rights, and a second class system of justice abound, notably amongst lawyers.[15] Assessing the concerns, it is not always easy to distinguish between genuine anxieties for the wellbeing of clients and lawyers' own professional self-interests. To some extent these concerns, whatever their origin, filter through the varying practices and processes which currently exist. Folberg and Taylor[16] have suggested that the history of mediation 'only begins to define what it is ... Mediation is first and foremost a *process* that transcends the content of the conflict it is intended to resolve'. Nevertheless, all processes are shaped and influenced by their past, and family mediation is no exception. Its history has both allowed space for experimentation and innovation, and at the same time set boundaries and limitations which have constrained professional development.

---

15 Law Society, *Fairness for Families: The Law Society's Blueprint for Resolving Disputes on Family Breakdown*, 1995, London: The Law Society.

16 Folberg, A and Taylor, A, *Mediation: A Comprehensive Guide to Resolving Conflicts without Litigation*, 1984, San Francisco: Jossey-Bass.

THE ORIGINS OF FAMILY MEDIATION

The plight of one parent families and the detrimental impact of acrimonious divorces, particularly for children, provided the impetus for the development of family mediation in England. In 1974, shortly after the implementation of the Divorce Reform Act 1969 which was expected to respond to the many concerns surrounding marriage breakdown, the Finer Committee on One Parent Families recommended that mediation (referred to at that time as 'conciliation') should be available to assist families with the consequences of divorce in a more civilised way than that which exists through the adversarial process.[17] The committee envisaged the introduction of a family court structure and a new approach to matrimonial proceedings. Successive governments chose not to follow the committee's recommendations, leaving it to a small but dedicated group of enthusiastic and committed lawyers, counsellors and social workers to spearhead the development of family mediation. It was piecemeal and fragmented and initially followed two quite distinct routes.[18] On the one hand, family mediation became a new extension of the statutory work of the probation service which has had responsibility for investigating matrimonial disputes since 1937. As a result, mediation began to develop within the divorce courts, with judges as well as probation officers frequently playing a leading role.[19] On the other hand, the voluntary social work sector seemed eminently well-placed to include mediation amongst its community-based services. Many charities which were originally established during the latter years of the Victorian era to support children, have been central to the welfare support for disadvantaged and 'problem' families throughout the 20th century. A deeply-embedded child-saving philosophy enticed some of these organisations to take a lead in developing new mediation services. In the past 20 years, over 60 voluntary family mediation services have been established in England and Wales, most registered as charities. They have been characterised by a recurring struggle for financial solvency, surviving on scarce, meagre resources obtained through donations, small grants and a variety of fundraising activities. The constant search for financial backing has taken both a disproportionate amount of mediators' time, and raised many questions amongst the more established professions about the credibility and standards of what appears to be a most insecure activity. That mediation should be provided free of charge has rarely been questioned by practitioners, although, increasingly, services have invited their clients to make donations.

The pioneers of family mediation traditionally worked in their parent professions with a focus on protecting children's interests. Not surprisingly, this focus was

---

17   Finer, Sir, M, *Report of the Committee on One-parent Families*, Cmnd 5629, 1974, London: HMSO.

18   Walker, J, 'Divorce Mediation - An Overview from Great Britain', in McCrory, J, (ed), *The Role of Mediation in Divorce Proceedings: A Comparative Perspective*, 1987, South Royalton: Vermont Law School.

19   Ogus, A, McCarthy, P and Wray, S, 'Court-annexed Mediation Programmes in England and Wales', in McCrory, J (ed), *The Role of Mediation in Divorce Proceedings: A Comparative Perspective*, 1987, South Royalton: Vermont Law School.

carried over into mediation since it was primarily the impact of divorce on children which had encouraged the search for alternative processes. Although the Finer Committee had envisaged that mediation could be used to settle all kinds of matrimonial disputes, mediators in England confined their approach to those disputes involving the custody of and access to children. This rather narrow focus did not challenge the traditional role of the legal profession as gatekeepers to the divorce process, and provided a useful route towards which they could channel the rather 'messy' contests about children while retaining supremacy in relation to the settlements about money and property. Although mediators in the United States tended to be less restricted in their approach, the early developments in Canada were more akin to those in England, particularly with respect to court-connected programmes.

Although a division between child-related and finance-related disputes appeared to make sense for the professionals concerned, it became apparent that it was not necessarily in the best interests of the couples using mediation. While couples were being encouraged to be civilised and cooperative in settling matters to do with children, they frequently had to be adversarial in their attempts to make decisions about all the other issues. The absurdity of couples talking together about their children one day, and fighting money matters out in court through their respective lawyers on another was starkly revealed in our major study of mediation carried out in the late 1980s.[20] Couples who could not agree about arrangements for children were equally likely to be in dispute about other matters. At the end of our study as many as 25% of couples who had successfully mediated child issues were still in dispute about child maintenance payments, and some 27% about property matters. Furthermore, the lastingness of settlements mediated in isolation from other disputes was problematic. In consequence, we recommended that not only should mediation be all-embracing, capable of dealing with all the issues consequent on separation and divorce, but also that it could not be considered as a true alternative dispute resolution mechanism while parties are obliged to settle other disputes at arms' length through lawyer negotiation and litigation.

Mediators in England and Canada had already begun to realise the limitations of a child-focused approach and were aware of the many comprehensive programmes developing elsewhere. An important catalyst for change was the recognition that many of these programmes were located in the private sector. In 1985 the Department of Justice in Canada estimated that some 55% of mediators, many of whom were either lawyers or psychologists, were operating privately, and offering mediation on all issues. Not until the late 1980s did family mediation develop in the private fee-for-service market in England, but when it did it was to offer a new model for mediation based on a partnership between family lawyers and social work professionals training together in order to co-

---

20 Conciliation Project Unit, *Report on the Costs and Effectiveness of Conciliation in England and Wales*, 1989, London: Lord Chancellor's Department.

mediate all the issues in dispute. Shortly afterwards, community-based mediation services began to experiment with a range of approaches to extend the remit of mediation beyond its child focus. All involved lawyers working in some way or another with skilled mediators from the mental health professions. There are now some 400 mediators, half of them practising family lawyers, working within the private sector, and a growing number working in community-based services, all of whom are trained to mediate all issues.

So, between 1978 and 1996, family mediation in England and Wales has developed in three fairly diverse ways: as an adjunct to court services, in many ways similar to mediation services attached to the courts in the USA, Canada, Australia and elsewhere; within newly established voluntary agencies based on the good will of volunteer counsellors, social workers and others, in an arrangement which is largely peculiar to this country; and, latterly, within the private sector, where lawyers and mental health professionals increasingly choose to work side-by-side to offer a comprehensive mediation service in much the same way as may be found in Canada and elsewhere. Yet, despite the numbers of couples divorcing in England and Wales each year – about 165,000 – the number using mediation to settle disputes has remained disappointingly low. In 1994, about 8,500 couples used either the voluntary agencies or the private sector; and of these, 6,800 mediated only children's issues; 400 mediated only finance and property issues; and 1,300 mediated all issues. Because it is not always easy to identify 'mediation' within the courts, and because the court-based mediators typically combine mediation with their statutory duties it is difficult to estimate how many couples experience mediation as part of the court process in separation and divorce proceedings, but the number is unlikely to be high.[21]

Although it would be wrong to suggest that such an ad hoc development of mediation is totally unique to England, the process has reached a point of consolidation in other countries rather more quickly and easily. Concerns to protect the best interests of children, particularly following the seminal work of Wallerstein and Kelly in the late 1970s,[22] focused attention on the limitations of an adversarial legal process and the relative advantages of more informal and consensual approaches. In Canada, court-connected mediation schemes began in 1972 with the first family mediation service in Edmonton, Alberta. Since then, mediation services offering a variety of programmes have been introduced in all 10 provinces (for a comprehensive review see Alberta Law Reform Institute 1994).[23] In addition, although there are voluntary mediation organisations, much mediation is conducted by private practitioners paid for by

---

21 In Canada, too, usage has been variable, with no obviously high demand for mediation, although as it becomes more widely understood as an alternative to adversarial processes, researchers are confidently predicting an increase in the numbers choosing mediation (Irving, HH and Benjamin, M, *Family Mediation: Contemporary Issues*, 1995, Thousand Oaks, Calif: Sage).

22 Wallerstein, JS and Kelly, JB, *Surviving the Breakup*, 1980, London: Grant McIntyre.

23 Alberta Law Reform Institute, *Court-connected Family Mediation Programs in Canada*, Research Paper No 20, 1994, Edmonton: Alberta Law Institute.

the clients using the service. In common with developments in the United States, practitioners and researchers in Canada have focused their attention on clinical practice issues, training and skills development.[24] In contrast, the development of charitable community-based family mediation services as the dominant form in England has resulted in a peculiar focus on organisational issues, rather than an emphasis on practice, and it is the former which continue to dominate the debate as to the viability of mediation within a reformed legal system, although process issues do, of course, give rise to concerns also.

THE SEARCH FOR HARMONY

With such an uncoordinated and drawn-out development of family mediation in England, it is perhaps inevitable that mediation practice and process have been very variable, much influenced by setting and by the professional orientation of the mediators. In contrast to developments in other countries, they have been influenced far less by the wider application of mediation as a consensual dispute resolution process with its long history of usage in a variety of cultures and social contexts. In contemporary discussions about family mediation it is easy to overlook the fact that most of the communities in Africa, Asia, Latin America, China and Japan have developed informal mechanisms for settling disputes through mediation, which is normally characterised by the use of a neutral third party whose task is to meet with the disputants, facilitate negotiation, and enable settlements to be reached. In addition, extended family and kinship circles have provided a mediation resource in many cultures;[25] and although they may not always have been neutral in their approach, there is evidence that in the 17th and 18th centuries in England, parents, family, friends and neighbours regularly intervened to arbitrate, advise and mediate between spouses.[26]

Although the primary aim of mediation is to resolve disputes, it is frequently coupled with expectations of reducing conflict and improving communication between the parties for the future. Japan, with its long cultural tradition of mediation, emphasises the importance of restoring harmony, and of mutual apology and pardon.[27] Zehr[28] has talked about the 'restorative lens' in bringing

---

24 Irving, HH and Benjamin, M, 'Therapeutic Family Mediation: Ecosystemic Processes and the Linkage between Pre-mediation and negotiation', in Rodway, M and Trute, B (eds), *The Ecological Perspective in Family-centred Therapy*, 1993, Lewiston, MA: Edwin Mellen; Irving, HH and Benjamin, M, *Family Mediation: Contemporary Issues*, 1995, Thousand Oaks, Calif: Sage.

25 Vroom, P, Fassett, D and Wakefield, RA, 'Mediation: The Wave of the Future?' (1981) *American Family*, 4, at 8–13.

26 Stone, L, *The Road to Divorce: England 1530–1987*, 1990, Oxford: Oxford University Press.

27 Schimazu, I, 'Procedural Aspects of Marriage Dissolution in Japan', in Eekelaar, JM and Katz, SN (eds), *The Resolution of Family Conflict: Comparative Legal Perspectives*, 1984 Toronto: Butterworths. Wagatsuma, H and Rossett, A, 'The Implications of Apology: Law and Culture in Japan and the United States' (1986) *Law and Society Review*, 20, at 461–98.

28 Zehr, H, *Changing Lenses* Scottsdale, 1990, Pennsylvania: Herald Press.

the reintegrative emphasis into focus. The creation of harmony between disputants who share or have shared an intimate relationship, or who have continuing responsibilities together (as parents, for example) would seem to be an eminently sensible goal of any dispute resolution process. True resolution must involve some level of mutual acceptance, forgiveness and a desire for cooperation.[29] Gehm[30] has emphasised the need to 'let go' of conflict and to 'make amends' for past hurts. Unfortunately, the dual aims of resolving conflict and reaching settlements have resulted in protracted and vehement debates in England about the appropriateness or otherwise of therapeutic skills and systemic theoretical perspectives.[31] These debates have heavily influenced policy and practice in family mediation, often to their detriment. Mediators elsewhere, including in Canada, appear to have experienced far less anxiety about mediation being a therapeutic process,[32] perhaps reflecting a grater acceptance of and respect for therapy and counselling in the promotion of mental health generally, and a willingness to try new ideas in a pioneering spirit which is often lacking in England. Indeed, the anti-therapeutic stance adopted by some mediators in England[33] is somewhat surprising given the undisputed rationale for promoting mediation in family matters in preference to adversarial processes: mediation has developed in family matters precisely because of social rather than legal concerns.

Despite the uncoordinated way in which family mediation has developed, and the existence of a variety of practice models, most mediators appear to share a common set of principles relating to the process which do indeed break new ground in the approach to matrimonial disputes. Mediation is conducted in private and discussions are confidential and may be legally privileged; the disputants retain responsibility for formulating their own agreements based on their own needs and circumstances, with an emphasis not on rights and wrongs but on establishing a workable solution; mediators remain neutral as to outcomes, but take responsibility for encouraging direct communication between the parties, balancing power and reducing conflict; and mediation focuses on future relationships and arrangements, believing that those couples with dependent children will know what is best for their children and are concerned to protect their interests. Based on these principles, the mediation process needs to enhance communication, maximise the exploration of alternatives, address the needs of all parties, help participants to reach agreements

29 Walker, J, 'Mediation in Divorce: Does the Process Match the Rhetoric?', in Messmer, H and Otto, H–U (eds), *Restorative Justice on Trial*, 1992, Dordrecht: Kluwer Academic Publications.

30 Gehm, JR, 'The Function of Forgiveness in the Criminal Justice System', in Messmer, H and Otto, H–U (eds), *Restorative Justice on Trial*, 1992, Dordrecht: Kluwer Academic Publications.

31 Walker, J and Robinson, M, 'Conciliation and Family Therapy', in Fisher, T (ed), *Family Conciliation within the UK: Policy and Practice*, 1990, Bristol: Family Law.

32 Irving, HH and Benjamin, M, *Family Mediation: Contemporary Issues*, 1995, Thousand Oaks, Calif: Sage.

33 Roberts, M, 'Mediation with Families in Separation and Divorce in the UK: Links with Family Therapy' (1988) *The American Journal of Family Therapy*, Vol 16, No 1, at 60; 'Systems or Selves? Some Ethical Issues in Family Mediation' (1990) *Journal of Social Welfare Law*, No 1, at 6–17.

perceived by them as fair, and provide a model for future conflict resolution.[34] To achieve this, practitioners have developed a number of practice models many of which provide a structure to the process. The diversity, however, has created an impression that family mediation is a practice in search of a theory[35] rather than being grounded in well-respected theoretical discourses.

Much time and effort has been put into describing what mediation is *not*, distinguishing it from negotiation, arbitration, counselling and therapy, rather than into attempting to develop a coherent theoretical framework. Moreover, Lisa Parkinson,[36] one of the pioneers of family mediation in the UK, suggested that short training courses in mediation 'cannot cover extensive amounts of theoretical material, and in any case it may be questioned whether [mediators] need to be aware of any particular theories, and if so, which ones'. In her view, theories about individual and family functioning are prone to vary according to fashion and prevailing beliefs, although she admitted that provided mediators question and review received wisdom, 'their awareness of different theories can extend their perspectives and encourage a flexible, wide-ranging approach with access to a variety of methods and skills'. Indeed, her interest in theory is focused primarily on its ability to draw attention to concepts and techniques which may be relevant to practice, always providing that they are adapted carefully so that the mediation task 'is not lost sight of and merged with other interventions'. She goes on to refer briefly to conflict management theory; communication theory; theories of marital interaction; family systems theory; crisis theory; and attachment theory. But the message is a clear one: training in mediation has primarily been about learning appropriate methods and skills. The lack of an agreed theoretical framework has meant that mediators have not been provided with explanatory models that inform their practice and enable them to take account of research findings which require practice to be revisited and modified.

To a large extent this remains a challenge for the future, and one which will have to be satisfactorily addressed before family mediation can be truly described as a discrete profession, if this is what is sought. Nevertheless, despite an early marginalisation of theory, two theoretical perspectives in particular, systems theory and communications theory, appear to have most influenced mediation practice.

Most mediators find it helpful to have a framework which views the family as an interacting system.[37] Negotiating future arrangements has an impact on, and will be impacted by the actions of each family member.[38] In North America and in England, many of those training in mediation have previously trained and

---

34   Folberg, J, 'Mediation and Child Custody Disputes' (1985) *Columbia Journal of Law and Social Problems*, 19 (4) at 1–36.

35   Taylor, A, 'A General Theory of Divorce Mediation', in Folberg, J and Milne, A (eds), *Divorce Mediation: Theory and Practice*, 1988, New York: The Guilford Press.

36   Parkinson, L, *Conciliation in Separation and Divorce: Finding Common Ground*, 1986, London: Croom Helm.

37   Gee, I and Elliott, D, 'Conciliation - A Family Model', in Fisher, T (ed), *Family Conciliation within the UK: Policy and Practice*, 1990, Bristol: Family Law.

38   Saposnek, DT, *Mediating Child Custody Disputes*, 1983, Los Angeles, Calif: Jossey-Bass.

practised in family therapy which itself evolved from the field of mental health in the 1960s as psychiatry shifted its focus from the individual to the family. The approach has had considerable influence on social welfare practice to the extent that a systemic perspective is unhelpfully equated with a therapeutic modality. Successive practitioners in mediation have been at pains to stress that the goals of mediation and those of all forms of therapy are different.[39] Therapy implies pathology, whereas mediation is not addressing any form of dysfunction. However, those who argue that mediation should be protected from a systemic orientation[40] in order to safeguard it from any link with therapy, deny the enormous value of systems thinking and unfairly condemn many of the practice skills and interventions which can be used to much beneficial effect both in family therapy and in mediation. The experience of divorce can only be fully understood within a family context, so that interventions which fail to acknowledge family dynamics will be severely limited in their utility. As Gee and Elliott[41] have pointed out, a systems perspective assumes that even a small change in one party's position can have a profound effect on the rest of the family, including children, extended family members and new partners.

Practitioners have long appreciated the central role that communication plays in any process of dispute management. Communicative behaviour, verbal and non-verbal, creates, reflects and remediates conflicts.[42] Central to this perspective is the realisation that conflict is a socially created and communicatively managed phenomenon. Mediation emerges as collaborative problem solving.[43] Resolving conflicts means finding solutions through effective communication that meet the needs of all the parties concerned. But mediation does not take place in a vacuum: there are contextual issues which shape interventions and outcomes. While traditional methods of dispute resolution pay particular attention to outcomes, often insensitive to the relationships between the parties, alternative mechanisms have seen as critical the interpersonal conflicts inherent in disputes in the private domain of the family. Putnam and Roloff[44] have identified three

39 Parkinson, L, 'Conciliation in Separation and Divorce', in Dryden, W (ed), *Marital Therapy in Britain*, Vol 2, 1985, Harper and Row; Parkinson, L, *Conciliation in Separation and Divorce: Finding Common Ground*, 1986, London: Croom Helm. Haynes, JM and Haynes, GL, *Mediating Divorce: Casebook of Strategies for Successful Family Negotiations*, 1989, San Francisco: Jossey-Bass. Walker, J and Robinson, M, 'Conciliation and Family Therapy', in Fisher, T (ed), *Family Conciliation within the UK: Policy and Practice*, 1990, Bristol: Family Law.

40 Roberts, M, 'Systems or Selves? Some Ethical Issues in Family Mediation' (1990) *Journal of Social Welfare Law*, No 1, at 6–17.

41 Gee, I, and Elliott, D, 'Conciliation - A Family Model', in Fisher, T (ed), *Family Conciliation within the UK: Policy and Practice*, 1990, Bristol: Family Law.

42 Folger, JP, Poole, MS and Stutman, R, *Working Through Conflict: Strategies for Relationships, Groups and Organisations*, 1993, New York: Harper Collins. Hocker, JL and Wilmott, WW, *Interpersonal Conflict*, 3rd edn, 1992, Dubique, IA: William C Brown. Folger, JP and Jones, TS (eds), *New Directions in Mediation: Communication, Research and Perspectives*, 1994, Thousand Oaks, Calif: Sage.

43 Fisher, JP and Ury, W, *Getting to Yes: Negotiating Agreement Without Giving In*, 1981 Boston: Houghton-Mifflin.

44 Putnam, LL and Roloff, M, 'Communication Perspectives on Negotiation', in Putnam, LL and Roloff, M (eds), *Communication and Negotiation*, 1992, Newbury Park, Calif: Sage.

features of a communication approach applicable to the study of family mediation: examination of micro-elements of behaviour with emphasis on patterning; a focus on dynamic, developmental features of negotiation; and an effort to uncover how meaning is dependent on relational, social and cultural contexts. Grimshaw[45] has suggested that all communication to resolve disputes involves *some* negotiation of identities and of the appropriate nature of interpersonal arrangements. A communication perspective has emerged as well-suited to the practice of family mediation, not least because of its emphasis on process, and it is this which has proved to be so relevant to practice and to research.

STEPS IN THE MEDIATION PROCESS

Kaslow[46] has described mediation as 'an intricate modern dance that includes legal, economic, and emotional themes'. As in all dances, mediation has identified steps, variations on which are constantly being perfected. Whatever theoretical or professional orientation influences the mediator, the mediation process is usually characterised as a set of steps or stages[47] each of which has its goals, tasks and attendant skills. Most mediators adhere to a structured approach to the mediation process, although this needs to be balanced with a degree of flexibility to accommodate the unique characteristics and experiences of each family. Two practitioners, OJ Coogler and John Haynes, have had a fundamental influence on mediation practice in the USA and in England, and a third, Howard Irving, has significantly guided the developments in mediation in Canada. All have developed brief, structured models, although Haynes and Irving are more unashamedly therapeutic in their approach. Coogler[48] advocated a more rigidly controlled process with detailed rules about the amount of time that could be spent on each stage of the mediation. A number of basic ground rules are followed by the mediator: there cannot be any separate negotiation with either party; children are not involved in the process; the mediator helps to shape the agenda and ensures that both parties actively participate; and the mediator maintains control over the manner in which the negotiations are carried out.

Coogler's rather unbending structure is designed to establish an orderly process and procedural fairness; high ethical standards; and a secure emotional environment, so that rational exchange is possible at a time when

45 Grimshaw, AD, 'Research on Conflict Talk: Antecedents, Resources, Findings, Directions', in Grimshaw, A (ed), *Conflict Talk*, 1990, Cambridge: Cambridge University Press.

46 Kaslow, F, 'The Psychological Dimension of Divorce Mediation', in Folberg, J and Milne, A (eds), *Divorce Mediation: Theory and Practice*, 1988, New York: The Guilford Press.

47 Moore, CW, 'Training Mediators for Family Dispute Resolution' (1983) *Mediation Quarterly*, No 2, San Francisco: Jossey Bass. Folberg, A and Taylor, A, *Mediation: A Comprehensive Guide to Resolving Conflicts without Litigation*, 1984, San Francisco: Jossey-Bass.

48 Coogler, OJ, *Structured Mediation in Divorce Settlement*, 1978, Lexington, Mass: DC Heath & Co.

communication may well be poor.[49] Following Coogler's work a number of practitioners, mostly in the United States, described various models of mediation.[50] Most were based on a process of negotiation of facts, issues and positions, with little attention given to relational aspects and variations. Many practitioners now find Coogler's model overly rigid and impersonal, so to a large extent it has been rejected in favour of a more therapeutic approach in which relational variations are taken into account. Practitioners such as Haynes and Irving describe a number of well-defined steps which may be tailored to individual needs, but all of which need to be addressed during the mediation process. While the terms used to describe these steps may vary, the purpose of each one is fairly well accepted in Canada, England and the USA.

A brief glance at these steps will demonstrate the logic of the mediation process as well as indicate the knowledge and skills required by the mediator to guide the couple through the different sequences, particularly if they are somewhat less than enthusiastic about having to 'face the music and dance'. The process followed by most practitioners can be divided into several main stages. Although models of mediation arbitrarily distinguish between about four and twelve identifiable stages, the following seven–step model, and variations on it, is one which is in common usage.

Engagement

The first step in mediation is crucial to the establishment of a relationship which will facilitate the rest of the process. Described by Haynes[51] as the 'intake' process, the emphasis is on describing what mediation is, how it works, what is expected of the couple and setting some ground rules. Folberg and Taylor,[52] who call this initial stage 'creating trust and structure', use it to gather relevant information about the participants' perceptions of the conflict, their goals and expectations, and the situations in which the conflict manifests itself.

Part of the mediator's task is to gather data which can be used to assess the parties' motivation and ability to negotiate together. They include information about communication styles and patterns; the extent and level of conflict; incidents of domestic violence and abuse; the preparedness of each partner for the decision to separate; parental functioning; and financial, emotional and social resources. This initial stage is complete when the mediator has a clear picture of the manifest and underlying issues, and the couple have a clear understanding of mediation and can determine if they wish to proceed.

---

49   Davis, G and Roberts, M, *Access to Agreement*, 1988, Milton Keynes: Open University Press.

50   Grebe, SC, 'Structured Mediation and its Variants: What Makes it Unique', in Folberg, J and Milne, A (eds), *Divorce Mediation: Theory and Practice*, 1988, New York: The Guilford Press. Moore, CW, *The Mediation Process: Practical Strategies for Resolving Conflict*, 1986, San Francisco: Jossey-Bass.

51   Haynes, JM, 'The Process of Negotiation' (1993) *Mediation Quarterly*, 11, at 75–92.

52   Folberg, A and Taylor, A, *Mediation: A Comprehensive Guide to Resolving Conflicts without Litigation*, 1984, San Francisco: Jossey-Bass.

Fact-finding and planning the agenda

Although much relevant information will have been shared during the engagement phase, the next step is to ensure that all the data relevant to the case is 'on the table'. From the mediator's perspective, knowledge about family composition, living arrangements, and the steps either or both might have made to seek a divorce and obtain legal advice, needs to be clarified. The mediator helps each partner to describe the conflicts and disputes between them, to assess their immediacy, duration, intensity and to discern areas of potential rigidity in the position each of them holds. Clarifying areas of agreement and disagreement in this way enables the mediator, in collaboration with the couple, to set the agenda for mediation.

Exploring options and alternatives

According to Taylor[53] the key question in this stage is 'How can you do what you want to do in the most effective way?'. To answer it, each party is helped to articulate the options they know or want, and to develop new alternatives. These then need to be assessed and evaluated by anticipating their implications, workability, limitations, and costs and benefits to each party and to their children. Mediators need to be both facilitative and creative during this part of the process. Taylor describes the mediator as a resource person, an expert who can suggest new options based on a more extensive knowledge and experience of divorce and its effects. Mediation moves to the next phase when there has been a full discussion of all the possible options, without prejudicial or judgmental attitudes impeding it.

Negotiation and decision making

Having explored all the options, the couple are helped to negotiate towards making some decisions, which frequently entails compromise on both their parts. What matters is that both can accept the decisions, even if they are not what they had hoped for originally, and believe them to be fair and just. It is in this phase of mediation that negotiation and bargaining take place with the intention to reach a win–win solution. Maintaining some sort of balance and equality in communication is essential to effective bargaining, as is resisting the urge to reach settlements too hastily. The mediator needs to ensure that each party is ready to make a decision.

Clarifying and summarising agreements

This stage in the mediation process has as its goal the production of some sort of document or draft agreement, frequently referred to as a Memorandum of Understanding in England. It is a summary of the agreements reached and not reached which should be capable of forming the basis of court orders if necessary, and of being used as a working document for the parties concerned. Most importantly, the document is not a legal one, it is written in everyday language, and it should be open to modification as circumstances change. The signing of

---

53 Taylor, A, 'A General Theory of Divorce Mediation', in Folberg, J and Milne, A (eds), *Divorce Mediation: Theory and Practice*, 1988, p 69, New York: The Guilford Press.

the document by each party is a symbolic step and provides tangible evidence of cooperation and closure. Sometimes children are invited to mediation at this point so that their parents can talk through the arrangements they have made. Not only does this ensure that children are properly and adequately informed of decisions affecting their lives, but also it can be very reassuring for them to see their parents cooperating and planning their future jointly.

Review

Mediators are well aware that the best negotiated plans may still falter in practice. Time is often given to the couple to try arrangements out and then to review them. Each may wish to take legal advice about the settlements to ensure that they are not seriously prejudicial to one person's best interests. In England, the majority of those mediating their disputes seek independent legal advice before and/or after the mediation process. Since it is not usual for advising lawyers to attend the mediation sessions, mediators always encourage their clients to take the Memorandum of Understanding to their lawyers for scrutiny. Our research indicates that this acts as a safeguard against either party making agreements which could have unforeseen adverse consequences, and is much appreciated by the users of mediation. In practice, few agreements get unpicked by lawyers at this stage.

Some people refer back to their lawyers throughout the mediation process. Although a few of the early court-based schemes encouraged the attendance of advising lawyers at mediation, this model has largely disappeared. Most mediators do not want parties' lawyers to be quite so influential during the mediation, but welcome the support they offer their clients before and after.

Implementation and reviewing agreements

Many mediators will not expect to see a couple again if their respective lawyers are content with the agreements reached and they are capable of being put into practice. For most couples, the mediation process ends with the review stage. For others, however, mediators may offer a follow-up appointment some months on. They recognise that the weeks and months after mediation are likely to be difficult and may involve several transitions in living arrangements. At the very least, each party has to adjust to new situations and arrangements which may be strange and emotionally painful. Rarely does everything run smoothly, hence the offer of a further appointment to review the outcomes of mediation. Such a practice can, in Taylor's experience, 'put out brushfires of discontent and provide positive reinforcement for the continuance of the mediation plan'.[54] In her view, mediation is unique among conflict resolution processes because it can create a process for future review and revision regardless of whether there are any problems or concerns. Of course, people are encouraged to return to mediation at any time if concerns, problems or further disputes emerge. The door to mediation is always left open. Divorce requires families to manage and adjust to a

---

54 Taylor, A, 'A General Theory of Divorce Mediation', in Folberg, J and Milne, A (eds), *Divorce Mediation: Theory and Practice*, 1988, p 69, New York: The Guilford Press.

series of transformations[55] each of which may be complex and stressful. Mediation must, therefore, be flexible and sensitive to individual needs, and most mediators emphasise the importance of process and not merely outcomes.

A structured process of mediation clearly takes time. Although it is a relatively brief, focused intervention, nevertheless if disputes are to be fully explored and a range of options for settlements considered and agreed, it is difficult to see how the process can be hurried. Inevitably, the time taken for each stage is dependent on the number of issues in dispute, their complexity, the extent and severity of conflict between the parties, each party's willingness to compromise, and the barriers to negotiation which the mediator may need to address. Mediators inclined to a more therapeutic and flexible process might take up to 16 sessions to complete mediation, while others aim to reach a Memorandum of Understanding after about six sessions, each one typically lasting two hours. Mediation on all issues including arrangements for children, and the division of money and property, is likely to take some four to six months to complete.

DEVELOPING SKILLS

Describing mediation as a six or seven stage process is disarmingly deceptive since it suggests a simplicity which masks the high level of professional expertise needed to help couples through it. It fails to acknowledge the array of skills required by the mediator and the variety of practice techniques which will be employed during the process. For the most part they derive from the clinical literature in mediation[56] and family therapy[57] and the literature on labour-management dispute resolution.[58] As Kaslow[59] points out, mediators must be fully cognisant of the psychodynamics of marriage breakdown, its emotional vicissitudes and accompanying anguish; they must be knowledgeable in behavioural dynamics and family systems; and they must have a thorough knowledge of family law as it affects their clients. Above all, mediators must be skilful directors of a complex and demanding process, capable of remaining detached enough to function as mediators, not counsellors or therapists despite needing to employ the skills of both.

---

55 Robinson, M, *Family Transformation through Divorce and Remarriage: A Systemic Approach*, 1991, London: Tavistock/Routledge.

56 Felstiner, WLF and Williams, LA, 'Mediation as an Alternative to Criminal Prosecution' (1978) *Law and Human Behaviour* 2 (3) at 223–44. Haynes, JM, 'The Process of Negotiation' (1993) *Mediation Quarterly* 11 at 75–92. Irving, HH and Benjamin, M, *Family Mediation: Theory and Practice of Dispute Resolution*, 1987, Toronto: Carswell; Irving, HH and Benjamin, M, 'An Evaluation of Process and Outcome in a Private Mediation Service' (1992) *Mediation Quarterly* 10 (1) at 35–55.

57 Fisch, R, Weakland, JH and Segal, L, *The Tactics of Change: Doing Therapy Briefly*, 1982, San Francisco: Jossey-Bass. Minuchin, S and Fishman, HC, *Family Therapy Techniques*, 1981, Cambridge, Mass: Harvard University Press.

58 Bomers, GBJ and Peterson, RB (eds), *Conflict Management and Industrial Relations*, 1982, Norwell, Mass: Kluwer-Nijhoff. Fisher, JP and Ury, W, *Getting to Yes: Negotiating Agreement Without Giving In*, 1981, Boston: Houghton-Mifflin.

59 Kaslow, F, 'The Psychological Dimension of Divorce Mediation', in Folberg, J and Milne, A (eds), *Divorce Mediation: Theory and Practice*, 1988, New York: The Guilford Press.

While the ultimate goal of mediation is the same as the adversarial system, that is to effect the settlement of matters in dispute, the way in which this is achieved is fundamentally different. Mediators define divorce disputes in mutual, cooperative terms[60] using a process of reframing. It involves redefining and interpreting a problem or situation in such a way that renders mutual problem-solving more feasible.[61] Statements and positions which are expressed in a negative way are recast so as to define a positive position. For example, a wife who constantly criticises the way in which her husband looks after their children (feeding them 'junk' food, spoiling them, and letting them stay up late to watch videos: accusations frequently hurled at fathers who do not have the day-to-day responsibility for their children) and who is therefore seeking to limit the amount of time he sees them on access or contact visits, may have her frustration reframed as a natural concern for her children's welfare, a concern which her husband is likely to be able to share. By focusing on what they can both do as parents to ensure consistency in and age-appropriate parenting, their respective roles and responsibilities can be highlighted in the search for agreed solutions. This move away from adversarial positioning towards consensual decision-making is the key feature of the mediation process. Achieving it requires the mediator to be competent in a range of skills, including directing the flow of communication, active listening, careful questioning, positive connotation, observation, clarification and confrontation.[62] None is necessarily easy, particularly in the emotionally-charged atmosphere of the mediation session.

Another important task for the mediator is that of balancing power between the couple. Within the adversarial model bargaining power is viewed as a strength, each party weighs up their relative strengths in order to win. Traditionally, men have had greater power in marriage in relation to finances and decision-making while women have had more power over the upbringing of children and family relationships. In a typical adversarial divorce the husband uses his power to call the tune on the distribution of money and property, while the wife normally controls her husband's access to his children. The result for so many post-divorce families has been a marked drop in the standard of living for wives with the custody of children,[63] and declining contact between fathers and their children.[64] The thrust in recent reforms in family law in England and elsewhere has been to reverse these negative and disadvantageous outcomes, and mediation

60   Erickson, SK, 'The Legal Dimension of Divorce Mediation', in Folberg, J and Milne, A (eds), *Divorce Mediation: Theory and Practice*, 1988, New York: The Guilford Press.

61   Moore, CW, 'Mediator Communication and Influence in Conflict Management Interventions: A Practitioner's Reflections on Theory and Practice', in Folger, JP and Jones, TS (eds), *New Directions in Mediation: Communication, Research and Perspectives*, 1994, Thousand Oaks, Calif: Sage.

62   Irving, HH and Benjamin, M, *Family Mediation: Theory and Practice of Dispute Resolution*, 1987, Toronto: Carswell.

63   Maclean, M, *Surviving Divorce: Women's Resources After Separation*, 1991, Basingstoke: Macmillan.

64   Kruk, E, *Divorce and Disengagement: Patterns of Fatherhood Within and Beyond Marriage*, 1993, Halifax, NS: Fernwood Publishing. Simpson, B, McCarthy, P and Walker, J, *Being There: Fathers After Divorce*, 1995, Newcastle upon Tyne: Relate Centre for Family Studies, Newcastle University.

is viewed as a competent way in which to effect the change. In mediation, attempts are made by the mediator to balance power so that the couple can negotiate on a level playing field, as far as is possible. The mediation process gives each party the opportunity to explore whether they have something to gain from reaching agreement and less to lose than they might have imagined.[65] Feminist critics of mediation have expressed concerns, however, that unless the imbalance of power is addressed, women in particular may be bullied during face-to-face negotiations into unfair settlements by domineering or even abusive husbands.[66]

In reality, when mediators begin to work with divorcing couples the traditional power divisions are revealed as much more subtle. Rarely are men totally in control of the family finances, nor are their wives able to wield complete power over decisions about their children's upbringing. Such a dichotomy is far from helpful in a process which is designed to encourage couples to share responsibility for all the consequences of the dissolution of their marriage. As Haynes[67] pointed out, the critical matter for mediators is in analysing how each party accrues and uses power within the family, and how the distribution of power impacts on the negotiations. By determining the power attributes that each party has, and how these are used in negotiations, the mediator can then attempt to ensure that power is balanced during the mediation process, and that neither party is overwhelmed by the other. There are various techniques for achieving this, and no shortage of practice examples of these and others in mediation training texts.[68] Typically, at the beginning of the mediation process, mediators set 'ground rules' such as ensuring that each party can speak without being interrupted by the other; or that different views or versions are to be respected. Such simple devices provide a framework for preventing dominant, overly pushy or talkative partners from crowding out or dismissing the comments of the other. If one partner is seen to put the other down (which often results in withdrawal or tears) the mediator might identify with the person under attack, focusing on the relative impact of the behaviour and intervening to prevent repetitions but without chastising the perpetrator.

Sometimes it is necessary for the mediator to forbid the discussion of a particular issue or situation, a new partner to one of the spouses, perhaps. It is not uncommon for one spouse to use the existence of a new relationship to inflame the issues in dispute so deflecting from the negotiations. Since the key players are the couple in

---

65 Parkinson, L, *Conciliation in Separation and Divorce: Finding Common Ground*, 1986, London: Croom Helm.

66 Grillo, T, 'The Mediation Alternative: Process Dangers for Women' (1991) *Yale Law Journal* 100 (6) at 1545–1610. Hart, BJ, 'Gentle Jeopardy: The Further Endangerment of Battered Women and Children in Custody Mediation' (1990) *Mediation Quarterly* 7 (4) at 317–30.

67 Haynes, JM, 'Power Balancing' in Folberg, J and Milne, A (eds), *Divorce Mediation: Theory and Practice*, 1988, New York: The Guilford Press.

68 Haynes, JM, and Haynes, GL, *Mediating Divorce: Casebook of Strategies for Successful Family Negotiations*, 1989, San Francisco: Jossey-Bass.

the room, it is relatively straightforward for the mediator to suggest that other people do not belong in the process and should be excluded from discussions.

Couples who come to mediation know each other well: they each know what buttons to push to wind the other up. A skilled mediator observes the interactions and patterns of behaviour so that if one partner is constantly 'programming' the other, the mediator can intervene to shift the pattern, so disempowering the dominant spouse and rebalancing the power sufficiently for negotiations to continue. Such interventions assume that each partner is capable and competent, which in Haynes' view has the effect of encouraging more competence in the way weaker spouses respond to and take part in the discussions.

LIVING UP TO EXPECTATIONS

Mediation has been described by Gulliver[69] as 'the gradual creation of order and co-ordination between the parties'. Given the complexity of matrimonial disputes and the strong emotions which normally surround them, this is no mean feat. It is not difficult to make the case for family mediation 'as a better way' in which to resolve intensely personal and private disputes. There can be few advocates of an adversarial process in such circumstances. Perhaps because of the 'obvious' advantages of a conciliatory approach, practitioners have not always understood or acknowledged the emphasis placed by policymakers on the need for empirical evidence. Until the mid-1980s there was little systematic research on the effectiveness of mediation, and those studies which did exist were largely monitoring the work of a particular local service[70] and few attempted a wider comparison. Kressel and Pruitt,[71] in a volume which brought together much of the North American research, concluded that the sustained study of mediation is still in its infancy, although it is way ahead of equivalent research on the effectiveness of the long-established adversarial system.

Early attempts to answer the question 'does mediation work?' concentrated on measuring settlement-rates. Judged solely on this criterion, mediation appears to have been respectably successful, with agreements on some issues being achieved in well over half of the cases in every recorded study. However, simply counting the number of agreements reached is a most unsatisfactory measurement of effectiveness given the focus in mediation not only on outcomes but also on process. Furthermore, settlement rates can only be accurate if it is possible to clearly define the issues in dispute and the outcomes, but we have found that it is not unusual for issues to be confused, blurred, vague and overlapping.[72] Hence a

69 Gulliver, PH, *Disputes and Negotiations: A Cross-cultural Perspective*, 1979, London: Academic Press.

70 Davis, G and Roberts, M, *Access to Agreement*, 1988, Milton Keynes: Open University Press.

71 Kressel, K and Pruitt, DG, *Mediation Research: The Process and Effectiveness of Third Party Intervention*, 1989, San Francisco: Jossey-Bass.

72 Walker, J, 'Family Conciliation in Great Britain: From Research to Practice to Research' (1989) *Mediation Quarterly* 24 at 29–55.

growing recognition that research on mediation must be sufficiently sensitive to be able to tease out the impact of process as well as evaluate the quality of outcomes reached, their durability and usefulness over time.

In a recent review of family mediation research, Irving and Benjamin[73] group the studies into three categories: process studies; outcome studies; and those which consider predictors of successful mediation. As they themselves comment, process studies ought, ideally, to be able to determine what interventions on the part of mediators have what sort of effects, with which kind of clients, in what types of contexts. Studies to date fall short of this, but they have shed important light on what takes place in mediation. Some of the more interesting studies of process have involved the analysis of audio-taped sessions.[74] They demonstrate that although mediator styles vary, 'successful' practitioners tend to intervene actively in couple interaction, shaping communication towards settlement seeking and away from polarised and conflictual positions. Some researchers have questioned the neutrality of the mediators in their 'active' interventions, arguing that in their orchestration of settlements, mediators subtly ensure certain sorts of outcomes.[75] While these may be both socially highly desirable and legally acceptable outcomes, they nevertheless reflect a particular value system which is not always made explicit to clients, and may work against the real potential for couples to find their own mutually acceptable solutions individually tailored to their own unique circumstances. More research is needed on larger samples if these concerns are to be carefully assessed.

Process studies show also that practice setting makes a difference, and that mediation practice is dependent to some extent on local statutory arrangements. Setting seems to act as a significant constraint, shaping what mediators do or do not do. There is little doubt that court-based mediation restricts the time available, with little opportunity for a more therapeutic process spread over several months. We found that the stress on settlement-seeking in the courts put pressure on mediators and clients alike, with reaching agreements seeming to take precedence over any attempts at reducing conflict and improving communication between the parties. Bargaining in the very obvious 'shadow of the law'[76] might have the effect of prompting settlements 'at the door of the

73   Irving, HH and Benjamin, M, *Family Mediation: Contemporary Issues*, 1995, Thousand Oaks, Calif: Sage.

74   Pearson, J, 'An Evaluation of Alternatives to Court Adjudication' (1982) *Justice System Journal* 7 at 420–44. Pearson, J and Thoennes, N, 'A Preliminary Portrait of Client Reactions to Three Court Mediation Programs' (1985) *Conciliation Courts Review* 23 (1) at 1–14. Donohue, WA, Drake, L and Roberto, AJ, 'Mediator Issue Intervention Strategies: A Replication and Some Conclusions' (1994) *Mediation Quarterly* 11 (3) at 261–74; Donohue, WA, Lyles, J and Rogan, R, 'Issues Development in Divorce Mediation' (1989) *Mediation Quarterly* 24 at 19–28. Dingwall, R and Greatbatch, D, 'Behind Closed Doors: A Preliminary Report on Mediator/Client Interaction in England' (1991) *Family and Conciliation Courts Review* 29 at 291–303.

75   Dingwall, R, 'Empowerment or Enforcement? Some Questions About Power and Control in Divorce Mediation', in Dingwall, R and Eekelaar, J (eds), *Divorce Mediation and the Legal Process*, 1988, Oxford: Oxford University Press.

76   Mnookin, R and Kornhauser, L, 'Bargaining in the Shadow of the Law: The Case for Divorce' (1979) *Yale Law Journal* 88 p 950.

court' but the process is one which seems to provide rather less satisfaction for disputants and mediators than one which is not operating to a judicial timetable.

Outcome studies usually provide data relating to one or more of six indicators: agreement rate; client satisfaction; gender differences; coparental relationships; costs; and longer term durability and change. As Irving and Benjamin[77] show, agreement rates tend to be broadly consistent, between 50% and 80%, across a range of studies in different jurisdictions and settings. We and others have long argued that client satisfaction is a most important factor in relation to outcomes, and the majority of studies report high satisfaction[78] often unconnected to the level of agreement reached.[79] Furthermore, the majority of people describe their agreements as fair, durable, workable and comprehensive.[80] Studies which consider gender differences, coparental relations and longer term outcomes are particularly critical to the debate about the future role of family mediation since they strike at the heart of many of the concerns voiced about family disputes and their resolution. I shall return to them, therefore, in the final section of this paper.

Determining the costs associated with mediation has proved to be more elusive, often because accurate hard data are difficult to obtain, and because it is not always clear what the legitimate components of cost should include. Nevertheless, Kressel[81] estimated that projecting the available data onto a national basis for the United States translated into a very significant financial saving. Certainly, the perception amongst mediation users in England is that it does reduce the amount spent on lawyers' fees and court costs.[82]

It is clear from Irving and Benjamin's review of the research that there is no consensus among the studies as to the best predictors of mediated agreements. Whereas Camplair and Stolberg[83] found that agreement is related to the content of disputes, their relative importance to the parties concerned and their

77 Irving, HH and Benjamin, M, *Family Mediation: Contemporary Issues*, 1995, Thousand Oaks, Calif: Sage.

78 Kelly, JB and Duryee, MA, 'Women's and Men's Views of Mediation in Voluntary and Mandatory Settings' (1992) *Family and Conciliation Courts Review* 30 (1) at 43–49. Irving, HH and Benjamin, M, 'An Evaluation of Process and Outcome in a Private Mediation Service' (1992) *Mediation Quarterly* 10 (1) at 35–55.

79 Conciliation Project Unit, *Report on the Costs and Effectiveness of Conciliation in England and Wales*, 1989, London: Lord Chancellor's Department.

80 Chandler, DB, 'Violence, Fear and Communication: The Variable Impact of Domestic Violence on Mediation' (1990) *Mediation Quarterly* 7 (4) at 331–46.

81 Kressel, K, *The Process of Divorce: How Professionals and couples Negotiate Settlements*, 1985, New York: Basic Books.

82 Walker, J, McCarthy, P and Timms, N, *Mediation: The Making and Remaking of Cooperative Relationships*, 1994, Newcastle upon Tyne: Relate Centre for Family Studies, Newcastle University. Walker, J, 'Is There a Future for Lawyers in Divorce?' (1996) *International Journal of Law, Policy and the Family* Vol 10, No 1, at 52–74. McCarthy, P and Walker, J, *Evaluating the Longer Term Impact of Family Mediation*, 1996, Newcastle upon Tyne: Relate Centre for Family Studies, Newcastle University.

83 Camplair, CW and Stolberg, AL, 'Benefits of Court-sponsored Divorce Mediation: A Study of Outcomes and Influences on Success' (1990) *Mediation Quarterly* 7 (3) at 199–213.

willingness to compromise, Emery and Wyer[84] saw the ability of husbands to accept the ending of the marriage as particularly critical. Kelly[85] found that relatively equal financial acumen, a clear commitment to divorce, and emotional stability were important factors. Studies which have attempted to look at more complex predictors do begin to show that the interaction between clients and mediators is an influential variable[86] But of particular significance, it seems, are the findings from a number of studies, including our own, which point to the importance of process. Kressel *et al*[87] concluded that mediators who favoured a problem-solving approach are more effective than those whose model is settlement-oriented. Pearson and Thoennes' earlier research[88] found that agreement was more likely when clients perceived that the mediator could help them gain insight into their feelings; when disputes were relatively recent and less severe; and when clients possessed good communication skills and were willing to cooperate. Certainly, these findings accord with many of our own and have fundamental implications for mediation practice.

FROM RESEARCH TO PRACTICE

Janet Rifkin[89] has drawn attention to the fact that the dispute resolution movement has been the subject of investigation by a broadly-based research community, much of which has been critical of contemporary mediation practices and has raised concerns about a number of difficult areas including professional rivalries,[90] power and neutrality,[91] coercion,[92] and justice.[93] Rifkin

---

84 Emery, RE and Wyer, MM, 'Child Custody Mediation and Litigation: An Experimental Evaluation of the Experience of Parents' (1987) *Journal of Consulting and Clinical Psychology* 55 at 179–86.

85 Kelly, JB, 'Mediated and Adversarial Divorce: Respondents' Perceptions of their Processes and Outcomes' (1989) *Mediation Quarterly* 24 at 71–78.

86 Donohue, WA, Lyles, J and Rogan, R, 'Issues Development in Divorce Mediation' (1989) *Mediation Quarterly* 24 at 19–28.

87 Kressel, K, Frontera, E, Forlenza, S, Butler, F and Fish, L, 'The Settlement-orientation versus the Problem-solving style in Custody Mediation' (1994) *Journal of Social Issues* 50 (1) at 67–83.

88 Pearson, J and Thoennes, N, 'A Preliminary Portrait of Client Reactions to Three Court Mediation Programs' (1985) *Conciliation Courts Review* 23 (1) at 1–14.

89 Rifkin, J, 'The Practitioner's Dilemma', in Folger, JP and Jones, TS (eds), *New Directions in Mediation: Communication, Research and Perspectives*, 1994, Thousand Oaks, Calif: Sage.

90 Walker, J, McCarthy, P and Timms, N, *Mediation: The Making and Remaking of Cooperative Relationships*, 1994, Newcastle upon Tyne: Relate Centre for Family Studies, Newcastle University. Walker, J, 'Is There a Future for Lawyers in Divorce?' (1996) *International Journal of Law, Policy and the Family* Vol 10, no 1, at 52–74.

91 Cobb, S and Rifkin, J, 'Practice and Paradox: Deconstructing Neutrality in Mediation' (1991) *Law and Social Enquiry* 161 at 35–62.

92 Conciliation Project Unit, *Report on the Costs and Effectiveness of Conciliation in England and Wales*, 1989, London: Lord Chancellor's Department. Northrup, TA and Segal, MH, *Subjective Vulnerability: The Role of Disempowerment in the Utilization of Mediation Services by Women. Final Report to the Fund for Research on Dispute Resolution*, 1991, Washington DC: Fund for Research on Dispute Resolution.

93 Auerbach, J, *Justice Without Law*, 1983, New York: Oxford University Press. Bryan, PE, 'Reclaiming Professionalism: The Lawyer's Role in Divorce Mediation' (1994) *Family Law Quarterly* 28 (2) at 177–222.

goes on to suggest that despite such intense research activity, there has been remarkably little ongoing interaction between researchers and practitioners, noting, instead, a number of tensions. She explains this phenomenon partly with reference to the lack of explicit theoretical frameworks evident in mediation training and the consequent focus on teaching skills, which, in her view, implies to mediators that the hallmark of good practice is mastery of technique. The subsequent challenge to practice through research studies is then said to 'stun' practitioners who are forced to re-examine and reject many of the principles which have shaped their training, activities which are both uncomfortable and unsettling when mediators have no theoretical paradigm within which to make shifts. Hence, in Rifkin's analysis, the recommendations of researchers are simply ignored or met with cynicism rather than used to redefine practice and improve process.

Interestingly, although these tensions are clearly in evidence in England, the relationship here between practitioners and researchers seems to have fared rather better than in North America. We have witnessed significant changes in practice as a result of research studies, perhaps the most far-reaching relating to the development of mediation on all issues (including property and financial matters) in the late 1980s which was much influenced by the findings of our own government funded research. Furthermore, the problems associated with many of the court-based services exposed during that study resulted in many probation services rethinking their involvement in mediation and channelling resources into the community-based services in a number of successful partnership arrangements. Certainly, family mediation's future in England is not likely to be within the court-based services.

But, in our experience, research has played an even more important role than promoting one kind of mediation (eg, community-based) in preference to another (eg, court-based). It has been critical in giving weight to the voice of the consumer who could be considered to offer a more important perspective than any professional, and whose opinion is almost certainly more likely to influence practitioners in the long run. Our most recent evaluation of all issues mediation enabled us to balance the experience of mediation from the perspective of consumers, mediators and lawyers, using a range of research methods including direct observation of the mediation process, following the fate of some couples week by week over several months.[94] Not only did the research demonstrate the effectiveness of the process in terms of outcomes, but it also revealed just how demanding the process is for clients and their mediators. 'Experience', Aldous Huxley remarked, 'is not what happens to you; it is what you do with what happens to you'.[95] Clients we spoke to experienced fatigue, looked for guidance and advice from mediators (perceived as 'experts'), called for the availability of

---

94 Walker, J, McCarthy, P and Timms, N, *Mediation: The Making and Remaking of Cooperative Relationships* 1994, Newcastle upon Tyne: Relate Centre for Family Studies, Newcastle University.

95 *The Reader's Digest*, 1956.

single interviews as opposed to strict enforcement of joint interviews when partners must be present, valued safety and fairness, disliked the heavy future focus and often felt constrained by a structured process. Their personal accounts provide mediators with much food for thought.

What the consumer studies do in a powerful way is put the case for the broader objectives associated with mediation: indeed, they justify the emphasis on restoration of harmony so much in evidence in other cultures. We found that mediation can assist in the reconstruction of friendship and create circumstances whereby couples can negotiate outside of mediation appointments. Mediation appears to be effective at helping people cope with the severe stresses and strains associated with separation and divorce; it reduces resentment towards the other party; it lessens tension; and it improves communication. Since users rarely talk in the language of lawyers (rather than refer to the resolution of disputes they talk about 'sorting out troubles'), we concluded that what people value most about family mediation is its ability to enable them to work out their own arrangements and assist their decision-making. What the process is called and how it is defined and organised is far less important than what it does, whether it can meet the very variable needs of divorcing couples, and whether the mediators are professionally competent. No one is looking for cheap and cheerful services, clients want a thoroughly professional service, and the standard they frequently use in making this judgment is the same as the standard they apply to lawyers.

PROMOTING COOPERATIVE RELATIONSHIPS

Mediators have been at the vanguard of a new 'improvement' in the way couples might come to an agreement about matters over which they could not agree on their own. Establishing cooperation in troubled relationships is not easy, and the search for the 'middle ground' has sent mediators from different backgrounds off on their own quest for compromise. It has long been claimed that mediation crosses professional boundaries, but the development of family mediation has been characterised by a level of mutual mistrust between the long established practice of law and the relatively new professions related to social work and counselling. Hence the deal to carve up the various matrimonial disputes into packages which could be labelled either as more suitable for lawyers (money and property) or as more relevant to social workers (arrangements for children). The development of mediation for the entire range of disputes threw this neat and essentially 'English' solution into disarray. While existing mediators, most of whom had social work backgrounds, were deferential to the knowledge and skills of lawyers, and lawyers recognised that social work training results in greater competence in conflict management and dealing with emotional issues, mediation as a true alternative to the adversarial process seemed to cause both groups to feel threatened: each could develop the skills of the other and so effect a 'take-over' of the matrimonial dispute field. The alternative scenario, of course, is one in which a new hybrid profession, that of mediation, might emerge.

Both lawyers and non-lawyers engage in a rhetoric of cross-disciplinarity, but the rhetoric is not very detailed. It has to cope with the fact that while law has a clear identity, the other is more vaguely described as 'social work', and the knowledge that while lawyers are normally viewed as helpful and held in high regard by their clients, few people choose to consult social workers or invest the level of trust and authority in them as they do in members of the legal profession. There is also a marked differential in their level of income, and by implication, the value placed on their services. As Davis[96] has pointed out, not to consult a lawyer during divorce is seen as risky, and this has served to create a dependence on their services. Lawyers provide both technical competence and act as a safeguard against injustice resulting from conflicts of interest which arise in divorce. As they have begun to train and practise as mediators, their technical expertise is absorbed into the mediation process. Mediation users in our study appreciated the knowledge and skills brought by lawyers to a complex process, and the sense of 'security' and 'legitimacy' their presence engendered.[97] It is also clear that notions of guidance, reconciliation and counselling remain a leitmotif in the expectations of those who use mediation services.

Mediation, then, represents a complex process of accommodation in the face of changing views about what a dispute resolution mechanism can and should achieve. After some 10 years of research in this area we have been forced to suggest that the confusion, ambivalence and conflict which mark matrimonial disputes cannot be adequately addressed by providing a catholic but confused service. The distinctive objectives of mediation require specification in an overall description, and the ability to move between the various procedures necessary for their particular achievement. There are inevitable implications for the way in which mediation is organised, and for its position as a profession in its own right. The users of family mediation increasingly come to see it as a distinctive service, separate from counselling and from legal representation. Yet elements of both are important if a degree of healing is seen as important in the process of reaching just and fair settlements. There is both a public and a private interest in the making and remaking of cooperative relationships, and we all have an interest in the furtherance of civility. We have argued, on the basis of all our research in mediation and post-divorce relationships, for the establishment of a coordinated and coherent network of services for families experiencing divorce which can be accessed through a single door. Mediation is valued as one of a number of important services which, between them, meet a variety of needs. A multi-disciplinary approach has considerable merit, especially as there is no evidence that mediation can or will take over from other professions, nor offer a panacea for all the ills and traumas associated with the ending of a marital relationship.[98]

96   Davis, G, *Partisans and Mediators: The Resolution of Divorce Disputes*, 1988, Oxford: Clarendon Press.

97   Walker, J, McCarthy, P and Timms, N, *Mediation: The Making and Remaking of Cooperative Relationships*, 1994, Newcastle upon Tyne: Relate Centre for Family Studies, Newcastle University.

98   Walker, J, 'Is There a Future for Lawyers in Divorce?' (1996) *International Journal of Law, Policy and the Family*, Vol 10, No 1, at 52–74.

Both couples and professionals bring contentious pasts to mediation, and unless these are satisfactorily addressed vested interests will hamper the quest for cooperative futures.

In a recent survey of practising family lawyers in England and Wales,[99] we found that 75% declared themselves to be in favour of the greater availability and use of family mediation. Far fewer believe that mediation should attempt to resolve all issues, however, and the majority of lawyers remain sceptical of its role extending beyond disputes relating to children. It is clear that lawyers view mediation as a useful adjunct to the traditional lawyer-led process, not as a substitute for it. Indeed, a large contingent expressed the view that mediation would not be necessary at all if all lawyers adopted a conciliatory approach to matrimonial disputes. Even lawyers trained as mediators see the future of mediation as dependent to a large extent on how issues concerned with funding, organisation and training are managed, and while they value the sharing of skills with social workers and counsellors, nevertheless regard legal expertise as an essential ingredient in the mediation process.[100]

LOOKING TO THE FUTURE

The promotion of civilised negotiation requires there to be an atmosphere of calm, trust and respect. Unless this prevails amongst the professionals involved, it is unlikely to be distilled through the divorce process and impact on couples themselves. Mediation, as it has been organised in England, has been dominated by the search for authority which has remained the property of the legal profession. With relatively few couples opting to mediate their matrimonial disputes, mediation has remained the 'Cinderella' of the divorce process: useful, able to mop up the miseries of custody and access battles, but holding a somewhat menial position despite a strong belief in the value of its work. A number of concerns and policy decisions, however, have recently elevated mediation to a centre-stage position, forcing a reconsideration of its merits and its limitations.

There is serious anxiety about the numbers of marriages which end in divorce. There is convincing evidence that divorce is not good for children, and that the personal and social consequences are high. The breakdown of family life incurs enormous economic costs, not least being the rising expenditure on legal aid; the public cost of divorce in England has been put at £4 billion each year (House of Commons 1996). The public agenda, then, is one of attempting to stem the tide of marriage breakdown; reduce the antagonism and conflict inherent in the divorce process; re-establish cooperation and conjoint

---

99 McCarthy, P and Walker, J, 'Mediation and Divorce Reform: The Lawyer's View' (1995) *Family Law*, Vol 25, at 361–64.

100 McCarthy, P and Walker, J, 'Mediation and Divorce: The FMA View' (1996a) *Family Law*, Vol 26, at 109–12; McCarthy, P and Walker, J, 'Involvement of Lawyers in the Mediation Process' (1996b) *Family Law*, Vol 26, at 154–58.

responsibilities between parents; and reduce the financial cost of divorce. It is a complex scenario and family mediation is not able to tackle it all. Dingwall and Eekelaar[101] have pointed to the difficulties of fusing cost–saving, welfare paternalism, and self-reliant dispute resolution in a movement for reform. Goldberg, Green and Sander[102] defined an effective dispute resolution mechanism as 'one that is inexpensive, speedy and leads to a final resolution of the dispute. At the same time it should be procedurally fair, efficient (in the sense of leading to optimal solutions) and satisfying to the parties'. No one could describe the current divorce process in England and Wales as meeting such objectives. Indeed, by 1990 the Law Commission had concluded that:

> The present law and procedure are confusing and misleading; discriminatory and unjust; unhelpful because they distort bargaining positions; and thus minimise the chance of achieving amicably negotiated settlements; likely to increase hostility and bitterness; unlikely to save 'saveable' marriages, but may make things worse for everyone, especially children.[103]

As a consequence, divorce reform became a matter of some urgency in England. The government consulted widely, and put forward its proposals in a White Paper in April 1995. In the government's view, the objectives for a better divorce process should be fivefold: to support the institution of marriage; to include practicable steps to prevent the irretrievable breakdown of marriage; to ensure that the parties understand the practical consequences of divorce before taking any irreversible decision; where divorce is unavoidable, to minimise the bitterness and hostility between the parties and reduce the trauma for children; and to keep to the minimum the cost to the parties and to the taxpayer. These objectives are to be achieved through a wholly new approach to the legal process and cultural context of divorce.[104] Instead of a process dominated by lawyers and litigation, emphasis is placed on providing couples with clear, comprehensive information about the impact and consequences of divorce and the various services available including marital counselling, mediation and legal advice; encouraging people to reflect on the decision to divorce and to attempt to save the marriage wherever possible; removing the possibility of alleging fault to prove marital breakdown; ensuring that arrangements for children and all other matters are settled before divorce is granted; and introducing family mediation as a central component of the divorce process, the preferred method of dispute resolution for making future arrangements. The key message is that no longer should divorce legislation be merely concerned with the dissolution of a legal contract, but it must take account of the need to protect and preserve primary family relationships.

The proposals represented a radical shift away from adversarial positioning towards an informal, individualised system of justice. The abolition of fault-based facts as

---

101 Dingwall, R and Eekelaar, J, *Divorce Mediation and the Legal Process*, 1988, Oxford: Clarendon Press.
102 Goldberg, SB, Green, ED and Sander, FEA, *Dispute Resolution*, 1985, p 7, Boston, Mass: Little, Brown.
103 Law Commission, *Report on the Ground for Divorce*, Law Commission No 192, 1990, London: HMSO.
104 Family Law Act 1996.

evidence of breakdown has proved to be the most controversial element, and one which has deeply divided members of both Houses of Parliament. There are many who believe that divorce without fault seriously undermines the sanctity of marriage, and that it should not be possible to obtain a divorce 'easily' or quickly. The majority opinion, however, is that alleging fault in a divorce petition does nothing to resolve the personal feelings of hurt or disappointment, but rather that it escalates hostility thereby minimising the chances of couples being able to reach consensual agreements. Dealing with the emotional consequences is central to coping with the breakdown of marriage and the parties' need to find a more acceptable means of giving effect to their continuing responsibilities toward each other, and their children. Hence the focus on family mediation.

It is the centrality of mediation in the Family Law Bill which attracted a good deal of criticism from some critics, notably lawyers. What is emerging is a changing perspective on the role of lawyers in divorce, away from fighting for their own clients as partisans, in favour of providing legal advice in support of mediation. It emphasises co-working and cooperation and a multi-disciplinary approach. It is most unfortunate that during its formative years mediation has been seen as all that is civilised and decent in dispute resolution, positively contrasted with negotiation by lawyers which is viewed as overly antagonistic and confrontational. Such polarity has merely served to fuel the antagonism expressed by some lawyers to the proposals for reform, particularly since many would argue that what is applauded in mediation constitutes the very essence of what enlightened family lawyers have been trying to achieve in recent years. So the debate has been variously cast within arguments which run as follows: 'it's a treasury-based option with the sole aim of reducing public expenditure'; 'the poor will be forced into mediation while the rich will be able to buy (more superior) legal services'; 'people will be denied access to competent legal services, and may make decisions they subsequently regret'; and, 'it's a mediation takeover – from a respected long-established legal profession to an unknown bunch of well-meaning volunteers'. So the spotlight is on mediation: its credibility and potential are being scrupulously challenged and investigated, and penetrating questions asked. Is its structure and organisation robust enough? Are mediators sufficiently skilled and professional in their practice? How is quality in service delivery to be guaranteed? Will women be disadvantaged? What will mediation cost? How is value-for-money to be measured? These are questions which cause considerable frustration to mediators, but which undoubtedly require convincing answers, particularly as legal aid is to be made available for mediation. Mediators are facing major challenges as they prepare themselves for legal aid franchise. Who is to say that mediation services in England should continue to look as they do now? One service coordinator has speculated that mediators may become self-employed, or go into partnerships, perhaps with other professionals,[105] thus resembling organisational arrangements familiar to

---

105 Posey, J, 'Looking to the Future: Observation on Government Proposals: A Coordinator's Response' (1995) *Family Mediation*, Vol 5, No 2, at 14.

North America. She goes as far as suggesting that small voluntary mediation services may be disappearing by the year 2000. Certainly they are likely to be transformed as requirements for practice standards are set and accreditation issues addressed. Perhaps the greatest challenges, however, are to do with process.

The government White Paper set an agenda for mediation which extends its remit beyond a minimalist approach to dispute resolution. The belief is that family mediation can identify marriages capable of being saved and encourage those couples to seek marital counselling; help couples to accept responsibility for the ending of the marriage by acknowledging conflict and hostility and allegations of fault and blame; deal with feelings of hurt and anger, and address issues which may impede a couple's ability to negotiate settlements amicably, particularly the conduct of one spouse; and focus on the needs of children rather than on the personal needs of the parties concerned. This is a tall order, and argues for a more therapeutic approach than has been practised so far. There is also an increased expectation that in mediation parents can be encouraged to cooperate and share in the upbringing of children, perhaps indicating the use of parenting plans as in Canada and elsewhere. Although in the past there has been an implicit assumption within family law that both parents are important to the well-being of a child, divorce has normally resulted in one parent (usually the mother) being awarded custody of the child, and the other being granted periods of access to or contact with the child. Increasingly, joint or shared custody has been promoted as a more favoured and favourable arrangement, particularly in the United States, although just what this has meant in practice has varied widely. For many families it has been a mechanism for paying lip-service to the expectation that both parents should be involved in decisions about their children's upbringing; and for a few it has resulted in children spending almost equal time living with each parent, moving between two homes. Whatever the reality, it is now acknowledged that sharing parenting after divorce is less easy than it may sound, and that parents frequently need help constructing workable and beneficial arrangements. The critical task is not to determine preference for one custody option over another, but to create a parenting plan that best matches the needs of each child.[106] Such plans are highly practical and detailed documents, describing arrangements for day-to-day living; contact with each parent; the responsibilities of each parent separately and jointly; the matters which parents will confer on such as education and health; agreements about variations and special occasions; and the mechanisms which will be used by parents to review and modify arrangements and resolve any disputes which may arise. In many ways, drawing up such a plan promotes a shift from parenting within a personal, intimate relationship, to parenting within a business-like working relationship.[107] This requires not only a more therapeutic approach by mediators, but also a more directive and interventionist one.

---

106 Emery, RE, *Renegotiating Family Relationships: Divorce, Child Custody and Mediation*, 1994, New York: The Guilford Press.

107 Ricci, I, 'Mediation, Joint Custody and Legal Agreements: A Time to Review, Revise and Refine' (1989) *Family and Conciliation Courts Review* 27 at 47–55.

Protecting the best interests of children is a principle which runs throughout family legislation, although operationalising it has often been elusive. Mediators are conscious of the need to consider the position of children and are addressing this in training and in the preparation of practice standards. Rarely are children directly involved in mediation since it is primarily a decision-making process, the responsibility for which rests with adults. So mediators need to remind parents of their parental responsibility and of the importance of taking into account the views and concerns of their children. When necessary, mediators do invite children to meet with them, perhaps when arrangements for the future are being rehearsed and finalised. Interestingly, a number of mediation services now offer counselling support for children. There is a danger, however, that mediators who adopt a therapeutic/interventionist model will convince themselves and policymakers that the majority of divorced and remarried families will be able to develop an ideal post-separation parenting arrangement 'that attempts to approximate as closely as possible the parent-child relationships in the original two parent home ...'.[108] Calls for mediation to include a much stronger educative and affirmative stance in promoting an ideal-type coparenting arrangement begin to border on a welfarist model of intervention which flies in the face of mediator-neutrality. Furthermore, promoting a vision of 'happy-ever-after' post-divorce families ignores the complexity of the transitions involved, the emotional, social and economic stresses, and the real difficulties associated with non-residential parenting.[109]

In the current political climate which upholds marriage and the family, any suggestion that mediation might 'recreate' 'normal' family relations after marriage breakdown is highly seductive. It is also overly optimistic, and may set both the process of mediation and those who undertake it up to fail. Critics such as Dingwall and Greatbatch will have greater cause to accuse mediators of applying moral pressure on parents in the quest to reassert traditional family values and patterns of parenting. Our research found that pressure exerted by 'experts' was rarely welcomed by mediation clients. The belief that with the 'right' legislation and the 'right' processes, families can be helped to function in an integrated, amicable, cooperative fashion, whatever the relationships, household structures and living arrangements, is almost certainly flawed. This may be especially evident in relation to those families where domestic violence has been perpetrated and has contributed to the breakdown of the marriage.

A recent national survey of domestic violence in Canada[110] found that 50% of divorced women reported violence by a previous spouse. A fifth of these women reported that the violence occurred following or during separation, and indeed, the divorce may have the effect of increasing the violence. Repeated or ongoing

---

108 Kruk, E, 'Promoting co-operative parenting after separation: a therapeutic/interventionist model of family mediation' (1993) *Mediation Quarterly*, Vol 15, No 3, at 235–63.

109 Walker, J, 'Cooperative Parenting Post-divorce: Possibility or Pipedream?' (1993) *Mediation Quarterly*, Vol 15, No 3, at 273–93.

110 Statistics Canada, *Violence Against Women Survey. Survey Highlights*, 1993.

abuse was commonly reported in marriages that had ended. This is borne out in other studies, and the violence is frequently associated with access and contact visits.[111] There is growing realisation that mediators must screen for and provide adequate safeguards in relation to domestic violence. Most mediators do not believe that mediation is appropriate for couples where violence has been a persistent feature or is severe and ongoing. Much of the feminist criticism of mediation is based on mandatory, settlement-oriented programmes in the United States where women may be coerced into reaching unsatisfactory agreements precisely because of the threat or fear of violence. It argues for a more considered assessment process in mediation.[112] Mediation may be acceptable if the process is individually tailored, separate interviews are offered, concurrent counselling is available for either or both partners, and legal protection is accessible.[113] Increasingly, researchers and practitioners argue that the key question is not whether to mediate in spousal abuse cases, but what special steps must be taken to protect an abused partner who wishes to mediate.[114] Whatever the situation, the rights and safety of clients and mediators must be of paramount concern.

As family mediation moves from the margins to the mainstream of matrimonial procedures, theory and practice issues are being refined and contextualised. The enthusiasm for mediation, not just in family matters, has frequently meant that new practices have been adopted before all the implications for procedure and institutionalisation have been carefully thought through. Terminology has inclined to be imprecise, and the aims of mediation have not always been clearly articulated or understood. Confusion has resulted, thus undermining the potential opportunities for mediation to emerge as a new profession. As Mackie pointed out in 1991[115] the danger has been that mediation services would become an 'unhelpful mish-mash of vague schemes and half-baked optimism with little substantial merit or applicability, and little likelihood of permanence'. However, this rather pessimistic scenario seems to have less support as the millennium approaches. Our most recent follow-up study of couples mediating all the issues surrounding their divorce shows that they are less likely to carry bitterness and resentment towards each other into post-divorce life. Many professionals and researchers believe that mediation has much to offer divorcing couples and the case for family mediation would now appear to be made.

---

111 Walker, J and McNicol, L, *Policing Domestic Violence: Protection, Prevention or Prudence?*, 1994, Newcastle upon Tyne: Relate Centre for Family Studies, University of Newcastle. Hester, M and Radford, L, *Domestic violence and child contact arrangements in England and Denmark*, 1996, Bristol: The Policy Press.

112 Koss, MP, 'Violence Against Women' (1990) *American Psychologist* 45 at 374–80. Steinmetz, SK, 'Family Violence: Past, Present and Future', in Sussman, MB and Steinmetz, SK (eds), *Handbook of Marriage and the Family*, 1987, New York: Plenum Press.

113 Corcoran, KO and Melamed, JC, 'From Coercion to Empowerment: Spousal Abuse and Mediation' (1990) *Mediation Quarterly* 7 (4) at 303–16.

114 Erickson, SK and McKnight, MS, 'Mediating Spousal Abuse Divorces' (1990) *Mediation Quarterly* 7 (4) at 377–88.

115 Mackie, K (ed), *A Handbook of Dispute Resolution: ADR in Action*, 1991, p 279, London: Routledge and Sweet & Maxwell.

The diversity in mediation practice remains both a strength and a weakness. Mediators' orientations undoubtedly contribute to the way conflict within the mediation process both unfolds and is dealt with. There are many challenges ahead, and much ground for scholars and practitioners to cover together. As Dingwall and James[116] have argued, family law

> exists in a constant tension between recognising the family as a self-contained disputing arena and intervening ... to regulate the impact of disputes on non-participants.

Walter Langley, a senior lawyer in Canada, described alternative dispute resolution as 'a breath of fresh air'. Family mediation has come a long way in just a short time, and its attraction may indeed rest with its apparent simplicity:

> One cannot help but be fascinated ... by something that can encourage men and women to sit down and try to just talk. (James Durrell, Mayor of the City of Ottawa 1990).[117]

---

116 Dingwall, R and James, A, 'Family Law and the Psycho-social Professions: Welfare Officers in the English County Court' (1988) *Law in Context* 6 (1) pp 61–73.

117 Durrell, J, 'The Proclamation: "Justice is ... Just Us"', in Tannus, M (ed), *A Tribute to Conflict Resolution Day of Ottawa-Carleton*, 1990, North York, Ontario: Captus Press.

4 ALTERNATIVE DISPUTE RESOLUTION IN LABOUR RELATIONS: A TALE OF TWO PROVINCES

*JUDITH MCCORMACK and STAN LANYON**

INTRODUCTION

Alternative dispute resolution and labour relations have had a long and fruitful relationship. The opposing interests of employees and employers, the intimacy of the workplace setting and the fluctuating nature of work relations provide an obviously fertile ground for conflicts, and the economic toll of labour disruptions adds a public interest element to this picture. As a result, the early designers of collective bargaining systems were quick to conclude that dispute resolution would necessarily play an important role in the viability of effective labour relations. So well-established is mediation in this setting, for example, that in the negotiation of collective agreements mediation has been mandatory in many provinces across Canada before a strike or lockout for many years. Alternative dispute resolution is not confined to collective agreement negotiations however. Rather, a variety of innovative programmes have been developed for use at different points in the labour relations cycle. In this article we provide a glance at some of those programmes in British Columbia and Ontario, together with some observations arising out of that experience.

THE IMPETUS FOR ALTERNATIVE DISPUTE RESOLUTION

Dispute resolution in labour relations was originally handled by the courts, despite the fact that their structure and formality meant that they were not particularly well-suited to this task. Proceedings were typically lengthy, complex and expensive, and parties were often required to pursue a dispute through several levels of litigation. Certain issues in labour law were also poorly developed or inconsistently applied, and courts were sometimes considered insensitive to the interests and perspective of labour.

The solution was twofold: statutory tribunals with specialised expertise in labour relations such as the Ontario and British Columbia Labour Relations Boards were established for matters involving legislated rights, and grievance and arbitration systems were developed for disputes arising out of collective agreements. In this sense, both Labour Relations Boards and private arbitration boards were originally designed as alternative forums for adjudicating disputes in

---

*   Judith McCormack is former Chair of the Ontario Labour Relations Board; Stan Lanyon is former Chair of the British Columbia Labour Relations Board

The authors wish to thank Peter Gallus, Manager of Field Services, Paul Gardner, Director of the Office of Mediation, Barbara Dresner, Senior Labour Relations Officer and Michele Ryan, Mediator, in Ontario and Jane Mallen and Eric O'Brien, law students, in British Columbia for their assistance.

labour relations. In addition, mediation was introduced into collective agreement negotiations as a method of minimising strikes and lockouts.

These changes provided distinct advantages for parties to a dispute. Proceedings became more informal and flexible, the speed of adjudication was increased, and costs were reduced. Boards and arbitrators also brought considerable knowledge in labour relations to the disputes, and their appreciation of both the underlying principles and the strategic aspects involved meant that they were better equipped to resolve them.

In recent years, however, these once alternative forms of adjudication have begun to suffer from some of the problems plaguing the courts. As in other fields, litigation has mushroomed, and the process has become increasingly legalistic. While still less formal than the courts, both arbitration and Board proceedings have become significantly influenced by judicial processes. There are a number of reasons for this. Parties are frequently, if not usually represented by lawyers, who exert a constant pressure on the proceedings to conform to a familiar process with tried and true safeguards. This development also adds a level of complexity that makes adjudication less accessible. Adjudicators are charged with deciding the legal rights of parties and must handle sophisticated legal arguments in high stakes cases, requiring increasing comfort and adeptness with legal analysis and reasoning. At the same time, the courts exert a powerful influence through judicial review of the decisions made by labour adjudicators. This combination of lawyers, courts and the legal training of adjudicators conspires towards a creeping judicialisation in labour adjudication, resulting in greater delays and higher costs. In addition, the increasing technicality of the process estranges parties from their own dispute by converting it into a legal idiom presented and considered by professionals.

This judicialisation affects not only the process of adjudication, but the content as well. The right/wrong dichotomy of law reduces dispute resolution to a series of battles, and the parties to winners or losers. Linear legal reasoning is not well-equipped to address ambiguity or differing versions of reality except in a relatively simplistic way. Moreover, recognition of the nuances of human behaviour and the search for solutions must often give way in adjudication to attempts to stuff facts into legal pigeon holes, find fault, and award remedies that can be limited in their flexibility.

Of course, some of these difficulties beset litigation in many fields. However, the particular landscape of labour relations means that they are especially problematic in this context. In a volatile environment such as a workplace during a union organising campaign, even a few weeks of delay can be fatal to a party's rights in real terms, and lengthy proceedings can distort the administration of justice significantly. In fact, it is axiomatic in labour jurisprudence that protracted proceedings can destroy the appetite of employees for collective bargaining and increase the possibility of statutory violations by panicked or ill-motivated employers. Moreover, where delay is perceived of as being in the interests of one constituency as it often is in labour relations, the credibility of the adjudicative process is also at risk.

It is also true that litigation may foster unnecessary antagonism. The traditional hearing process, for example, relies on advocates to argue contrary positions, often setting the credibility of one witness against that of another. This style of dispute resolution may promote hostility, particularly where sensitive issues are involved or hearings are lengthy. The effect may be damaging to the parties' nascent or continuing relationship. This is exacerbated by the winner/loser dichotomy which does nothing for the ongoing interaction necessary in labour relations, often leaving one party triumphant and the other licking its wounds. Finally, the shrinking resources of statutory tribunals on the one hand, and parties on the other, has provided added urgency in the search for less expensive alternatives.

All of these factors have made the development of further alternative dispute resolution mechanisms a pressing task. Such mechanisms can be faster and less expensive than formal adjudication, and can be more finely-tuned to the parties' practical needs. Mediation, for example, involves the parties more closely and directly in the resolution of their own disputes, and the settlements reached may be more effective and durable than resolutions constructed by adjudicators. This flexibility or capacity for specificity together with the collaborative process which brings agreements into being means that settlements are more likely to be viable on a day-to-day basis and more likely to be honoured. It is often the case that parties feel greater satisfaction in the settlement as well, and greater loyalty to it as a result of their involvement in fashioning it. If alternative dispute resolution settles a dispute without a hearing, or simplifies and shortens the hearing, the capacity for litigation creating bitterness may be minimised. Moreover, each instance of mediation at different stages gives the parties practice in dispute resolution which facilitates their ongoing relationship.

At its most advanced, alternative dispute resolution is more than a change in method or form; it is a fundamental change in approach to dispute resolution. While the proceedings of both arbitrators and labour relations boards are less formal than those of the courts, they both depend on advocacy. In contrast mediation, for example, steps outside of the advocacy model and provides consultation, negotiation and consensus. The parties are no longer delivered to a form of ritualised combat. Rather, they are required to assume ownership of the process, and responsibility for their own resolution. The advantage of this approach is that the parties move beyond simply representing their interests in opposition to one another. Instead, they work together to build a common context within which they can explore a resolution. In this sense, mediation is also consistent with the theory of self-government by the parties which underlies collective bargaining and the making of workplace rules through a collective agreement.

The issues are different for mediation in the collective bargaining process itself. Here mediation functions not as an alternative to litigation, but as a method of minimising the use of the sanctions of a strike or lockout. In many cases, the financial losses to parties involved in this kind of economic warfare may be considerable, and in others, there may be a significant impact on the public as well. And while in some cases labour conflict may be cathartic, in others it may create long lasting bitterness, leading to a deterioration in the relationship and sometimes further strife.

It is also important to emphasise that when alternative dispute resolution takes the form of case management or alternative hearing models, it is not a lesser expedient on some scale of adjudicative purity. Rather, it fulfils the promise of a justice that is accessible, affordable and understandable. Moreover, an open and accessible process has an impact on the power of each party to a dispute. 'Deep pockets' are less likely to determine either the process or the result.

With this general overview in mind, we now turn to the experiences of Ontario and British Columbia. In each province, a variety of programmes provide alternatives to cumbersome formal hearings, including mediation, streamlined case scheduling and management processes and leaner, more expeditious models of adjudication.

ALTERNATIVE DISPUTE RESOLUTION IN ONTARIO LABOUR RELATIONS

Alternative dispute resolution plays a major role in Ontario at almost every phase of the labour relations cycle. To illustrate this point, we shall describe four major programmes which address the collective bargaining relationship at different key points, although these are by no means the only programmes. Our description starts with the Ontario Labour Relations Board which adjudicates cases involving the entry to and exit from a collective bargaining relationship, as well as those involving the structure of that relationship and a variety of statutory rights and obligations. The Board has developed a comprehensive mediation programme and a variety of case management techniques, in addition to a number of alternative hearing models. The second programme involves the Office of Mediation of the Ontario Ministry of Labour which provides mediation to assist the parties in reaching a collective agreement without a strike or lockout, an agreement. Thirdly, during the life of that collective agreement, the Ministry's Office of Arbitration offers mediation for grievances proceeding to arbitration. Fourthly, the Office of Mediation also provides a preventative mediation programme to address more systemic difficulties in the labour relationship.

THE ONTARIO LABOUR RELATIONS BOARD AND DISPUTE RESOLUTION

The Ontario Labour Relations Board was established 50 years ago, and now administers some 14 statutes, mostly centred on labour relations in different sectors. Chief among these is the Labour Relations Act which provides a series of statutory rights and obligations for employees, and employers, including the right of employees to join and be represented by a union and the right to terminate such representation. It sets out a framework for collective bargaining which provides for entry to the system, the negotiation of collective agreements, the timing and conditions of strikes and lockouts, picketing, the designation of essential services, and various other matters. Approximately 5,000 cases a year are filed with the Board under these various statutory provisions.

Mediation

The primary emphasis of the Board with respect to alternative dispute resolution is centred on its mediation programme. In recent years, the strength of this emphasis has been reflected in the Board's efforts to change the legal culture in which it functions to reflect the central role of mediation. Rather than thinking of mediation as a step in the process on the way to adjudication, the Board has indicated that mediation should be considered the dominant mode of handling cases, with adjudication available as a back-up if mediation fails. Because the programme is comprehensive and well-established and because of its many benefits, it has been widely accepted in the community served by the Board, even though it is not mandatory. Indeed, a significant number of cases are now filed because the parties want a mediator, not because they want a hearing.

Access to mediation is virtually automatic, in the sense that approximately 95% of the Board's cases are routinely assigned to mediators in the Board's Field Services programme upon receipt of the application commencing the case. The only general exceptions are complaints involving jurisdictional disputes between unions in regard to work assignments, where the strategic and political implications of litigation make settlement highly unlikely. For the rest, there is no initial evaluation of the suitability of individual cases for mediation because experience has indicated that most cases will benefit from it, and because the mode of mediation is informal enough to allow the mediator to withdraw quickly after he or she begins the process if it appears that the case is unlikely to respond to mediation. Cases are reviewed at the point of assignment to endeavour to make a good 'match' between the case and the mediator where the workload allows for this. There are 25 mediators employed by the Board with the title of labour relations officers. The settlement rate for the mediation programme is between 85% to 90%.

A labour relations officer usually commences the process by contacting the parties by telephone. In some cases such as applications for union representation or termination of union representation, mediation discussions are conducted primarily over the telephone. In other cases, the initial telephone contact helps the mediator to assess the situation, obtain information, decide how to structure one or more meetings, prime the parties and set up certain issues. For representation cases, a protocol has been developed with respect to the order in which certain standard issues are addressed to promote efficiency and to prevent the parties from manipulating the process for strategic reasons. In other cases, the labour relations officer has great flexibility with respect to the form mediation takes. Usually, however, this will involve at least one meeting. On average, a labour relations officer will spend a day or more on each case, including telephone calls, research and preparation, one or more meetings, and some follow-up activity.

The time a labour relations officer has in which to effect a settlement varies a great deal. Cases involving illegal strikes and lockouts, which are usually heard within 24 to 36 hours after filing, provide a restricted window of time. Interim order applications, which are scheduled within two or three days, provide a slightly greater period for settlement. Certain kinds of unfair labour practice hearings will start within two weeks, while other kinds of hearings may not commence for four weeks, allowing for a more leisurely mediation process. Interestingly enough, variations in the time available do not appear to affect the settlement rate. For example, illegal strike and lockout applications and interim order cases have a higher rate of settlement than many with more time permitted for settlement. To the extent that it is possible to identify patterns in settlement rates, they appear to relate more to factors such as the nature of the case, the strategic context of the application and the consistency of the jurisprudence in the particular area.

Hearing dates for adjudication where the case has not settled are set in the vast majority of cases when the application is filed. The Board's experience indicates that this plays a salutary role in attracting the attention of busy lawyers and providing a deadline. For cases that have not settled by that hearing date, the labour relations officer will often work with the parties at the hearing room door. Approximately 10% to 25% of cases settle on the day of hearing, Even after the hearing begins, the labour relations officer will sometimes keep in touch with the proceedings and offer his or her services after a significant preliminary ruling or a definitive turn in the evidence makes the climate more receptive to settlement.

Parties are represented by lawyers during the mediation phase in some 70% of cases. This can be either quite beneficial to the process or highly problematic. Experienced labour relations lawyers often help to ascertain their client's needs, to moderate their expectations and to diffuse some of the emotional content of the dispute. The labour relations officer can also be of assistance to the lawyer or representative by conveying news or information to clients that they would find unpalatable coming from their lawyer or representative. Counsel who are skilled and experienced with mediation may find themselves in a role that blends advocacy and mediation as they buffer, filter and moderate the interaction between their client and the other participants in the mediation. At the same time, an inexperienced or inept lawyer can raise unreasonable expectations in a client and become so preoccupied with the legal issues that he or she skews the process. Nevertheless, officers will try not to embarrass a lawyer in front of his or her client, occasionally a challenging task.

All mediation discussions are confidential in the sense that the contents are not communicated to the adjudicators who may hear the case if it does not settle. In addition, the Board will not generally hear evidence in a hearing with respect to the nature of settlement negotiations, and the Labour Relations Act provides that information furnished to labour relations officers shall not be disclosed except to the Board or with the consent of the Board. To add to this, labour relations officers cannot be required to testify in civil or administrative proceedings. These measures are all designed to support the mediation process by creating an environment in which the parties will feel they can speak freely, and have confidence in the objectivity of the mediator.

A wide range of styles and approaches are utilised by labour relations officers in the mediation process. Generally speaking, however, it is fair to say that they tend to play quite an active role, with a significant educational and evaluative component. They see themselves as having carriage of the proceedings and are relatively interventionist, although they try to ensure that the process will leave the parties feeling that it is their settlement and not something imposed upon them. Often a case will represent an employer's first exposure to unionisation and collective bargaining, and frequently it is not a welcome event. The labour relations officer will sometimes spend a considerable amount of time introducing a party to the collective bargaining system, explaining how it works, providing reassurance that the end of the world has not arrived, and describing what will happen next. In some cases, the labour relations officer will also supply a common sense perspective on labour relations, pointing out the likely consequences of different courses of action in terms of the effect on the workplace. In this sense, the mediation provides a longer term investment in the parties' relationship as well as a more user-friendly and efficient means of resolving a particular case.

Labour relations officers are familiar with the various statutes the Board administers and its case law, and will use this knowledge to assist the parties in considering settlement. Providing some evaluation of their respective cases is an important tool in encouraging parties to be open-minded and receptive to settlement ideas. In part this is because the mediation takes place in the context of litigation about statutory rights and obligations, with these matters necessarily capturing the attention of the parties to some extent and crystallising their bargaining power. The primary focus, however, is usually on eliciting the underlying issues and crafting a resolution which addresses them. Indeed, often the labour relations officer will also try to steer the parties away from concentrating on their legal positions so that their practical interests can be identified.

Although the process is largely tailored to the nature of the case and the parties, it is usually fast, fluid, and flexible, and likely to involve the following components: collecting information, allowing some opportunity for parties to vent their frustrations, creating rapport between the parties and the mediator, drawing out the needs and limits of the parties, generating and eliciting ideas with respect to settlement possibilities and fashioning an agreement. Settlements will be reduced to writing and are enforceable by application to the Board. Where a settlement is not possible, the labour relations officer may assist the parties in narrowing the issues in dispute and agreeing upon facts to shorten the litigation.

The skills and experience of the labour relations officers are as diverse as their personal styles. On the whole, however, they tend to be people who relate to others easily, listen well, are both diplomatic or blunt as the situation requires, have considerable patience and stamina, are creative and persuasive, and have a keen sense of timing. With respect to the latter point, they are likely to know when to be funny, when to be forceful, when delicacy is required, when to put the parties together, when to separate them, when to be persistent and when to allow a party time to digest an offer or reconsider their position. Often they will be able to see the solution to a problem at the start of the process, but may spend a number of hours or days in helping the parties to arrive at that point or conceive of it themselves. Among other things, the time spent listening during those hours or days provides the parties with a kind of 'day in court' which may obviate the necessity of actually getting into the hearing room.

Another important quality shared by labour relations officers is the ability to backtrack skilfully when he or she may have made a mistake or misread the situation. Similarly, the ability to deliver bad news in a way which does not box a party into a corner is critical. They tend to be analytical in the sense of knowing what is relevant and what is not, both legally and otherwise, although very few of them are lawyers. Their own professional reputation and credibility may play an effective role in the process as well, particularly in terms of the evaluation component.

One function they do not perform is attempting to remedy or offset any power balance between the parties. This is in part because the parties are often corporate or institutional such as companies or unions, and in part because the more highly-charged environment of labour relations would mean that this kind of role might jeopardise their credibility as neutrals. They will try to ensure that a weaker party has sufficient information to make considered decisions and that he or she understands the possibilities and the consequences involved. Beyond this, however, they do not perceive it is part of their mandate to equalise the parties' positions.

Nevertheless, it is possible that the process itself has something of a levelling impact. To the extent that it moves the conflict to a forum where the identification of interests and problem–solving are the primary mode of conflict resolution, the process itself may dilute the effect of the parties' respective power stemming from their legal or financial positions, although these may still play a significant role.

In recruiting labour relations officers, the Board looks for extensive labour relations experience in addition to a bundle of skills which includes sensitivity, creativity, listening and analytical abilities, poise and persuasiveness. Because of the need for labour relations experience, labour relations officers tend to come from either labour or management, making it imperative they can transform themselves into neutrals and present themselves as objective within a short period of time. Even after they establish themselves, their credibility as neutrals is something which requires ongoing attention. Self-confidence is critical as well because the informality of the mediation lends a degree of intimacy which can leave the mediator vulnerable if the process collapses. In addition, officers who depend on their work for too high a degree of self-definition may seek a settlement too desperately, and in coaxing the parties may cross a line which impairs their effectiveness.

In other words, an element of detachment is necessary, for these reasons and also because the need to tailor the officer's approach to the variables of each case requires a level of deliberateness from time to time. Persistence is also a requirement, since it is not uncommon for parties to announce an offer as their last, or to say that they have reached the end of what is possible. In this situation, the labour relations officer may engineer a break or change of pace, or may even make small talk with a party for a while, trawling for openings which might offer ways to resume the discussions. Similarly, self-control can be a major asset in dealing with difficult or antagonistic lawyers or parties.

Training consists of a mentoring programme where trainees are assigned to an experienced officer for a six month period. During this time, they observe both their mentor and other officers in action to expose them to a range of styles and maximise the inventory of techniques available to them. They also work through a supervised programme of cases of gradually increasing difficulty until they are ready to manage them on their own. A reading programme includes material on both mediation skills and substantive labour law. Continuing education is provided in part by monthly meetings with the Board's solicitors who provide information about legislative and regulatory changes, and the Board's cases, policies, and rules of procedure. Recently, the field services programme was also reorganised to provide greater opportunities for continuing mentorship and peer support.

In addition to the training provided by mentors and colleagues, in 1994 the Board began organising exchange initiatives for labour relations officers with client organisations or other mediation programmes. The exchanges involve the labour relations officers, individuals with private sector unions and employers, and the Office of Mediation collective agreement mediators whose functions are described below. In the case of exchanges with unions and employer groups, the advantage to the labour relations officer is to provide a particular kind of hands-on experience either to fill in his or her own background or to update it. The exchanging party has the opportunity for one of their staff to acquire mediation skills and learn about the Board's processes. The exchanges with the Office of Mediation give both participants exposure to another type of mediation at a different stage of the labour relations cycle.

It is worth noting here that there are some kinds of cases where the mediation efforts of labour relations officers and collective bargaining mediators may overlap. For example, cases involving first collective agreement disputes, the designation of essential services, the use of replacement workers during a strike or lockout or allegations of bad faith bargaining may involve collective bargaining mediators initially or simultaneously. When cases are filed with the Board, labour relations officers will begin settlement discussions, which of necessity may include negotiations with respect to the collective agreement. In these circumstances, the labour relations officer and the collective bargaining mediator will keep in touch to co-ordinate their activities.

The Board works to make its accumulated institutional expertise available to others as well. For example, the manager of field services now participates in a mediation design consultancy project in which he assists other tribunals to develop a blueprint for their own mediation services, and he has been involved in training mediators at other labour boards in Canada. The field services programme also provides some technical or common sense information on an informal basis for lawyers and parties who call in for this purpose. Within the obvious limits imposed by being part of an adjudicative institution, some of this information can be useful in preventing or addressing problems at an early stage.

While the Board's field services programme is the principal forum for mediation at the Board, there are also mediation services available which involve the adjudicators as well. In certain cases, for example, a more formal pre-hearing conference may be scheduled, usually on the request of the parties, at the suggestion of a labour relations officer, or as a result of case screening. These are presided over by an adjudicator who will not hear the case if it subsequently proceeds to a hearing. Although there is great flexibility in the structure of the pre-hearing conference, generally it is fair to say that the evaluation of the parties' cases tends to play a more significant role than at an earlier stage of mediation. Frequently labour relations officers or parties will feel that an authoritative view from an adjudicator may be of assistance in making settlement more attractive to a recalcitrant party or an unrealistic lawyer. The Board has also had some success with combining an adjudicator and a labour relations officer for pre-hearing conferences. In this situation, the adjudicator plays a greater role in the evaluation component, 'softening up' the parties, and the labour relations officer then moves in to help the parties fashion an agreement. Because the skills involved in mediation are often quite different from those used in adjudication, the Board has conducted mediation training sessions for adjudicators to enhance their effectiveness in a settlement role.

Cases are usually adjudicated by panels of three, including labour and management Board Members and a neutral vice-chair. In some circumstances, cases may also be assigned to a vice-chair sitting alone. From time to time the panels or vice-chair may also mediate settlements in cases upon which they are sitting. Sometimes this may involve only the labour and management Board members in discussions. This is because the vice-chair's views are likely to be determinative in tripartite adjudication of this nature, and excluding him or her from settlement negotiations insulates the adjudicative function of the panel from the process to some extent. In other cases, however, the vice-chair may play an active role. If settlement does not take place, on infrequent occasions the panel or vice-chair alone may also go on to determine it, providing a version of what is often referred to as 'mediation-arbitration'.

There are some obvious dangers to this process. The roles of mediator and adjudicator are not always compatible, and to be effective as a mediator in this situation, it may be necessary to make assessments and receive information which are not appropriate for an adjudicator. The melding of roles may confuse the parties, can affect the credibility of the institution and is generally frowned upon by the courts.

This means that the risks are high for this form of mediation. At the same time, it can be remarkably effective in the right case, and it can save the parties a great deal of time and money by putting a lengthy but ill-fated case out of its misery in a timely manner. Generally adjudicators are of the view that it is a useful form of mediation but one to be used with great caution and the consent and full understanding of the parties. The decision to engage in it will involve careful consideration of the nature of the case, the type of parties, the identity of the counsel, and the skills of the adjudicators.

Because of the range of mediation options available at different stages of the litigation process, in 1995 the Board established a mediation team to ensure that they were integrated into a coherent and efficient overall programme. Among other things, the team has looked at the possibility of duplication of efforts where a hearing panel intervenes after labour relations officer discussions or a pre-hearing conference, the importance of communication between different levels of mediation, and the risk of judicial review. Currently it is in the process of developing a checklist to guide such interventions.

Finally, the Board in its adjudicative capacity strives to create a highly supportive environment for mediation. As noted previously, it will not hear evidence with respect to settlement discussions to ensure that the parties will feel they can talk freely. Agreements are enforced, and the Board will not allow a party to re-open a matter once agreement has been reached in the absence of extraordinary circumstances. Adjudicators will endeavour to maintain a degree of consistency in the case law for a variety of reasons, not the least of which is the positive effect this has on settlements and the ability of employers and unions to arrange their affairs with some confidence. In addition, in certain kinds of cases which are likely to involve a large number of issues, the Board has developed rules of procedure which require a party to file an agreement it would be prepared to sign with its application, for the purpose of jump-starting the settlement process.

Streamlining litigation

Despite the Board's array of mediation services, there is little question that not all cases can be settled. The nature of the issue, the temperaments of the parties, the experience of counsel or the strategic environment surrounding the dispute may mean reaching agreement is not possible. For those cases, the Board has developed a series of initiatives designed to streamline the adjudicative process.

When applications are filed with the Board, they enter an informal screening process in which some are diverted into a case management system. While the nature of the process may vary with the type of application, generally cases will be reviewed by adjudicators who will consider, for example, whether the application makes out a case on its face for the relief requested, whether document production orders would be useful, whether certain types of investigation by labour relations officers are warranted or whether a pre-hearing conference would be productive. An application which does not make out a case for the remedy requested (on the assumption that all the allegations can be proved) may be dismissed without a hearing. The purpose of a pre-hearing conference in this context is to assist the parties in narrowing the issues in dispute, obtain agreement on facts, direct disclosure of particulars or evidence, and otherwise structure the litigation in difficult or complex cases. Similar discussions may be held over the telephone with the parties instead or in addition to the conference.

In 1993, the Board developed new rules of procedure, the product of extensive consultation with adjudicators, mediators, lawyers and the labour relations community. The changes were precipitated in part because of the need for a fresh look at its litigation procedures and the necessity of synchronising them with substantive legislative amendments. The new rules were designed to be easier to read and reflect increased emphasis on early and complete disclosure to minimise 'trial by ambush'. They also promote expedition in the scheduling and conduct of hearings. These changes were coupled with the establishment of a fast track to reduce delays for types of cases considered particularly time-sensitive or urgent.

These measures resulted in significant reductions in the time taken for matters to be heard and decided. However, the Board has also attempted to monitor their impact to ensure that they did not have an adverse effect on the settlement process. Among other things, quick scheduling decreased the time between the filing of an application and the hearing date for many cases. There was some apprehension that shortening that period of time might result in a fall in the settlement rate at the mediation stage, because parties would be too busy preparing their cases to settle. As it turned out, moving the first date of hearing forward appeared only to result in cases settling earlier, not less often.

A related issue involved the question of whether early disclosure hindered or helped settlements. There were at least two reasonable possibilities: that early disclosure would focus the parties and their counsel on the case at an earlier point, and that their respective strategic strengths and weaknesses would crystallise sooner and facilitate settlement. On the other hand, there was some concern that the preparation of this material might result in a kind of litigation momentum, making the parties less interested in settlement. Setting out the facts in writing might also fix a party into a version of events which would be offensive to the other party, and difficult to unravel. Again, it seems that early disclosure has not hindered settlement in the sense that the rate has held steady. On an anecdotal basis, it seems reasonable to think that in different cases or even within the same case, both the advantages and disadvantages of early disclosure on the settlement process might be operative. It is also true that even unsuccessful mediation, either by a labour relations officer or at the prehearing or hearing stage, often provides a degree of informal disclosure to the parties which can facilitate the progress of the hearing.

In some areas, the Board is authorised by legislation to resolve disputes without formal hearings and the new rules of procedure maximised these opportunities. For example, in handling jurisdictional disputes between unions with respect to the assignment of work, the Board began holding 'consultations', in which the parties are required by the rules to file considerable material in advance. The subsequent consultation involves the parties making abbreviated presentations to a panel of the Board, which then renders a brief decision, either at the hearing or within a day or two. Consultations rarely last longer than a day, in contrast to hearings in these cases which sometimes took up to a year to complete. While predictably not all decisions resulting from consultations have been welcomed, the process itself has largely met with considerable approval by employers and unions alike.

Another new model of hearing involves the Board's power to award interim relief. The nature of interim relief requires a speedy adjudication, and the Board designed new rules for these matters which required the parties to file their evidence in advance in the form of declarations. Hearings are usually held two or three days after the application date, at which time a panel of the Board will hear arguments only. Typically these hearings take several hours, again with decisions delivered either at the hearing or shortly thereafter.

Interestingly enough, it was initially contemplated that interim relief cases might eventually be determined without a hearing at all, simply on the basis of the written material filed. In practice, however, the Board found that scheduling a hearing provided a time frame and a focus for mediation efforts by the labour relations officers, which promoted settlement. Ultimately, it appeared that the usefulness of this structure, coupled with the high rate of settlement in these cases, meant that scheduling an oral hearing was more efficient than a 'paper hearing'. Paper hearings are often held, however, in other kinds of cases, including determinations on employee status or reconsideration requests.

To reduce costs, especially for parties located in centres away from the Board's facilities in Toronto, the Board has developed a practice of using telephone conferences to hear and adjudicate brief matters such as adjournment requests or preliminary motions. Other forms of electronic and paper hearings are contemplated.

Where formal hearings are held, the Board strives to provide a process which is both reasonably fast and fair, not always an easy mix To promote both these goals, the Board has held training sessions for adjudicators to maximise their inventory of skills in effectively managing hearing dynamics. In addition, the Board has also explored procedural avenues to cut short dysfunctional hearings, including, for example, the panel initiating the equivalent of a non-suit on its own motion, or indicating to a party that it would entertain such a motion without the need for an election with respect to the calling of evidence.

Another approach is to require a party to state its best case, rather than hearing all the evidence, where it appears that such case is very weak and that it is likely to be unsuccessful even if all its allegations are proven. The Board may then determine the matter on this basis, but only, of course, if the determination is in favour of the other party. Similarly, the Board will sometimes direct a party to provide 'will–say' statements for witnesses it anticipates, with the same purpose in mind. Another option is to decline to call upon a party to respond in argument to a weak case or motion. Of course, some of these kinds of hearing management techniques are simply the strategies that experienced and skilful adjudicators have been using for years, in the courts as well as in the administrative justice system.

In some cases the Board may provide a mix of adjudication by the panel and mediation by a labour relations officer on the day of hearing. For example, if settlement discussions have reached a sticking point, the parties may go into the hearing to have the Board decide that issue on the spot. They will then return to the labour relations officer to continue discussions until they reach another snag, at which point they may go back into the panel for further adjudication. A more formal version of this process has been utilised in the designation of essential services for strikes and lockouts, where the Board has adjudicated upon certain key issues or provided overriding principles for the parties to consider in attempting to reach agreement in this area.

Ultimately, however, the usefulness of these kinds of alternative models or hearing management techniques must always be balanced with the importance of ensuring that parties both receive a fair hearing, and perceive it that way.

COLLECTIVE BARGAINING MEDIATION BY THE OFFICE OF MEDIATION

A thumbnail sketch of the legislative scheme set out in the Labour Relations Act in Ontario is useful in understanding the pivotal role played by the Office of Mediation in collective agreement mediation. After a union has been certified by the Ontario Labour Relations Board to represent employees, the union and the employer are required by the Act to enter into negotiations with each other, to bargain in good faith and to make every reasonable effort to reach a collective agreement. The fact that negotiations take place in the shadow of economic sanctions such as a strike or lockout is considered to promote opportunities for settlement through each party's desire to avoid economic pain. However, parties cannot strike or lock out in the course of their collective agreement negotiations without going through an initial mediation process referred to as conciliation. This process is conducted by one of 28 mediators provided by the Office of Mediation. After conciliation, the Minister of Labour will typically issue a report indicating that he or she has decided not to appoint a Board of Conciliation. These Boards are rarely used, but the issuance of the 'no–Board report' starts the clock ticking toward a deadline 16 days later when the parties are permitted to use economic sanctions. During this period, parties may voluntarily request mediation, which normally takes place within two or three days of the strike or lockout deadline and is also provided by the Office of Mediation. The timing of mediation in this regard is deliberate in the sense that experience has shown that the deadline has a productive effect on the parties' efforts. Mediation is generally lengthier, more intense and more highly-pressured than conciliation because of its proximity to the period in which economic sanctions can be used. When parties do strike or lock out, they will usually (although not always) do so at the first legal opportunity.

The combined conciliation and mediation activity of the Office of Mediation involves approximately 4,000 to 5,000 disputes a year, covering anywhere between 500,000 and 600,000 employees. Overall, approximately 95% of these disputes result in collective agreements without strikes or lockouts. Of those, some 30% to 40% settle at the conciliation stage. Another 20% settle subsequent to conciliation without further intervention by the mediator, and the remainder settle at the mediation stage.

The process is initiated by one or both parties applying for conciliation. The Office of Mediation checks certain preliminary matters, such as ensuring that the union involved actually has bargaining rights, but makes no assessment as to the appropriateness of conciliation at that point. The other party has five days to object, but the only objection accepted is a technical one, for example, to the effect that the application has not been made during the proper statutory time window. There are a number of reasons why there is no evaluation at this stage of the process, including the fact that conciliation is mandatory, and that applications and objections may form part of the strategic manoeuvring in bargaining. The mediation process which may follow conciliation is available simply on request.

The Office of Mediation will match mediators to cases in terms of expertise where this is possible in relation to the workload. Among the 28 mediators, there are six mediation specialists who have accumulated specific knowledge, experience and credibility in particular industries. For example, a mediation specialist in the forest products industry will have approximately 60% to 70% of his or her cases in that area. Since the skills of the specialists are generally conserved for mediation, the mediation specialist will also coordinate the activities of other less specialised mediators at the conciliation stage in the industry. In other areas, the Office will try to arrange to have the same mediator conduct both the conciliation and the mediation on a file.

Meeting dates for both conciliation and mediation will be set with the agreement of the parties. In most cases only one day will be scheduled, as experience has shown that setting more than one day will sometimes prolong the process, with the parties only getting down to serious work on the last day. However, more days may be set subsequently if it appears necessary. The average time spent on either a conciliation or mediation session is a day and one-quarter.

This kind of mediation presents different challenges than litigation mediation. The role of the mediators is to help the parties reach agreement on issues such as wages, discharge rights, seniority, and so forth. Mediators in this area have a different substantive knowledge base, centred more on collective bargaining trends, economic data and collective agreement language than on statute and case law, and substantive evaluation plays a smaller role. This may in part reflect the difference between a rights-based litigation context and one which involves interest-based economic conflicts. In any event, the evaluation of a party's position is more likely to be provided upon request, rather than volunteered. Of course, generic mediation skills such as listening, identifying interests, eliciting and creating options are similar, but they can take different forms in this context. Among other things, the multiplicity of issues means that configuring trade-offs is likely to feature highly in the bargaining.

The fact that the parties may have already spent considerable time in negotiations or that they may have collective bargaining experience has mixed implications for the process. On the one hand, they can be skilled negotiators themselves, with attendant advantages. On the other, the disputes they have been unable to resolve may be particularly challenging. In addition, the dynamics within a party can become critical, and the mediator may spend considerable time helping a union staff representative or a company negotiator to bring the rest of the negotiating committee to a particular point or conclusion. In this way, there may be bargaining within a negotiating committee, particularly on the union side where the ratification process and the elected status of committee members can bring a highly political element to the process as well. In this context, the timing and duration of mediation may play a role in the acceptance of the results. For example, an 11th hour settlement after around-the-clock negotiations may be more likely to suggest to ratifying employees that every effort has been made by their negotiating committee and that the best settlement possible has been obtained. A trend towards centralised bargaining in Ontario may also increase the stakes for some sets of negotiations as the number of workplaces covered by them expands accordingly. Similarly, centralised bargaining often means bigger negotiating committees encompassing more diverse interests, and the internal dynamics can be more complex on both sides. Timing is also crucial in terms of prioritising the issues at stake. The parties do not have an infinite degree of energy, and mediators try to ensure that it is not expended on less important issues first.

Generally speaking, the collective bargaining mediators do not approach mediation with the same degree of carriage that labour relations officers bring to the process. The underlying philosophy in collective bargaining mediation is that it is the parties' dispute, and that the best settlement is one where the parties did not notice the mediator was there. Among other things, experience has indicated that it is important to keep the focus on the parties' responsibility for the proceedings, as otherwise they may start viewing the conflict at least to some extent as the mediator's problem. Mediators also see the process as an opportunity for the parties to learn to communicate with each other, particularly where the labour relationship is relatively new. As a result, the session will usually be convened with the parties together, and there is increased emphasis on encouraging the parties to continue to meet face to face for as long as possible. At the very least, the mediator will usually bring the parties together when they exchange positions. In more pragmatic terms, this also has the advantage of minimising the possibility of misunderstanding and subsequent conflicts with respect to interpreting and administering the collective agreement.

Of course, this less interventionist perspective will depend on the circumstances. Like labour relations officers, collective bargaining mediators retain a great deal of discretion to tailor the process to the parties' needs and the dynamics of the situation. For example, although the process is essentially the same for both conciliation and mediation, the more volatile context provided by the strike and lockout deadline means that mediation will be more intense, often extending to the small hours of the morning. As the deadline approaches, mediators may become more active in their approach. This is true as well where the process appears to be bogged down, either in conciliation or mediation.

Even after a party strikes or locks out, the mediator will continue to stay in touch with the parties and convene meetings where this seems likely to be productive. Sometimes this may mean waiting for a period until the toll of economic warfare has put the parties in a more conciliatory frame of mind.

Settlements usually take the form of written memorandums of settlement which the parties agree to recommend for ratification. On the union side this involves a vote by employees. Parties are encouraged to draft the memorandums themselves to strengthen their ownership of the settlement and minimise misunderstanding. Once the memorandum is ratified, the mediator's involvement is completed. If the memorandum is not ratified by one or both parties, negotiations generally recommence or a strike or lockout occurs. Enforcement of the settlement takes place through the Ontario Labour Relations Board which will not permit strikes and lockouts where a collective agreement is in force, and through the grievance and arbitration procedure with respect to disputes arising out of the collective agreement. Again, information furnished to mediators is protected from disclosure by law.

In recruiting mediators, the Office of Mediation looks for extensive experience as the chief spokesperson in negotiations for either labour or management, with a established track record of credibility. This does not necessarily imply a search for individuals with a conciliatory bargaining style. On the contrary, a candidate may have been a tenacious negotiator, but one who is considered honest and trustworthy by his or her bargaining opponents. As in the case of labour relations officers, the ability to make the transition to being a credible neutral is important in a context where mediators are likely to come from either the employer or union constituency. The mediators themselves tend to be charming, gregarious people who can engage the parties' interest in the process even at two o'clock in the morning. In addition to the skills and qualities described earlier with respect to labour relations officers, they must be adept at working with groups of people on both sides with varying degrees of experience and ability, and differing interests.

The primary feature of the training programme of three to six months is a mentorship programme, which includes rotated assignments to expose the trainee to a broad range of styles and techniques. After three to four months, new mediators may start taking their own cases with some supervision. Part of the goal of the mentoring process is also to expose the new mediator to as many parties as possible, with a view to building up his or her profile and professional credibility. As we noted earlier, the Office of Mediation participates in exchange programmes with the Ontario Labour Relations Board. In addition, it arranges similar exchanges for its mediators with the Office of Arbitration. Mediators are provided with a monthly update on settlement patterns from the Office of Collective Bargaining Information, where parties are required to file copies of their current collective agreements. In addition, mediators can request specific data from this office whose staff of 13 provides various kinds of research. There are approximately 10,000 collective agreements filed with this office at any particular point in time.

Lawyers and professional labour relations consultants are often involved in this form of mediation, but normally only on the employer side of the table. As in other forms of mediation, lawyers and representatives who are experienced can assist the process, while those who are under the illusion they are litigating a collective agreement may obstruct it.

The collective bargaining mediators share the views of labour relations officers with respect to the inappropriateness of attempting to balance the power relationship between the parties. To do so would introduce an element of advocacy to the role which might impair the mediator's objectivity, or at least affect the perceptions of the parties in this regard.

GRIEVANCE MEDIATION BY THE OFFICE OF ARBITRATION

Once there is a collective agreement in place, disputes with respect to the application and interpretation of the agreement are channelled into the grievance and arbitration process. The grievance procedure is set out in the collective agreement and will usually involve a series of discussions between the union and the employer moving up a vertical decision-making hierarchy in each organisation. If the grievance is not settled during this procedure, a party may decide to send it to arbitration. In Ontario, the Labour Relations Act requires collective agreements to contain an arbitration mechanism. In addition, the Act provides for an expedited form of arbitration where a hearing will commence within 21 days. In either case, a party can request mediation from the Office of Arbitration prior to the arbitration hearing. For expedited arbitrations, the Office itself takes the initiative to contact the parties and set up a mediation session. While the process is not mandatory, some 90% of parties agree to utilise it. Since mediation for nonexpedited arbitrations requires the initiative of the parties, it is more sporadic, although the number of requests has steadily increased in recent years. If mediation is unsuccessful, an arbitration hearing will be conducted by a private arbitration board or arbitrator.

The Office of Arbitration employs 13 mediators with the title of grievance settlement officers who mediate approximately 6,000 grievances a year. Each session averages between two and four hours long and takes place as close to the shop floor as possible, usually at the employer's premises. The settlement rate varies between 85% to 87%. While there is an attempt to fit the expertise of the grievance settlement officer to the cases, availability is also a major consideration in the assignment system.

As in the case of labour relations officers, the approach of grievance settlement officers is relatively active, and neutral evaluation plays a significant role. However, the grievance settlement officer will generally have little advance material or information, and there is unlikely to be prior telephone contact. Rather, the officer will commence the session with the parties together, and cull information about the case either in this format or after separating the parties. He or she will then try and ascertain or identify any problems underlying the grievance and brainstorm with the parties to find solutions. Arbitral jurisprudence or in its absence, the uncertainty of litigation, is used by the grievance settlement officer to enhance the attractiveness of a mediated resolution and assist the parties in assessing their respective positions.

Discipline and discharge grievances tend to offer the most flexibility in terms of settlement options, while disputes over contract language may be more intractable if the implications of a particular interpretation have broader application. Generally speaking, however, one of the most important benefits of mediation in this context is the fact that often the grievance language does not necessarily represent the real issue or the whole picture. Mediation provides an opportunity for such problems to emerge and be addressed in pragmatic ways that may be unrelated to the legal framework employed in arbitration. Like the discussions with a labour relations officer, there is a substantial educational component to the process as well, although it may take different forms in this context. For example, the grievance settlement officer may assist an employer in understanding the principles of graduated or progressive discipline, or may help a party analyse patterns and systemic problems in the workplace giving rise to grievances.

In roughly 25% of cases, the parties will be represented by lawyers, and again, whether or not this helps or hinders the process will depend on the individual counsel. In some cases, the presence of counsel may heighten either a party's feeling of responsibility or satisfaction in relation to a settlement. In others, a party who has already retained a lawyer may feel he or she has less to lose by proceeding to a hearing. As in the case of labour relations officers, the grievance settlement officer may also be in a position to convey awkward information to a party in a manner which would be difficult for the party's representative. Settlements are reduced to writing and are enforceable by arbitrators who are reluctant to allow parties to re-open proceedings where there has been an agreement.

Like their colleagues, grievance settlement officers do not perceive their role as adjusting an inequitable deal or compensating for a party's power deficit. Aside from ensuring that the weaker party understands his or her situation and the agreement, officers are reluctant to interfere, in part because experience indicates that parties are quite capable of proceeding to complete the agreement in the hall without them if they perceive that the officer is standing in their way in this regard.

Grievance settlement officers usually come to their positions with at least five years of experience in labour relations, such as collective bargaining or collective agreement administration. The skills employed are similar to those used by labour relations officers and collective bargaining mediators, with perceptiveness, creativity, eloquence, perseverance and a keen sense of timing highlighted. Their substantive knowledge base will be focused on arbitral case law, rather than statutes or wage trends. The training period includes an internship of two to three weeks coupled with a reading programme. Grievance settlement officers then maintain their knowledge base by monitoring the arbitration outcome of those of their cases which do not settle, and by the circulation of current or interesting arbitration decisions to and from their colleagues. Approximately 2,000 arbitration awards are filed with the Office of Arbitration each year, representing decisions on both expedited and nonexpedited cases.

As a result of recent legislative amendments, the Ontario Labour Relations Act also provides for the appointment of a mediator–arbitrator for grievances on the agreement of the parties. Because this is a relatively new provision, evaluation of its use at this point is difficult, particularly because the Act gives other arbitrators a similar power. However, some arbitrators have practised mediation-arbitration in Ontario for many years before these amendments. Like mediation by adjudicative panels at the Labour Relations Board, this can be a challenging and tricky proposition, fraught with pitfalls. The success of these arbitrators can be directly traced to their specific talents, skills, experience, and intuitive senses of fairness.

PREVENTATIVE MEDIATION BY THE OFFICE OF MEDIATION

The Ontario Ministry of Labour's Office of Mediation also offers an innovative preventative mediation programme directed at parties that are having difficulty with their overall labour relationship. The purpose is to build a constructive labour management relationship and to replace hostility and distrust with a problem-solving approach. The programme reflects the view that while the labour relationship may involve some degree of inherently opposed economic interests, there is an interpersonal or psychological dynamic operating as well which can have a significant effect on either minimising or maximising conflict. Even within the limits imposed by the parties' differing economic interests, preventative mediation presumes that some structural changes may be possible and that in any event, the parties benefit from more skilful managing of their remaining conflicts.

There are four distinct branches of the programme: joint action committees, joint training sessions, a 'relationship by objectives' programme, and mediator consultation. All of these options are provided by the same mediators who conduct collective bargaining mediation in Ontario.

The first branch involves the provision of a mediator to assist the parties in creating a joint action committee to provide an informal communication forum in which the employer and the union can address day-to-day problems. A mediator will help the parties constitute the committee and establish guidelines for it, including the purpose of the committee, its structure and chairship, the nature of appropriate agenda items, and the time, place and duration of meetings. The mediator will also attend the first few meetings to provide guidance and help the parties manage their interaction. At this point, although the mediator will typically cease to play an active role, he or she will continue to be available for consultation where necessary. Meetings are generally scheduled on a monthly basis, and while the agenda may be flexible, the parties usually try to avoid getting caught up in either grievances or collective bargaining. Usually there are co-chairs, one from each side, who alternate in conducting the meetings. Minutes are taken and distributed. A successful committee can improve communication and understanding, address issues before they turn into full-blown disputes and help to defuse a strained relationship.

The second branch of preventative mediation, the joint training programme, is predicated on the basis that supervisors and union stewards need similar skills, and that learning those skills together helps to break down barriers. A common understanding of their respective roles can also contribute to the overall health of the labour relationship. The training programme involves a one day session led by two mediators, which includes discussion of common grievance and communication problems, case studies and various labour relations subjects. The purpose is to develop the skills and insight of front-line management and union personnel, with a view to preventing or reducing unnecessary conflict or friction.

Perhaps the most well-known is the third branch of the preventative mediation programme which uses the 'relationship by objectives' approach to allow parties in a difficult or hostile labour relationship to redesign it. In a location away from the workplace, a team of four or five mediators will lead the parties' representatives through a process of identifying and discussing problems, and setting objectives. The programme takes two to three long, hard days of discussions, and experience indicates that 18 to 24 participants is the optimum number to support the dynamics of the programme, which involve taking certain kinds of risks in those discussions. Union and management representatives work through a series of steps including the identification of problems in the labour relationship, a comprehensive and candid discussion of those problems, the establishment of objectives to address them, the development of an action plan to obtain the objectives, and monitoring and follow up in this regard. In this sense, the programme is considered to be a first step, rather than an end in itself.

The 'relationship by objectives' programme is not a panacea and requires extensive commitment on the part of both parties to be successful. The Office of Mediation will hold exploratory meetings prior to conducting the programme to ensure that there is a reasonable chance that it will be productive. If the parties have requested the programme for the wrong reasons, it may not be provided.

Those reasons might include an employer who wants to soften up a union prior to bargaining, a union attempting to use the programme to recoup losses suffered in negotiations, or either party responding to head office directives to improve the relationship. Generally the programme will not be conducted in proximity to collective bargaining negotiations. The mediators approach the sessions with the idea that their job is to provide a sophisticated process, while the parties provide the content to that process.

In some cases, the action plan agreed to by the parties is pursued with enthusiasm and may evolve into other activities. In others, however, staff turnover and other intangible factors mean that the benefits of the programme taper off after two to three years. It may be that building a particular culture with respect to managing conflict requires a considerable degree of sustained and ongoing effort. There has been some suggestion that more monitoring and follow-up by the Office of Mediation might be helpful in those cases. At the same time, the parties need to take responsibility for the relationship and to develop a degree of self-reliance in managing their relationship as well, and scarce resources provide added emphasis for this proposition.

Finally, the Office of Mediation provides mediator consultation during the term of a collective agreement on specific relationship or bargaining needs. This may include anything from starting mid-contract study committees on various topics to comprehensive workplace restructuring.

All of these programmes are available only by the mutual agreement of the parties, and are initiated by one or more of them applying to the Office of Mediation. The office is flexible in its approach to the parties' needs, and may combine different aspects of the programmes to create new or blended options suited to their particular requirements. Experience has shown that the programmes are effective in reducing tensions, improving the labour relationship, facilitating subsequent collective bargaining and minimising grievances. Among other things, this may also have a positive effect on later grievance and collective bargaining mediation. In this sense, the spectrum of mediation programmes available in Ontario may provide a more systemic investment in the parties' relationship.

ALTERNATIVE DISPUTE RESOLUTION IN BRITISH COLUMBIA LABOUR RELATIONS

The Labour Relations Board of British Columbia was established in 1973 to adjudicate labour relations disputes under the Labour Relations Code. It administers a statutory scheme of labour relations similar to that regulated by the Ontario Labour Relations Board. One significant difference between the Boards however, is that collective bargaining mediation comes under the aegis of the British Columbia Board itself, rather than a separate body as it is in Ontario.

This has interesting implications for the relationship between the Mediation Division of the Board, which handles both collective bargaining, and other forms of mediation, and the Adjudication Division which deals with the hearing and determination of cases.

THE MEDIATION DIVISION OF THE LABOUR RELATIONS BOARD

The Mediation Division of the Board provides a spectrum of mediation services including collective bargaining mediation, essential services mediation, grievance mediation, and two programmes directed at improving the parties' ongoing relationship. Before reviewing those services in more detail, we will look first at the mediation process followed in most of them.

The mediation process

The process of mediation is not bound by rules of procedure and substantive law, and as a result, the parties are free to negotiate a settlement in accordance with their own methods and priorities. There is, however, an approach to mediation designed to facilitate productive negotiations between the parties applicable to several of the kinds of mediation provided by the Mediation Division. This process, which is described below, reflects the fundamental principles that underlie mediation: an understanding and appreciation of the issues confronting the parties; the ability to dissuade the parties from pursuing unreasonable positions; and the ability to encourage the resolution of issues in dispute.

Prior to the commencement of negotiations, the mediator endeavours to understand each party's perspective on the issues in dispute. This may be accomplished by reading summaries prepared by each side, or by meeting separately with the parties in pre-mediation conferences. In addition, the mediator may begin to formulate settlement options based on what they perceive to be the real interests of the parties. Finally, the mediator ensures that all parties needed to approve and implement an agreement will be present during negotiations.

In the introductory phase, the mediator familiarises the parties with the mediation process and stresses the importance of commitment to the process, the issue of confidentiality, and bargaining protocols. During the next stage, the parties attempt to formulate the negotiation agenda. This generally begins with the identification of the issues by the parties. Once the issues are identified, they are summarised by the mediator and presented to the parties. The mediator ensures that each party understands the issues formulated and uses them to develop a neutral framework for negotiations.

After setting the agenda the parties engage in an information-gathering process. They identify their needs, interests and concerns and the importance of addressing these issues. Through the exploration of the parties' positions, areas of common concern should emerge. This common ground will form the basis of the settlement agreement.

During this process, the mediator facilitates the exchange of information by maintaining a positive negotiating climate. He or she also engages the parties in 'reality testing' by challenging the reasonableness of their positions. Finally, the mediator ensures the parties remain focused on the resolution of the issues in dispute and are not distracted by promotion of personal or political ideologies.

After the parties' interests have been explored, negotiations should focus on the conclusion of an agreement. At this stage, the mediator assists the parties in generating possible options for settlement. The parties then assess the options and determine which option is most practicable and desirable. Upon settlement the mediator ensures it is written in specific terms; any ambiguity will undermine its effectiveness. To further guarantee the successful operation of the agreement, the parties should consider how the agreement will be implemented and monitored. This ensures the settlement agreement fits the workplace.

With this general process in mind, we now turn to the different types of mediation offered by the Board's Mediation Division.

Collective bargaining mediation

Collective bargaining mediation has a long and successful history in British Columbia and continues to engage a majority of the Division's resources. It is available simply by either party applying to the Board, which will result in the appointment of a mediator to facilitate the conclusion of an agreement.

Applications for collective bargaining mediation may arise in a number of circumstances, but are most common when the parties are aware of the issues in dispute but cannot reach an agreement due to a breakdown in the lines of communication. In this situation, the mediator acts as a new line of communication between the parties and puts pressure on them to reach agreement. The parties expect the mediator to aggressively attempt to facilitate the resolution of the dispute, and are very critical if the mediator does not take an active role in the settlement process.

In recent years, the collective bargaining process has become much more complex. This increased complexity is reflected in the mediation process, which has also changed significantly over the years. For example, the issues facing labour and management today tend to be more numerous and difficult. In addition, parties are often more inflexible and unwilling to be pushed into compromises that they do not perceive to be consistent with their interests. Moreover, in an increasing number of cases, particularly first collective agreements, mediators are requested to provide the parties with recommended terms of settlement. As a result of these changes, mediators are required to be much more creative and imaginative, and they must have the ability to formulate reasonable and logical solutions to complicated issues.

When an application for collective bargaining mediation is made to the Board, the appointment of a mediator is automatic, except in circumstances where a party has given strike or lockout notice. When such notice has been given, both parties must agree to the appointment of a mediator. In 1994 over 350 applications for mediation were filed with the Board, of which 295 involved appointments under the general mediation provisions of the British Columbia Labour Relations Code, mostly for renewal agreements. The remainder of these applications concerned first collective agreement situations. Mediated settlements were reached in the majority of the disputes, using the process described above.

Before the enactment of recent legislation, the Board rarely intervened in first collective agreement disputes. When it imposed a first agreement, it did so to compensate for the unfair labour practices of an uncooperative party. This failed to foster collective bargaining relationships, and in every case where a first agreement had been imposed, the unions were subsequently decertified. The addition of s 55 to the Labour Relations Code allowed the Board to adopt a different approach to the negotiation of first collective agreements.

Section 55 provides as follows:

55(1) Either party may apply to the associate chair of the Mediation Division for the appointment of a mediator to assist the parties in negotiating a first collective agreement, if

(a) a trade union certified as bargaining agent and an employer have bargained collectively to conclude their first collective agreement and have failed to do so, and

(b) the trade union has taken a strike vote under section 60 and the majority of those employees who vote have voted for a strike.

(2) If an application is made under subsection (1) an employee shall not strike or continue to strike, and the employer shall not lock out or continue to lock out, unless a strike or lockout is subsequently authorised under subsection (6)(b)(iii).

(3) The associate chair must appoint a mediator within 5 days of receiving an application under subsection (1).

(4) An application under subsection (1) must include a list of the disputed issues and the position of the party making the application on those issues.

(5) Within 5 days of receiving the information referred to in subsection (4), the other party must give to the party making the application and to the associate chair a list of the disputed issues and the position of that party on those issues.

(6) If the first collective agreement is not concluded within 20 days of the appointment of the mediator, the mediator shall report to the associate chair and recommend either or both of the following:

(a) the terms of the first collective agreement for consideration by the parties;

(b) a process for concluding the first collective agreement including one or more of the following:

      (i) further mediation by a person empowered to arbitrate any issues not resolved by agreement and to conclude the terms of the first collective agreement;

     (ii) arbitration by a single arbitrator or by the board, to conclude the terms of the first collective agreement;

   (iii) allowing the parties to exercise their rights under this Code to strike or lock out.

(7) If the parties do not accept the mediator's recommended terms of settlement or if a first collective agreement is not concluded within 20 days of the report under subsection (6), the associate chair shall direct a method set out in subsection (6)(b) for resolving the dispute.

(8) If the associate chair directs a method set out in subsection (6)(b)(i) or (ii), the parties shall refrain from or cease any strike or lockout activity and the terms of the collective agreement recommended or concluded under that subsection are binding on the parties.

In the case of *Yarrow Lodge Ltd*, BCLRB No B444/93 (1994), 21 CLRBR (2d) 1, 94 CLLC para 16,047, the Board emphasised that the purpose of s 55 was to facilitate the achievement of a first collective agreement by employing the processes of collective bargaining and mediation. The mediator is therefore a key component of the Board's first collective agreement policy.

If a mediator is unable to facilitate the resolution of a first collective agreement, he or she may make recommendations, either in regard to the terms of settlement, or with respect to a process for concluding the collective agreement. In order to give effect to the purpose of s 55, the recommendations with respect to the terms of settlement will generally form the basis of a settlement agreement, even when the dispute proceeds to interest arbitration. There are a number of reasons for this approach. First, if the mediation process contemplated by the section is seen merely as an interim step, with interest arbitration to follow, the parties may not be willing to compromise, because to do so would prejudice their positions before the arbitrator. In other words, parties might continue to adopt uncompromising and unreasonable positions in the hope they will be awarded some of their demands before an arbitrator. Second, parties might frame their bargaining positions according to what they perceived to be their best legal position in relation to arbitration. Thirdly, even if the parties were willing to negotiate, there would be less incentive to accept the mediator's recommendations if the parties believed they had a second chance to argue their positions before an interest arbitrator. In some cases, this may cause a 'chilling' or 'narcotic' effect on the collective bargaining process.

Recommendations by the mediator in regard to a process for concluding a collective agreement will depend on the circumstances. The strike/lockout option will most often be recommended where the parties have made reasonable efforts to conclude an agreement and the problem is simply one of hard bargaining. Arbitration will generally only be recommended when one party has engaged in impugned conduct including bad faith or surface bargaining, the adoption of an uncompromising bargaining position without reasonable justification, failing to make reasonable or expeditious efforts to conclude a collective agreement, and making unrealistic demands, either intentionally or due to inexperience. Where there is a bitter and protracted dispute and the parties are unlikely to reach settlement themselves, this may also result in a referral to arbitration. In addition, where one party has accepted the recommendations of a mediator there may be a reference to interest arbitration. Finally, mediators may also make recommendations for limited issue arbitration or final offer selection when only a few issues remain in dispute.

The Statute (s 55(6)(b)(i)) allows for the mediation/arbitration (med/arb) of interest disputes, for the resolution of a collective agreement. The informal policy of the Board is not to impose this form of settlement. However, it is the preferred route to resolve such disputes. The advantage of med/arb relates not only to the economy of process but also to the fact that no interest arbitrator will have anywhere near the knowledge of a collective bargaining dispute that a mediator has, nor the range of positions taken by the parties and the disclosure they have made in relation to them, nor the compromises made and the delicate balance struck. Mediation is thus consistent with the dynamics of collective bargaining, the negotiation rather than the litigation of a collective agreement. However, it is this very knowledge of the mediator that can be the basis of an objection to the med/arb process. When, in some circumstances, disclosure and compromise can be seen as prejudicial to a parties' legal position, that party will want an arbitrator who has no prior involvement or knowledge of that dispute. They simply desire an adjudication of their position. There is, of course, the additional issue of natural justice, of deciding matters based only on the evidence adduced and the legal positions adopted.

The process involved in the mediation of first collective agreements is different from that used to mediate renewal collective agreements. For example, in first collective agreement situations the parties are new to the bargaining, and as a result, the mediator spends more time on education and orientation. In addition, there are usually more issues in dispute at the commencement of the mediation process and it therefore takes more time and effort to get the process going. Finally, the mediator is called upon more often to develop actual contract language and a framework for settlement.

In 1994 there were 39 mediator appointments under s 55, with eleven appointments carried over from the previous year. These figures can usefully be seen against a backdrop of over 400 certifications in 1994. In addition to the s 55 applications, a number of first agreements were concluded as a result of appointments under the general mediation provisions of the Code. Mediation of this nature also took place prior to s 55 applications in approximately one quarter of the disputes. A majority of the applications were filed by unions in the private sector.

Of the 50 appointments handled under s 55 during 1994, 12 were resolved by mediated settlement, six ended with the parties' acceptance of the mediator's recommendations for settlement, three resulted in a direction for binding arbitration following one party's acceptance of the mediator's recommendations for settlement, five were resolved by voluntary binding arbitration, and three ended with a direction for limited issue arbitration. Unions were ultimately decertified in four of the applications and seventeen applications were outstanding at the end of the year. Work stoppages occurred in only two disputes, and these were subsequently followed by mediated settlements.

Essential services mediation

Like the Ontario Board, the British Columbia Board is responsible for the designation of essential services during strikes or lockouts. In British Columbia, however, the number of sectors in which this function must be performed is greater than in Ontario where the right to strike and lock out is more limited. These services have been defined as those deemed necessary to prevent immediate and serious danger to the health, safety or welfare of residents of British Columbia in the event of a strike or lockout.

When the Minister of Labour makes a direction to the Board to designate essential services, the Associate Chair (Mediation), may appoint one or more mediators to assist in reaching agreement on essential services levels that will continue to be provided in the event of a strike or lockout. If no agreement can be reached, the mediator reports to the Associate Chair (Mediation) and provides recommendations as to the appropriate levels of designation. The Adjudication Division then makes a designation order, incorporating the recommendations of the mediator.

As a result of a high volume of these cases in the health care sector, the Board recently experimented with a more systemic and innovative approach to essential services designation. This included the organisation of a conference involving health care sector stakeholders, for the purpose of building consensus between them with respect to the identification of essential services. This turned out to be a highly successful initiative from the point of view of both the Board and the participants, and represents an alternative approach which might also be useful in other areas of labour relations.

Grievance mediation

Grievance mediation in British Columbia is provided by the Mediation Division as well, and is initiated by the written request of both the union and the employer. A mediator then meets with the parties, either jointly or separately, and assists them in resolving the issues in dispute, using the process described above. As in Ontario, mediation in this area offers the benefits of flexibility, informality, speed and ownership of the process, often in contrast to an arbitration hearing. Again, neutral evaluation and the generation of settlement options play a major role in its success.

Of course, if grievance mediation fails, the parties are free to proceed to arbitration under the provisions of their collective agreement. If the parties choose to arbitrate, attempted settlement through mediation still serves a useful purpose, as it allows the parties to focus on the issues in dispute. This tends to expedite the arbitration process with the benefit of reducing costs. Negotiations undertaken during the mediation process are without prejudice and cannot be introduced in the arbitration proceeding without the mutual consent of the parties.

Labour Management Consultation Committees

Under s 53 of the British Columbia Labour Relations Code, a mediator may be appointed to assist parties in establishing or rejuvenating a labour management consultation committee. The section provides as follows:

53(1) A collective agreement must contain a provision requiring a consultation committee to be established if a party makes a written request for one after the notice to commence collective bargaining is given or after the parties begin collective bargaining.

(2) The consultation committee provision must provide that the parties consult regularly during the term of the agreement about issues relating to the workplace that affect the parties or any employee bound by the agreement.

(3) If the collective agreement does not contain the provisions described in subsections (1) and (2), it shall be deemed to contain the following consultation committee provision:

On the request of either party, the parties shall meet at least once every 2 months until this agreement is terminated, for the purpose of discussing issues relating to the workplace that affect the parties or any employee bound by this agreement.

(4) The purpose of the consultation committee is to promote the cooperative resolution of workplace issues, to respond and adapt to changes in the economy, to foster the development of work related skills and to promote workplace productivity.

(5) The associate chair of the Mediation Division shall on the joint request of the parties appoint a facilitator to assist in developing a more cooperative relationship between the parties.

Like Ontario's joint action committees, the purpose of the consultation committee is to provide a non-adversarial forum in which parties can discuss items of mutual concern. In providing a mechanism for open communication, the committee seeks to facilitate cooperation between the parties in the hopes of improving their ongoing relationship. The success of the committee is premised on the notion that where union and management endeavour to resolve problems through cooperative and informal discussion as they arise, the number of grievances will be reduced. Moreover, when a collective agreement comes up for renewal, there is a greater chance of settlement when the issues have already been discussed by the committee.

In order for a consultation committee to be effective, there must be a clear definition of the committee's purposes and objectives, open and constructive discussions and an effective method of following through with proposals and recommendations. In furtherance of this objective, the committee's terms of reference is one of the first items addressed by the parties. The terms of reference should cover the following: a preamble; the name of the committee; purposes and functions; membership and terms of office; frequency of meetings; duties of officers; provisions for subcommittees and satellite committees; and amendments.

The relationship by objectives programme

The 'relationship by objectives' programme in British Columbia is similar to that in Ontario, and is intended for employers and unions who are experiencing serious difficulties in their ongoing relationships. Upon a joint request for assistance, a mediator will hold a series of exploratory meetings with the parties. These meetings are designed to ensure the commitment of the parties and to determine whether the relationship by objective programme will achieve the desired results.

Once a commitment has been made, a relationship by objective session is scheduled, generally for two days in a location away from the workplace. The programme starts with the identification of each individual's expectations of the programme. These expectations are recorded by a mediator and reviewed at the completion of the programme. The next step, called 'suggestions for improvement', refers to the division of the participants into union and employer representatives. Each group then meets with a mediator to discuss specific suggestions on how each party can improve the relationship. During this process, each party is asked what it could do, and what the other party should do, to improve relations in the workplace. These suggestions are then reviewed by all participants and common objectives are established based on the 'could' and 'should' lists. Finally, all participants assist in the joint development of specific action steps. Each action step includes a description of the required action, identification of the individuals responsible for the implementation of the action, and a time frame for its completion.

After the two-day working session has been completed, a summary document is drafted by a mediator containing the relevant information generated during the session. The summary is then issued by the parties to those individuals involved in, or affected by, the action plans. The progress of the parties is monitored through follow-up meetings with a mediator. These generally take place three and six months after the relationship by objective session.

The Mediation Division conducted its first relationship by objective programme in 1993. Since that time, a number of organisations of varying sizes in both the private and public sectors have successfully utilised the programme to improve their relationships. For example, in March 1994 the Division facilitated a two day working session between representatives of BC Transit and the Independent Canadian Transit Union. Historically, the parties had been consistently unable to establish a productive bargaining relationship, a fact which had resulted in a number of bitter labour disputes. In an effort to improve the ongoing relationship, the parties agreed to participate in the relationship by objective programme.

Employer and union representatives met for two days to discuss issues of primary importance to the relationship and to develop strategies to deal with those issues. Specifically, the parties identified 13 broad issues that needed to be addressed. They then developed concrete action plans accompanied by target dates and follow-up mechanisms to ensure that the objectives would be met.

As a result of the programme, the parties were able to achieve their goals of recognising the need for improved working conditions and the working relationship, confirming a mutual desire to bring about positive changes, and making the commitment to achieve and sustain an improved relationship. The parties further recognised that a significant step had been made in addressing key concerns and establishing a more open relationship.

THE ADJUDICATION DIVISION OF THE LABOUR RELATIONS BOARD

Beginning in 1993, the Board began a series of ongoing discussions with the labour relations community focused on the expanded use of alternative dispute resolution by the Adjudication Division. The Board emphasised developing common objectives and a consensus on the appropriate steps to advance such initiatives.

The first step it took was to conduct an internal audit to identify problem areas that could benefit from improved alternative dispute resolution. This audit revealed that between 63% to 70% of the applications dealt with by the Adjudication Division were cases that required adjudication on an expedited basis.

The audit also revealed that the Board was keeping pace with the number of applications being received, but that a backlog had developed in 1992. Because of the number of expedited applications, this backlog was carried forward, and could not be easily addressed. Consequently, a central problem for the Board was the time required to adjudicate these expedited applications.

Based on the kinds of concerns with respect to the length, complexity and cost of proceedings described earlier in this chapter and coupled with the audit information, the Board identified two objectives relating to alternative dispute resolution: to attempt to resolve disputes without any formal adjudication, and to simplify and expedite proceedings where hearings were necessary. A number of general proposals were developed as a basis for discussion with the labour relations community. The Board's proposals were reviewed by a broad spectrum of the labour relations community, including management and labour representatives and legal counsel. The result was significant consensus on many appropriate changes, including the manner in which applications were initiated, earlier and more deliberate settlement attempts, pre-hearing conferences, alternative forms of hearings and expedited hearings.

The next step for the Board was to develop amendments to its rules governing practice and procedure that reflected the general consensus. The amendments were submitted to those who participated in the consultation process for final input and received broad based support. Acting on this consensus, the Board implemented the new amendments in August of 1994.

In general, the amendments to the rules created a number of alternative dispute options for each stage of the adjudicative process. Many of these require the agreement of the parties, but the amendments also grant considerable discretion to the Board as to how the options may be employed. The overall framework for these options is reflected in the Board's rules, which provide that their purpose is to secure the just, speedy and inexpensive settlement or adjudication of every proceeding, having regard to the real substance of the matters is dispute and the respective merit of the parties' positions.

The alternative dispute options in the Adjudication Division can be loosely grouped into pre-hearing mechanisms such as case management and settlement conferences, and alternative models of adjudication at the hearing stage. The pre-hearing initiatives have been the most successful and quickly advanced in the Adjudication Division, and are considered to be the first step in reducing undue delays in processing applications and conserving the Board's limited resources.

Pre-hearing initiatives

Case management activity starts when applications to the Adjudication Division are received by the Registry. The registrar first ensures that all applications comply with the Board's rules of procedure governing the commencement of proceedings, forms for applications, filing of replies, service and delivery and related matters. Once an application is found to be in order, the registrar determines whether an application must be processed on an expedited basis. Expedited matters include applications for certification, unfair labour practice complaints, essential service designation requests, and complaints involving strikes, lockouts, picketing and replacement workers. Expedited applications are directly set down for a hearing. The scheduling of the hearing may depend on the type of application. For example, unfair labour practice complaints must be heard within a statutory time frame of three days; strike and lockout cases are often heard within 24 hours.

If the registrar determines an application need not be heard on an expedited basis, the application is assigned to an administrative assistant by geographic area. The administrative assistants are responsible for coordinating the submission process, including granting extensions to the time limits for filing submissions. Extensions of up to five days are granted where there is a reasonable basis for the request.

Once the time for filing submissions has passed, the associate chair (adjudication) refers the file to a panel, which develops an appropriate case management strategy. The most common step is to hold a case management meeting, which does not require the consent of the parties. These meetings attempt to narrow the issues in dispute and provide for the disclosure of particulars and the production of documents. The parties may be asked to develop an agreed statement of facts. Experience has shown that these conferences are likely to reduce the hearing time. The parties are also forced to consider the case long before the hearing dates, and as a result, one party is less likely to be 'ambushed'. Settlement opportunities are an inherent result of all case management meetings.

Some of the other purposes of a pre-hearing conference, and the options that are available, are set out in the Board's rules:

17A(1) Without limiting s 126 or any other provision of the Code, a pre-hearing conference may be scheduled by the board on its own motion or at the request of a party in any proceeding for one or more of the following purposes

(a) directing the pre-hearing disclosure of documents by a party or by any other person who may be called as a witness in the proceeding,

(b) directing a party to provide further facts or details of the position it is taking in the proceeding;

(c) developing an agreed statement of facts, obtaining admissions which might facilitate the hearing, or preparing a sworn statement of the evidence which will be elicited from a witness in the proceeding;

(d) directing that an investigation be conducted and a report be prepared respecting any aspect of the proceeding;

(e) directing that a written submission be filed respecting a report prepared in the proceeding, or respecting any aspect of the proceeding;

(f) attempting to simplify the matters in dispute between the parties, including achieving the resolution of some or all of those matters;

(g) directing the parties to attend a settlement conference;

(h) discussing the conduct of the hearing, including the order in which the parties will proceed, the number and identity of witnesses, and the estimated length of time required; and

(i) directing any other pre-hearing step or initiative which is designed to aid in the disposition of the proceeding in accordance with rule 1(2).

(2) Where the board makes a direction under sub-rule (1), it may specify terms and conditions, including prescribing time limits, to be complied with by a party in respect of that direction.

Another option in pre-hearing alternative dispute resolution is the use of settlement conferences as a structured and Board-supervised method of encouraging settlements between the parties to a dispute. They may be initiated by the Board or may be held at the request of one of the parties. Sometimes they are held in conjunction with a pre-hearing conference or an investigation by a special investigation officer, or they may be scheduled independently. Settlement conferences are generally conducted by either a special investigation officer or a vice-chair who will not hear the case subsequently.

These special investigation officers can be called upon for informal assistance by the parties and/or adjudicator at any stage of proceedings up to and including any hearings which may be in progress.

Informal settlement discussions are held on a 'without prejudice' basis, ie a party cannot subsequently raise what was said in those discussions in any formal proceeding. However, should the parties reach an agreement of the issues which results in a settlement agreement, that agreement is binding on the parties and will be enforced by the Board.

A significant proportion of the special investigating officers' workload is distributed among such areas of the Code as Part 2 (unfair labour practice complaints). In certain circumstances, for example in essential service designation applications, special investigating officers may also be required to complete investigative reports. Special investigating officers may also participate in case management meetings attended by the parties and the panel assigned to adjudicate an application.

The settlement rate by these officers is high. For example, in excess of two-thirds of all unfair labour practice complaints referred to the officers are settled and thus are not adjudicated. In the very sensitive areas of Part 5 of the Code (illegal work stoppages), the settlement rate is consistently over 70%.

The informal dispute resolution process assists the Board and the parties in making effective use of resources and personnel. The process substantially reduces the time needed to conclude cases and reduces expenditures. This process reflects the negotiating nature of labour relations and emphasises resolution of disputes in accordance with the purposes of the Code. The Board recognises the importance of minimising, where practical, decisions imposed by a third party and encourages the parties to make use of the Board's informal processes.

Settlements that are reached through this process are binding, but the discussions are held on a 'without prejudice' basis. In other words, nothing that is said in such a discussion may be raised by either party at a subsequent formal proceeding. Expedited applications are routinely assigned to an Special Investigative Officer for settlement discussions and the success rate, for example, with respect to unfair labour practice complaints, is approximately 60%.

Compliance with these pre-hearing processes is provided for by the Board's rules, which set out various consequences for the failure to comply with the rules or a direction made under them.

Alternatives to formal hearings

There are a number of tools that the Board has created to reduce the length of hearings. The primary focus of these tools is on the calling of evidence, which is traditionally the most time-consuming part of a hearing. The most frequently used are the limitations on evidence given by witnesses. Depending on the facts of the case, a panel may accept oral evidence only on a narrow range of issues, or only for testimony that cannot be submitted by affidavit. The pre-hearing forms of alternative dispute resolution are crucial to this effort. Investigative reports by special investigation officers, affidavit evidence, and agreed statements of fact all help reduce the volume of evidence which must be submitted in hearings. Some of the more contentious forms of alternative hearing models involve time limits on evidence and arguments, the exclusion of legal counsel, or limits on the avenues of appeal.

Alternate forms of hearings are regulated by the Board's rules as well:

17C(1) Without limiting ss 124 and 126 or any other provision of the Code, the Board may make a decision in any proceeding

(a) on the basis of written materials on file with the board, including any report received pursuant to an investigation directed by the board;

(b) on the basis of an oral hearing where the parties will be given a full opportunity to present evidence and make submissions, subject to directions made at any point in the proceeding by the board or the panel to which the proceeding has been referred;

(c) after providing the parties with an opportunity to make oral submissions, which may include evidence and information relevant to the proceeding; or

(d) on the basis of an ADR hearing respecting which the parties may agree to one or more of the following

(i) the matter will be scheduled for an expedited hearing,

(ii) a brief written summary of each party's position will be exchanged in advance,

(iii) an agreed statement of facts will be prepared and/or limited viva voce evidence will be called at the hearing,

(iv) neither party will be represented by legal counsel at the hearing,

(v) a fixed time period will be established for the presentation of any evidence and argument,

(vi) limited reference will be made to legal or other authorities,

(vii) the panel to which the proceeding has been referred may in its discretion attempt to mediate a settlement of some or all of the matters in dispute,

(viii) a short decision without precedent will be issued as soon as possible if the matter cannot be settled,

(ix) any reconsideration of the decision will be limited to questions of natural justice, and

(x) any other step or procedure designed to facilitate an expedited decision in the proceeding.

Post-hearing activity

The Board's alternative dispute resolution initiative has offered few alternatives for the post-hearing stage of the process. In part, this is because much of the focus has been on reducing the number of applications that require hearings and reducing the length of hearings that are necessary. Moreover, the Board's internal audit revealed that delays were not caused by inefficiencies in the post-hearing process, but as a result of an accumulated backlog and the number of lengthy hearings. It is true as well that there are few alternatives to the process of drafting or issuing decisions. In response to concerns about the length and complexity of those decisions, however, the Board has adopted a shorter and more readable format for decisions. Where possible, the Board issues oral decisions or brief 'letter decisions' for cases that are not of general interest. Applications for leave for reconsideration are one example of common letter decisions.

Sample uses of alternative dispute resolution

When the Board began its alternative dispute resolution initiative in 1993, there was a period of adjustment for many in the labour relations community. Though parties may have been in favour of the idea when they believed it was to their advantage, they were generally wary of changes that affected their conduct of a proceeding. Case management meetings, for example, were seen by many lawyers as an intrusion on their traditional sphere. As we have noted, lawyers prefer a familiar process, and parties liked the traditional process of 'trial by ambush' because it fit their conception of adjudication. There was some reluctance to allow an opponent access to key evidence or knowledge of the issues that would be discussed in advance of the actual hearing.

Alternative dispute resolution is now accepted as commonplace. Experience and experimentation have dispelled many of these initial concerns and the advantages have become obvious to the parties. Parties to a dispute now frequently expect and request forms of alternative dispute resolution. It seems clear that acceptance was eased as well by the consensual manner in which the Board implemented its initiatives.

The experience of the Adjudication Division reveals that not all of the alternative dispute options in the rules are commonly used. Among other things, it is evident that these new options work most effectively with the parties' agreement and active participation. In practice, alternative dispute resolution in the Adjudication Division has been most consistent with the use of case management meetings, investigations by special investigation officers, and settlement conferences.

In the following section, we have described a typical approach to alternative dispute resolution for several types of applications. The first example, unfair labour practice complaints, reflects an alternative approach that is common to many types of applications. The second example involves strikes and picketing in which hearings must be concluded within 24 hours. The common elements that affect all uses of alternative dispute resolution include the nature of the labour relationship, the interests at stake in the dispute, the sophistication, or legal experience of the parties, the basis of the complaint, and the political or strategic reasons for adjudication.

Unfair labour practice complaints

One of the most common types of expedited applications is an unfair labour practice complaint. Briefly, the British Columbia Labour Relations Code sets out various forms of prohibited conduct that are considered to interfere with an employee's right to participate in the activities of a trade union. An employer, for example, may not use discipline, intimidation, coercion or threats to induce an employee to resign from a trade union or refrain from joining a trade union. In effect, the unfair labour practice provisions ensure free and fair access to collective bargaining. Because of their crucial importance and the frequency of these complaints, it is in this area that alternative dispute resolution was first used extensively.

The first question that arises when an unfair labour practice complaint is assigned to a panel is whether the dispute has a chance of being settled without adjudication. The facts of the dispute and the legal positions taken by the parties are central to this question. In general terms, there must be grounds for some negotiation or compromise and support for a non-adjudicative resolution. These criteria are not uncommon in unfair labour practice complaints because of the nature of the dispute. Often, unfair labour practices are committed unwittingly or instinctively. For example, when employers learn that a union certification drive is underway, they may automatically call a meeting of the employees and voice their opposition, or demand to know who is involved. Depending on the content of their messages, all of these actions may be prohibited by the Code.

If the panel believes that a settlement appears possible from the submissions, there are a number of ways to bring the parties together. A large number of unfair labour practice complaints are settled by holding a meeting with a special investigation officer, either before or after a case management meeting with the panel. The Board's experience in British Columbia is that the key to a settlement in an unfair labour practice complaint is intervention at an early stage of the process for several reasons. For example, many complaints are settled as soon as the parties become aware of the law. If representatives or lawyers do not have the opportunity to examine a case in advance, then this type of settlement will be delayed or even prevented. Pre-hearing case management before the actual hearing dates forces the parties to prepare their case and creates inherent settlement opportunities.

The Board has also found that early intervention is important because unfair labour practice complaints are largely based on credibility, and a hearing involves a direct confrontation between the parties. The further the adjudicative process develops, the more clearly the positions of the parties may be established and the less likely it is that the parties will turn their minds to conciliation. As one vice-chair put it, they arrive at the Board 'dressed for battle'.

This is to some extent in contrast to the experience of the Ontario Labour Relations Board. In that province, while early intervention can often be helpful or even crucial in individual cases, the Board has also found that there are unfair labour practice cases where the proximity of the hearing date plays a critical role in settlement. In general, no clear correlation between early intervention and the likelihood of settlement has emerged. Because of the multitude of factors involved, it is difficult to know why the experience in these two provinces has been different in this regard.

If the panel determines that an unfair labour practice complaint cannot be settled, the next question is whether the case can be decided without holding an oral hearing. This is rarely possible. The general rule is that a hearing is required where material facts are in dispute. Since these complaints often depend on circumstantial evidence and personal credibility, a full evidentiary hearing is often necessary.

Even if an oral hearing is required, alternative dispute resolution may simplify and expedite an unfair labour practice complaint. The pre-hearing forms of case management provide for the exchange of documents and particulars, so fewer issues will arise at hearing and both parties should be better prepared. An agreed statement of facts is rarely possible for these complaints, due to the prevalence of credibility issues; however, a case management meeting may reveal that certain witnesses are not required, or that there is no dispute over a particular incident. On the whole, a hearing is likely to proceed more efficiently once the issues are narrowed.

The use of alternative dispute resolution during unfair labour practice hearings is generally limited to recognising settlement opportunities when they arise. This effort requires a somewhat different approach for the first two stages of the hearing, the opening statements and the evidence. During the opening statements, the panel may adopt an active, questioning approach. This might involve simply asking what the central issue is, or how the submissions will proceed, or what the possible solutions are. In each case, the traditional and somewhat formal style of rhetoric will have been replaced by a dialogue or discussion. How this type of initiative proceeds is largely a matter of style, but the effort itself is non-biased, and must appear so. It is acceptable to challenge the parties on their submissions, but a panel cannot reach conclusions in advance of the evidence. For example, panels may talk of the strengths, weaknesses or consequences of a legal position, but do not refer to 'winning' or 'losing'. This is particularly important for unfair labour practice complaints, where the parties' credibility may be at stake, in addition to considerable legal interests. If alternative dispute resolution is to be accepted and effective, then the parties' legal positions must be treated seriously and they must feel that they have had the opportunity to be heard.

Several opportunities for alternative dispute resolution may arise during the submission of evidence that are common to all applications and are largely evidentiary, rather than interpretative. By necessity, complaints that proceed to a hearing are those that could not be settled and the outcome is likely difficult to predict. Many cases depend on a single witness or one crucial piece of evidence. One of the uncertainties of an oral hearing is that this evidence may not perform as anticipated, or may be discredited by unexpected events. In some complaints, an experienced panel will realise there has been a significant turning point, and may push for a settlement at that time, rather than proceeding with the rest of the case. Similarly, the panel may sense that the duration of a hearing has strained the parties to the point that a settlement is possible. In some cases, the actual formal decision is less important than the political value secured by pursuing the case to a hearing. Once the complainant has had an opportunity to publicly make their case there may be little reason to continue with the hearing.

Settlement opportunities that arise during a hearing must be approached with caution by the panel because intervention may create an appearance of bias or interference. There are several other options. Like the Ontario Board, where a panel of three hears a case, the two board members may meet with the parties without the vice-chair at a propitious point in the hearing. The panel may also call upon the services of a special investigation officer in similar circumstances. A less interventionist approach is to give the parties a day or two in the middle of the hearing to re-evaluate their positions. Even without the explicit involvement of the panel, the parties may realise the advantages of developing their own resolution.

It is also important to remember that alternative dispute resolutions cannot create a resolution or settlement in every case, nor can every hearing be appreciably simplified. Although a panel may take advantage of settlement opportunities during a hearing, they must also be aware of the fact that the parties may have made every reasonable attempt to come to an agreement and full adjudication is the only recourse. At this point the intervention of the panel may actually slow the adjudication of the dispute. Respect for the parties dictates that the panel limit its interference.

Other applications

Expedited applications involving strikes, lockouts, picketing, ally provisions and prohibited conduct such as the use of replacement workers are common in British Columbia, and the same general approach may be followed as with unfair labour practice complaints. However, there are several different considerations that apply because of the timing of these applications during collective bargaining. Any proceeding involving a strike or lockout puts not only significant material interests at stake but critical tactical or strategic considerations as well. For this reason, the adjudicative process must be adapted to ensure that the balance in negotiations is not affected or an unfair advantage created. A delay in adjudication during a strike, for example, may give the union a considerable benefit.

Many of these applications are heard within 24 hours, leaving little time for prehearing forms of alternative dispute resolution, or protracted settlement efforts. One common solution is to have the parties meet with an special investigation officer for an informal discussion in the half-hour immediately preceding the scheduled hearing. Unlike Ontario, few settlements are reached in advance of such hearings. There are several reasons for this that relate to the nature of the dispute. First, the gravity of these statutory provisions and the interests at stake mean that few applications are brought frivolously or without careful planning. Second, hearings in applications of this nature are generally very short and decisions are issued almost immediately, so the parties may be more inclined to follow the traditional adjudicative process to its conclusion. Third, and perhaps most importantly, these applications have a strong strategic, or political element. In the midst of a strike or lockout, neither side may be able or willing to compromise their position because of the perceived effect that a voluntary concession may have in negotiations. For political reasons, both sides may require an official order from a neutral third party before they can resolve the issues in dispute, even if the outcome is well-known, or a tacit understanding has been reached. The political aspect of labour relations adjudication is not confined to these applications, but there are few clearer examples.

As a result, these kinds of cases can be more resistant to settlement. At the same time, the experience of the Ontario Board is that illegal strike applications have a relatively high rate of settlement, while replacement worker and picketing cases settle at a similar level to that of the caseload generally. One reason the illegal strike cases are easier to resolve without a hearing is because the facts are often not in dispute and the law is clear. Of course, this does not necessarily mean that the problem that prompted the walkout is resolved; in some cases the settlement will involve rechannelling the conflict into the grievance procedure. Nevertheless, employees will be returning to work in the meantime, which is usually the primary issue in the application.

We are prepared to speculate that the varying experiences of Ontario and British Columbia in this regard may reflect different provincial cultures with respect to the use of economic sanctions in labour relations. A higher level of illegal strike applications *per capita* filed with the British Columbia Board than in Ontario may suggest a greater aggressiveness by unions in this regard, which may also explain a lower settlement rate.

Even where a hearing is required, the informal settlement discussions may have created common ground between the parties, narrowed the issues in dispute, or simplified the hearing. In addition, the act of bringing the parties together and forcing them to consider a resolution may have a positive effect on the parallel course of collective bargaining negotiations.

The manner in which alternative dispute resolution is employed in these matters is significantly different from its use in unfair labour practice complaints. Although both types of applications are considered expedited, the issues and evidence that arise are different. Unlike unfair labour practice complaints, applications under these provisions are rarely based on circumstantial evidence or conflicting witnesses. As noted earlier, often the facts are clear in a case, and if given the opportunity, the parties may be willing to concede those facts or limit the evidence. Evidence is traditionally the most time-consuming part of a hearing, so the process is shortened dramatically if a hearing can be confined to oral argument on any legal issues in dispute, possibly with only one or two witnesses. Of course, if one party sees a tactical advantage in delay, these forms of alternative dispute resolution may be difficult to implement. Generally, the process involves a certain give and take between the panel and the parties, but the Board has made it clear that this type of tactical advantage is not acceptable, and some forms of alternative dispute resolution may be imposed in the few cases where the parties have no valid reason to resist.

The post-hearing process for these kinds of applications is shorter than most other cases. Decisions are generally issued within one day of the hearing. Increasingly, however, the adjudication division has attempted to issue oral decisions where possible. Although the time saved to the parties is not significant, reduction in expedited decisions frees the Board for other non-expedited applications. For the parties to these applications, a formal decision is usually not required. Unless there is some precedental importance, an order and an oral decision of the Board is all that is required. Occasionally, parties may request a written decision because they want to embarrass the other party with written evidence of some illegal conduct. As with unnecessary delay, the British Columbia Board has decided this is not a proper reason to issue a written decision because this form of posturing is detrimental to labour relations and damages the collective bargaining relationship of the parties.

CONCLUSION

Alternative dispute resolution mechanisms are now so integral to the administration and regulation of labour relations that it is difficult to imagine life without them. As this chapter illustrates, extensive mediation programmes are available at various points of the labour relations cycle, and alternative models of adjudication have been developed to supplement or replace older models that have inherited some of the problems they were originally designed to prevent.

At a time when public sector resources are shrinking, it is also worth noting that these programmes were developed as a result of government initiatives, and that the kind of creativity and experimentation required flourished in this setting. While it is difficult to quantify precisely the cost-effectiveness of these programmes, their high settlement rates, the impressive degree of user satisfaction and the economic toll of both labour litigation and strife suggest that they are worthwhile investments. Taken as a whole, these programmes represent a broad range of dispute solving methods which have the potential of transforming the resolution of conflicts in labour relations.

5 MEDIATING BUILDING CONSTRUCTION DISPUTES

PETER FENN*

INTRODUCTION

This chapter discusses the application of mediation to construction disputes. The construction industry is of key economic significance in many national economies. It describes and analyses the special features of construction industries, which may exacerbate the potential for disputes. The received wisdom is that construction is plagued by disputes and it could be postulated that mediation should be broadly applicable as a dispute resolution mechanism. However, there is as yet little evidence that mediation is being widely adopted, although its use is growing. Construction industries have been creative in adapting ADR techniques to suit individual needs, however, and some of these hybrid techniques are outlined below.

WHAT IS THE CONSTRUCTION INDUSTRY?

Before considering the types of disputes that arise within the construction industry, it is instructive to first take a look at the construction industry itself. The construction industry is a large and diverse industry in many nations. In the UK, the standard industrial classification used by the UK government to define industrial categories for the purposes of official statistics includes the following:

> Construction: Erecting, repairing buildings; constructing and repairing roads and bridges; erecting steel and reinforced concrete structures; other civil engineering works such as laying sewers and gas mains, erecting overhead line supports and aerial masts, open caste mining, etc. The building and civil engineering establishment of defence and other government departments and of local authorities are included. Establishments specialising in demolition work or in sections of construction work such as asphalting, electrical wiring, flooring, glazing, installing heating and ventilating apparatus, painting, plumbing, plastering, roofing. The hiring of contractor's plant and scaffolding is included. It also includes other activities where the major elements of their work is building, civil engineering, other installation of products and systems either in buildings or in association with civil engineering works.

Construction is a very large industry. In 1994 in the UK its output on a value added basis was over £50 billion (almost 9% of gross domestic product), and construction employed a large percentage of the work force. The industry is highly fragmented, consisting of a large number of small firms. Construction data has to

*   Lecturer, Department of Building Engineering, University of Manchester Institute of Science and Technology (UMIST).

be treated with caution, not least because of the difficulties in defining the industry. The fragmentation of the industry creates further problems in measuring employment. Are persons engaged in fabrication of building products classified under manufacturing or under construction? Most professionals in the construction industry are included as part of the services sector and are not counted as the construction industry. There is also a problem with under-reporting, due to fraud.

The standard industrial classification definition recognises that building and civil engineering projects, unlike most other industries, are split into the separate operation of design and production. Further, the design and production operations are separated from the eventual use of the building. Architects and other design professionals working on their own account are classified as professional services. The manufacture of some components and materials, for example, bricks, cement, timber, doors and windows, falls under manufacturing, and the quarrying of gravel and sand under mining and quarrying.

ECONOMIC FEATURES

Many commentators on the construction industry point to its special economic features. Before examining the organisation and production methods used by the industry, it is useful to draw attention to the special features of the demand for, and the supply of, the product.

DEMAND

The particular demand features of the construction product can be summarised as follows:

- Most buildings are 'one-offs', bespoke or tailor-made to the client's individual specification. Further differences in site surroundings and user requirements mean that there is very little standardisation. This reduces opportunities for mass production and to a large extent determines the method of pricing.

- Building and structures are durable and because of this one half of the value of the output of the construction industry is repairing and maintaining these durable products.

- Durable goods are mainly capital goods. Borrowed funds are used to purchase buildings and structures, which are expensive relative to income. The demand for buildings and structures is therefore dependent upon the cost and availability of credit to fund these capital purchases.

- Demand is subject to fluctuations: seasonal and cyclical. In many countries activity is confined to spring and summer months. Cyclical fluctuations are often claimed to be more serious; as an investment goods industry, construction is vulnerable to fluctuations in demand resulting from changes in expectations.

- Since the construction industry often constitutes a major percentage of a country's economic output, it is also vulnerable to government intervention. Changes in taxes and subsidies can affect the rate of re-development. Since demand is dependent on the cost and availability of credit, governments are tempted to use the construction industry as a major 'regulator' of the economy.

SUPPLY

The distinctive features of the supply of construction products are as follows:

- Unlike most manufacturing industries which can carry out all their operations concurrently, construction is an assembly industry where the operations are consecutive.
- Production takes place in the open air on site. This gives rise to problems of weather protection, storage of materials, the movement of labour and equipment and supervision of the work.
- In economic terms, the minimum technical unit for most projects is small. A traditional UK house can be built by two brick layers, two labourers and a carpenter, with other tasks being subcontracted. The same is true for many large projects which can be completed by a relatively small labour force, by contracting work out to specialist firms (vertical disintegration).
- Construction is labour intensive; labour costs form a high proportion, between one-third and one-half, of total costs. Skilled labour accounts for some two-thirds of total labour costs. The casual and cyclical nature of the work results in a high rate of unemployment, and employment in the construction industries forms a higher percentage than unemployment of workers in general.

THE STRUCTURE OF CONSTRUCTION INDUSTRIES

The origins of all construction industries lie in man's primary need for shelter. Initially as society develops families build shelters for themselves and groups of neighbours cooperate to build common structures such as churches, bridges and other infrastructure for common needs. This spirit of co-operation remains in many developing and developed countries. Raftery[1] describes how people still play a significant role in personally providing labour for the construction of their own dwellings in countries like Germany, France, Portugal, Greece and Ireland. It is also a fairly common phenomenon in North America and Scandinavia.

---

1   Raftery, J, *Principles of Building Economics*, 1992, London: BSP.

This informal sector of construction often escapes legal regulation and statistical numeration. This introduces a shadow economy consisting of both an innocent informal sector, and an illegal sector. So-called 'black economies' in Western countries have been estimated to amount to 3–5% of gross domestic product in the UK and up to 5% in West Germany.[2] Many commentators have described the importance of illegal economies in poorer and developing countries and Raftery describes this as a reason why the World Bank plays a role in helping the development of informal sector construction activities in many countries.

The presence and size of an informal sector in the construction industry is further indication of the imprecision of quantitative descriptions of construction industries. It is evidence of further fragmentation and possibly a source of many disputes. The World Bank[3] describes the structure of the construction industries in various countries and points to variations in structure being dependent on three factors:

- Type of work to be done. This may depend on the size of a country and its climatic and geographical features, the dispersion and density of its population.

- The choice of technology. Again this may depend on physical and climatic conditions; and also on the state of technological development, the availability of resources, labour and materials and plant and governmental intervention in the overall development of the economy.

- Social and economic factors. These are often a function of cultural and historical conditions, the political and economic organisation of the country and the state of its economy.

The structure of construction organisations that is the production unit in the industry will be consequent on these three factors. Construction units normally fall into four types: state owned; private sector enterprises; informal sector individual enterprises and self-help or communal organisation.

IN THE UNITED KINGDOM

The economic factors outlined above have produced an industry dominated by a few large firms, with most of the construction activity being carried out by many small firms on a sub-contract basis. This trend towards small firms has increased recently, fuelled by a government committed to free market strategies and the encouragement of self-employment, and a move by firms to shed overhead cost. The structure of the UK industry is shown in Table 1 and demonstrates a dramatic growth in very small firms with less than eight employees.

---

2   Smith, S and Wiede Nebbeling, S, 1986, *The Shadow Economy in Britain and Germany,* London: The Anglo German Foundation.

3   *The Construction Industries: Issues and Strategies*, 1984, Washington DC: The World Bank.

Size of firm No of employees	1973	1978	1989	1993
1200+	80	35	48	33
600–1119	125	71	66	53
300–599	246	143	153	96
115–299	872	507	530	330
60–114	1440	849	871	577
25–59	4662	3027	2936	2164
8–24	15626	11559	10811	7759
1–7	73525	158904	86391	184095

Table 1: The changing composition of UK construction firms 1973–93

Source: Housing and Construction and Department of Environment Statistics

IN THE EUROPEAN UNION

It might be that the structure of the UK construction industry is a peculiarity of that country; a feature of its history and development. However, examination of EU statistics demonstrates that other countries have the same characteristic fragmentation. Table 2 shows the dominance of the small enterprises in construction.

Table 2: The dominance of the small enterprises in construction 1993
Source The European Commission

Country	No of Building Firms	No of Firms employing up to 20 employees	% of total
Belgium	26000	24000	92
Denmark	27600	25000	90
France	340000	327000	96
Greece	75000	71000	95
Ireland	N/A	N/A	85
Italy	410000	398000	97
Luxembourg	1494	1264	85
Netherlands	18680	16208	94
Portugal	28400	26800	94
Spain	182000	178000	98
Switzerland	35822	31530	88
United Kingdom	209000	203700	97
West Germany	280000	260000	93

OPERATIONAL AND ORGANISATIONAL FEATURES

The organisational features of construction result in a plethora of contractual arrangements. Furthermore, these arrangements are often between parties of widely different commercial strengths. This is fertile ground for conflict and dispute.

Operational and organisational features have evolved different solutions in different countries. The organisational features of all countries, however, share some common themes. Organisational features may be divided into:

- initiating and funding
- design
- construction and supervision management
- construction activities

The arrangements whereby the client (who initiates and funds the proposed building or structure) deals with the construction industry have been described as procurement. Procurement arrangements may be classified into three types: the so-called traditional system; design and build procurement; and management type procurement systems. The organisational and contractual arrangements for these three systems are shown in Figures 1, 2 and 3.

The traditional system (characteristically used in the UK) involves the client or building owner in a number of separate contractual relationships. The range of consultants with whom the client contracts might include an architect, quantity surveyor, structural engineer, services engineer, interior designer and a building contractor. Traditionally, the architect took the lead and it was his job to liaise with the client and to ensure that the building met with the client's expectations.

A claimed advantage of this system is that the client has an array of specialist advisors on hand. These specialist advisors are all members of separate professional institutions. However, the vested interests of those institutions often meant that little collaboration took place between consultant specialists. For this reason the traditional system fell into some disrepute, the lines of responsibility and authority were notoriously unclear and Higgin and Jessop in 1965[4] described immense difficulties in communication. By the 1970s in the UK, the traditional system had developed a reputation for delivering buildings which were over-budget, over-programme and not to the desired quality.

---

4   Higgin, G and Jessop, N, 1965, *Communications in the Construction Industry*, The Tavistock Institute, London.

Figure 1: The traditional procurement system

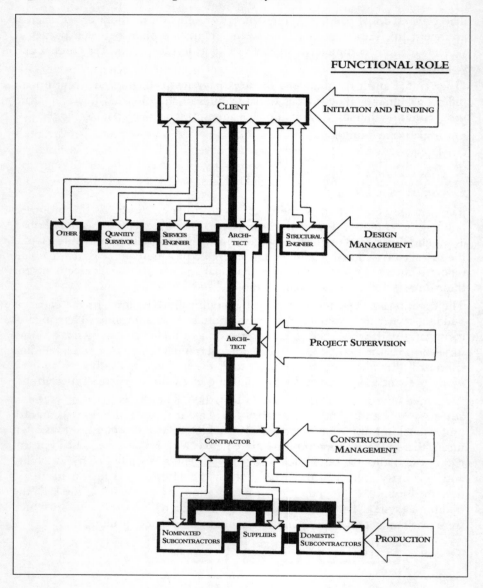

FUNCTIONAL ROLE

CLIENT — INITIATION AND FUNDING

OTHER | QUANTITY SURVEYOR | SERVICES ENGINEER | ARCHITECT | STRUCTURAL ENGINEER — DESIGN MANAGEMENT

ARCHITECT — PROJECT SUPERVISION

CONTRACTOR — CONSTRUCTION MANAGEMENT

NOMINATED SUBCONTRACTORS | SUPPLIERS | DOMESTIC SUBCONTRACTORS — PRODUCTION

KEY

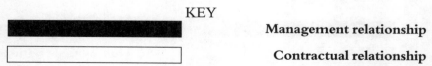

Management relationship

Contractual relationship

The increasing internationalisation of the construction in the 1970s meant that pressure for change in the traditional system was brought to bear on the UKindustry both by international clients, and as result of marketing by international contractors. These pressures resulted in the so-called alternative arrangements of design and build and management systems, established procedures in other countries which were now tried for the first time in the UK.

Figure 2 shows the arrangements for design and build procurement. The salient feature is the replacement of many separate contractual arrangements with one link between client and contractor. This system is closer to the traditional model in many countries (for example, the US) where the professional demarcations characteristic to the UK industry did not develop. The advantages claimed for this system include single point responsibility, producer input into design and speed when compared to sequential approaches.

Figure 2: Design and build procurement

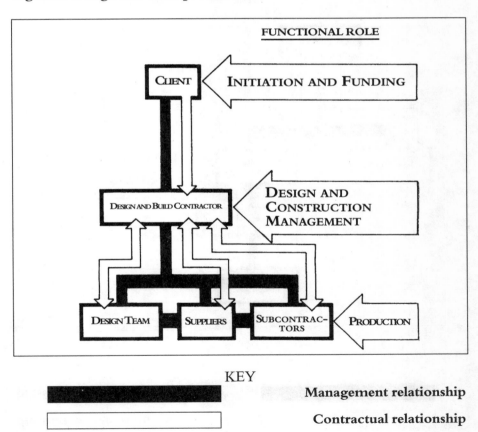

Figure 3 shows arrangements in a third management procurement model. There are many variants but essentially the contractor offers the client a consultant-based service, and charges a fee for coordinating and planning the construction and managing and executing the process. The benefits claimed for the systems are centred on the early involvement of management expertise, ensuring maximum construction experience being fed into design and production.

In figure 3, the contracts are held by the management contractor. The other major system is construction management, where the contracts are held by the client.

Figure 3: The management procurement method

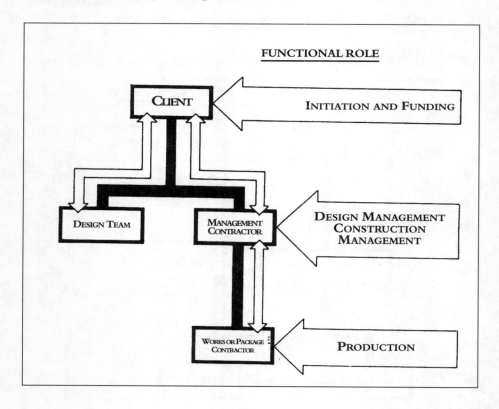

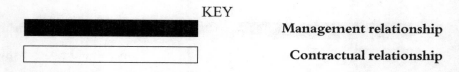

HOW DISPUTES ARISE

As described earlier, construction demand and supply have particular features which are likely to cause disputes. These include the bespoke nature of design, unique ground conditions, inexperienced clients, the desire for early completion to reduce finance costs and the uncertainties of the weather. Construction contracts are unique in the sense that negotiations continue throughout the project; it might be argued that construction contracts are in fact one long negotiation from beginning to end. The contract requires the parties to agree a whole host of matters, including evaluations of variations, extensions of time and quality of workmanship.

Researchers[5] have produced a taxonomy of the root causes of construction disputes, and their related proximate causes (immediate apparent causes that trigger claims and disputes).

Table 3: Root causes: a list of the root causes which generate disputes by themselves or through interactions

unfair risk allocation
unclear risk allocation
unrealistic time/cost/quality targets (by clients)
uncontrollable external events
adversarial (industry culture)
unrealistic tender pricing
inappropriate contract type
lack of competence of project participants
lack of professionalism of project participants
client's lack of information or decisiveness
unrealistic information expectation (contractors)

---

5   See Kumaraswamy, M, *Conflict, Claims and Disputes in Construction, Engineering and Architectural Management*, 1996, London: E & FN Spon, in press, for a summary of this research.

Table 4: Proximate causes: related proximate or immediately apparent causes which generate disputes by themselves or through interactions

inadequate briefs
poor communications
personality clashes
vested interests
variations or changes by client
slow client response
exaggerated claims
errors in estimating
internal disputes
inadequate contract administration
inadequate contract documentation
inaccurate design information
incomplete tender information
inadequate design documentation
inappropriate contractor selection
inappropriate payment modalities
inappropriate contract form

The following tables show the common categories of construction claims and the causes of claims, listed in descending order of overall significance.

Table 5: Categories of construction claims

Variation due to site conditions
Variations due to client changes
Variations due to design errors
Unforeseen ground conditions
Ambiguities in contract documents
Variations due to external events
Interference with utilities
Adverse weather
Delayed site possession
Delayed design information

Table 6: Causes of claims

Inaccurate design information
Inadequate design information
Inadequate site investigations
Slow client response
Poor communications
Unrealistic time targets
Inadequate contract administration
Uncontrollable external events
Incomplete tender information
Unclear risk allocation

Source, Tables 5 and 6: Kumaraswamy, 1995[6]

Most disputes or disagreements are settled by negotiation without recourse to other dispute resolution techniques. However, the fact that some negotiations fail is evident from the prevalence of disputes. The question might be asked: why do negotiations fail?

Negotiations fail primarily for the following reasons, or perhaps a combination of these reasons:

- *Communications failure.* Intuitively one could postulate that this is the number one cause of construction disputes. Examples of communication failures include failures to explain properly what is required with regard to the construction of the works, for example, ambiguities or unclear areas in the documents forming the contracts, or correspondence which does not explain clearly what is required. Contractual conditions may require that particular matters of importance are given in writing, for example, variation orders, architects' instructions, notices of delay, etc. Often written notices are unclear and the simple misinterpretation can lead to an escalation of the situation, which in turn, will lead to a dispute. Communication failures which lead to total breakdown in relationships can often be corrected by using a neutral third party, and in these circumstances mediation is particularly appropriate.

- *Poor negotiation skills.* Some people are incapable of compromise or are just bad negotiators. Many act as positional negotiators, exaggerating their demands or claims in the hope of reaching agreement somewhere in the middle. This negotiation style often creates a considerable gap and this is perceived as impossible to bridge. Again, a neutral third party mediator can usefully assist in overcoming a negotiation breakdown caused by poor negotiation skills.

---

6   Kumaraswamy, M, *Common Sources of Construction Disputes*, 1995, Inside Asia: Hong Kong.

- *Lack of information.* In many construction negotiations there is a surprising lack of information, either on what really happened or on how much, or how long, is required to carry out a particular process or to rectify a defect. If negotiations are to be successful, the negotiators must have access to the relevant information. This is a particular problem in construction contracts involving specialist work, where those holding the key information (for example, specialist sub-contractors and specialist designers) are often not present in the main contractor/architect negotiations. The use of a third party neutral can identify information gaps in the course of explaining the dispute. Often the neutral can arrange for those with the specialist knowledge to attend the negotiations.

- *Emotion.* Disagreements often generate emotional factors which escalate a simple disagreement into a serious dispute. Emotion can cloud the true issue and make it very difficult for parties to reach negotiation settlement. The dominance of the male culture and male gender values which are inherently more conflictual than female gender values has been said to add to the problem.[7] Certain mediation processes allow for 'venting' and/or the separation of the parties during the negotiation process, and in this way a mediator is able to ensure that negotiations continue.

- *Good-faith disagreements about legal outcome.* Often situations arise where both parties genuinely believe that they are correct in their interpretation of the legal merits of the case. In many instances their belief will be reinforced by advice they have received by their lawyers or contract advisers. These are very difficult negotiations for a third party to help resolve, as the neutral person may need to evaluate the merits of the situation and indicate what they believe the results would be if the matter were litigated or arbitrated. It is only human nature that often the more the party pays for the advice, the more strongly they will believe that advice. Good faith disagreements of this kind are sometimes associated with poor communications, for instance, a one-sided explanation of the dispute may have been given by the lawyers or contract advisers. In many cases, the person providing the information to the lawyers or contract adviser does not have the first hand knowledge of disputes and will themselves have already been given a distorted view of the dispute. Negotiations impasses of this nature are susceptible to resolution by structured mediation such as the mini-trial (or executive tribunal).

- *Wrong people.* It is crucial that negotiators have settlement authority, are skilful negotiators and have all the right attributes. Neutral third party intervention can often help in this situation, either by assessing the position of the individuals or by assisting in overcoming the deficiencies. Often a third party can help by tactfully suggesting that negotiators be replaced or assisted by others.

---

7   Gale, A, 'The Construction Industry's Male Culture', in Fenn, P and Gameson, R (eds), *Construction Conflict: Management and Resolution*, 1992, London: Chapman Hall.

- *Need for an authoritative ruling.* If the matter of the dispute is such that a ruling on it will provide a precedent for other disputes, then non-binding ADR processes will do little to assist. The preferred route for such impasses is usually litigation.

- *Bad faith.* If one or both sides do not wish to settle the dispute, and there is bad faith in the negotiation, then it is unlikely that the use of a non-binding ADR technique will be suitable. In this situation mediation can often be counterproductive and may even be suggested by one side merely as a delaying tactic to gain commercial advantage, and/or to delay 'the day of judgment'.

ESTABLISHED PROCESSES FOR DEALING WITH CONSTRUCTION DISPUTES

The evolution of standard form contracts

In the UK, the traditional arrangement for buying buildings and structures was via an architect or masterbuilder controlling craftsmen, journeymen and labourers. The architect and the workforce made their name by repute. The scope for dispute was limited, formal contracts were few and the contribution of individuals could seldom have a dramatic effect on the overall scheme. The risk of the cost and duration of the construction remained with the client; normally the crown, aristocracy or the church. Nevertheless, disputes still sometimes arose. Ferry and Brandon[8] have described how building Blenheim Palace almost bankrupted the Duke of Marlborough; and one would imagine that many tradesmen and labourers came and went due to disputes during construction. The industrial revolution changed this. Building projects became business-led and the need arose for risks to be apportioned between the parties to the contract, the client and the builder. A concept of the builder bidding a price in advance of construction of the works developed; contractors would bid in competition for schemes based on the designs produced by architects and engineers.

As the concept of a price in advance developed following the Industrial Revolution, there were calls for standard forms of contract in building work. From about 1870, the bodies representing contractors began to discuss the issue of a standard contract with the Royal Institute of British Architects (RIBA). As a consequence RIBA and the contracting bodies issued their own form of contract. However in 1903 a settlement was finally reached following the intervention of the then Institute of Builders. An agreed form of contract was issued. Further amendments were discussed and the revised form was issued in 1909.

There were problems, however, in connection with this 1909 form and dissatisfaction grew. In 1909 the contracting bodies gave notice to RIBA. They rescinded their agreement to the 1909 form and issued their own building

---

8   Ferry, D and Brandon, P, *Cost Planning of Buildings*, 1983, London: Granada.

standard code. Following this, in 1922, a contract conference was held between representatives of architects, surveyors and contractors and the joint drafting committee was established under independent chairmanship with an arrangement for any points of difficulty to be referred for final decision to Sir William McKenzie GBE, KC. It was reported in this period that the main area of disagreement was whether the architect should be the sole judge between the contractor and the client upon aspects affecting the financial aspects of the contract. In 1928, the contract conference approved a draft form of contract which provided for arbitration on all matters.

Relationships within the industry having been restored and confidence and goodwill re-established, discussions continued and from these the 1931 Form of Contract emerged. A tribunal mechanism was introduced by the Joint Contracts Tribunal (JCT) as a recognition by the sponsoring parties that the most experienced committee of practitioners working with the most skilled legal draftsmen could never anticipate every difficulty which might arise during building. The JCT was therefore established to discuss difficulties and agree amendments to the standard form contract. In 1937, an adapted version of the 1931 form was issued for use in the public sector. A further revised edition was published in 1939 and terms were further revised during the Second World War to meet all the conditions likely to experienced after the war had ended. In 1955 the JCT announced a general revision of its forms of contract and invited comments and proposals from all those interested. It was reported that some 1,400 points of interest were raised, indicating the degree of interest within the construction industry in the standard form. These revisions resulted in the 1963 edition of the JCT standard form of building contract.

Following the development of the standard form of building contract the JCT went on to design and produce a wide range of standard forms of contracts to meet the needs of industry clients. The JCT is a widely representative body which now issues a vast spectrum of standard forms ranging from a jobbing agreement for works on smaller scale to management contract documentation. In 1990 some 217,000 copies of JCT documents were purchased.

Arbitration

As a system of main contracting developed, building organisations used their skills to manage labour and materials. At first firms directly employed but more recently a system of sub-contracting has developed, in a highly competitive tendering market. The result is a fragmented market of poorly qualified firms, with the scope for disputing vastly increased.

Initially the primary methods of settling disputes within the industry were litigation and arbitration. As the industry developed and became more sophisticated, less formal procedures became available. For example, standard forms of contract (above) introduced an employer's agent, architect or engineer. This employer's agent became responsible for the administration of the contract and was given varying powers to decide on contentious matters as they arose in the course of construction.

Arbitration has been traced back to ancient Greece although most sources credit the Romans with originating arbitration via the praetorial system. This system was used throughout the Roman Empire and found favour with merchants and traders in England. This law of the merchants was eventually administered via the Courts of Pie Powder; a corruption of the French *Pieds Poudres*, the court of the dusty feet. The industrial revolution and the advent of limited liability brought the formation of corporate bodies. Once again the civil courts failed to meet the needs generated by these commercial developments. Following the industrial revolution, it became apparent that the procedures of the civil courts were hardly the ideal place for the resolution of corporate disputes. Business complained of the vagaries of the system and took their disputes elsewhere, notably to arbitrators. The construction industry in particular was quick to take on board the developing process of arbitration. Baden Hellard[9] describes the formation of the Chartered Institute of Arbitrators in the UK which included several construction professionals on the founding committee.

Arbitration in the UK became the preferred method of resolving disputes in the construction industry. Litigation and arbitration continued in an atmosphere of mutual distrust; occasionally legislation upheld arbitration awards as the agreed method of resolving disputes. All the widely adopted standard forms of contract for construction works include an arbitration agreement. Today, arbitration is generally seen as the usual method for resolving disputes. Its advocates claimed its major advantages include speed of proceedings; cost of proceedings; privacy; and the technical expertise of arbitrator.

However, more recently, arbitration has been accused of suffering from the same problems which afflicted the civil courts after the industrial revolution; the very problems which originally provided the environment for arbitration to flourish.[10] The perceived advantages of cost, speed, and technical expertise have all but disappeared as arbitrators have increasingly mimicked the High Court for arbitration procedures. Parties are very frequently represented by senior counsel, the rules for evidence and proof follow High Court procedure and proceedings have become protracted. Parties to arbitration have increasingly turned to the courts for appeals against the decision of their arbitrators. Some industries now propose arbitration as an 'alternative dispute revolution' technique, demonstrating how an established technique in one area can be seen to be new in another. However construction professionals would hardly consider arbitration to be an 'alternative' technique.

---

9   Baden Hellard, R, *Managing Construction Conflict*, 1988, London: Longman.

10   Acland, A, *A Sudden Outbreak of Common Sense*, 1990, London: Hutchinson Business Books. Tillotson, J, *Contract Law in Perspective*, 1996, London: Cavendish Publishing.

ALTERNATIVE DISPUTE RESOLUTION TECHNIQUES

Site based v non-site based techniques

An important dividing point in the dispute resolution process in construction disputes is the stage at which the dispute passes from the site (out of the hands of those involved with the success of the project) and into the hand of third parties. These third parties may be head office based or external consultants. The importance of this distinction was confirmed by research in the United States carried out by the Construction Industry Institute.[11] Once this line has been crossed, the site based personnel lose control of the resolution of the dispute, leaving the issues of entitlement and quantification to be dealt with by those less familiar with the project. The head office staff or external consultants are often not sensitive to the on-site relationships and argue in an environment where adversarial techniques are the norm and the dispute is likely to escalate. This adds to the cost and time for resolution of the dispute and in many countries it has become normal for large construction disputes to be resolved off-site by a costly, after the fact, determination.

It has long been recognised that once the dispute resolution process passes from the site, matters can soon become out of hand, and construction projects and contractors make conscious attempts to resolve the disputes on site. A variety of techniques and procedures have been implemented to attempt to resolve the dispute at site level. These techniques are described in more detail below.

Mediation

Mediation is the leading ADR technique in construction contracts and consists of a neutral person, the mediator, assisting the parties in dispute reach a negotiated settlement. Mediation is quick, cheap and usually effective and advantages have been described in terms of the five C's: Commercialism; Consensus; Continuity; Control and Confidentiality.

- *Commercialism* – at the heart of ADR lies the concept of helping commercial people make commercial decisions.

- *Consensus* – a joint objective to find the commercial and business solution.

- *Continuity* – a desire to find a solution in the context of an ongoing commercial and business relationship.

- *Control* – the ability to tailor a solution that is geared towards a business and commercial result rather that a result governed by a rule of law which may be restrictive or inappropriate.

- *Confidentiality* – maintaining confidentiality in commercial matters, no washing of dirty linen in public.

---

11 Disputes Potential Index, Construction Industry Institute Special Publication 23–22, Dispute Prevention and Resolution Research Team, CII, The University of Texas at Austin USA.

Parties to mediation are free to talk in confidence to the mediator in private sessions or caucuses, where they are able to focus on what they would really like to achieve in negotiation. The true interests of the parties are often different from the position presented to the other party in the negotiation. It is usual for the mediation process to be treated as privileged and this means that nothing said or done in a mediation may subsequently be directly admissible in arbitration or litigation proceedings, should the mediation fail.

The use of mediation in construction disputes is growing. For example, in Hong Kong mediation is written in as an option to arbitration in the Government Standard Form Construction Contract and the Royal Institution of Chartered Surveyors (RICS) Minor Works Form Contract. In a major airport redevelopment in Hong Kong an attempt at mediation is a pre-requisite before proceeding with one of the binding options for resolving disputes. In 1992 The International Confederation of Consulting Engineers (*Fédération Internationale des Ingénieures Conseils* (FIDIC)) carried out a survey of FIDIC member association countries and their use of the mediation clause contained in the FIDIC conditions of contract for works of civil engineering and construction (4th edn 1987) known as the red book.[12] This survey included a status report from corresponding members in 17 countries and a synopsis is included at Appendix A.

In addition to mediation, a number of other non-binding, consensual approaches to settlement have evolved throughout the construction industry.

Dispute review boards (DRBs)

In the United States, DRBs have been an outstanding success. The DRB is an expedited non-binding ADR procedure whereby an independent board, usually three persons, is established to evaluate disputes and make settlements recommendations to the parties. The Board members become knowledgeable about the project by periodically visiting the site. The Board meets at regular intervals and hears presentations on the dispute which have arisen since they last met.

The goal of the DRB process is not only to resolve disputes, but also to prevent them. The same Board will sit on all disputes occurring during the project and the parties will soon become familiar with how DRB members look at particular types of issues. Parties will then be able to predict how the Board will react and will take that into account when negotiating between themselves and as a consequence many disputes will settle before reaching Board level.

A form of DRB was used to resolve disputes between English and French contractors during the Channel tunnel project and DRBs are being used successfully on several major projects in the US. The World Bank insists on the use of DRBs in connection with infrastructure projects around the world where the World Bank provides finance for the project.

12　Fédération International des Ingeneurs-Conseils (FIDIC) *Conditions of Contract for Works of Civil Engineering*, 4th edn, 1987, Geneva: FIDIC.

The dispute resolution adviser (DRA)

The DRA system is a flexible pre-contract and post-contract dispute avoidance and resolution system. At the pre-contact stage it is used for identifying commonly occurring problem areas and unrealistic risk allocation in the project documentation or proposed project structure. Suggestions are made by a neutral person, following a confidential information gathering exercise on how contract documentation or contract arrangements might be modified in order to reduce the potential for conflict. At the post-contract stage, the employer and the contractor choose a mutually acceptable construction industry professional who is well versed in dispute resolution techniques to serve as the DRA. In a similar manner to a DRB (Board member), the DRA visits the site on a regular basis to keep abreast of construction activities and to advise the parties on how best to deal with disputes or disagreements as and when they occur. The DRA also has a proactive role in focusing the parties' attention on potential problem areas; in this way matters can be addressed in a construction manner and mitigating measures introduced as soon as possible. The DRA also acts as a facilitative mediator and will attempt the persuade the parties to resolve their disputes by non-binding means if at all possible.

As a further incentive for the parties to resolve their own disputes, short form arbitration is built into the DRA system as a swift and cheap method for resolving those disputes which the parties are unable to negotiate either by themselves or with the assistance of a neutral person. The DRA system also uses partnering and step negotiating techniques (below).

The mini-trial

The mini-trial or executive tribunal is not a trial at all but a highly structured form of mediation, and like the dispute resolution adviser system it is a hybrid ADR system. Mini-trial combines evaluative and facilitative mediation with negotiation. The mini-trial typically involves two chief executives and a neutral person who listens to an exposition from both sides of a particular dispute. The procedure follows that of an arbitration or trial in that arguments are presented, and witnesses called and cross-examined on both sides. Unlike a full trial, the presentation normally takes place within a relatively short time frame, often half a day, and provides the chief executives and the neutral person with a good overview of the dispute. The chief executives then attempt to resolve the matter by negotiation, using the neutral person as an evaluative mediator if they reach an impasse.

The mini-trial has been used successfully in the US and Hong Kong for resolving construction disputes.

Partnering

Partnering is a technique pioneered by the US Army Corps of Engineers. It is essentially a consensus–building process that reorientates the parties from a 'them and us' mentality to a 'we' approach. Partnering is a long-term commitment between two or more organisations for the purposes of achieving specific business objectives by maximising the effectiveness of each participant's resources. Parties to partnering agreements enter into long-term arrangements for mutual benefit.

Partnering is not normally based on a single project but operates over a period of time (this is particularly important in construction where traditional organisational features are built around single projects). The concept is one of team building which again is not normal in construction. Partnering has been used successfully in Hong Kong and in the UK where major retail clients have, for a long time, entered into arrangements with preferred contractors which are not project-based (ie built around a single project). Partnering arrangements often utilise a technique known as step negotiation. In step negotiation, the representatives of the parties to whom the dispute is referred are required, in the event that they cannot resolve the problem, to refer the matter to their superiors in both organisations. This provides an additional incentive to the representative to resolve problems without having to involve their superiors.

THE FUTURE FOR ADR IN CONSTRUCTION

Miles[13] describes how, despite a concerted effort by the organisations involved, it is fair to say that throughout commerce generally and the construction industry in particular there is still a general lack of awareness of what ADR is and what it seeks to achieve. Even in the legal profession, a number of leading lawyers think of ADR only in terms of arbitration, involving a traditional adversarial approach and an adjudicatory award of some kind.

Once there is an awareness and an understanding of alternative processes, it is easier to encourage parties to use these procedures. Probably the first hurdle that has to be overcome in the construction industry is the traditional male culture[14] which surrounds the resolving of disputes. Whilst the majority of disputes are still resolved through commercial negotiations, there is an incorrect perception that the suggestion of ADR could be taken as a sign of weakness.[15] That perception ought to disappear with a better understanding of the process and with the establishment of a track record of successful settlement in the

---

13   Miles, D, 'The Problems of Using ADR in the Construction Industry, in Fenn, P and Gameson, R (eds), *Construction Conflict: Management and Resolution*, 1992, London: Chapman Hall.

14   Gale, A, above note 7.

15   Stipanowich, TJ and Henderson, D, 'Mediation and Mini–Trial of Construction Disputes', in Fenn, P and Gameson, R (eds), *Construction Conflict: Management and Resolution*, 1992, London: Chapman Hall.

construction field. Of course, the need for arguments to be made in each case for using ADR processes can be overcome by the inclusion of ADR clauses in standard forms of construction contracts, and it is encouraging to note the world-wide trend for the adoption of such clauses.

The advantages offered by ADR for the construction industry are widely quoted. The 5 Cs (commercialism; consensus; continuity; control and confidentiality) provide a useful summary. In most construction contracts the contract period is of a significant length and in the major construction projects can go on for many years. Major dam projects, the Channel Tunnel and bridge contracts are excellent examples. If a dispute occurs early on in the project, it is vitally important to maintain harmonious relationships between the parties if at all possible. If the parties fall out with each other early on, it is not satisfactory from either parties' point of view for a contractor either to walk off site or to be ejected. The parties have to learn to live with each other and co-operate with each other to see the project through to a successful completion. The existence of a dispute which may not be resolved until many years after completion of the project will not help relationships on site. If the dispute can be resolved at an early stage, there is less scope for parties to take up entrenched positions, retreat from which may be perceived as being a sign of weakness or loss of face. If the parties can establish a precedent for settling disputes this can only enhance the relationship on site so that a constructive atmosphere, with the parties working together to achieve completion as a team, can be established rather than what is often an acrimonious and adversarial climate on site.

Whilst there may be points of law and fact to be argued in construction cases, more often than not the issues between the parties narrow down to those of a technical nature. The reinvolvement of businesspersons in dispute resolution via the ADR process, therefore, brings back into the arena those most naturally suited and trained to argue matters of a technical and commercial nature.

How then does the growing use of ADR affect the positions of the potential parties to a construction dispute?

The sub-contractor

The prevalence of sub-contracting in construction industries has been described above. The advantage to a sub-contractor in embarking upon ADR is that this may give him a route to the ultimate payer, the employer, in circumstances where no direct route exists (his claim can only be brought in contract against the main contractor). Often an employer will make deductions against a main contractor which the main contractor then seeks to pass on to the sub-contractor. The unfortunate sub-contractor, being kept out of his money, has no means of persuading the employer to pay. It may even be that the main contractor has the benefit of a 'pay when paid' clause in his contract with the sub-contractor.

The sub-contractor will not necessarily favour ADR. He may feel he has an 'open and shut case', a straight forward entitlement to a set sum of money. He may perceive ADR as a pressure upon him to make concessions and to compromise. However, it should be remembered that even where there is an indisputable sum due, there may still be advantages in negotiation. There is no point in obtaining judgment against a party for a sum if that party is likely to go into liquidation if judgment is executed. In such circumstances there is scope for negotiating payments by instalments, thereby easing the pressure upon the payee's cash flow.

The main contractor

Main contractors can hold contracts in two directions; one with the client and one with the sub-contractors and suppliers. It has been thought in the past that main contractor's principal resistance to ADR is a perception that the procedures may result in their having to make earlier payments to sub-contractors. In the UK many main contractors make their money by delaying payments to sub-contractors and the cost, delays and expenses of arbitration and litigation deter sub-contractors taking action against defaulting main contractors. Relatively inexpensive ADR processes may encourage sub-contractors to press defaulters for earlier payment. Undoubtedly, this will be the main contractor's principal source of resistance to ADR.

On the other hand, main contractors will see the benefits of ADR so far as any dispute they have against their employer and client. The benefits of early private resolution of disputes will also have the attraction of confidentiality for contractors who may not care to gain a reputation for being claims-oriented.

The employer

Employers have the power at their fingertips to introduce ADR into any contractual arrangement by simply including clauses in their standard forms of contract. Even if the standard form does not contain a standard clause, there is nothing to stop employers introducing one or incorporating arbitration rules which also allow for mediation or conciliation. The international arbitration rules produced by ICC and UNCITRAL include such clauses. Again, there may be a reluctance on the part of employers to introduce any procedure which may increase the prospect of an early payment. However, there is an increasing awareness amongst employers that the cost of traditional adversarial processes are excessive and the often unpredictable nature of litigation or arbitration means that no one can be certain of the outcome. The benefits in terms of commercialism should be apparent to all employers.

The insurer

Where matters of law and precedent are central to some disputes, it may be that ADR processes are not appropriate for insurers. Insurers have traditionally been resistant to early settlement but surprisingly, in some jurisdictions – notably the

US – insurers have been amongst the strongest institutional supporters of ADR. A driving force behind this interest in ADR are statistics showing that of sums paid in settlement, 60% of those costs have gone towards fighting the case. Again the confidential nature of ADR may prove attractive, particularly in the area of professional indemnity, where few professional advisers want their mistakes aired in public.

End users

ADR techniques, particularly mediation, are becoming increasingly well-known in other fields including neighbourhood and environmental issues. Construction developments can often be faced with protest groups and ADR may be suitable to address conflict between the industry and user groups.

Construction professionals

It is axiomatic that many construction projects reach completion and all parties receive satisfaction. The client receives the building she requires to the desired quality, on-time, and within budget. The contractor, on the other hand, achieves these objectives and makes a profit. The construction professionals (architects, engineers, surveyors, construction managers) deal with these two parties and achieve remarkable successes. Many do this by using, informally, the techniques of ADR. Many do it without realising that the formalisation of these processes will help them to more consistently achieve their principal objectives.

Legal representatives

In many jurisdictions there is a disenchantment with the law and this dissatisfaction manifests itself via the vilification of lawyers. There is nothing new in this: 'The first thing we do, let's kill all the lawyers'.[16] Everybody knows at least one joke attacking lawyers or their profession.

Ultimately, lawyers need satisfied clients, like anyone, if they are to obtain repeat business. A client is not readily going to subject himself to any process if he has bitter experience of going through the mill and losing. It is incumbent upon the lawyers to devote their creative talents towards exploring the options. ADR is one such option. Many hold a cynical view that lawyers' support of ADR is merely a matter of defensive marketing. This is for clients to chose. If lawyers offer clients a better service by a defensive marketing, those lawyers will thrive.

---

16   William Shakespeare, *Henry VI* (Part II).

CONCLUSION

This chapter has argued that the construction industries, via their organisational and contractual features, promote and produce conflict and disputes. There is little evidence that, to date, mediation is being used to any great extent in construction disputes. However, construction industries have been creative in adapting hybrid ADR techniques to suit individual needs and this demonstrates the applicability of ADR to disputes arising within the industry. It is anticipated that the use of mediation in construction disputes will show a steady increase over the coming years.

APPENDIX A

THE USE OF MEDIATION IN CONSTRUCTION DISPUTES

In 1992 the International Confederation of Consulting Engineers (Federation Internationale des Ingenieures Conseils (FIDIC)) carried out a survey of FIDIC member association countries and their use of the mediation clause contained in the FIDIC conditions of contract for works of civil engineering and construction. This survey included a status report from corresponding members in 17 countries:

Australia
Canada
Finland
Germany
Hong Kong
India
Ireland
Japan
Korea
New Zealand
Norway
Peru
South Africa
Surinam
Sweden
United Kingdom
United States of America

A brief synopsis of the report from each country follows.

Australia

Mediation processes have not been taken up as enthusiastically as was hoped. It is thought that this is a result of conservatism amongst professionals and contractors. There was also a feeling amongst the contractors that they had tried mediation only to find that the other party was using it as a delay mechanism, with no intention of resolving the dispute.

In December 1991, the Australian Government endorsed a construction industry reform strategy via a report 'No Dispute'. It is expected that the dispute resolution clauses recommended in the 'No Dispute' report will be progressively adopted throughout the building and construction industries.

Canada

Enthusiastic support was reported for any process which simplified and speeded up dispute resolution while including savings in money. However, there were very few examples of mediations taking place. The standard construction contracts used in Canada are those prepared by the Canadian Instruction Documents Committee and whilst the three current documents include provision for arbitration, there is no provision for mediation.

Finland

A similar report to Canada. Again enthusiasm expressed for mediation but little practical use.

Germany

This report describes the situation of the old federal countries before unification between West and East Germany. It notes that due to the expense and delays associated with civil court actions and often unpredictable results, mediation is being used in an increasing number of cases. The standard form of contract in Germany (VOB) includes provision for the intervention of an administrative office within a Government district to help settle disputes but beyond that the next stage is arbitration.

Hong Kong

Mediation is an important feature of dispute resolution in both the Peoples Republic of China and Hong Kong. Mediation has had a new lease of life in the Hong Kong construction industry as a result of the Hong Kong Government's agreement to the inclusion of mediation provisions in all construction contracts.

India

Mediation is not in systematic use in India and is not referred to in local standard forms of contract. Again, there has been some enthusiasm regarding introducing mediation processes before arbitration and litigation is resorted to, but this enthusiasm has had limited practical consequences to date.

Ireland

The report claims that mediation techniques have become more popular in Ireland recently. Moves towards the more widespread use of mediation have been initiated by the Chartered Institute of Arbitrators.

Japan

Mediation appears to be widely practised in Japan. The history of mediation is traced back to the feudal period or even earlier. This tradition survives today in the way that government agencies deal with citizens and as well as in the settlement of disputes amongst both companies and individuals. Mediation has been established by legislative act or local government regulation for a wide range of matters, including construction disputes.

Korea

Again, mediation is the preferred method of dispute resolution in Korea. It has statutory recognition under the Civil Conciliation Law (CCL) promulgated in 1990.

New Zealand

It was reported that in New Zealand mediation has been used for some time to resolve labour, neighbourhood and family disputes, and that recently there has been increased interest in the use of mediation within commercial and construction disputes. The standard form of contract for construction in New Zealand includes the option of mediation prior to arbitration.

Norway

There is no officially established procedure for mediation in Norway and therefore no rules governing the processes. The general conditions of contracts of construction and building now include a clause advocating mediation for all disputes.

Peru

In Peru, mediation processes are seldom if at all used to settle disputes arising from construction contracts, whether these involve private or public agencies.

South Africa

The rising costs of arbitration and litigation processes have given rise to a growing interest in mediation. The Government is beginning to show an interest and mediation is now provided for in all standard building and engineering contracts, prior to resorting to arbitration and litigation.

Sweden

Once again there is perceived to be a future for mediation process owing to the enormous costs involved in court cases and arbitration. The standard form of construction contract provides for binding arbitration; there is no provision for mediation. Nevertheless, the parties sometimes decide to consult an experienced professional for guidance.

United Kingdom

The report claims that the growth of construction litigation in the United Kingdom is nothing less than epidemic. There is a long history in the United Kingdom of dissatisfaction with civil litigation procedures, and indeed all forms of construction contract contain binding arbitration clauses as evidence of this. However, arbitration processes themselves have now started to be seen in the same light as litigation (lengthy, costly, etc). Naturally with this background there has been considerable interest in mediation processes. However, there are few reports of its use in construction disputes and it is viewed with suspicion by potential disputants.

United States of America

Litigation in the US construction industry is described as reaching epic proportions. The general dissatisfaction and frustration with the prohibitive delays and costs inherent in litigation and arbitration have seen an explosion in the use of mediation. It is claimed there has been an exponential increase in the use of ADR techniques over the last 10 years. Federal and state courts have moved vigorously towards settlement of claims using mediation. Construction contracts contain provisions for a range of ADR procedures, including mediation.

6 MEDIATING COMMERCIAL DISPUTES: EXCHANGING 'POWER OVER' FOR 'POWER WITH'

GENEVIEVE A CHORNENKI*

Mediation is a process which offers commercial disputants meaningful, creative solutions at a fraction of the cost of the litigation system. But, to enjoy mediation's benefits, commercial parties must learn how to screen for and select appropriate disputes. A large component of this screening involves an honest self-awareness of attitudes towards conflict and a readiness to adopt a new approach to power which emphasises shared as opposed to competing efforts.

This paper focuses on the kind of shift that is fundamental to the successful application of mediation to commercial disputes and sets out seven criteria for parties to review as a precondition to participating in mediation.

Example 1

Ramero Desantos was very angry. He had arranged to withdraw $50,000 US on an urgent basis from his account at Worthington Savings and Loan, only to be told at the last minute that his grandfather, the beneficiary of the money, had to be personally present at the bank. But his grandfather lived in their country of origin and the money was to be used as an illicit payment to preserve a large land holding there. This new condition of the bank was impossible to meet and resulted in loss of the land, valued at many hundreds of thousands of dollars. Ramero Desantos could not take Worthington to court for this would make matters public, thus endangering his grandfather, a persecuted minority at the hands of the state.

Worthington Savings and Loan had steadfastly refused to acknowledge Mr Desantos' claim. Why should it? Ramero Desantos had no real leverage. He would never go to court.

And yet, Mr Desantos returned from an all day mediation some time later with a measure of reimbursement by the bank for the loss of the land.

Example 2

When Vanity Propane won the tender for the supply of propane to the prestigious Twinnings Golf & Country Club, it was a banner day. The contract provided an entree into an important new national market segment worth millions of dollars a year if properly exploited. Imagine

* Founding partner, Mediated Solutions Incorporated, Toronto.

Vanity's dismay, however, when a club member, Everet Latos, started litigation to attack the resolution of Twinnings Board of Directors granting the Vanity contract, on the grounds that it was outside the scope of their powers.

Latos' attack was nonsensical and the Twinning's Board told him that, but Mr Latos doggedly pushed on, demanding that the Vanity contract be set aside.

And yet, some weeks later, Vanity, Latos and Twinnings emerged from a three-hour mediation with a simple agreement – to paint the Vanity propane tank on the Twinnings' property white.

Example 3

Eldercare Nursing Homes Limited and Osborne Construction each resented the other. Eldercare alleged unauthorised and fraudulent deletions from the design of its flagship nursing home, the value of which Marcus Osborne, the contractor's principal, pocketed to make up for cost overruns. Osborne, in turn, alleged interference and harassment in the performance of the job.

The moral indignation of one side was matched only by that of the other. Days of disputing turned to months. Months turned to years. Venom accumulated.

And yet, under the guidance of a mediator, Osborne ultimately delivered and Eldercare graciously accepted a statement acknowledging changes to the construction design which 'constituted an acute embarrassment to your Board.'

Example 4

Samuel Nickles runs a large manufacturing company, Nickles' Precision Products. Started by him as a part-time business in the late 1970s, it has grown into a multi-national undertaking with annual sales in excess of $5 billion. Samuel is determined to have the company survive him and ultimately devolve to his grandchildren. He has repeatedly called meetings of his adult children to inform them of their roles in his succession plan. The children persistently decline to attend and resent being summoned and told how they will spend their working lives.

And yet, following a weekend meeting with a mediator, the children and Samuel departed exhilarated and exhausted with a plan for how decisions will get made and implemented for the continuity of Nickles' Precision Works.

These are examples of the 'promise' of mediation with its compelling potential to bring about resolutions that are truly responsive to the parties' wants. Such outcomes are not uncommon in 'interest-based' mediation, where a mediator establishes useful communication, seeks to uncover the parties interests and crafts with them a solution that meets as many of those interests as possible.

Interests (synonymous with needs, wants or concerns) are not always easily discernible or understood, even to the party who experiences them. Interests can be vague, undeveloped, unconscious or conflicting. They can emerge unexpectedly in the face of new information that often comes forward at a mediation.

In the Desantos & Worthington case, for instance, while Ramero Desantos could not enjoy the leverage of litigation, he was manifestly a person of means with the potential for other business at the Worthington Savings and Loan. When the mediator enabled Worthington to learn the purpose of the $50,000 withdrawal and to appreciate the financial situation of Ramero Desantos, Worthington looked at the matter in a different light. It was able to strike a deal with Desantos for partial reimbursement of the value of the land without formal proof of loss, in order to restore his goodwill as a client.

Interest-based mediators urge commercial parties to articulate and understand their real needs, wants and concerns as opposed to their stated or public ones. Mediators search for and clarify those needs and craft solutions that satisfy them. Sometimes parties see or experience their respective needs as competing or mutually exclusive, but the interest-based mediator examines those needs dispassionately to see if in fact they do conflict, or if they are shared.

In the Vanity Propane case, for instance, the mediator learned that Everet Latos, an active member and avid golfer at Twinnings Golf & Country Club, was also a major shareholder of Fontana Fuels, a competitor of Vanity Propane. Mr Latos did not object to the fact that Vanity had won out over Fontana in the tender. That competition had been fair and square. Instead, Mr Latos objected to the fact that the Vanity propane tanks were positioned near the club house at the end of the course, so that members and guest completing a game of golf concluded with a striking view of the Vanity trade mark. What Mr Latos wanted, and both Vanity and Twinnings could easily give, was removal of the free advertising available to Vanity, not revocation of the contract for the propane supply. Hence, the solution was devised of painting the propane tanks white.

Depending on aptitude and inclination, an interest-based mediator can surface a need, want or concern that has not been stated. Such a need, although unarticulated, can be powerfully operative among commercial parties. It can surface indirectly again and again and, until dealt with, can sabotage negotiations. An interest-based mediator works with the parties to find a palatable way of expressing that need and having it met.

In the Eldercare & Osborne case, board had been warned not to use Osborne as a general contractor, and the acute embarrassment that they experienced when the predicted risks materialised, that was the key to unlocking an acrimonious and persistent dispute. Until the board's need for acknowledgment and public apology was identified and addressed, the parties were doomed to continue their litigious dance.

The interest-based mediator converts a binary choice, my way or your way, into a joint problem-solving statement to which all parties may subscribe. In the case of Nickles' Precision Works, this involved a change from whether or not Samuel's children would follow his succession plan, to whether and *to what extent* the children were prepared to get involved in the company.

In each of the foregoing examples, the mediator intervened where the parties were polarised or at an impasse. Relationships were strained or broken. Negative repetitive behaviour occurred. Time had passed. Money had been spent. Executive time had been used. Opportunity costs mounted. Mediation ended that, producing 'elegant', efficient and economical settlements that sometimes seem simple and obvious in retrospect.

This is the 'satisfaction story' of mediation, the one that is told and retold by proponents and vendors of the process to inform commercial users of its benefits and to induce them to participate. It is a compelling story, for the negative costs and consequences of conflict often equal or exceed the value of the matter in dispute. The frustration of an impasse is a familiar feeling to commercial negotiators everywhere. What mediation practitioners and proponents fail to tell commercial parties with the same frequency that they recount mediation's benefits is that interest-based mediation demands a set of unfamiliar attitudes and a fundamental change *on the part of participants* in the way that power is thought of and used.

Power, to a commercial player, is the ability to get one's way or to unilaterally bring about results or change, despite resistance. It is control of something or someone. It is predominantly competitive in nature. Strict adherence to this form of power by any of the parties in the examples would not have produced the outcomes that they enjoyed. Worthington Savings would have continued to marginalise Ramero Desantos. Latos and Twinnings would have litigated the legitimacy of the authorising resolution. Eldercare would have continued to accuse and Osborne to deny. And Samuel Nickles would have persisted in promoting his own succession plan. Instead, mediation required each party to withdraw from crude attempts at influence or control and to move to a deeper level within each dispute in order to get access to its 'rewards'.

However, power as influence or control is a necessary and long standing ingredient of a competitive economic system which values individual initiative, earned status, the acquisition of resources and an essentially distributive view of the world. Such a context entails particular attitudes or unspoken rules which are known and observed by commercial players. These include beliefs that:

- Parties are principally motivated by their own self-interest. Where the self-interest of another party conflicts with that of the business, the party will inevitably act in its own self-interest to the detriment of the business.

- Vulnerability (actual or perceived) is undesirable and is to be avoided at all costs, as it exposes a business to the unbridled pursuit of self-interest by an opposite party.

- Trust entails vulnerability and involves the suspension of judgment. Thus trusting is a high risk and undesirable activity. It is safer to doubt a party's *bona fides* than to trust because it is only in retrospect that one can tell whether trust was appropriately given, by which time the harm has been done.

- Power equates with dominance and dominance is strength. Power means the ability to unilaterally bring about outcomes and is desirable as it reduces vulnerability. Hence, the object of most commercial exercises is dominance or winning, and winning is infinitely preferable to losing.

- Exclusivity in the marketplace and elsewhere is a condition devoutly desired wished, subject only to societal norms against monopolies. Exclusivity enables access to limited resources (of which the world consists).

- People and organisations are either for you or against you. If the actions of any particular person or organisation are detrimental to the business, they must have been preceded by an intention to do harm.

- Information is a valuable commodity. It can be compartmentalised and owned, and its distribution must be controlled among those who will act in the business' favour.

- Emotion is irrelevant and absent from commercial undertakings because after all, 'it is just about money at the end of the day.' It is imperative to observe a strong, unstated taboo against the identification and recognition of emotion.

While on one level these traits look like a commercial caricature, on another they express the most fundamental values upon which the commercial world is based. These are 'cultural' values which inform and sustain commercial activity and are perpetrated without a significant degree of conscious action. Where they become important in the context of mediation is in extent to which they can be aligned with the values inherent in the interest-based mediation. At present, the two coexist with some degree of discomfort.

The idea of power as influence or control has been transported into the culture of mediation but not as a desirable and necessary ingredient. Rather, it is understood as a phenomenon to be controlled. The most prevalent view among mediators is that power is, primarily, a mediator's responsibility and that she ought to undertake power-balancing between or among disputants. Very often, this analysis is centred on differences between or among disputants in how much information they have or control, in how they speak and behave, in whether they exhibit more extreme behaviours such as threats, coercion, or physical or verbal abuse which may negate a party's ability to give voluntary and informed consent. Prescriptions for mediators list sources or kinds of power and identify 'power imbalances' that they can do something about, and those that they cannot alter.

Mediators frequently write and talk of 'balancing' power and the mediator is enjoined 'to either disempower the overly powerful party or empower the powerless party'.[1] Mediators are said to 'manage' power relationships and to:

> [attempt] to strike a balance between the negotiators' total power positions … Doing so lowers the probability the stronger negotiator will attempt to exploit the weaker and that the weaker will abandon the relationship or seek to undermine the stronger's position. To strike the balance, the mediator provides the necessary power underpinnings to the weaker negotiator – information, advice, friendship – or reduces those of the stronger. If he cannot balance the power relationship, the mediator can bargain with or use his power against the stronger negotiator to constrain the exercise of his power.[2]

Such a view of power is entirely consistent with Anglo-Canadian jurisprudence. The concerns of both mediators and judges relate to one party having an unmatched advantage or form of dominating influence over another that is not benign. Power is 'the ability of one person to dominate the will of another, whether through manipulation, coercion, or outright but subtle abuse of power'.[3] Protection is available in extreme cases for those who are intellectually, economically or situationally 'weaker'. However, arm's length commercial parties are almost always presumed to be of equal bargaining power, regardless of their differences, and any vulnerability is presumed to be preventable through more prudent exercise of their bargaining power.[4]

Unfortunately, this preoccupation with power as control or influence provides commercial parties with little meaningful information about the attitudinal change that interest-based mediation requires. It suggests that mediation is but an extension of commercial norms and that if one could only do away with troublesome excesses and abuses of power, then the benefits of mediation could be enjoyed by all. In practice, interest-based mediation takes the emphasis off power as influence or control and places it on a different kind of capability, that of the 'collective'. It is the voluntary joining together of parties in the pursuit of a joint problem-solving exercise rather than their successful domination of another that is at the heart of interest-based mediation's true 'promise'. When such joint efforts take place, the parties do exercise power, but not as influence or control. Instead, they are engaged in the power of the collective, here referred to as 'power-with'.

Power-with is the power of association, or the power of the team. It is a whole-is-bigger-than-the-sum-of-its-parts phenomenon. *Power-with* is not the absence of conflict, but the focusing of individual abilities on a common goal. In the case of mediation, that goal is the creation of an agreement that meets needs on each

---

1   Goss, JH and Taylor, K, *Mediation: Theory and Skill, Level II* (1990) Alberta Arbitration and Mediation Society at 45.

2   Wall Jr, JA, 'Mediation: An Analysis, Review, and Proposed Research' (1981) 25 (1) *Journal of Conflict Resolution* 157, at 164.

3   *Geffen v Goodman Estate* [1991] 2 SCR 353.

4   *Frame v Smith* [1987] 2 SCR 99; *Norberg v Wynrib* [1992] 2 SCR 318.

side of the table, insofar as this is possible. Thus, *power-with* is the laser, as opposed to the dispersed light. It is the virtual corporation, the think-tank, the surgical team. It is not one disputant unilaterally compelling another to unwillingly do its bidding. When *power-with* occurs, one can observe:

> ... the aims, processes, methods, or behaviour that create order, stability and unity of direction ... [not] simplistic notions that [it] ... is peace and that peace is the absence of conflict ...[5]

For commercial users of mediation, *power-with* is the phenomenon that must prevail in mediation for its benefits to accrue. It occurs in a mediation when the parties begin, eventually, to answer the same joint problem-solving question or to bargain in order to bring about a mutually acceptable readjustment of their interdependence. The question becomes, 'How can the problem with this software be remedied', instead of 'Who is responsible for the fact that something went wrong?' Or, 'What price can we both agree on as being fair for the extra work?' instead of 'How can I contribute or do as little as possible?'

Power-with takes place when Worthington Savings and Loan stops insisting that Mr Desantos' claim is entirely illegitimate and when Mr Desantos stops insisting that he is entitled to 100% of an unprovable loss. It manifests itself when their joint question becomes: given that Ramero Desantos is a client of means and that the bank declined access to money that was rightfully his, what can the bank give and what will Mr Desantos accept that will restore his good will in the institution while at the same time compensating him for his loss?

Where *power-with* in mediation differs from that of the virtual corporation, the think-tank, or the surgical team, is that parties involved in those activities are interdependent by choice and generally perceive themselves as benefiting from the interdependence. Disputants in mediation, such as Eldercare and Osborne, however, are often interdependent against their will or are linked in a way that they experience as intolerable. In mediation, Eldercare and Osborne seek to terminate or restructure that interdependence and they are able to do so through their willingness to be open to each other's needs.

The most profound, and most difficult, activity that must occur at an interest-based mediation of a commercial dispute is the conversion of that dispute from an 'either/or' situation, a binary choice, to a focused, joint problem-solving exercise. It is this aspect of mediation, the voluntary participation of parties in a collective as opposed to an individual effort, which is within the unilateral control of every commercial party contemplating or engaging in mediation. A commercial party's primary willingness to do this is infinitely more important to the success of a mediation than any amount of screening for mediator aptitudes or orientation, or matching of disputes and disputants to the process, or the relative '*power over*' of the parties.

---

5   Folberg, J and Taylor, A, *Mediation: A Comprehensive Guide To Resolving Conflicts Without Litigation*, 1988, p 24, San Francisco: Jossey-Bass.

A willingness to engage in *power-with* is critical for commercial parties in mediation. It entails the conversion of a situation from one that pulls participants away from each other (the Twinnings' resolution is valid/the Twinnings' resolution is invalid) to one that moves them together, at least for the purposes of resolving a defined controversy or dispute: for example, how can the playing field for Vanity and Fontana be levelled with respect to advertising in a way that does not negate Vanity's contract with Twinnings? Bundled up in this undertaking may, and often will be, questions of who can coerce whom on what basis and for what purpose. *Power-with* does not negate or eliminate power as influence or control. But the parties' task at the mediation is so much larger and more complex than exercising or responding to conventional power.

Power-with is not something that a mediator can foster or create without the assistance of the parties and the flaw in a great deal of mediation promotion and description is that it can create the impression that the process, and/or the mediator, are able unilaterally to bring about (through technique, skill, good judgment, intuition) the kinds of conditions that will lead to elegant, economical and efficient resolutions. Nothing could be further from the truth. The mediation process requires not only a measure of cooperation with the opposite party, but at least the same measure of cooperation with the mediator and the mediation process itself. If this were more clearly understood, it would promote more appropriate case selection for mediation, for it would screen out (by self-identification) parties that are clearly unsuitable for interest-based mediation.

So how can a commercial party determine whether and to what extent the values of interest-based mediation are compatible with its own goals? The following factors are intended as a guide. The more willing each party is to participate or accept these conditions, the more likely it is that interest-based mediation will have something to offer. If these conditions prove to be unacceptable to a commercial party, no adverse judgment is intended. Mediation is not the only dispute resolution mechanism apart from litigation. Other forms, such as binding or advisory arbitration, dispute review boards, or fact-finding with recommendations, are all alternatives available to commercial parties in dispute. These often provide more controlled environments, less risk-taking disclosure, and more rule-oriented ways of proceeding. At the same time, they excuse parties from the necessity of accepting responsibility for outcomes and from surrendering their conventional approaches to power.

In an interest-based mediation, participants in commercial mediation can anticipate demands to:

- Focus individual energies on a collective problem, not an individual one. The problem may be no more elegant than 'on what basis can the plaintiff give and the defendant receive a release?' Or, it can be more complex, 'how can we foster respect and human dignity in the workplace?'.

- Form a genuine commitment to examine whether and to what extent the collective problem can be solved. This need not be commitment to definitely achieve a result, but commitment to the effort entailed in constructing an outcome.

- Accept mutual influence in the sense of willingness to try and persuade others, and openness to being persuaded by others. This relates to being understood and to understanding, rather than to convincing and converting.

- Engage in overt behaviour, but not necessarily private belief, that is respectful and non–obstructionist in the sense that it does not detract from the focused energy of the group.

- Maintain a willingness to foster or at least tolerate a level of capability on the part of each individual participant in the mediation process. This involves their ability to identify and actualise goals, options, skills, resources and decision-making. While there is no requirement that the parties be equal in their abilities here, rough parity of capability is a necessary prerequisite to the kind of negotiating undertaken at an interest-based mediation.

- Sustain an ability to recognise other points of view, other interpretations, other inferences, other versions of the controversy; the ability to paddle around in the other party's canoe. Known as recognition, this is an important condition:

  From the starting point of relative self-absorption, parties achieve recognition in mediation when they voluntarily choose to become more open, attentive, sympathetic, and responsible to the situation of the other party, thereby expanding their perspective to include an appreciation for another's situation.[6]

  The hallmark of recognition is letting go – however briefly or partially – of one's focus on self and becoming interested in the perspective of the other party as such, concerned about the situation of the other as a fellow human being, not as an instrument of fulfilling one's own need.[7]

  As a condition of *power-with* in a commercial mediation, however, recognition need not take the form of true compassion and connection. It could merely be an expression of enlightened self-interest. What does matter is that recognition is expressed overtly in words or actions. Mere alterations in belief, while valuable, are insufficient to bring about the active, kinetic phenomenon of *power-with* described here.

- Honesty. Engage in honest, authentic communication. If a commercial party tells the mediator that something is important to it when it is not, or advances an interest as a foil to hide what is truly important, this is counterproductive. It will busy the mediator in trying to achieve what has been stated as being important, for no useful end.

In the end result, these seven points concern the attitudes that commercial parties need to bring to the mediation process. Attitude is vital to the successful

---

6   Baruch Bush, RA and Folger, JP, *The Promise of Mediation*, 1994, p 89, San Francisco: Jossey-Bass.
7   *Ibid*, at 97.

outcome of any mediation and is a factor directly within the control of any particular party. Unless a commercial party is able and willing to accept the values and attitudes that interest-based mediation requires, then it is an unlikely candidate for the process. With its emphasis on information exchange, power-with (as opposed to raw unilateral influence and control) and recognition, interest-based mediation may, in fact, require a stretch that is uncomfortable or unacceptable for many commercial parties. The truth is that it does entail some element of vulnerability and 'letting-go' in order to bring its rewards within reach. To disguise this aspect of mediation is to do a disservice to users or potential users. For commercial parties who are able and willing to suspend reliance on power as unilateral influence and control and to participate in a collective problem-solving effort, the mediation process has much to offer. It is a measured understanding of mediation's demands as opposed to its benefits that will lead them there with more realistic expectations.

7 COMMUNITY AND NEIGHBOURHOOD MEDIATION: A UK PERSPECTIVE

*MARIAN LIEBMANN**

When people talk about community and neighbourhood mediation, for the most part this concerns disputes between two neighbours. However it can also include other disputes such as wider neighbourhood matters, disputes between groups and organisations, or extended family disputes; in short, any disputes which cause problems between people in the broader community. It does not usually include commercial disputes, or those family disputes which involve the divorce and separation of couples and ensuing problems surrounding children, property and money.

THE ORIGINS OF COMMUNITY MEDIATION IN THE UK

Although mediation is a traditional method of resolving conflict and practised widely in Asia and Africa, the influences on mediation in the UK have come mainly from North America and Australia. In the early 1980s, several well-known leaders in mediation and conflict resolution from the US and Australia spoke in the UK. This spread information about mediation, and also brought together those in the UK who were interested in pursuing mediation, both in the community/neighbourhood context, and with victims and offenders in the criminal justice context. American training material began to be widely available in the UK, in particular the *Mediator's Handbook – Peacemaking in Your Neighborhood* (1990) from the Friends' Suburban Project, Philadelphia.[1]

The first main interest in the UK was in victim/offender mediation and reparation, in which victims and offenders meet to discuss the crime and to work out how the offender can make amends. The National Association of Victims Support Schemes (NAVSS, now called Victim Support) held a conference on reparation in 1981, and carried out the first survey of British developments in mediation and reparation. A project was established in South Yorkshire in 1983, and four services were funded and researched by the Home Office between 1985–87.[2]

Conflict resolution in schools also started around this time, with the Kingston Friends Workshop Group in 1981, developing methods of teaching children

*   Project Director, MEDIATION UK. I would like to acknowledge help from the following members of MEDIATION UK in providing material or making helpful comments on drafts: Gavin Boby, Carey Haslam, Peter Whitehead and Martin Wright.

1   Beer, JE, *Mediator's Handbook – Peacemaking in Your Neighbourhood*, 1990, Philadelphia, US: Friends' Suburban Project.

2   Marshall, T and Merry, S, *Crime and Accountability*, 1990, London: HMSO.

how to resolve conflict peacefully. Their work was based on the American *Children's Creative Response To Conflict*.[3]

The first community mediation service was Newham Conflict & Change Project. This project grew out of the initiative of several members of the local community in Newham, London, and some professional psychologists at the Tavistock Institute, London, who came together to look at conflict and violence in the community. They ran several workshops and one of the developments from this was a community dispute resolution scheme.[4] Newham Conflict & Change Project continues to thrive and now offers additional services in mediation, education, training and consultancy. Among other early mediation services were Sandwell Mediation Scheme in the West Midlands and Southwark Mediation Centre in London. Most of the early mediation services were largely dependent on the vision of particular people or groups, including professionals from probation services and psychology, and religious groups such as Anglican clergy and Quakers.

Parallel to these developments were similar initiatives in the field of family mediation and commercial mediation. These resulted in similar networks of mediation services and experienced people. In addition, ACAS (the Arbitration and Conciliation Advisory Service) was set up by the government in 1974 to help resolve conflict between employers and employees.[5]

THE CREATION OF A NATIONAL ORGANISATION

From 1983, NAVSS held regular meetings of the Reparation Forum, an informal group of probation officers, academics and victim support workers. This group became known as the Forum for Initiatives in Reparation and Mediation (FIRM). At about the same time, Tony Marshall of the Home Office Research and Planning Unit undertook two surveys of projects, looking at both victim/offender and community mediation projects, which resulted in the directories *Reparation, Conciliation and Mediation*[6] and *Bringing People Together*,[7] including both victim/offender and community mediation projects. A magazine/newsletter was started, edited by Yvonne Craig, who remained the editor until 1992.

Although the roots of FIRM were in victim/offender work, there was growing interest in neighbourhood mediation, and this found its expression in the increasing number of community mediation services.[8] In 1991 FIRM changed

---

3   *Mediation takes a FIRM hold: The first ten years of MEDIATION UK*, 1995, Bristol: MEDIATION UK.

4   OPUS, *Newham Conflict and Change Project, Evaluation Report*, 1989, London: OPUS.

5   Trade Union and Labour Relations Bill, July 1974.

6   Marshall, T, *Reparation, Conciliation and Mediation*, RPU paper 27, 1984, London: HMSO.

7   Marshall, T and Walpole, M, *Bringing People Together: Mediation and Reparation Projects in Great Britain* RPU paper 33, 1985, London: HMSO.

8   MEDIATION UK, *Mediation takes a FIRM hold: The first ten years of MEDIATION UK*, 1995, Bristol: MEDIATION UK.

its name to MEDIATION UK, to enable it to be more readily understood.

MEDIATION UK's aims are to bring conflict resolution skills to every individual as part of his/her basic education for citizenship in a democracy. As part of this, it helps individuals and organisations to identify methods and policies for working through conflicts, and works to build up resources to provide skilled third party intervention in current and potential conflicts.[9]

MEDIATION UK activities include putting people in touch with others who are interested in mediation generally, and helping people with neighbour problems to find a local mediation service. It assists with setting up new services and putting people in touch with experienced mediators and trainers. Its quarterly publications *MEDIATION* and *MED-News* keep people in touch with training and development opportunities and news from the field. A growing part of its work is providing access to documents for research, through its library and filing system. Media work, giving talks and writing articles help to promote and build the image of mediation across the UK and internationally. It is also concerned to help achieve high standards in any field of work associated with mediation and conflict resolution.

MEDIATION UK's day-to-day work also includes organising events, including an annual national conference, and briefings for MPs and the press. Increasingly it is involved in liaising with government departments and local authorities, and developing policies and procedures associated with mediation and conflict resolution in practice. To accomplish its aims, it operates through working groups to take forward particular mediation initiatives, and create effective strategies for the future. One current project is facilitating the development of regional networks within the mediation field, and also with organisations outside it.[10]

MEDIATION UK currently has a membership of about 450, of which 150 are organisations and 300 are individual members. Hundred and ten of the organisations are mediation services. Of this total, 75 are community/neighbourhood mediation services, 25 are victim/offender mediation services, and 20 are concerned with conflict resolution work and mediation in schools (some services do more than one kind of work).

One of the largest areas of work for MEDIATION UK is helping new services develop, especially community mediation services. It does this by providing information, for example, the *Guide to Starting a Community Mediation Service* (collated from existing best practice),[11] samples of literature from other mediation services, and by putting them in touch with the nearest similar mediation service. MEDIATION UK also tries to help with advice on fund-raising (but cannot itself provide funding), and ongoing training. It often

---

9   MEDIATION UK, *Information leaflet*, 1993.

10   MEDIATION UK, Annual Report 1994/95.

11   MEDIATION UK, *A Guide to Starting a Community Mediation Service*, 1993, Bristol: MEDIATION UK.

provides speakers for exploratory discussions and public meetings.[12]

To accomplish this work, MEDIATION UK has a small staff based in a national office (two full-time, four part-time, plus several volunteers) and an Executive Committee of 15 drawn from different projects throughout the UK. Recent developments include regional and topic networking groups (above), of which the community mediation network is the newest. This network meets twice yearly to bring together all those involved in community mediation, to discuss their work and develop good practice.

MEDIATION UK has acted as a catalyst in helping the start-up of many new community mediation services, by providing as a central information point and resource to those wanting to start a community mediation service.

EXPANSION AND GROWTH

Over the past two years, there has been a substantial expansion of community mediation in the UK. This has in part been a response to the growing incidence of neighbour nuisance. Local authority environmental health services (responsible for regulating noise, pollution and other local environmental hazards) are becoming deluged with neighbour noise complaints. In 1992/93 there were 3,137 domestic noise reports per million of the population,[13] a 20% increase over the previous year. The mid-term trend also shows a sharp increase, with nearly double the number of complaints being received compared with 1985/86.[14]

A research paper on disputes between neighbours reported in 1986 that Birmingham City Council received over 8,200 cases of neighbour nuisance each year. Housing assistants each received, on average, nine new cases every month, and spent about seven hours every week dealing with neighbour disputes. They had experienced a steep increase in the number of cases over recent years; they had also predicted that things were going to get worse.[15] The Birmingham report also highlighted the inadequacy of traditional approaches to neighbour nuisance, and suggested that more use should be made of mediation, with its potential for changing the complainant-offender relationship. It quoted encouraging results from the first two mediation services in the UK, in Newham and Sandwell (see above).

Another more recent report[16] confirmed this picture, and suggested that the focus be shifted away from trying to determine what constitutes 'anti-social

---

12 MEDIATION UK, Information Leaflet, 1993.

13 IEHO, *Environmental Health Statistics 1992/93*, 1994, London: Institute of Environmental Health Officers.

14 Hughes, D, *Environmental Law*, 1992, London: Butterworths.

15 Tebay, S, Cumberbatch, G and Graham, N, *Disputes between Neighbours*, 1986, Birmingham: Aston University.

16 Farrant, S *et al, Managing Neighbour Complaints in Social Housing: A Handbook for Practitioners*, 1993, Aldbourne: Aldbourne Associates.

behaviour' or who is a 'problem tenant', towards responding to complaints which are made about that behaviour. Another handbook published at about the same time by the Institute of Housing[17] also surveyed complaining behaviour, and both books evaluate the possible responses from social landlords, including mediation.

The increasing number of complaints reflects the perception on the part of many people that neighbour disputes are on the increase. There are many reasons which may account for this:[18]

- Lifestyle clashes, especially between generations, or between elderly people and families with children, are more common as different generations often have different values and needs.

- A shortage of housing which means that different generations are more frequently housed side by side or above one another.

- The 'right to buy' council houses[19] means that many areas have a much more mixed population, and owner occupiers are sometimes less tolerant of neighbours' behaviour than council tenants.

- The 'care in the community' policy for mental health[20] means that there are many more vulnerable people in the community, often inadequately supported. Some of them are more likely to get into disputes, or to have perceptions which differ significantly from their neighbours.

- Over the past few years it has become more difficult to move house in the UK, whether as a tenant or as an owner occupier, either because of a shortage of housing or because the housing market is very static.

- More people are spending more time at home, due to unemployment, sickness, early retirement or part-time work, so that neighbour problems affect them more than if they were out at work all day.

- The increased number of noise disputes may be due to the availability of much louder noise-making equipment, together with poorer building standards and thinner walls.

- The increase in general stress, poverty and social dislocation makes difficulties with neighbours seem like the 'last straw'.

---

17 Karn, V, Lickiss, R, Hughes, D and Crawley, J, *Neighbour Disputes – Responses by Social Landlords,* 1993, Coventry: Institute of Housing.

18 Farrants *et al,* above note 16; Karn *et al,* above note 17.

19 Tenants who rent houses from their local authority now have the right to buy the house they are living in on very favourable terms. Many council house tenants have taken up this offer, so that housing estates which used to consist of houses belonging to the local authority and let to council house tenants who paid rent, are now much more mixed in terms of ownership.

20 'Care in the community' is designed to provide more care in the community for people with mental health problems. As a result of this policy, many large psychiatric hospitals have closed, with the intention that funds should be transferred to provide care for psychiatric patients in the community. In practice, hospitals have closed and community resources have not entirely replaced them, so that there are many vulnerable people in the community, often quite poorly supported. They are often the focus of neighbour disputes, either because their perceptions differ from those around them, or because neighbours find their behaviour rather strange and are prejudiced against them.

Local authorities are interested in mediation for a variety of reasons. The expense and often failure of legal remedies to deal with neighbour conflict leads to a need to provide an alternative to existing methods of resolving disputes. There is also a growing belief that mediation is more appropriate for certain types of disputes, and has a real potential for rebuilding communities.

Local authorities, especially housing and environmental health departments, have come to see community mediation services as cost-effective ways of dealing with neighbour nuisance. This means that they are often willing to fund or part-fund mediation services (either by grant or contract) in order that such services can be enabled to do this work and relieve local authorities of an increasing burden which they feel they do not have the expertise to undertake. The Department of Environment has now produced (in conjunction with MEDIATION UK) a booklet called *Mediation: Benefits and Practice*,[21] which encourages local authorities to look seriously at the possibility of providing funds to help initiate local mediation services.

Whereas the first community mediation services were almost all to be found in very urban areas, some of the newer ones are based in small towns and rural areas. While it is widely acknowledged that some of the rise in neighbour disputes may be due to the stresses of urban living, there are also many types of neighbour disputes which are found in all sections of the community, both urban and rural; for example, boundary disputes and noise disputes. Rural living also gives rise to a whole range of other issues. For instance, in some rural districts, the issue of 'travellers' can cause serious disputes. In more remote areas, there may be friction between long-standing residents and 'incomers'.

Some community mediation services are also bases for other kinds of mediation, such as elder mediation, which concentrates on disputes likely to affect older people, particularly in institutions but also in the community. Medical mediation, environmental mediation, organisational mediation, and public services mediation are further areas which are beginning to grow, and many of them form links with, or are developed from, existing community mediation services.

TYPICAL DISPUTES

There are many cases of neighbour disputes which cause untold misery to both sides, and seem quite intractable. Some of the most dramatic reach the newspapers at regular intervals, and the following cases are a selection from recent years.

A man was fined for strangling his neighbours' noisy parrot, which had made their lives a misery for more than three years with its dawn-to-dusk din. As a result of his action, he was fined £600 and ordered to pay £350 costs.[22]

---

21 Department of the Environment, *Mediation: Benefits and Practice*, 1994, London: DoE.
22 'Man fined for strangling neighbour's noisy parrot', *The Independent*, 10 October 1992.

Two neighbours were engaged in a four-year feud concerning an extension to a bungalow, built by a new neighbour who was a builder. The ensuing court case resulted in an order to tear down the extension for which planning permission had not been obtained. Meanwhile, relations between the neighbours had soured completely.[23]

More seriously, many neighbour disputes end in violence. Two brothers were jailed for life for murdering a neighbour in a dispute about his dog.[24]

A painter and decorator killed two young women by setting fire to their building after they complained about noise coming from his flat. He was jailed for nine years.

In another case, a man was found guilty of manslaughter and jailed for eight years, after a neighbourhood feud over noise turned violent, leaving one person dead and three others injured.[25]

Altogether, over a period of six years, 17 people died through murder or suicide at the end of noise disputes between neighbours.[26]

Another kind of community dispute also ended in death. A motorist shot dead a car salesman after he accused him of 'inconsiderate parking'. The motorist had apparently acted in self-defence when he was threatened with a knife by the salesman for parking directly outside the car showroom.[27]

Other cases come to the notice of housing associations, housing departments or environmental health departments. The following examples are taken from a book on responding to neighbour disputes, recently published by the Institute of Housing.[28]

Clash of life styles

A housing association took over some property from a local authority. Some tenants felt that the housing association's policy was different from that of the local authority, with housing being allocated to 'undesirable' tenants. There was dissatisfaction with some neighbours who caused general nuisance including vandalism, litter in communal areas, and disturbances from dogs and car repairs. These problems were largely a product of a clash of life-styles. What for new tenants moving into the area constituted normal and acceptable behaviour was deemed unacceptable by longer-standing residents.

---

23   Braid, M, 'Sir Bernard's four-year battle with the builder next door', *The Independent*, 21 December 1992.

24   'Brothers get life', *The Guardian*, 4 March 1994.

25   'Noise feud led to neighbour's death', *The Independent*, 25 October 1994.

26   Victor, P, 'Neighbourhood noise: 17 people have died from it', *The Independent on Sunday*, 18 December 1994.

27   'Motorist who killed in parking row fined £1,000', *The Guardian*, 29 October 1992.

28   Karn, V *et al*, above note 17.

Dispute exacerbated by bureaucratic response

Often disputes are allowed to run on with no consistent policy being followed by housing managers. A complaint was made to a housing association by a pensioner about his neighbour's children, one of whom was cycling on the footpath and nearly knocked the pensioner over. The boy's father overheard the pensioner telling the boy off, and reacted by using abusive language. The pensioner claimed that the boy's father poked him, insulted his wife and threatened to harm him and his wife and home. The pensioner slammed the door shut and the boy's father kicked it in temper. The police were called but no action was taken.

The pensioner made an oral complaint to a housing assistant and then a written complaint to the area housing manager. A stream of letters passed between the housing department and the pensioner, with little actual action being taken. Eventually the pensioner and his wife involved the local MP and others, but they only referred the matter back to the housing department. The housing manager spoke to the boy's father, but he said his children were not responsible for the incident complained about. The pensioner was advised to deal directly with his next door neighbour.

Things went on this way until a new area housing manager arrived. She replied to the pensioner's continued letters, and visited him to discuss the case. After doing this she also visited the next door neighbours, and no more was heard from either party. This more personal approach, similar to 'shuttle' mediation, achieved something which all the letters and bureaucratic responses had failed to achieve.

Moving away from the problem

Sometimes cases of harassment result in the victims feeling obliged to move. A local authority tenant was the victim of harassment from her next door neighbour, who abused her verbally, broke her windows and threw bricks at her when she was in the garden. She erected a high fence but the neighbour broke it down. She complained to the housing department, but the housing officer said all they could do was talk to the neighbour, who denied all the allegations. After this the victim claimed that her neighbour's behaviour was even worse than before. She contacted the police, who simply advised her to call a truce. She then contacted a solicitor who wrote to the council on her behalf. When the council did not respond, she was advised to proceed with a court action. The neighbour was bound over for two years but continued to harass her. At this point she accepted a transfer from the council although she felt that this might imply that she was at fault. She could not stand living with the aggressive behaviour of her neighbour any longer, and also feared that further intervention from housing staff might cause another escalation of the harassment.

HOW A DISPUTE ESCALATES

The tendency of neighbour disputes to escalate is well illustrated by the typical case of a dispute over the issue of noise. The neighbour may contact the other party to complain about the sound of their CD system; if that does not sort out the problem, they will then contact their landlord. If the landlord does not do anything about the matter, the neighbour would then try the environmental health department, the police, the council, the citizens' advice bureau and anyone else they can think of who might be able to assist. When they have exhausted all those avenues and still not got what they want, they might take the matter to court.

By this time, the dispute will probably have been going on for many months and what started out as a disagreement over noise will most likely have mushroomed into a conflict that borders on an obsession. It will now include a catalogue of incidents, allegations, frustrations and grievances on both sides.

So the neighbour will take the case to court, armed with diaries and records documenting the disturbance and it is likely that an injunction will be granted ordering the second party to stop playing their music. However, this does not necessarily mean that the neighbour will stop. They might feel aggrieved by the decision and now choose to play their music louder or later at night. They may even take the matter into their hands and resort to violence.

Many people think that going to court is the only option available to them to get what they want, and they can be disappointed with the outcome. Mediation offers people in dispute a common sense alternative.[29]

ANALYSING NEIGHBOUR DISPUTES

Neighbour disputes are often complex. The first task for a mediator is to define the various elements in disputes, identifying the facts and then the issues, and defining them in terms of interests. It is also important to listen to and take note of any past history which may give insight into the present feelings and reactions of the parties.

Secondly, the real problem may not be the presenting problem. Sometimes when people complain about a neighbour dispute, it covers up a much larger problem, such as a recent personal bereavement or changed financial circumstances. Careful listening and open-ended questions will usually help the mediator to discern what the real problem is.

Thirdly, disputes can sometimes be based on perceptions and misunderstandings rather than intended injuries or hurts. The vital task here is clearing up these misunderstandings and opening communication lines between neighbours.

---

29 MEDIATION UK, Submission to Lord Woolf's Review, *Access to Justice*, 1995, Bristol: MEDIATION UK.

There are four characteristic elements to neighbour conflict. Territoriality leads to arguments over fences, hedges, parking spaces, children trespassing. Commodities can lie behind conflict, when neighbours argue over the possession of something; this may be linked to territoriality. Prejudice and stereotyping can often inflame disputes, and result in moral judgments which perceive all actions in a particular light. This may give rise to racism, or prejudice against so-called 'problem families', leading to attempts to get them evicted. Disputes where these are factors can often result in entrenched positions, which can be difficult to shift. Finally, relationships are often a significant factor in conflict. For instance, when there has been a change in the relationship, the complaint may be more about the loss of this relationship than about the matter in question.

Sometimes conflicts seem to be relished by one or both parties, and all attempts to resolve them are sabotaged. They take on aspects of game-playing. In the 'excitement game', the dispute gets someone attention they would otherwise not have, so there is little incentive to resolve it. In 'housing games', complaints are sometimes made about neighbours in order to secure a house transfer, or to persuade the council to evict their neighbours. There may also be psychological factors at work. Sometimes neighbours who complain manifest paranoid behaviour and feel that everyone is against them. This may be due to mental health problems. It can also happen with elderly people who may be suffering from senile dementia.[30]

WHY DOES MEDIATION WORK?

Instead of polarising parties into two enemy camps, mediation encourages them to focus on the problem between them and not on each other. Parties are encouraged to look at their needs and feelings in the particular situation they are facing. Mediators do not have to spend time looking at flaws in the arguments of either side, but instead focus on common ground between the disputants and the way forward.

Mediation gives both parties an opportunity to tell their version of events fully and to hear what the other party has to say. There are always two sides to the story and both sides will have legitimate concerns and grievances. People are more likely to change their actions if they hear about how their behaviour is affecting the other person, than if they are told not to do something.

Disputing parties are more likely to keep to a solution that they have been involved in than one imposed by an outside person. A solution imposed by the court generally makes one party a winner and the other party a loser. Mediators believe that both sides can win, that there is likely to be a solution which will meet most of the needs of both sides involved. People are able to reach agreements that are

---

30   Hinton, A, *Factors in Neighbour Disputes*, conference paper, 1993, Bristol: MEDIATION UK.

appropriate to their particular situation and their needs might be quite different from the requirements of others with a similar type of dispute.

Mediators ask people what they want to resolve the conflict. In many cases what people might want is simply an apology from the other person for the distress that they have caused. However once they have taken the matter to a solicitor, they find themselves on a rollercoaster ride they cannot stop.

Mediation is a confidential process which enables people to say whatever they want without the fear that it will be taken down and used in evidence against them. The English Court of Appeal has ruled that admissions or conciliatory gestures made during mediation are not admissible in court following an unsuccessful mediation. The only exception to this is where someone has indicated that he has caused, or was likely the cause of, severe harm to a child (*In re D (Minors)* (1993)).[31] This protective confidentiality means that parties in mediation can express their emotions, and mediation can provide a safe place for people to vent their anger.

The resolution of the conflict depends on finding out the real cause, which may be lost in the involved legal history of the case. Mediation is more likely to get to the root of the problem, particularly in neighbour disputes – quite often one minor incident may have been the cause of a long-running neighbour dispute. Some cases thrown out of court when it was deemed that the dispute was caused by 'six of one and half a dozen of the other' have been subsequently successfully solved by mediation. Disputes have many strands or aspects to them. The courts, however, can only deal with matters of law, which means that in many cases they cannot deal with the whole picture.

Although mediation looks at the past, its focus is on the future – what do the parties want the situation to be from now on? This is important because usually, when neighbours take each other to court, they have to go back home to carry on living next door to each other.

HOW A COMMUNITY MEDIATION SERVICE IS ORGANISED

Several different approaches to organising community mediation services have been tried in the UK, each with its own advantages and disadvantages. Broadly speaking, there is now a consensus that the independently organised community mediation service is the option that best fulfils the dual needs of independence of operation and community involvement. However, other organisational options have their applications, and will be mentioned briefly first.[32]

- *Training existing staff to be specialists in mediation.* Several housing associations and local authorities have adopted this as an interim measure after identifying

---

31 *In re D (Minors)* [1993] TLR 12 February.

32 Crawley, J, *Neighbours, Nuisance and Mediation: A Study for Hackney Housing*, 1994, Baldock: Conflict Management Plus.

the need for mediation. The advantages of this approach are that the service is kept under the control of the host organisation (which usually funds it), and is relatively quick to implement. However the disadvantages are that there can be a possible clash of roles for the mediators, between being independent mediators on the one hand and enforcement officers (of local authority regulations) on the other. This means that housing officers, for instance, are not seen as impartial. There is also a problem of ensuring community involvement.

- *Using freelance mediators.* In this model, external freelance mediators are brought in to resolve neighbour disputes. This can work in situations where there are few disputes, and the main groundwork has been done previously. The advantages of this type of organisational approach are that the mediators are preserved as independent and impartial, and it does not require a large organisational infrastructure. The cost is also directly related to the number of cases handled. However, such mediators may be seen as remote from the community, and problems of access and availability may increase the cost and lead to frustration.

- *In-house mediation service.* In this model, the mediation service has a co-ordinator who is subject to the management structures of the host organisation, but will usually recruit volunteer mediators from the community to undertake the actual mediation of disputes. The advantages of this model are that managerial control remains with the funding organisation, while maximising community involvement through community-based volunteers. The mediators are also seen as independent, as they do not have other roles within the funding organisation. The disadvantages of this model are that, because of its links to the funding organisation, the service may have difficulty in being seen as impartial, although this can be achieved to some extent by an independent multi-agency steering committee to oversee independence of operation as far as the mediation of disputes is concerned. There is also the danger of 'co-option' of the mediation service towards the aims of the host organisation, and coming to be seen as the 'soft arm of enforcement'.

- *Independent community mediation service.* In this model, the local mediation service is set up as an independent organisation, often a registered charity, with an independent management committee which oversees the general running. A coordinator manages a group of mediators, usually volunteers from the local community. There are several advantages of this way of organising community mediation. In the first place, it guarantees community involvement both in the management committee and through the volunteer mediators. It also helps to build skills in the community by training volunteers and thus spreading mediation skills. The service is seen as independent and impartial. Its independence means that many different agencies can refer cases to it, and all these agencies will be able to save the time of their officials.

The major disadvantage of this model is mainly its vulnerability to funding pressures. With no statutory organisation to undertake long-term funding of the community mediation service, much effort has to be put into raising funds, often from charitable trusts and businesses, as well as from statutory sources. (On the other hand, the fact that they draw funds from many sources may sometimes be a source of strength and independence, since no one source of funding becomes critical.) New services often have to rely on short-term government project funding, which is made available for new initiatives, but which is then not replaced by longer-term funding after one or two years. Thus many initiatives start but become short of funds after a few years, just when the benefits of mediation are becoming better appreciated in that community. Recent developments in the UK may alleviate this problem, with more local authorities now prepared to make contracts with local community mediation services to handle a certain number of disputes per annum.

FUNDING A COMMUNITY MEDIATION SERVICE

The first three organisational options outlined above will usually be funded by the host organisation (eg, a local authority housing department) because the mediation service is generally started at its initiative, to fulfil needs which cannot be met in other ways. Even so, host organisations may apply to other sources of funding to help with cost, in particular special project funding from national or local government.

Independent mediation services are usually funded from a variety of sources. Often they attract start-up funding for six months to three years from national or local government special project funding for urban areas, crime prevention or environmental action (noise). Some government funds now require three-way partnerships between voluntary organisations, local government and local business.

Community mediation services may also attract on-going local government revenue funds, especially from housing and environmental health departments. Occasionally social services, probation and health authorities may also help; and the local education authority for any schools-related work. Community development funds are also sometimes available.

Until recently, most of such funding was given in the form of a local government agency grant for a period of one to three years. Now many local authorities are being required to purchase services by way of local contracts, and more recently still, by compulsory competitive tendering (CCT). The advantage of contract-based funding is that community mediation services can expect much more secure funding in return for providing services. The disadvantages can be that there are serious implications of failing to complete the contract, and there may be far more requirements from the local authority. Another possible disadvantage is that different departments may wish to make different contracts for the work, for example, the local housing department may wish to make a contract for disputes concerning local authority housing tenants only, and the environmental health department may wish to make a contract in respect of noise disputes only, leaving other kinds of neighbour disputes unfunded. However, several local authorities have coordinated their efforts towards funding a community mediation service for all citizens in a particular locality. A further recent development, since housing associations have taken over the provision of social housing from local authorities in some areas, is for housing associations to make contracts with local community mediation services.

Most community mediation services receive some funding from the charitable sector. This may either be start-up funding, or to supplement funds from the sources already mentioned. As mediation has gained a higher profile in the UK, so charitable trusts and foundations have been more willing to fund such services. However, this funding tends to concentrate on innovative work, for example the first rural mediation service, the first mediation service to undertake a particular kind of work, and so on. Most charitable trusts are not willing to pay for a community mediation service '*ad infinitum*'.

Many community mediation services, once they are running well, develop training and publications as a supplementary service which brings in some money towards funding the service. However, there are no community mediation services which can fund themselves entirely in this way, without diverting all their effort into training and ceasing to offer mediation services. Local mediation services also look to local companies to help in a variety of ways, with grants, secondment of staff or with gifts in kind, such as office furniture and computers. The mediation service may also have a membership scheme, and try to raise funds from members of the community, local churches and fund-raising events.[33]

HOW A COMMUNITY MEDIATION SERVICE OPERATES

Referrals to a community mediation service come from many agencies and quarters. Some services insist that disputants refer themselves, but most are happy for agencies to make referrals, provided that the disputants have agreed. This can be helpful where disputants do not have access to telephones and are not comfortable writing letters. Agencies making referrals can include housing departments, environmental health departments, housing associations, police, social services, probation services, race equality councils, victim support, tenants'/residents' associations, citizens' advice bureaux, advice centres, law centres, solicitors, doctors, health centres and religious organisations. Referrals may also be made by friends or relatives.

---

33   MEDIATION UK, *A Guide to Starting a Community Mediation Service*, 1993, Bristol: MEDIATION UK.

A telephone call or letter may go no further than a request for information. However, once it is established that the first party is interested in the possibility of mediation, usually two volunteer mediators are assigned to the case, and make an appointment to visit the first party in their own home. In some mediation services, this stage is undertaken by visitors who may not be fully trained mediators. This visit is an opportunity for the first party to tell their story, and for the mediators to get an idea of the nature of the dispute. It is also an opportunity to discuss the various options open to the first party, including: do nothing; bring a complaint to a statutory agency; try mediation. If mediation is the chosen option, the mediators then ask permission to visit the second party. If the first party does not agree to this, the case goes no further.

If the first party agrees, the mediators then write to or telephone the second party and state their intention to visit. They are very careful not to assume that the description of the dispute from the first party is the whole story. So a typical letter will talk about 'a situation or problem between them and their neighbour' and ask for their views of the situation. Initially many second parties are wary of mediation, feeling that they have been unjustifiably complained about, and it is part of the skill of mediators to reassure them that their views are genuinely sought, and that no judgment is being made as to 'who is in the wrong'. The mediators then visit the second party and try to obtain their view of the dispute, and the options that they are willing to consider.

If the second party is willing to consider mediation, a face-to-face mediation is arranged. If not, further work can still be done by shuttling between the two parties, and reaching an agreement this way. This approach is sometimes described as 'shuttle diplomacy', after its similarity with international mediation.

If a face-to-face meeting is arranged, this takes place at a neutral venue agreeable to both sides, often a community centre in their neighbourhood, or the mediation centre if it has the facilities. Volunteer mediators usually work in pairs, sometimes matched with disputants in relation to age, gender, race or culture.

The mediation process concentrates on getting both sides of the story, making sure that all the issues are brought out, and helping disputants to express their feelings and what they would like to happen. Mediation sessions involving neighbour disputes can get quite heated, and mediators may need to enforce ground rules about not interrupting. When everything has been aired, mediators then help the disputants to look to the future, to identify common ground, and to look at all the different options that might provide a workable solution. They then encourage them to select one of these options on an experimental basis and help them write it up into a concrete and workable agreement. Disputants may still be sceptical as to whether things are going to work once the mediation session is over, and follow-up is often built into the process, so that if the chosen solution does not work, disputants can come back and make another attempt at resolving the conflict (see Figure 1).

Figure 1: How a Community Mediation Service Operates

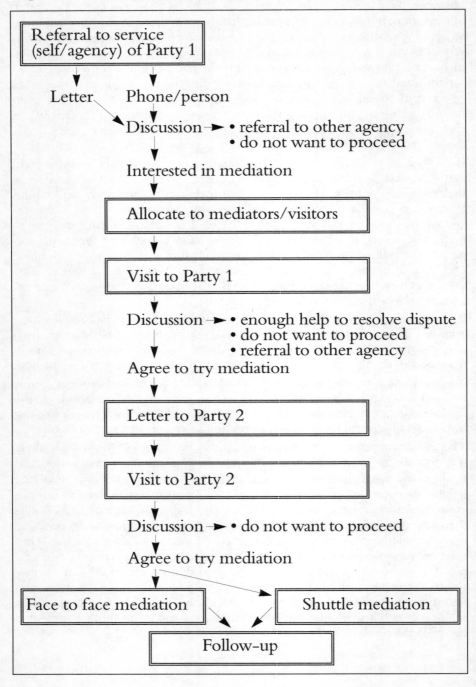

In keeping with the confidentiality of the process, mediators' notes are destroyed at the end of the session, and only the agreement (or lack of) is left as a record of the meeting. If the referral has come from an agency, then the mediators inform the agency whether an agreement has been reached or not, but do not disclose details of the conversation, or generally the precise nature of the agreement (at least not without the parties' consent).

The mediators then follow up the case after an agreed interval. In our experience, the agreement holds good in about 90% of cases which reach face-to-face mediation. Research in the United States suggests a high level of compliance with agreements made via community mediation services[34] (see also the case studies, below).

The community mediation service usually records basic statistics, including the source of the referral and the nature of the dispute. It may also record (for both parties) housing, employment, sex, age, any disability, and ethnic origin. Some services also record the mediator's ethnic origin, sex, age and any disability. Obviously services record the number of referrals, although this may not be a simple matter, and there is great variation between services as to how they do this. A mediation service may also record the total number of enquiries, the number of enquiries which turn into 'mediation cases', and what happens to all of these along the way ie where visits are made to first party, second party, and those cases which proceed to face-to-face mediation. A current project being undertaken by MEDIATION UK is to coordinate these local recording systems, with the aim of producing a national database and agreement on how to record referrals and what happens to them.

Services also record their evaluation of success, although the indicators chosen can vary quite significantly. The MEDIATION UK project hopes to coordinate consensus on how to do this nationally. Records will also show the number of agreements and any follow-up that is undertaken, such as a measure of whether agreements are still holding after a period of, say, six months.[35]

Only approximately 20% of disputes referred to community mediation services reach face-to-face mediation.[36] At first there was disappointment that this figure was so low. Now there is a recognition that the prior stages of the mediation process are just as important and valid. The new MEDIATION UK *Training Manual in Community Mediation Skills*[37] reflects this in providing training for the whole process of mediation, from the first telephone call to the last follow-up.

Most local mediation services are lively, active and often over-stretched organisations. The coordinator is often the only paid person and may be part-

---

34 See, for example, Roehl, J and Cook, R, 'Mediation in Interpersonal Disputes: Effectiveness and Limitations', in Kressel, K and Pruitt, D (eds), *Mediation Research*, 1989, San Francisco: Jossey-Bass.

35 MEDIATION UK, *A Guide to Starting a Community Mediation Service*, 1993, Bristol: MEDIATION UK.

36 A generally quoted figure from many community mediation services.

37 MEDIATION UK, *Training Manual in Community Mediation Skills*, 1995, Bristol: MEDIATION UK.

time or full-time; sometimes there is also some help with administration. The service usually has a small office in a central part of the town or city, so that mediators can come and go as they fetch leaflets, bring reports, or ask for advice. The telephone rings frequently, with calls from distressed neighbours (often taking an hour of listening), mediators checking in or other agencies wanting to liaise. Coordinators usually have to turn their hands to many tasks including the recruitment and support of volunteer mediators, allocating cases, fundraising, giving talks to various agencies such as police and housing departments, as well as conducting some mediations. Mediators usually meet monthly for in-service training and discussion of cases, and for occasional social events to celebrate their work as a team.

CASE STUDIES

The following mediation case studies are taken from recent Annual Reports of MEDIATION UK,[38] from local community mediation services around the country.

From monsters to saviours

Pensioners Mr and Mrs Foster complained to the housing department about the noise when a single parent and her toddler moved into the flat above. As well as the toddler's noise, they complained of Sharon and her boyfriend Paul entertaining visitors well into the night. The housing department referred the case to the local mediation service.

The parties met in the mediation office. Mr Foster suffered from terminal cancer, and Sharon had not realised how ill he was. She agreed to rearrange her entertaining/social hours and ask her visitors to be quieter. The Fosters heard that Sharon needed a baby-sitter sometimes and offered to look after the child.

When the mediators checked with the Fosters a month later, they found that Mr Foster had died. However the agreement had held, and they had looked after the child several times, which had given Mr Foster great pleasure. When Mr Foster was taken ill, Sharon and Paul had helped to look after him, and they also attended his funeral. Mrs Foster said that the mediation had made it possible for her to turn to them, and emphasised how much this had meant to her.

Friends' quarrel healed

Rebecca's flat is below Emily's, in a block where you can hear the click of your neighbour's light switch. On the whole they got on well, but one weekend

---

38   MEDIATION UK (1993), Annual Report 1992/93; (1994), Annual Report 1993/94; (1995), above note 10, Annual Report 1994/95.

Emily's nieces and nephew were visiting, and Rebecca couldn't stand the noise of the children upstairs any longer. She asked Emily if they could keep the noise down. Emily said she didn't see why they should be restricted. They became abusive to each other and were hurt and angry. Over the next weeks there were other incidents, such as music being played deliberately too loud. Rebecca asked for a transfer to another flat, but the housing department referred them to mediation. They didn't think it would do any good but agreed to try.

At the mediation session they were forthright and angry about how they saw the problem. The mediators clarified the issues. It was the disputants themselves who brought about the turning point: one said 'We're two women on our own. We should be looking after each other.' They reached an agreement and walked back home together.

Children's teasing escalates

Mrs G's 12 year old daughter Jane had been teased and provoked for some time by Vicky W, a girl of the same age who lived in the neighbourhood. Both sets of parents became angry, accusations started flying and the situation threatened to become worse.

Mrs G approached a community police officer who organised a meeting between the girls and their parents, then asked if a mediator could attend from the local mediation service.

The meeting took place at the local police station with a mediator guiding the process. It ended with both girls being able to put things behind them and agree about future behaviour. Three months later there had been no further problems.

Police refer neighbour case to mediation

Ms A was referred by the police. Her neighbour had threatened her and had assaulted friends and members of her family. The problem had been going on for several years but was escalating. Mr B admitted shouting, swearing and fighting with a male neighbour but regarded Ms A's behaviour as unreasonable. She ran a business from her home which involved people collecting equipment early in the morning, especially at weekends, they made a lot of noise, blocked up the driveways and road. She had a caravan parked off the road opposite and people stayed in it, making a lot of noise and urinating in the bushes.

During a face-to-face mediation it was necessary to point out on a number of occasions that if each party was not prepared to believe that the other party was making offers in good faith, then everyone was wasting their time. Eventually an agreement was reached in which Ms A would try to ensure that her business caused less interference with her neighbours, would try to keep early calls to a minimum and take more control if people slept in her caravan. Mr B agreed not to threaten or abuse Ms A, to avoid provocative behaviour and if he had a complaint in the future to put it in writing. Three months passed without a further referral from the police.

Elder mediation

An elderly refugee, and his wife with tinnitus, were never able to talk with the young business couple next door about their large overhanging trees. So they kept writing notes about the matter, which irritated the neighbour. Mutual distress and conflict increased but the Elder Mediation Project, through shuttle diplomacy, enabled them both to reach an amicable agreement about sharing the costs and work of lopping the tree. Later the old man reported happily that their relationship with their neighbours was now excellent.

A whole street in conflict

Teenagers were playing football in the street; parents of younger children, and older couples in the street, objected and considered the response of the teenagers to be abusive.

Counter-allegations of abuse and threats of violence were made and the police were called several times. Cars and gardens suffered minor vandalism, and tempers rose when some adults used video cameras to record alleged actions.

Five families were visited by the mediation service, and three long mediation sessions were held in a local community centre. At the end, an agreement was drafted that established times and places where the children could play. All parties agreed to cooperate in the future, should further difficulties arise.

A joint letter was sent to the council, requesting conversion of local waste ground into a play area. All dog owners on the street were contacted, requesting that they ensure the play areas were not fouled.

Twelve months later the agreement still held.

Misinterpretation of 'odd noises'

A house divided into two housing association flats had two men as tenants. Downstairs lived an unemployed man in poor health, who was HIV positive. The upstairs tenant worked shifts at a restaurant, and had his young children to stay at weekends. The downstairs tenant interpreted the frequent noises as a malicious game of dropping things to annoy him. He complained to the health authority, and asked the housing association for a house move. The tenant upstairs called the mediation service.

The mediators listened to both sides, and suggested a meeting, to which both came. Initially they were very cold towards each other but, prompted by the mediators, began to reveal their personal circumstances. It turned out that the noises were caused by one of the children who was disabled and frequently fell on the floor. The upstairs tenant also had no idea of the stressful circumstances of the other tenant. There was a 'rush of emotion' as they both acknowledged each other's difficulties.

They were then easily able to make agreements concerning the children, the upstairs tenant's shift work, and the downstairs tenant's letters of complaint. Just as important was the new tolerance that emerged. Three months later the agreement was still holding well.

Mental health problems affect dispute

A woman suffering from mental health problems derived great comfort from her two dogs, who were then kicked badly by burglars and barked more than before. The woman and her mother were also very upset about the burglary.

Next door lived a self-employed businessman, whose business was failing, and who had moved to the house following a divorce. The increased barking affected him more and more, until he contacted the environmental health services, who in turn contacted the neighbours. The owner of the dogs then slashed her wrists from worry that the dogs would be put down.

The case was referred to a specialist Noise Counselling Service, attached to the local mediation service. After several visits from the noise counsellor to both parties, to gain their trust, mediation went ahead, with support from the psychiatric services. Agreements were made concerning management of the dogs for a trial period of a month, when both parties said they were much happier about being neighbours.

The following cases are detailed in a 1990 report by FIRM.[39]

Noise problem escalates to assault

Amanda moved into a terraced house, and celebrated with friends, only to find her next door neighbour Bruce on her doorstep complaining about the noise. She apologised. This was repeated on two further occasions when Amanda had friends round.

On the third occasion, Bruce ended up assaulting Amanda, and one of Amanda's friends assaulted Bruce, who needed five stitches. Both men were arrested. After hearing both sides the police felt the case was appropriate for mediation and the charges were dropped.

Several visits by the mediators were made to both parties, who both regretted their actions on the evening when 'it just got out of hand'. They then met at the mediation offices, and explained their hopes and fears. Amanda had hoped for good relations when she moved in, and Bruce felt he had acted out of character.

---

39 FIRM, *The Need for Community Mediation Services*, occasional paper 5, 1990, Beaconsfield: FIRM, now available from MEDIATION UK.

Bruce asked for consideration concerning noise after midnight. If Amanda told him in advance that she was having friends round, he was happy to arrange to stay with friends.

Both agreed to swap telephone numbers so that if there were any further problems they could ring each other. Both said they felt relief from the resolution of their conflict.

Three parties, a dog and some noise

A single mother and her daughter started on the wrong foot when they moved in between two older female neighbours. There were arguments over a dog belonging to one of the older residents, and noise made by the child and TV. After several months of problems, the housing office suggested mediation.

After many difficulties, a face-to-face mediation was arranged, and the mediators encouraged all three parties to think about how they could live together in the future.

It emerged that the child had been bitten by a dog and was very wary of any dogs, so the owner agreed to keep the dog on the lead when the child was in the garden.

Despite their remaining anger, the three parties agreed to talk to each other if there were future problems, or contact the mediation service again. One party did this when the dog was let off the lead, and it turned out to be a misunderstanding. When the mediators checked a few months later, things were working out well, and everyone was talking to each other.

Four families at loggerheads over children's behaviour

This dispute involving four families had almost come to blows. Mrs Hazel Short lived on one block of the estate with her husband and two younger children. Her elder son, John, had a flat in another block. 'Whenever we passed through a certain part of the estate on our way to see John we'd get taunted and shouted at by about seven children,' she said. 'They come down on me because I'm not local, I don't talk like them. One Sunday, I was walking through and I got hit on the back by two bottles. I thought, that's it! We called the police, but they said they couldn't do anything. We didn't think it was worth talking to the parents, we thought we'd get the same as we'd got from the kids. So we wrote a letter to the three families we thought were involved, asking them to stop it.'

That wasn't quite how Mrs Lisa Vernon saw the situation. 'The first I heard of any trouble was when I got a letter saying that my kids had been running around, being cheeky and swearing. They threatened to write to the council and take us to court. Three families got the same letter. I was particularly angry because I knew it wasn't my kids. I went round to her house to find out what was going on, but she didn't want to know, and there was a bit of an incident.'

It was at this point that the police referred the case to the local mediation service. Mediators went round to see the families, and reported later, 'Two of them admitted that their kids were in the wrong. They felt that kids were acting dangerously on the estate, but that Mrs Short should have come to them first. Nevertheless they agreed to meet her and have a chat. Their attitude took a lot of steam out of the situation, because previously Mrs Short had felt that they didn't like her, and had a grudge against her. Mrs Vernon demanded an apology, which Mrs Short sent through us, and things seemed to quieten down'.

After the mediators had helped the neighbours to meet and sort things out, they reported that 'The two parties don't exactly socialise, but at least they are united in their praise for the mediation service'. Mrs Short added 'I didn't hold out much hope when the mediators said they'd visit the other families, but their response surprised me and there's been no trouble since then. I hate to think what would have happened ...'. Mrs Vernon agreed, 'If it wasn't for the mediation service, we'd have ended up in court, and there might have been physical violence too'.

Cross–cultural misunderstandings

Nek and Salah lived next door to each other, along with their respective families, on the top floor of a block of council flats in London. Until the intervention of the mediation service, they had swapped nothing but insults for over two years. Nek was retired, had two children and a bad heart. Salah held down two jobs, worked seven days a week and had three children, the youngest being only two. Nek had lived there for 14 years, Salah and his family had moved in about two years previously, and it was shortly after this that the trouble began.

First Nek: 'The first few days he was here, I was friendly with him, and then, after two or three weeks, he came here and started arguing about my son; he said he was smoking and was one of the worst boys in the area.'

Salah's version of the story is as follows: 'Immediately there was trouble. They had a dog, and his son would feed it on the pavement outside the house, he would release the dog to chase my children. That boy was a bad boy. I asked them if they could feed the dog in their flat but they refused to do that. They said it had been left by squatters and they fed it because they felt sorry for it. I wrote to the council and they came, but there was nothing they could do. I took it into my own hands and got rid of the dog. I threw stones at it. After that they were not happy. They were not talking to us and that went on for a long time.'

At no point in his account did Nek mention the dog. He was, however, concerned at the number of visitors Salah received, and complained that there had been many lodgers. It is easy to see how, with lack of effective communication, the situation gradually deteriorated. Nek, describing his frustration, said: 'That business of being angry, it can drive you to a lot of things. It snowballs, grows bigger and bigger.'

It was to avoid further escalation that Nek contacted the mediation service, after seeing a poster in his doctor's surgery. Mediators then visited Nek, heard his side of the story and then contacted Salah.

Salah said: 'Somebody rang us from the mediation service and they wanted to have a word with me. They said they tried to bring neighbours together. I don't care what other people do. I'm a proud man and here to make money. But when I got letters from the council saying I had been a nuisance, playing music, disturbing neighbours, I became offended and wrote to my solicitor.'

After agreeing to take part in mediation, Salah first talked to the mediators and then went along to their office at the same time as Nek to thrash out their problems. What emerged from the session was a series of misunderstandings which had not been helped by stubbornness and aggression on both sides. They discussed their respective backgrounds and cultures in Sri Lanka and Africa, and Nek came to realise that it was normal practice for Africans to have many visitors. He came to understand this, even if he did not like it. Salah was able to accept that Nek's son, Arif, was a responsible young man, even though he was still bitter over earlier incidents. At the end of the session an agreement was signed, which set down the issues, and what both parties now believed to be true.

There were obviously still points of dissent between Nek and Salah, but they were now on civilised speaking terms. The one thing did unite them was their praise for the mediation service and its workers. In Salah's words: 'There was going to be a battle because I wanted to stay here. Everything has cooled down now because of the mediation service.'

MEDIATION AND CRIME PREVENTION

Several community mediation services in the UK have been funded by the Home Office Safer Cities Scheme, in the hope that mediation might prevent crime and fear of crime, especially on high-crime housing estates.

Neighbour disputes can sometimes escalate into violence, as instanced in the cases already quoted from newspapers. Some of these neighbour disputes surface in victim/offender mediation services, in the areas where these are available. The following two examples, from victim/offender mediation services in the UK, illustrate how neighbour disputes can escalate to assault, and may be more effectively resolved using mediation than criminal court procedures.[40]

Clearing up the mess

A group of young men used to hang around in an underpass in an urban area, causing inconvenience to nearby residents. This included foul language, minor

---

40   MEDIATION UK,1993, 1994, 1995, see above note 39.

theft, criminal damage and urinating. One evening, unable to stand it any longer, a resident challenged this behaviour, on behalf of his family. Words were exchanged and two members of the group assaulted the resident.

When they were arrested and interviewed, both offenders were remorseful and ashamed of their actions, having failed to appreciate the problems their behaviour had been causing others. They acknowledged the assault on the resident was uncalled for and wanted to make amends.

The resident related a saga of victimisation, including abuse to his family, thefts from their washing line and fear of his children using the underpass. He recognised his anger had 'boiled over' on the night of the assault.

After considered thought and some anxiety, the parties met at the Adult Reparation Bureau. The offenders' apologies were accepted and a full discussion took place. Following the mediation session, the offenders cleared the underpass, and shared the problems caused with their peers, who in turn appreciated the harm caused by their behaviour. The victim was happy with the outcome and there were no further problems. The case was legally disposed of by way of a formal police caution.

Malicious wounding and neighbour mediation

A man was charged with malicious wounding. This incident occurred after his son was reprimanded by the victim for misbehaving at his son's birthday party. When the offender heard about this, he went round to the victim's house, picking up a steel tube on the way. An argument ensued and the offender head-butted the victim and struck him with the steel tube.

Mediation and reparation enquiries revealed two separate conflicts: the surface tensions relating to this case, and also a dispute between the wives. This dispute had a 'knock-on' effect, creating conflict between the children of the two families.

A meeting was first arranged with the wives, where problems were discussed openly. The wives agreed to go back and talk with their husbands and families. This resulted in a mediation meeting between both couples, in which the offender apologised for his actions. Both sides confirmed that the incidents would now be forgotten and assured each other that there would be no further repercussions between the two families. At court the offender was bound over for 12 months in the sum of £50.

Although none of the UK mediation services presently have funding for the necessary research, there is concrete evidence from elsewhere that mediation can indeed prevent crime, especially assault. For example, a study in New South Wales, Australia, focused on disputes between neighbours which led to violence. This study was carried out in four areas, two with a Community Justice Centre providing a mediation service, and two matching neighbourhoods without one.

The study showed that there was a lower incidence of neighbour violence in those areas where mediation was available.[41]

IS MEDIATION COST-EFFECTIVE?

One of the arguments that is advanced for mediation is that it saves time and money. In the case of neighbour disputes, this is very difficult to prove. Neighbour disputes can circulate through so many different departments that it is very difficult to put a figure on time and money saved. For instance, the same neighbour dispute in various guises can surface through a complaint to the housing department, the environmental health department, police, the local race equality council, the citizens' advice bureau, or the local magistrates' court or county court. It can also lead to disputes between different local authority departments, such as the housing department (which may want to evict a family) and social services (whose role is to ensure vulnerable families keep their accommodation).[42]

One of the first efforts at measuring cost-effectiveness was undertaken by Southwark Mediation Centre in London.[43] They produced a document estimating the costs of continued conflict as opposed to the cost of mediation. The example below shows a typical case.

Cost savings through mediation

A dispute between long-standing neighbours had raged for six months before coming to a successful mediation. It concerned noise and allegations of racism. The following columns show the approximate costs before mediation and the probable further costs if the mediation had not taken place:

Agencies involved	Work over six months prior	Costs (£)	Projected work over further one year if no mediation	Costs (£)
Police	6 Visits	120	12 Visits	240
Housing	4 Visits		7 Visits	
Department	2 Phone calls		3 Phone calls	
	2 Letters	110	3 Letters	160
Environmental	5 Visits		7 Visits	

---

41 Faulkes, W, *Mediation as a Crime Prevention Strategy*, conference paper, 1991, Bristol: MEDIATION UK.

42 Simpson, R, *Promise and Pragmatism: Community Mediation into the Nineties,* conference paper, 1992.

43 Southwark Mediation Centre, *Cost Savings through Mediation*, 1994, London: Southwark Mediation Centre.

Agencies involved	Work over six months prior	Costs (£)	Projected work over further one year if no mediation	Costs (£)
Services	2 Phone Calls 1 Letter	130	3 Phone calls 2 Letters	185
Race Relations	1 Phone call	5	2 Phone calls	10
Community Centre	1 Visit	10	2 Visits	20
Advice Centre	2 Visits	20	4 Visits	40

Approximate Costs to Date: £395

Potential Savings Over Further One Year: £655

Total Potential Savings If Mediation Involved at Outset: £1050

With an approximate cost of £300 per case for mediation, this case would have saved over £700 by going to mediation. Furthermore, the Faulkes study[44] showed that in two similar neighbourhoods, the cost of neighbour violence in areas without a community justice centre was four times that of the areas with the community justice centres.

More recently MEDIATION UK has set up a cost-effectiveness research project, currently being undertaken by Sheffield University. This project is funded jointly by a charitable trust and the Department of the Environment, and has commenced a survey of all community mediation services in the UK, in order to gain up-to-date information. The first phase of the project has also collated this data towards a national consensus on statistics and criteria of success.[45] The next phase of the research is to compare inputs and outputs of all the possible processes being used to handle neighbour disputes, including mediation. The average cost of a mediation is generally agreed to be about £300, if volunteer mediators are used (above). It is hoped that a comparison can be made between the cost of mediation and the cost of other processes used to resolve disputes, and also of the cost of disputes which are allowed to continue without resolution. This report should be available in 1996.

---

44 Faulkes, W, above note 41. See above discussion, p 194.

45 Dignan J et al, First and Second Interim Reports on the Findings of the Community Mediation Service General Survey, 1995, Sheffield: University of Sheffield. See discussion above, p 185.

THE RELATIONSHIP BETWEEN MEDIATION AND LEGAL REMEDIES

Legal remedies have become very expensive in both time and money, and legal action is almost always more expensive than mediation. There are many stories of neighbour disputes which have cost thousands of pounds. Mediation could have helped in most of these cases.

For instance, a couple from Buckinghamshire went to court over cricket balls from a neighbouring village green coming into their garden. They lost their case and were faced with a legal bill for £12,000.[46]

Another case in which two families sued each other concerning a whole host of complaints, including noise, dogs, rubbish, verbal abuse and much more, cost a total of £50,000 for an 11 day court case. The legal bill for one of the disputants, £27,000, was covered by legal aid, and thus ended up as a cost to tax payers.[47]

Court cases brought by environmental health departments can also be extremely costly. One recent case concerned noise from budgerigars, which the neighbours said was completely intolerable. The environmental health department took the budgerigar breeder to court, but lost the case, and had to pay £60,000 from local council funds. The defendant's costs of £40,000 were paid from legal aid from central funds. Many of these costs might have been avoided with mediation.[48]

The court process is an adversarial one, so that even when a neighbour wins a court case against another neighbour, the resentment that has already built up does nothing for neighbourly relations, and in many cases makes things worse. Sometimes, where neighbours have been fined or even imprisoned as result of court action, the dispute still carries on.

Given the advantages of informality, speed and ability to take both parties' interests into account, it makes sense for mediation to replace legal solutions wherever possible. There is some evidence[49] that this may be more feasible at the beginning of the dispute, when neighbours still have a reasonable relationship with each other; and also when the dispute has eventually 'run its course', and both sides are heartily sick of the dispute, especially if court costs are escalating out of hand.

A recent survey carried out by the National Consumer Council showed that about three-quarters of those who had experienced a serious dispute felt that the present legal system is too slow, too complicated and off-putting for ordinary people.[50] All those who had experienced a dispute were then given three

---

46 Drummond, M, 'Settling it out of Court', *The Guardian*, 31 May 1994.

47 Tavener, R, 'Sue Thy Neighbour', *Western Daily Press*, 17 March 1995.

48 Key, I, 'Going cheep costs fortune', *Today*, 27 April 1994.

49 Faulkes, W, above note 41. National Consumer Council, *Civil Law and the Public*, 1995, London: National Consumer Council.

50 National Consumer Council, *Civil Law and the Public,* 1995, London: National Consumer Council.

alternative ways in which the case could be resolved and asked which they preferred. Only 8% preferred 'a full trial in court'; 23% opted for 'sitting round a table with an independent expert who makes the decision'; the largest majority, 53%, chose 'sitting round a table with an independent expert who helps you to reach an agreement between yourselves'. Those with recent experience of going to court made similar choices.

Nevertheless, there are some important *caveats* to simply replacing all legal processes by mediation. It is important to know when mediation is appropriate and when it is not. There are several indicators which may help to determine this. Mediation can help when both parties want to keep on good terms with each other, and there is good-will on both sides, especially if it is in both parties' interests to sort things out. It can also help when the law is not clear, and when both parties are tired of the dispute. Mediation is not appropriate if either party is unwilling, or it is not really in one party's interest to settle. Mediation is also not viable if there are threats or fear of violence, and police action may be indicated; or where the dispute needs a public judgment.[51]

There is also fear that mediation will simply result in the least powerful party agreeing to the demands of the other party, because they 'fear the worst' outside the mediation setting. There is also anecdotal evidence from the US that mediation may be used as 'cheap justice'. Poorer citizens may be diverted to mediation, because it is cheaper on the public purse, while citizens who can afford a lawyer have the choice whether to go to mediation or to go to law. Compulsory mediation may result in parties just 'going through the motions' when they have been directed to mediation rather than choosing it voluntarily. Most mediators feel that mediation has to be a voluntary process to stand a chance of working properly.

Many community justice centres in Australia, and some in the US, have found a useful compromise formula. The court may direct neighbours to attend a compulsory information session given by the mediation service, after which the parties may choose whether to go for mediation or to come back to the law court. In this way mediation is described by the people who will act as mediators, while also giving parties the chance to ask questions and to check out the mediation service for themselves.

This approach is also part of the recent Family Law Act 1996, in which greater use of mediation is encouraged when couples decide to divorce. Those seeking divorce will be required to attend a compulsory information-meeting which outlines all their options, including mediation, before starting the divorce process.[52]

---

51 Liebmann, M, *Neighbours' Quarrels*, 1994, London: Channel Four Television.

52 Lord Chancellor's Department, *Marriage and the Family Law Act – the new legislation explained*, 1996, London: LCD.

The increasing costs of civil litigation and the length of time taken to deal with cases, have led to the Woolf Inquiry on *Access to Justice*. The Woolf Inquiry heard from a number of local mediation services, and MEDIATION UK made a written submission. In the interim report published in April 1995, Lord Woolf highlighted the benefits of alternative dispute resolution and especially mediation:

> A number of organisations including MEDIATION UK and schemes run by local authorities, provide mediation services which are designed primarily to resolve and defuse disputes between neighbours. These have made a considerable contribution to the resolution of disputes, resulting in a significant saving to the court system. Almost without exception the bodies who provide these mediation services are under-funded. This is not in the interest of their clients or of the court service. I recommend they are funded more appropriately. I would very much hope in any review of legal aid the need of bodies of this nature will be taken into account. In many situations, they provide the only way that the citizen can obtain access to justice, and in any event they may offer a better and less confrontational way of dealing with disputes between neighbours, when a continuing relationship is often important.[53]

Following on from the Woolf Inquiry, the Lord Chancellor has published a Green Paper on legal aid, *Legal Aid – Targeting Need*.[54] This paper proposes that there should be block funding from legal aid for a variety of non-legal services. There is no reason why mediation should not be one of the services supported in this way.[55] This would provide a possibility of funding local mediation services to take cases which would otherwise go to court.

There is a definite movement towards mediation as an alternative to formal legal remedies. There is also a growing realisation that if such a movement is to be encouraged, there needs to be a way of paying for it. It is important that mediation services for neighbour disputes are free at the point of delivery, just as (filing fees aside) adversarial complaints systems are.

Legal remedies are primarily concerned with settlements rather than the process of settlement. There has been a tendency for mediation in some places, mainly in the US, to focus on the achievement of a settlement as the only aim (so-called 'settlement-led' mediation). However, one of the most significant aspects of mediation is its ability to focus on relationships and the increased understanding achieved through talking together, whether or not an agreement is reached or not (described as a 'process-led' model). Most mediation in the UK is 'process-led' rather than 'settlement-led' – and agreements are also reached on many occasions.

---

53   The Rt Hon the Lord Woolf, *Access to Justice*, Interim Report to the Lord Chancellor on the Civil Justice System in England and Wales, IV, 21, June 1995, London: Woolf Inquiry Team.

54   Lord Chancellor's Department, Legal Aid Reform Team, *Legal Aid – Targeting Need*. Cm 2854, May 1995, London: HMSO.

55   MEDIATION UK, submission by MEDIATION UK to *Legal Aid – Targeting Need*, 1995e, Bristol: MEDIATION UK.

CONCLUSION – THE FUTURE OF MEDIATION

Community/neighbour mediation has made great strides over the last 10 years. The trend has moved from small groups of dedicated individuals starting mediation services to local authorities faced with escalating neighbour problems seeing the results and potential of mediation, and being prepared to provide funding. Central government too is taking an interest, especially the Department of the Environment concerning domestic noise disputes, and the Home Office in the use of mediation in crime prevention. The Lord Chancellor's Department is also keen to look at the possibility of mediation as an alternative to civil litigation in order to make savings of time and costs.

The future for mediation for neighbour disputes is very promising. In the midst of the organisational changes necessary to help this come about, and debate over the many complex issues raised by use of mediation, our focus must continue to be the ways in which mediation can help neighbours to communicate with each other better, and lead happier lives alongside one another.

8 SENTENCING CIRCLES: MAKING 'REAL DIFFERENCES'

BARRY D STUART*

So we make mistakes – can you say – you (the formal justice system) don't make mistakes ... if you don't think you do, walk through our community, every family will have something to teach you ... By getting involved, by all of us taking responsibility it is not that we won't make mistakes, we would be doing it together, as a community instead of having it being done to us ... . We need to find peace within in our lives, in our families, in our communities. We need to make *real differences* in the way people act and in the way they treat others. I'm not saying the only way, but an important way is to empower ourselves ... empower others, especially those caught in this justice trap. Only if we empower them and support them can they break out of this trap.

We have seen that by empowering each person to take responsibility ... people can really begin to change because beginning the healing path means having the power to act for themselves in a process that treats them like people who are cared for.

Yes they (offenders) need to take responsibility, even go to jail if need be, but making all these decisions as a community means doing it in a good way – as a community, families, elders, everyone taking a part. Communities heal through helping others and by giving support. We start developing peace within by making the person know they are cared for, know they can have a better relationship with their families, with their communities, then we begin to see *real differences*.

(Rose Couch, Kwanlin Dun Community Justice Retreat, 1994)
[Emphasis added]

INTRODUCTION

Circle sentencing offers no new or miracle cures. It is one means of empowering communities and people affected by crime to participate in responses to crime and to the attendant social problems. Many cases are more appropriately processed with more community and no less cases are more appropriately processed through the formal justice system without active involvement of the community. I do not believe any one system can ensure an effective response to the diverse circumstances surrounding crime and criminals.

Too often the processes used to redress conflict within our communities exacerbate underlying differences, intensify animosities, weaken important

* Yukon Territorial Court Judge. Squeezing out the marrow from the bones of my experience with circle sentencing has not been easy. I owe much to Maria Dupuis for her indefatigable patience and support, to Judge Heino Lilles for sharing the challenge, to Debbie Johnston for taking the time and care to help me find the way and to Dr Julie Macfarlane for waiting so long for me to arrive.

relationships, and heighten tensions among the parties, within their families and communities.[1]

How conflict is processed profoundly influences the potential for constructive change. Who participates, and how they participate, in any conflict resolution process shapes the relationships among participants, and the content and durability of outcomes. We fail to invest enough time, care and resources in developing processes to fit either the particular circumstances surrounding disputes, or to align steps within a conflict resolution process to achieve effective results for parties and for society. While courts have an important place in society's response to conflict, currently too much public expenditure and too much public reliance is invested in formal court processes. Many informal community based processes have far greater potential to constructively change attitudes, build, rebuild relationships, promote mutual respect for different values, empower parties to resolve differences, and generally improve the well-being of everyone affected by crime, or by any conflict.

This paper discusses how preparatory steps for court circle sentencing[2] can be designed by participants to mine the potential for constructive change that conflicts offer, and for integrating social justice concerns. In designing all steps in circle sentencing the primary objective within Yukon communities is to achieve 'real differences' in the behaviour, attitudes, life style and conditions of all parties, and to make 'real differences' in the well-being of the immediate

---

1   Throughout this paper the use of 'community' in the context of circle participation can refer to a local area, and or the immediate personal circle of friends, family, school or work associates of parties to a dispute. In this sense, circles and family conferences are equally relevant and useful in smaller communities as they are in large metropolitan areas since everywhere there are either identifiable neighbourhoods or a community of family, friends, work or school associates. The latter form of community, personal communities, are much more important in achieving the 'real differences' discussed in this paper. Consequently, circles are often better suited to conflicts in large metropolitan areas where, in addition to personal communities, access to a rich array of remedial resources exist. The appropriateness of circles and other forms of community justice in large urban areas is often tragically ignored due to a combination of dated concepts of 'community' and romantic, but erroneous, notions of small communities as 'Camelot'.

2   There are many different kinds of circles: talking, healing, community and court sentencing circles, family and community conferences, and many different approaches to each kind of circle across Canada. These differences are essential to fully embrace the circumstances of each community. This discussion draws on the processes found in Yukon *court sentencing* circles and particularly from Kwanlin Dun, the only community with some full and part-time staff working on community justice. Unlike community sentencing circles or community conferences, which involve local Justices of the Peace, police officers, court workers, families and the community, court sentencing circles involve a judge, Crown and defence counsel as well as all others involved in community sentencing circles. As experience grows with circle sentencing, two important and encouraging trends are evolving:

   •   in court circle sentencing the dominant roles of judges, Crown and defence counsel are diminishing as keepers, court workers, local police, victim and offender support workers, and others in the community gain confidence to take greater control of the process, and as professionals recognise the need to step back to empower others. The diminishing roles of professionals is especially evident when offenders and victims are supported and prepared to speak on their own behalf.

   •   greater use is being made of other informal processes. Community circles and conferences are being used more often, and more cases are diverted completely out of the system, to mediation, diversion, healing and talking circles.

personal and geographic communities affected by a crime. This discussion addresses the vital contributions of preparatory steps. What happens *before* a circle hearing, profoundly influences what happens *in* the hearing.

The first part of the paper gives some context and meaning to the nature of 'real differences'. The second part briefly sets out the steps taken prior to a circle sentencing. The final part of the paper explores some of the contributions preparatory steps make to advancing 'real differences'.

First a quick detour. Understanding why I believe pre-circle preparation is so important, requires that I begin by sharing my perception on the respective contributions circle and courts make to resolving conflict. The criminal justice system currently reaches beyond its competence and far beyond what it was designed to do. The adverse impact the criminal justice system has on individuals, families and communities is not a consequence of inadequate professional resources, but of using the formal justice process when other community based processes are more appropriate. The criminal justice system simply cannot achieve, especially acting by itself, what the public, especially politicians, ask. By trying to do too much, the criminal justice system fails to competently do what it is designed to achieve.

Yes, we use jails too much, but equally we use police, lawyers and judges too much. The excessive use of jails is directly connected to the excessive reliance upon justice professionals. We need a better balance, a balance that can only be achieved by transferring back to families and communities much of the responsibility appropriated by government in the past century.

In many cases, social and criminal justice concerns must be integrated. The senseless, unnecessarily expensive truncation of responses to social problems into highly defined departmental divisions of responsibility precludes the collective action necessary to make a 'real difference'. Circles view crime holistically; pulling together health, education, social service and economic resources to redress the underlying problems of crime. By enhancing the working relationships among all participants, by empowering families and communities, circles strive to promote the overall well-being of communities. When all agencies use the potential of circles to integrate their services at the community level, the full potential of circles, of partnerships with the community will be realised. In this sense, the circle process is not just about restorative justice, but about restoring families, restoring communities, and thereby significantly contribute to restoring participatory democracy.

THE ESSENCE OF 'REAL DIFFERENCES'

Civil courts by imposing a judgment, criminal courts by imposing a sentence, may settle a conflict, yet such settlements often do little to resolve personal differences between the parties, or to enhance relationships among parties. The conflict is often exacerbated by an adversarial court process focused on narrowly defined legal issues. Courts may change the focus of a conflict but rarely enhance relationships among the parties, mitigate warring attitudes, reveal common ground to foster respect for different values, or inspire creative problem-solving to find mutually beneficial outcomes. Courts have a place, but not the predominate place now secured by public spending.

How often after a court case can the parties feel their differences are resolved? How many, win or lose, emerge from court, a settlement in hand, with a sense of being empowered, with new respect for the values, interests and plight of other parties, with a better working relationship with opponents, with a resolution of attitudes, and finally, how many leave the court confident a new conflict will not be provoked by the continuing 'bad' relationships among the parties? Courts by imposing a solution often do not end hostilities, do not resolve the deeper underlying conflict, do not make 'real differences'.

Real differences involve fundamental changes in lifestyles and attitudes. For most offenders, these changes involve a genuine desire to heal, to make positive connections to people, to families, to a community. Healing may involve tackling long-standing complex problems; severe substance abuse, deeply entrenched emotional and psychological trauma, uncontainable anger, violent propensities or a mixture of any of these conditions inducing criminal behaviour. Not just offenders, but victims and others affected by crime often must make fundamental changes in their lives to move beyond the trauma of crime. Making these changes requires courage, the courage to seek forgiveness, the courage to reach out for help and the courage to persevere. Making these changes requires the unswerving support of family and friends, and without this support even the most determined rarely sustain their healing journeys:

> You know – when I was down – really down – sick in the hospital – everything looked dark for me – my family was in trouble – real trouble – either sick real bad or in jail. Everywhere I looked, not much to hope for eh – I needed help. I'd given help for years to many others but I wasn't getting any help myself now ... I was down – then I got to thinking – you know – I was too proud to ask for help. When I did ask – I got it – that's what made the difference for me – it's what makes the difference for everyone. I've always seen that in the circle too.'
> [Elder – Kwanlin Dun – 1992]

Real differences embrace changes in relationships that enable offenders to become reconnected or connected in a positive manner for the first time to families, supportive friends and their communities. These changes in relationships mitigate the personal and physical damage caused by crime.

Families and communities often bear some responsibility for the conditions fostering crime. Many crimes do not solely injure the victim, but injure the victim's family, the offender's family, and many others and adversely affect communities. Accordingly, those affected have a right and, to some extent, an obligation to participate in finding solutions. Without their participation, solutions embracing 'real differences' for either families or communities are often out of reach. Real differences embrace changes in communities of the nature envisaged by the biblical sense of Shalom, 'repairing right relationships fractured by crime and restoring a community to wholeness'.[3]

Families and communities recognise the need for 'real differences' in individuals, in relationships and in communities. Without these 'real differences', the hostilities, anger and tensions provoked by crime will continue to unleash divisive forces within the family and community that are likely to spawn more crime. Communities that examine closely the causes of crime fully appreciate that the courts cannot eradicate crime. These communities know that removing criminals from the community does not remove crime. They recognise that to reduce the destructive influence of crime, to restore or build harmony, they must be involved. These communities see crime as a 'violation of people and relationships, creating obligations by all to make things right'.[4]

Preventing and responding to crime should never be the exclusive business of the State if 'real differences' are sought in the well-being of individuals, families and communities. The structure, procedures, and evidentiary rules of the formal criminal justice process, coupled with most justice officials' lack of intimate knowledge and connection to individuals, families and communities affected by crime, preclude the State from acting alone to achieve transformative changes. There are some exceptions. Most of these exceptions occur when justice officials step beyond the highly defined boundaries of their professional responsibilities.[5]

PRE-HEARING PREPARATORY PROCESS

THE IMPORTANCE OF PEACEMAKING PRINCIPLES

In circle sentencing, the peacemaking traditions of aboriginal cultures, currently adapted and popularly referred to as mediation and consensus-building principles, are pivotal. To what extent each community circle process respects the principles of peacemaking, primarily determines whether any 'real differences' can be achieved, *what* the circle sentence will contain, and *how* the circle sentence will survive in the real world. Much of the pre-circle process is dedicated to ensuring peacemaking principles are respected and govern the circle process.

---

3   Van Hess, D, in Galaway, B and Hudson, J (eds), *Criminal Justice, Restitution and Reconciliation*, 1990, Monsey, New York: Criminal Justice Press

4   Zehr, H, *Changing Lenses: A New Focus for Criminal Justice*, 1990, p 181, Scottsdale, Pa: Herald Press.

5   For example, the initial creation of probation officers, as well as the more recent conversion of probation officers to community facilitators in Vermont, the vastly new approach to incarceration in Oregon, the original offender-victim reconciliation project in Kitchener (see Gordon Husk's paper in this collection), and the numerous innovative projects with youth started by police in many places, are all creative community initiatives generated by justice officials who moved beyond the boundary of their position.

While striving to learn, I have a long learning road ahead before I could adequately explain how peacemaking principles permeate and influence the circle process at all stages. The following brief account of peacemaking principles is offered to provide a sense of the principles shaping circle sentencing.

- *'Peace within'*: Finding 'peace within' is an integral part of peacemaking. The success of each circle is directly linked to how all participants, (especially offenders and victims) have advanced in finding 'peace within'.

  If you don't begin the healing journey by dealing with yourself in a good way ... you cannot deal with anyone else in a good way ... It begins inside each person – yah – we can help – maybe even help get it started – certainly help keep it going – but it has to be the person who must want to change – if they don't really want this – it just can't happen – no matter how much others want it to happen –That's what we're doing in circle sentencing – Getting people to realise this and begin to build peace within themselves. [Rose Wilson, Court Worker, Vancouver Conference – 1995]

  'Peace within' is not a final destination, but a journey with constant challenges. It is a journey that begins by overcoming the excuses and denials used to elude responsibility for harmful conduct, to shrink from acknowledging a desperate need for help, and to postpone the pain of working through soul wrenching psychological injuries. 'Peace within' is not an easy journey, but one that nurtures a renewed belief, faith in oneself and in others.

- *'Right relations'*: 'Right relations' is another important component of peacemaking. 'Right relations' call for mutual respect, an understanding, but not necessarily acceptance of different values. To achieve 'right relations', the circle calls upon all participants to actively demonstrate genuine respect for others in what they say, and in how they listen. Creating 'right relations' equips parties to assume greater responsibility for resolving their differences.

  By an early, and steadfast, focus on 'right relations', the circle process recognises the importance of settling not just substantive issues but in building, rebuilding relationships.[6] Imposing a sentence is less important than producing change in a participant's self-image, self-esteem, attitude about themselves, about others and in generally improving relationships among all affected by the crime and its attendant conflicts. Most community participants see beyond the immediacy of the legal challenge of finding an appropriate sentence to focus on what can build healthier people, healthier relationships, and ultimately a healthier community.

- *'Harm to one is harm to all'*: Within a family, within a community, harm to any one member adversely affects all others. This notion, indispensable in maintaining the bonds within a family or community, finds little if any effective recognition within the criminal justice system. The circle

---

6   A growing constituency among professional mediators embraces the primordial importance of improving relationships. See Bush, R and Folger, J, *The Promise of Mediation*, 1994, San Francisco: Jossey Bass.

sentencing process depends upon a recognition by all participants that the well-being of any individual is directly connected to the well-being of the community.

While offenders must take responsibility for their injurious conduct, and demonstrate genuine remorse, the responsibility for peacemaking must be shared by family, and by others in the community. Sharing responsibility for a change within families and communities provides the essential foundation to build 'peace within' and 'right relations', and provides the basis for realising the equally important peacemaking principle, 'the joy of one is the joy of all'.

- *Consensus*: In circles, time is taken to move beyond the initial position of participants to discover underlying interests and to build the basis for consensus. Innovative solutions are sought to accommodate the interests of all participants. The process in striving to reach a consensus, recognises the validity of all interests, and promotes respect and understanding for differences.

- *Inclusive*: To ensure that all interests are included, the circle aspires to be as inclusive as possible. Special efforts are made to extend the base of participation. The strength of the process is directly related to the breadth of community participation. Unless their conduct manifests disrespect for the circle, no one is excluded. The inclusionary objective of circles is not a function of numbers as so much a question of balance. To reach a true consensus, all affected interests must be heard, respected, fairly treated and given an equal opportunity to participate.

- *Forward Looking*: Peacemaking chiefly concentrates on future relationships. In circles, the history of issues and of people are important guides for assessing requirements for building a different future. But, unlike court, circles give more attention to what will happen in the future.

Reliance upon all of these peacemaking principles constitutes for many aboriginal peoples the basis of dealing with conflict in a 'good way'.

There is an enormous spirituality emanating from a circle based on peacemaking and populated with courageous people striving to deal with profoundly personal issues. The potential of the circle can be limited by offenders lacking the integrity to be honest, by community people lacking the courage to take responsibility, or by professionals unable to treat all participants as equal, or whose scepticism closes them to the invitation of the circle to share openly. A long road lies ahead, full of many challenges before the potential of the circle to foster the well-being of all participants can be realised. Many circles thus far, even circles with participants lacking the openness to fully contribute, have revealed the enormous capacity of circle sentencing to resolve deeply divisive attitudes and issues, to build better relationships, and to deal with conflict in a 'good way'.

PRE-HEARING PREPARATION: CURRENT PRACTICES

In the early days of circle sentencing all parties came 'cold' into the circle hearing. There was little or no pre-hearing preparation. Everything was left to the 'magic' of gathering people together in a circle. Early circles were held, and some still are, without rigorous scrutiny of the offender's genuine desire to change, without mediation training for key resource people, without community justice co-ordinators, without a co-ordinated approach among justice agencies and often without support from key justice agencies. Everyone came uncertain about what might happen. Rarely was there any prior exchange of information, of plans, or of expectations with other participants. Nevertheless, when Crown or police supported the circle, and when community volunteers accepted the challenge, the circles often achieved 'magical' results.

Coming into a circle 'cold', without any preparation of the victim, offender or other relevant players, places far too much reliance, too much emphasis on the hearing. This approach generates fear and anxiety about what might occur in the circle. Assumptions prompted by fear in such emotionally charged circumstances can detrimentally affect the peacemaking and consensus building potential of circles. Without adequate preparation, circles can last for more than two hours. The emotional and physical drain of such long hearings on all participants, especially upon elders, is far too taxing.

Preparation for circles is critical, immeasurably improves outcomes, and ensures a balanced, active participation. The following pre-circle hearing steps improve the process, shorten hearings, generate meaningful involvement, empower victims, offenders and others to shape decisions affecting their lives and can produce in some cases a consensus recommendation to the court for a sentencing plan that is quickly adopted by the circle. These steps are instrumental in generating the conditions and responses necessary to make 'real differences'.

- Before the circle hearing the local *Justice Committee*[7] should:
    - (a) notify the victim of the offender's application;
    - (b) consider victim input in deciding suitability of circle process;
    - (c) assess support group for the offender;
    - (d) review the initial plan proposed by the offender support group;
    - (e) circulate all key information to participants;
    - (f) meet with the offender and the victim;
    - (g) monitor the progress of the offender;

---

7   Each local Justice Committee will differ in composition and practices. The committees may include a mix of justice officials and community volunteers or solely be composed of community volunteers. The richer the variety of community representatives, the stronger the committee will be (teachers, health officials, business people, religious leaders, etc).

(h) decide when and in what process case should be heard;

(i) ensure the offender has completed all application steps;

(j) set down a place and time for the hearing;

(k) encourage family and relevant community resource people to participate;

(l) appoint keepers of circle;

(m) post public notices of the hearing.

- To be accepted into a court sentencing circle the *offender* must:

  (a) accept full responsibility for the offences before the circle;

  (b) establish a balanced support group to assist them through all steps in the circle process;[8]

  (c) meet as often as required with the local Justice Committee;

  (d) develop a plan to take responsibility for the offence, reconcile with and compensate the victim, demonstrate appreciation for community assistance, and address their rehabilitative needs;

  (e) carry out all steps required by the support group or Justice Committee.

- Prior to a hearing, the *Crown* or *police* should:

  (a) apprise the Justice Committee and the court as soon as possible of any objections to a circle sentencing;[9]

  (b) provide all relevant information they possess to the community Justice Committee;

  (c) participate (especially local police) in community Justice Committee meetings assessing the offender's initial and continuing suitability;

  (d) review plans and progress reports from the Justice Committee, from victim and offender support groups;

  (e) contact the victim and the victim support group to ascertain the victim's interests, and determine what help is required;

- *The court worker* or *defence counsel* before a circle hearing should:

  (a) provide legal advice to the offender;

  (b) inform the offender of the circle process, the nature of participation and responsibilities expected of the offender and the potential advantages and disadvantages of the circle process;

---

8   The Justice Committee ensures the support group includes, in addition to family and friends, people who are stable, sober, reliable and others with skills and resources specifically needed for the offender's healing journey. The support group functions not just to 'support' offenders, but also to ensure each offender accepts full responsibility for their actions and diligently carries out their commitments.

9   Communities do respond to concerns raised, and in most cases remove the concerns of police or Crown. The decision and impetus to hold a circle primarily rests with the community Justice Committee.

(c) assist the offender in developing a balanced support group;

(d) help develop a plan for healing, for accepting full responsibility, and for repairing injury to the victim;

(e) assist the offender in converting intentions to change into action;

(f) prepare the offender to participate directly in circle hearing.

- Prior to the circle, a *community justice co-ordinator*[10] should:

  (a) advise an offender and victim of how to access community justice options;

  (b) provide help to offenders, victims and others in accessing community justice resources;

  (c) gather information from victims, offender, police and others necessary for community justice committee decisions;

  (d) carry out tasks assigned by the community Justice Committee in preparing the case for a circle hearing.

- *The judge* or *justice of the peace* should, prior to hearing:

  (a) review reports from justice officials, the Justice Committee and both support groups;

  (b) ascertain from keepers of the circle the order of cases to be called;

  (c) decide if the proceedings must be recorded;

  (d) develop familiarity with the community's circle sentencing procedures and guidelines.

- *Keepers of the circle*,[11] before the circle hearing, should:

  (a) ensure information available from justice agencies, justice committees and support groups has been exchanged and is available for public access;

  (b) contact victim and offender support groups to confirm readiness for circles;

---

10 A community justice co-ordinator, paid and properly trained, working for the community Justice Committee, can make an inordinate difference. The co-ordinator can do many of the tasks assigned to others much more effectively. This person can make community justice work. Recognising the importance of this position marks an important advance in my learning curve. Initially, I believed the partnership between communities and formal justice agencies could be built with only volunteers from the community. I was wrong. To marshal the vital energy and resources volunteers can contribute, the community Justice Committee must have some part-time or full-time staff. At the minimum, the Justice Committee needs a justice co-ordinator who lives in and is intimately familiar with the community. Without a justice co-ordinator reporting to the community Justice Committee, the partnership will fail, or will survive to primarily pursue the objectives of formal justice agencies. The principal advantages for both partners in a community-justice partnership flow from an emphasis on community objectives.

11 Keepers of the circle have mediation or consensus-building training, and are community volunteers chosen by the Justice Committee to facilitate a circle hearing.

(c) ensure the presence of key participants;

(d) arrange room for circle hearing;

(e) bring 'talking' feather, stick or stone;

(f) welcome and seat elders;

(g) remove anyone whose state of impairment or attitude reveals disrespect for the circle;

(h) select someone to say opening prayers;

(i) introduce themselves to strangers and make strangers welcome;

(j) answer any questions about the process.

Sometimes offender and victim support groups meet in advance of the hearing. This can be extremely helpful in preparing for the hearing. When time and effort are fully invested in pre-hearing preparation, a consensus among all parties can be achieved before the hearing. When this happens, the circle can enhance the plan by contributing ideas for accessing additional resources, or by broadening the base of a consensus.

THE IMPACT OF PRE-HEARING PREPARATIONS

The following influences highlight how pre-hearing preparation contributes in numerous ways to the achievement of 'real differences'.

CHANGING PERCEPTIONS

The feelings, attitudes and perceptions carried into the circle profoundly affect the success of the circle. The more care, support, information and attention invested in key participants before the circle, the more likely parties can move beyond fear, hostility, anger and other negative blockages to constructively advance their interests.

The nature and timing of pre-hearing preparation can significantly change how participant's view other participants, how they perceive their interests can be achieved, and how they will participate.

Victims' perceptions

In the formal justice system, victims are often reduced to pawns in the justice 'game'. They are left to their own devices, given little information about the process, rarely involved in decisions concerning setting or adjourning court dates, setting or revising bail conditions, staying or withdrawing charges, in plea bargaining or sentence submissions. Facing a combination of shrinking government funding and increasing caseloads, some professionals are too busy to actively attend to victims' interests, while others believe it is not their responsibility to involve or notify the victim.

Despite recent changes to help victims, the justice system continues to give more attention to the law that has been broken by a crime than it does to the harm done to others.[12] The justice system by itself can never afford the sustaining care for victims that a properly functioning community justice system can offer. A partnership between justice agencies and communities can provide the resources and personal attention necessary to empower victims, restore their dignity and a sense of being safe, provide the empathy and support they need to rebuild and restore their lives. The goal should not solely be to compensate victims, but to restore the victim's previous well-being, and their connection to family and community.

The timing of assistance for victims is crucial. A victim left to struggle alone while the community appears to rally to assist an offender, can feel their suffering and anger has been belittled or ignored. These feelings engender a sense of injustice, and a desire to see an offender severely punished. In many ways, the ability of victims to achieve 'real differences' is severely jeopardised if their needs are not immediately addressed. For victims to move beyond pain and anger and begin their healing journey, they must experience immediate significant empathy as well as tangible assistance.

In New Zealand, a minor but crucial change in the family conference pre-hearing process substantially increased the frequency and quality of victim participation, and enhanced victims' perception and expectations of family conferences. The co-ordinators provided emotional support and even financial assistance to overcome any immediate medical, work-related or other financial losses imposed by crime. This immediate attention to victim needs demonstrated that co-ordinators cared, were supportive and understood the plight of victims. Subsequent requests from the co-ordinator for the victim's involvement in a family conference were perceived by victims as a request from someone who would be supportive and understanding. In providing tangible and immediate assistance, co-ordinators helped reduce the trauma of being a victim and planted a foundation of trust that carried over into the family conference sessions.[13]

> It was simple really – we just showed we wanted to and could help. This was an important first step to generate positive feelings of the victim for the process. A feeling that is vital to the success of the conference. We doubled victim participation, and their satisfaction very quickly with this little change (Matt Hakiaha, Whitehorse speech, 9 November 1995).

Almost all financial assistance family conference co-ordinators provided to victims was recouped from offenders during the family conference process, thereby transferring responsibility to offenders and perhaps some good will as

---

12   Berzines, L, *New Directions in Sentencing*, Presentation to National Judicial Institute, 10 November 1995, unpublished. See also Berzines, L, *Is Legal Punishment Right?*, a seminal work that is a 'must read' for all. Available from the Church Council on Justice and Corrections, 507 Bank Street, Ottawa, Ontario K2P 1Z5, Canada.

13   Matt Hakiaha, New Zealand youth family conference co-ordinator, Presentation in Whitehouse, Yukon, 8 November 1995.

well. This practice in New Zealand illustrates how simple innovative pre-hearing measures can significantly enhance the potential to achieve optimal results for victims (as well as for offenders).[14]

Media reporting on crime, especially their coverage of victims' immediate response to serious crime, creates a widespread public impression that all victims seek justice measured in long prison terms. The longer the prison term, the more justice achieved. Yet experience in victim/offender reconciliation programmes and many research studies[15] concur with Lorraine Berzines, who as the victim of a very serious crime states:

> ... having been a victim of a serious crime myself, and having checked this out with many others, I can tell you that what victims want most is quite unrelated to the law. It amounts more than anything else to three things:
>
> — victims need to have people recognise how much trauma they've been through; they need to express that, and have it expressed to them;
>
> — they want to find out what kind of person could have done such a thing, and why to them;
>
> — and it really helps to hear that the offender is sorry – or that someone is sorry on his or her behalf.[16]

Support groups consisting of family, friends and lay resource people are vital to the circle process and can offer victims an empathetic ear to fully hear their trauma, and recognise their pain and the injustice experienced. Especially if engaged early, support groups can help victims avoid becoming entrenched as victims, abandoned to their own resources, while the justice system concentrates on offenders. Equally important, support groups help victims find answers about the offender, who the offender is, why the offender picked on them, what the offender feels, thinks about the crime, about the victim, and what the offender will do about the victim's injuries and losses. If this information and support is

---

14 The New Zealand Family Conference process depends extensively on volunteers to provide victim support from the moment of the crime throughout the entire process. While not paid for their time, they are compensated for all expenses, respected as key contributors, equal colleagues and given free extensive mediation and related skills training. The widespread commitment among New Zealanders to community service explains the sustaining success of their community based justice initiatives. This vital sense of community service must be once again pervasive throughout Canada to improve the quality of life within our communities.

15 Richmond victim–offender reconciliation program; *Victim meets Offender: An evaluation of Victim-Offender Reconciliation Programs*, Gates, R and Gehm, J, PACT Institute of Justice, 1985; *Restitution As Innovation of Unfulfilled Promise?*, Galaway, B in Federal Probation XII #3 September 1988. See also the excellent report by David Dauney as Chair of the Standing Committee on Justice – *Taking Responsibility – a Report* (available from Church Council on Justice and Corrections), and see also Zehr, above note 4, at p 205.

In a recent independent assessment of the Victim Offender Program directed by David Gustafson in Richmond, British Columbia – a program that focuses on very serious crimes involving extreme violence – the satisfaction rate of victims, or families of victims was 91%. What the press tell us victims want, and what experience in these programs reveals victims need and want, is quite different (David Gustafson, phone conversation, May 1996).

16 *New Directions in Sentencing*, A presentation to the National Judicial Institute by Lorraine Berzines, Church Council on Justice and Corrections, Toronto, Canada, 10 November 1995.

provided before a circle hearing, victims are more likely to participate, and participate in a manner that advances their well-being as well as the well-being of the offender and the community.

Victims must be heard and their needs met. Support groups prepare victims for whatever role they wish to play in the process, ensure their interests are incorporated and keep them informed. A lack of information, or worse, misinformation about the process, can be detrimental to a victim's perceptions of offenders, of the process and of themselves. Support groups invaluably prevent or reduce further victimisation by the process.[17] Support groups create an environment for victims to fully assess their best interests and thereby focus on how the process can serve their interests both immediately, and in the long-term.[18]

While victims' needs must be immediately addressed, victims may not be able to confront or interact directly with the offender for some time, and some may never be able or wish to do so. Each case and each victim will be different. The victim requires time and support to make choices about how they wish to be involved, and what they want to happen. Some victims, especially in less serious crimes, may need little time or preparation to participate. What is done during the pre-hearing preparation will dramatically affect if, and how, most victims will participate. A failure during pre-hearing preparation to ensure every opportunity is explored to safely engage victims as much as possible in the process will jeopardise the capacity for victims to realise 'real differences'. The ability to realise real differences in offenders and others affected by the crime will be restricted if victims do not participate.

Offenders' perceptions

The decisions and directions taken by offenders can significantly depend on the immediacy of support received.

> I knew I was going to jail, like the last time, so I planned to make it take a long time before I got sentenced so I could get – you know, stay drunk for a long time because I knew I would have probably a year or something like that to sober up again in jail. This is what I was going to do, then someone told me about the circle, said it was something new, would give me lots of support, like right away – I wouldn't have to wait, to depend upon government programs. He convinced me to try this different route, so I took it. I wanted a change, but I didn't think I could because I tried before, but never made 'er. But right away, right then I got help from all kinds of people, yeah, they made me believe it

---

17 All options a court provides for victims to participate are retained in a circle sentencing process. The circle process, especially the preparatory stages, enhances and adds to these options. Victims may participate by simply filing a victim impact statement, have the Crown or others speak on their behalf or take the stand. If they wish to testify in court, their testimony is included in the circle process.

18 Communication between the victim and offender support groups must be established *before* the hearing. Local people hired as co-ordinators can help facilitate exchanges or meetings. Adding volunteers to each support group who are not friends or family and switching volunteers in each case from victim to offender support groups can also help.

could happen, I could change – really convinced me to give it a shot (Kwanlin Dun Circle – Participant, Whitehorse, 1994).

From their support groups, offenders receive the help needed to begin their healing journeys. The personal attention offered by support groups generates the will and a supportive environment that promotes the difficult first steps in a healing journey. Within the offender's support group, and throughout the community justice process, the offender will clearly be told 'you did a very bad thing ... something we cannot tolerate'. At the same time, offenders hear offers to help and a recognition of their potential for change. They are reassured they are a valued, loved part of their community. A support group can instill the confidence and self-esteem essential for most offenders to find the perseverance to begin and endure the challenges of their healing journey. Support groups inspire and nurture the essential ingredients of change: 'I *want* to change, I *believe* in myself enough to make it'.

Preparing offenders to speak on their own behalf in the circle is crucial. Hearing from defence counsel or court workers, what an offender feels, how deeply remorseful they are or how earnestly they wish to make reparations or change their life, can never be as convincing as the same words directly from the offender. Accepting responsibility, apologising, asking for forgiveness, making a commitment to change and asking for help are all deeply personal matters, steps that cannot be taken by someone else without diminishing credibility, or losing empathy and acceptance from others. Unlike court, circles expect full participation from offenders. Many offenders in the circle have been to court numerous times. Very few say very much, if anything ever in court. Extensive help is required for offenders to overcome fear, move past false bravado, and to gain the self-confidence to speak effectively on their own behalf.

Yukon circles deal principally with repeat offenders, people who have been sentenced in court 10, 20, some over 30 times. They are fully conditioned to the formal justice system. For most, court is a game, a game played by others. If sentences are less than offenders anticipated, especially less than other offenders predicted, offenders feel they have won. This 'game' induces many offenders to falsely attest to a desire to change their lives. In court, being deceptive and fuzzy about the truth is encouraged in many subtle ways. In court offenders are shielded by judges and by lawyers from direct interaction with the pain and anger of victims.

Pre-hearing preparation is vitally important for recidivists to dramatically adjust to demands for their direct, honest, open participation. In the circle, with family, friends and others who intimately know the offender; there is no place to hide. The offender faces people who know them too well to be easily fooled by brinkmanship transformations. Without effective pre-hearing preparation, recidivist offenders lapse into old patterns; con, con, con, whomever, whenever you can, and blame others. The litany of reasons to elude or diminish responsibility is well known: the crime is not my fault – it is because of 'my childhood', 'my family', 'my drinking', 'my boredom', 'my friends'. Some will blame the system – 'the police have always had a thing to get me'; 'I've been to jail too much – I'm institutionalised'. Certainly some or all of these reasons do partially explain criminal behaviour. But to move beyond the past, to make 'real differences', the offender must find the courage to battle lifelong demons, to let go of the need for excuses or explanations, no matter how justified they may be. In the circle, the offender must muster the courage to speak for themselves and directly hear from victims, from others disgusted or disappointed by their conduct.

Offender support workers, hired full or part-time as in Kwanlin Dun, can make an enormous difference in getting offenders onto and keeping them on a healing path. During preparatory steps, a support worker can construct much of the basis for making 'real differences' in the offender's life. Using ex-offenders who have been through the circle to work as support workers for offenders has unique advantages for both offenders and support workers.

Pre-circle preparation can make the difference between an offender abusing the circle and using the vital chance to change that a circle can provide. Changing the perspective of someone who has become acclimatised to the court environment takes time and extensive support. Many of the pre-circle preparatory steps are critical for offenders to make the transition from a court process to a community process. Without adequate preparation, the circle can be reduced for offenders to a court with a unique seating arrangement.

Justice officials' perceptions

Not just offenders and victims can achieve 'real differences' in circle sentencing. Everyone who participates in the circle, including all representatives of the justice system can experience 'real differences', especially in their perceptions of others and of the potential of acting co-operatively with communities. As a judge, my perspective on many offenders, on many victims, on the value of family and community involvement and on what we can and cannot do effectively within the justice system has been substantially transformed by experiences in circle sentencing.

Securing a commitment by justice agencies and a community to a partnership requires an acute awareness of what both partners can achieve by working co-operatively. To mine the potential of this partnership, changes in perceptions held by professional justice officials about their responsibilities and about the potential contributions of communities are essential. Perceptions can and will change, but only if professional justice officials invest sufficient trust and time to work with the community.

Justice officials are rarely given adequate training, resources, clear directions, and especially, the time to explore and develop the potential of community justice. As a consequence, justice agencies fail to appreciate the value of a community partnership and thereby fail to devolve sufficient responsibility and invest adequate resources into the partnership to make it work. Just as the circle demands that participants 'walk the talk', until justice agencies do more than mostly talk about community partnership, their 'walk' will entail little more than symbolic tinkering with their overall daily operations, and a community partnership will be little more than a public relations ploy.

Police perceptions

To be effective, police need the respect, trust and support of the community.[19] Community trust is not secured by public policy statements, by fancy public relations, or by token gestures of community policing. Community trust, respect and support is built upon the work of each police officer in the community. The community circle sentencing process offers an invaluable opportunity for the police to get to know and be known by the community.

Of all professional justice officials, it is particularly important that the police experience a transformation in their perceptions. Without a genuine belief and commitment to community justice by the police, the partnership will not work. Police can and have been extremely creative in developing community initiatives. If given the freedom and training to work with communities, police can make community partnerships function very successfully. Police have the power, the influence to make the partnership work. Without police who know the community, are trusted by the community and are brought into the confidences of the community, the ability to build a co-operative, mutually supportive, trusting relationship becomes difficult, if not impossible.

If police do not know the community intimately, do not know who can be trusted, who can deliver key assistance and who can be influential in changing attitudes, perceptions and behaviour, they will resort to the 'book'; using formal justice resources to process all crime. This lack of knowledge can be expensive. Expensive not only due to the unnecessary drain on criminal justice resources, but expensive in lost opportunities to significantly change behaviour, build community resources, strengthen community connections, and to engage community based prevention resources. Police officers not integrated into the community are less likely to be approached for help, except to use their legal muscle to stop violence or investigate serious crime. If not known and not trusted, police primarily become a reactive force to respond to a crisis, rarely utilised as a pro-active resource used to prevent a crisis.

The story of police involvement in circle sentencing in the Yukon is a story replete with wonderful successes and some unfortunate, lamentable, avoidable disappointments. What can be gleaned from the successful part of the Yukon police story is the importance of engaging the police throughout the community circle sentencing process, but especially in the pre-hearing stages. As

---

19 See *An Evaluation of the Neighbourhood Foot Patrol Program of the Edmonton Police Service*, 1989, Canadian Research Institute for Law and the Family; Waller, I, *Current Trends in European Crime Prevention*, 1989, Ottawa, Department of Justice; but also, Clairmont, D, *Community Based Policing: Implementation and Impact* (1991) Can J of Criminology 469.

the pre-hearing stages unfold, police input is as important to community perspective as community inputs are to police perspectives. The police make significant contributions on many levels and equally benefit from a better appreciation of offenders, of the underlying causes of the crime, of the 'real' prospects for change, of what risks are posed to others. Equally important, police officers gain a better appreciation of the victim's needs, interests and perspectives on what happened and what they expect to be done. Armed with a more comprehensive understanding of the crime, the offender, the victim, and of the extent and reliability of community resources, police can make constructive contributions in the pre-hearing process and in the hearing.

> I am happy to see you here [in the circle]. We welcome you and the other police to be a part of what we are doing. It is a good thing to work together – Lord knows we've not done much good working against each other. I know about that eh – but that is in the past – what we got going here is something to help all of us – help you too – cause we know you have a tough job. Helps us – certainly helps me to see the person behind the uniform – does my heart good to see you do care for these people – that you are not just interested in arresting and putting people in jail – eh – makes a big difference how we welcome you here to this circle – to our community. Thank you truly for being here (Harold Gatensby, Keeper of Circle – Carcross 1993).

Without participating in pre-hearing preparation, the police are seen as a single-interest participant, focused solely on pursuing a punitive sanction. They enter the circle a stranger to most. Powerful strangers in a circle introduce tension, a tension that invites adversarial exchanges, and undermines the overall level of trust necessary for creative, co-operative problem solving.

Pre-hearing preparation offers unique opportunities for police and communities to appreciate the valuable contributions each can bring to a community justice partnership. Exposure on a personal level during informal exchanges woven into shared tasks in pre-hearing preparations fosters mutual understanding, respect and trust. Trust and respect is essential to achieve real differences in the perceptions the police and communities have about the respective contributions each can make.

Crown perceptions

In community circle sentencing conducted by justices of the peace with court workers or the support workers assisting offenders, the Crown's interests are best represented by local police. As with the New Zealand family conferences, 'much more work gets done without lawyers present'.[20] In court circle sentencing, the Crown is a key participant. Crown counsel, supportive of community justice, knowledgeable about the community, respected by the community and willing to invest time with community staff and volunteers, can do much to make the partnership between the community and justice system a success. In the Hollow

---

20   Hakiaha, M, Winnipeg Conference, 1 October 1995.

Water Sentencing Circles in Northern Manitoba, and in several other places in Canada, supportive Crowns have significantly helped to empower communities to regain responsibility over conflict and have been instrumental in advancing the objectives of community justice.[21] Conversely, a Crown not known by the community, ignorant of the community and opposed or indifferent to community justice, can almost single handedly undermine the partnership.

In many communities, especially Northern communities, Crown and police are constantly changing.[22] Crowns do not live in circuit communities, some work in a community once, some only a few times and rarely is a Crown assigned the same community for more than two years. Police do live in communities, but rarely for more than three years. The constant changes in justice officials makes pre-hearing preparation crucial. Without interaction through support groups, and justice committees, these justice officials have no effective means of knowing or trusting community insights on what will best serve all affected interests. Pre-hearing preparation can at least mitigate the very destructive impact on community justice partnerships of constantly changing key justice officials.

Lacking a good understanding and knowledge of the community, Crowns tend to draw heavily on traditional sentencing jurisprudence. This fills their submissions with references to appellate cases, with a litany of standard aggravating factors, and with a heavy reliance on the offender's criminal record. These submissions accord less respect to community factors than to sentencing precedents extracted from case law. Invariably, these submissions conclude with calls for jail sentences. Such submissions trigger non-productive, adversarial exchanges over the utility of jail sentences between the community and the Crown which polarise and entrench positions. In adversarial exchanges, honesty and trust are compromised as each side concentrates solely on circumstances that

---

21 Rupert Ross, a Senior Crown from Kenora, Ontario, and author of the many important works exploring the fundamentals of community justice (including *Dancing with a Ghost*, 1992, London: Butterworths – a model of what Crowns can do in the field to promote community justice). There are many others. The Yukon has been blessed in the early beginnings of community justice with excellent Crown counsel who invested their own time in helping communities (Bill Corbett, Don Avison, Pat Hodgkinson, Elizabeth Thomas).

22 While inadequate support for community justice from police or Crowns is perceived in communities as the fault of individual Crown and police, it is primarily management policies, not individuals, that cripple community based justice initiatives in the Yukon. Police stay for three years in a community, rarely for more, often for less time. Crown belong to the Federal Department of Justice and have an Ottawa or Southern Canada career path. Few come to the Yukon with any northern experience. Many stay for a few years and march on down their career path to a southern posting that bears little relevance to their 'northern tour'. The community has no meaningful input on who comes to the community. Just as a good relationship begins to blossom between Crown and community, a new Crown arrives. The constant parade of Crowns through a community is as devastating to community justice initiatives as is the constant parade of police officers.

Communities invest significant energy and time to get to know numerous police officers and Crown. Each time the official is replaced, the community must start all over again. Eventually, the community will not invest the same effort with the new 'cop' or 'Crown'. Community justice can simply not properly evolve with a constant parade of new key justice officials.

The exorbitant cost of constantly rotating professionals within communities, the disruption to communities, and ultimately the frustration of communities may someday bring this quasi-colonial practice in the North to a long overdue end.

favour their position. Possible common interests between the Crown and community are buried beneath heated positional wrangling. Such wrangling further isolates the Crown from the community, and prompts some Crown counsel to feel like 'the enemy' or the one 'most misunderstood'.

Many community people have a much greater intimate familiarity with the advantages and disadvantages of incarceration than the Crown, either by having served time in jail, or by knowing someone in their family or in their community who has been to jail. Many in the community know offenders who return to their families and communities less capable of finding or keeping employment, more socially dysfunctional and likely to intensify their criminal behaviour. Their personal experiences can precipitate intense passions about the inappropriateness of jail. Consequently, their emotions run high when confronted by a Crown extolling the virtues or suitability of a jail sentence, especially in terms that suggest a jail sentence will 'protect the community' or 'change behaviour'.

Exchanges in the circle which move beyond positional power plays and strident personal attacks promote a recognition by all that in some cases, jail sentences can be an appropriate part of an overall plan. Crown counsel who are engaged in and trusted by communities, and demonstrate an understanding and respect for community values and interests, have introduced the possibility of jail as an option without kicking off adversarial positional exchanges. Their constructive inputs promote the creative problem-solving necessary to generate outcomes embracing all interests. To move beyond counterproductive exchanges, to find common interests and the positive working relationship necessary to creatively search for solutions embracing all interests, there must be mutual trust and respect between Crown counsel and the community. To achieve this, Crown counsel must be more involved in communities and must become involved as much as they can in pre-hearing preparatory stages.

Without engagement in pre-hearing preparation, justice officials who enter into the circle 'cold' make it difficult to gain the common ground, trust and confidence that are prerequisites for effective participation in a consensus building process with 20 to 30 others over a two to three hour hearing. Equally, for others from the community, the presence of a 'stranger' in the circle can hinder open, frank discussion. To move past enthusiastic policy statements about community justice, and fully engage justice agencies in community partnerships, many perceptions must change. More talk will not change long standing justice agency practices. Change can only come by experiencing the potential of active involvement in a community partnership. Engaging local justice officials in all pre-hearing preparatory steps can constructively change perceptions and practices of justice officials, especially those of Crown counsel who are 'strangers' to the community. It is difficult, if not impossible, to build and maintain community partnerships with justice officials who are strangers.

Family and community perceptions

Families, if involved in pre-hearing processes, often gain a clearer picture of the magnitude of the offender's problems and become less defensive when the victim's story is heard and appreciated. They gain a better understanding of what they can and must do to make a difference in the offender's life. The extensive support from many others in the community implants new energy, new commitment to providing help to offenders in their family. Pre-hearing preparation also can change the community perspective of police, Crown and of the community's ability to make a difference. Similar dramatic transformations among others in the community can be precipitated by involvement in pre-circle preparation. The more participation, the greater the positive ripples through the community in gaining support for the challenges facing offenders and victims. Pre-hearing preparation can also change the community perspectives of police, Crown, and of the community's ability to make a difference.

The discussion above barely scrapes the surface in describing how pre-hearing preparation contributes to constructively changing the perceptions of all participants. The impact of effective pre-hearing preparation on probation officers, treatment officials, and on the friends of victims and offenders is equally vital in creating the foundation for innovative, holistic solutions embracing all interests.

As well as changing perceptions, effective pre-hearing preparation has a number of other, very significant, benefits for both the process and the outcomes of circling sentencing. These are described below.

INCREASING PARTICIPATION

Pre-hearing preparation significantly expands the breadth of participation in the circle and in community issues. A broad base of participation that includes family, friends, employers and others from the community, significantly helps to:

- extend community awareness, input and support;
- effectively engage community based resources;
- balance support for victim and offender;
- increase awareness and responses to the needs of *all* affected by crime;
- promote reconciliation;
- rebuild relationships;
- foster community security and safety.

Yukon circle sentencing experiences suggest that the broader the base of participation, the higher the likelihood of success. If the support comes from a mix of family, friends and others in the community, the support group's ability to persevere, to work through the hardships encountered on a healing journey is significantly enhanced.[23]

Pre-hearing steps allow the Justice Committee and support groups to identify and involve key people. The information shared during the preparatory stage can remove barriers for some, and induce others to participate.

ENRICHING INFORMATION

Pre-hearing preparation enriches the quality and quantity of information available to participants in circle hearings *before the hearing*. The earlier information is available, the less likely parties will form hardened positions. Little or no information fosters erroneous assumptions about what is not known. These assumptions generally conjure worst case scenarios prompting courses of action that deny finding optimal solutions for all, and lose opportunities to make 'real differences'.

Participants acting upon misinformation, based upon an understanding of one side or an awareness of only a small part of a much larger story, tend to adopt and fervently pursue positions that undermine their best interests. Examples of Crown, police, judges, offenders, victims and others doing so abound. The following example illustrates how exchanging information *before* a circle hearing can change the understanding and consequently the position of an offender's family.

Jim was in the circle for three offences, impaired driving, assaulting a police officer and refusing to provide a breath sample.

Jim had several employable skills. He always could get work. Sober, employers were anxious to hire him. From a big family, Jim married Belle, who also had a large family. The support of two large families, numerous friends and his easy going personality secured extensive support for Jim to press for a non-custodial sentence and to avoid any residential alcohol treatment that would interfere with his need to 'provide a living for his wife and three young kids'. Jail time or residential treatment were fiercely opposed. His family and supporters asked:

'Who would look after the family? Who would bring in the wood? Who would look after his elderly parents?'

'He's been to jail a couple of times – didn't do a damn bit of good – you know it made him worse.'

'He needs to get on with his life.'

'He has debts to pay, children to look after – hard work will keep him off booze.'

---

23 Understanding the dynamics of support groups will be a vital part of building successful community circles. Impressions thus far suggest relative strangers participating in support groups with family and friends strengthen support groups by offering fresh insights, and by motivating those close to offenders or victims to persevere. If relative strangers have peacemaking or mediation skills, they can be instrumental in overcoming old, entrenched attitudes among people close to offenders.

Jim's family and most of his support group began convinced that continued employment, not treatment, would serve his best interests.

The sentence given was dramatically different than his support group initially sought. Jim was sentenced by the circle to a short term in jail to be immediately followed by residential substance abuse treatment. All his family and all but one friend ultimately agreed that there should be a custodial sentence, as did Jim. This dramatic change in perspective by Jim's family and friends was caused by several factors – all produced by pre-hearing preparation.

- The contributions from all the circle participants portrayed a different picture of Jim than any one perspective revealed. Jim had initially denied the extent and frequency of his drinking and violence. Once the stories of all who knew him were put together, everyone began to appreciate he was clearly not 'coping with his problem'. Jim was facing his second impaired driving charge in eight years, but as information emerged, he drove many, many times impaired.

- The violence to the police officer was initially passed off by some supporters as a silly, out-of-character minor fracas caused by drink and misunderstanding. However, he'd had fights with friends recently and a few more with strangers in bars out of town. Belle began to share stories of violence in the home. Belle's ability to bring out what was happening at home derived from knowing she would be supported and Jim would get the help he needed.

- Realising the full story, influential people in Jim's life helped him recognise the depth and seriousness of his problems, offered the support he needed to take a different path and volunteered help to address the needs of his family while he was in treatment.

- A consensus grew among family and friends for a short jail sentence of 30 days that would dry him out and render him fit enough to commence a four week residential treatment program. A probation order ensured his treatment will be followed up by more counselling for anger management, psychological issues and substance abuse. Family and friends took up different parts in ensuring his wife and children were looked after, in providing the support, encouragement and company to keep him on a healing path. His employer ensured a good job awaited his successful completion of residential treatment.

This example illustrates how a frank and full sharing of information *before* the circle hearing can dramatically change perspectives and positions, and help shift from adversarial exchanges over conflicting positions to a co-operative search for a solution embracing everyone's best interests.

A full exchange of information during pre-hearing preparation can also influence:

- *Whether some parties will participate.* Victims and other key resource people, if not fully informed, often decide not to participate in circle sentencing. Their decision to stay out of the process is usually based on information derived from before the crime, or upon misinformation about the nature and directions of support provided for an offender.

- *What interests parties will pursue.* Absent full information, participants can construct positions that undermine their best interests. Before the circle hearing, without full information, positions will harden as parties develop and accumulate arguments to advance their initial positions.

- *Whether parties can change their perceptions and attitudes.* Once positions are ardently staked out in the circle hearing, the ability to change is further complicated by requiring the development of options that include 'face-saving' opportunities for participants to make significant public shifts in their positions. The courage and honesty of many to openly make significant changes in the circle is astounding. However, there is enough emotional intensity, enough serious work to do, and enough challenge in circle hearings without unnecessarily creating more by not fully developing and exchanging information *before* the hearing.

GENERATING COMMITMENT

Forging 'real differences' requires digging through many difficult layers of private hells. Not just victims and offenders, but all participants are profoundly affected by the fears, pain, anguish and frustration that permeate circle discussions. Circles are not easy, not pleasant detours around court hearings. Anyone who thinks so, either has not been through a circle, or has not been in a circle that penetrated the emotional ground where 'real differences' are harvested.

All participants, particularly the offender and victim, must be committed to the circle process to muster sufficient courage, honesty and perseverance to achieve 'real differences'. A commitment of this magnitude can only come from believing that the circle process offers a better alternative to pursue their interests than any other course of action. How can participants, justice officials, victims, offenders and others develop an adequate understanding of what circles offer to voluntarily make the necessary commitment to circle sentencing? The ever-changing 'guard' of professionals leaves little institutional experience of circles in justice agencies. If justice officials lack an understanding of the specific advantages circles offer, their commitment will be tenuous or superficial. A weak commitment by any primary party severely undermines the capacity to work through difficult issues in building a consensus. Until circle sentencing has had ample time to develop, and its strengths and weaknesses extensively appreciated, pre-hearing preparation offers the best if not only chance for all participants to evaluate whether the circle offers the best alternative to pursue their interests, and thereby make the commitment necessary to harvest the full potential of circle sentencing.

REMOVING SURPRISES

Surprises are rarely productive intruders into a consensual process. The tensions and fears arising from not knowing what is happening, not knowing what will be presented in circle hearings can sap commitment, engender defensive, even aggressive positions. Dealing with relative strangers adds tension, especially if the interest strangers wish to advance at the hearing is unknown.

By reducing or eliminating surprises, pre-hearing preparation creates a more constructive environment to prepare for the hearing and ushers participants into a circle hearing with less trepidation about what they will encounter. Reducing fears and tensions generates open, honest exchanges and maximises the creative problem solving potential of circle hearings.

RAISING THE COMFORT LEVEL

During pre-hearing preparation all parties gain a better familiarity about the process, about what is expected of them and about the expectations of others. Support groups can significantly raise the comfort level of victims and offenders. Support groups, by preparing them to participate, assuring them of their presence and support in the circle, and helping them access any treatment or other resources they need, contribute to easing the tensions victims and offenders experience in living through the processing of their case.

IMPROVING ACCESS TO SUPPORT SERVICES

The formal justice system kicks in most support services after sentencing. This can be six months or more after the crime. Especially for young offenders and their families, help is needed immediately. In all cases, delay in plugging in support or treatment services can be severely detrimental to victims, offenders, their respective families and communities. If unattended, the damage and trauma caused by crime can continue to mount long after the crime.

Pre-hearing preparation enables community justice processes to provide more support sooner. Timely access to support and treatment can profoundly improve the prospects for achieving 'real differences'.

ASSESSING OFFENDER SUITABILITY

In most circles, promises of what will be done by offenders carry little weight. Talk is cheap and easy. Actions speak louder, more persuasively within the circle. During pre-hearing preparation, offenders have an opportunity to act on their commitment to change. A failure to act or commence rehabilitative programs, or to curtail substance abuse will question the suitability of offenders for the community process, and may shift the offender from the community to the court.

Gaining acceptance by others in the circle of plans that replace or reduce jail sentences requires a belief within the circle that the offender is genuinely motivated, has the ability to persevere, and has the support and resources to succeed. Words alone, especially from repeat offenders with a long history of substance abuse, unemployment and a life full of broken promises will not generate consensus support for alternatives to incarceration. Action, especially immediate, extensive concrete steps toward rehabilitation, coupled with a full acceptance of responsibility during preparatory stages, secures broadly based support for alternatives to incarceration more effectively than words.

In assessing an offender's suitability for a community process, and ultimately assessing the suitability of alternatives to incarceration, what is done or not done during the pre-hearing steps can be determinative. To test the commitment of offenders and of communities to a sentencing plan, a circle hearing may be postponed and conditions imposed that protect the community and challenge offenders to 'walk their talk'.[24]

CLARIFYING THE BEST ALTERNATIVE FORMAL OR COMMUNITY SERVICE

Some cases are best processed through the formal justice system. Many are not. Creating community based alternatives overcomes the lunacy that one system (one size fits all) can competently process all criminal cases. There are far too many differences in the circumstances of offenders, victims and communities and in the circumstances surrounding crime to competently shove all cases through the doors of one process.

Whether the formal justice process, a community justice alternative or some combination of both serves the best interests of all participants will depend upon many factors. There is as much to be lost in processing the wrong cases through community justice options as in processing cases through the formal justice process that could be better served by a community process. Comprehensive pre-hearing preparation can be invaluable in making the right choice of the most appropriate process. Investment in pre-hearing measures increases the use of informal processes such as mediation, diversion and talking circles. The investment in preparation is recouped by minimising unnecessary reliance on expensive, formal systems. Preparatory steps can also reduce reliance upon formal justice resources by exposing potential for making 'real differences' within community processes not readily apparent, even to an 'experienced' eye.

Equally important, pre-hearing preparation can expose a lack of genuine potential for making 'real differences', and thereby avoid a misuse of community options. Often pre-hearing preparation is the only means of clarifying what the

---

24 See *R v N (D)* (1993) 27 CR (4d), at 114, setting out the grounds for and the importance of delaying the imposition of sentences in some cases.

circle offers and the only means for participants to make an informed choice of which process – court or circle – best serves their interests.

DETERMINING THE MOST APPROPRIATE COMMUNITY JUSTICE PROCESS

Circle sentencing should not constitute the entirety of the community justice process. Each community must have a range of options to respond to conflict, circle sentencing being but one of many choices. To everyone's benefit, an effective community justice process includes many options to respond to conflict. Having several options creates the invaluable ability to match the circumstances of each case to the process best suited to achieve enduring, practical outcomes. A comprehensive pre-hearing process hones the ability of the Justice Committee to determine which process is most suitable given *all* circumstances in the case. Ideally, a community ought to have the options for responding to crime set out in Figure 1.

In a fully operational community justice system, with police and Crown intimately involved in the community, many cases will be diverted at the front door of the community justice process and never formally referred to the Justice Committee. This is only possible if the police are an integral part of the community justice system, know who they can call on for help, who they can trust, and especially important, what the community expects and will support. Police, working closely with communities, can increase reliance upon warnings, formal cautions, informal referrals to mediation or diversion. Police either trained as or working with peacemakers can provide immediate, constructive interventions that resolve many matters within hours or days. The intervention of police with peacemaker skills, as a peacemaker at the earliest possible moment, can make an enormous difference in how the parties subsequently pursue their respective interests. Early intervention can increase the prospects of constructive resolution, and reduce processing costs.

Mediation is an essential tool in pre-hearing preparation. Mediation occurs implicitly in the justice committee, and in both offender and victim support group meetings. Mediation may be used explicitly when the Justice Committee calls upon a mediator or co-mediators to help offenders and victims and others caught up in the turmoil of the crime to improve their capacity to relate, understand and create solutions embracing all their best interests. In some cases, mediation may help prepare parties for a circle hearing, in many others, mediation may resolve all outstanding issues.

Diversion, healing or private talking circles, or community conferences with young offenders, may also be used in appropriate cases to assist in preparing for circles or to completely handle the conflict. All of these options as well as mediation may either conclude and implement an agreement, or develop a proposal for approval by a justice of the peace or judge or by a community or

Figure 1: Justice Committee Options

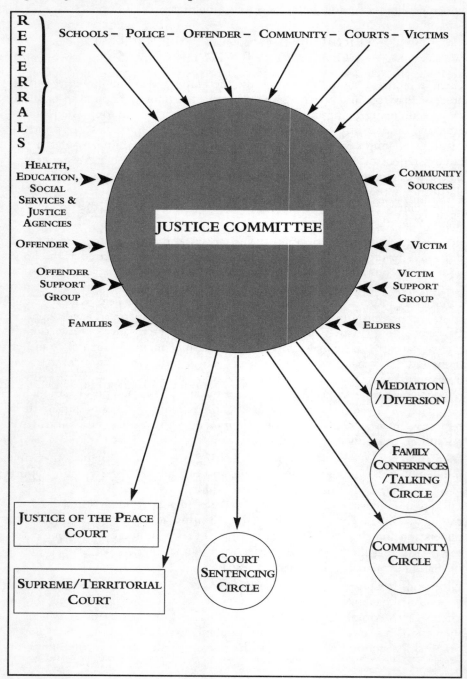

court circle. Finally, the Justice Committee may decide the case ought to be sent to the local justice of the peace court, or to the territorial or Supreme Court for sentencing. In any of the courts, Justice Committee members may make submissions, including detailed proposals.

Within all these alternatives and others, a community may develop the essential flexibility in each case either to combine options, or to shift from one option to another. For example, as a case progresses, the information revealed may change the attitudes and perceptions sufficiently to refer cases to less formal options. Conversely differences may polarise, or offenders may demonstrate they lack the fortitude to 'walk the talk' making it necessary to engage a more formal response. The flexibility to divert a case to mediation or informal processes at any time is as invaluable as the ability to take the case out of mediation and informal processes and refer it back to the court.

Community justice committees can significantly contribute to selecting the best options for processing each case and thereby make efficient use of both community and formal justice resources. To do so, community justice committees must be supported by justice agencies, serviced by a paid part-time justice co-ordinator and, as in New Zealand, community volunteers must have access to relevant training and be compensated for their expenses.

What happens at the hearing is significantly affected by what happens before the hearing. The more done before, the less needs to be done in the hearing, and the greater the prospects for achieving real differences. In Kwanlin Dun, the value of pre-hearing preparation is appreciated and increasingly utilised. Effective pre-hearing measures enable more cases to be diverted from the circle process to diversion committees, to talking or healing circles, or to mediation, and more cases come to circle hearings simply for approval of, or amendments to, plans already well underway. As recent experience in Fort St John has illustrated, comprehensive preparation, even in the eleventh hour, can profoundly influence what happens in a circle.[25]

The need for pre-hearing preparation is not a call for inflexible procedures. Rose Couch, the Director of the Kwanlin Dun Justice Project, fervently stresses that flexibility is a critical feature in designing all stages of a community justice process:

> The humanism – the individuals – their needs – feelings – their families – this is the most important thing – we need to be sensitive to what must be done in each case – having a strict-rigid process defeats what we are all about – each case will be different – we must be prepared to go with what each case takes to help (Rose Couch, Kwaulin Dun Community Justice Retreat, 1994).

---

25 Goerzen, MD, Counsellor and Project Co-ordinator, *A Diary of Circle Sentencing with the BC Supreme Court*, 14 September 1995, unpublished paper.

EVALUATING THE IMPACT OF CIRCLE SENTENCING

Community justice initiatives are often mistakenly evaluated on the same criterion as formal justice processes. It is not that using the same standards is unfair. It is that community justice initiatives are about much more than lowering recidivist rates. Far more so than formal justice processes, community processes such as circle sentencing contain the potential to:

- engender moral growth among all participants;
- foster positive attitudes about others;
- empower individuals, families and communities to take responsibility for conflict in their lives and constructively resolve differences with others;
- generate innovative, enduring solutions;
- remove underlying causes of crime;
- build a sense of community;
- create safe and healthy communities;
- educate participants about causes of crime and the importance of community prevention.

These deeper transformative impacts advance on many levels the well-being of individuals in communities. These contributions are overlooked by measuring circle sentencing or any community justice process by recidivist rates. Nonetheless, circle sentencing and other community justice processes can significantly reduce recidivism.[26] But focusing on recidivist rates loses sight of other invaluable contributions and ignores why these contributions need to be reinforced, staffed and funded in dramatically different ways than formal justice processes.

While reducing recidivism is an important goal, community justice processes designed exclusively for this purpose become merely adjuncts to formal justice processes, thereby extending the reach of the formal justice agencies into a community. Ideally, community justice systems diminish, not increase the use and reach of professional justice resources.[27] A partnership between the formal justice system and the community is vital to making the changes necessary to pursue community justice and make real differences. Without such a partnership, community justice systems will become simply an extension of a coercive, punitive state system. Successful community justice processes free up resources for justice agencies to focus on what they can do best, and remove from the grasp of justice agencies the cases communities can best handle.

---

26 While not yet complete, assessments of Yukon community circle sentencing indicate many offenders with histories of frequent serious crimes, have stopped offending, some do re-offend, but generally less frequently and less seriously. Some keep on trucking, their pattern of offences much the same as before. In New Zealand and in other communities using restorative community justice systems, the recidivist rates are significantly reduced. Matt Hakiaha suggests young offender recidivism has dropped by a third due to family conferences (presentation in Whitehouse, Yukon, 8 November 1995).

27 See Van Ness, D, 'Four Challenges of Restorative Justice' (1993) 4 *Criminal Law Forum* 251, at 272; and especially Blomberg, T, 'Widening the Net: An Anomaly in the Evolution of Diversion Programs', *Handbook of Criminal Justice Evaluations*, 1980, Klein & Teilmann.

Pre-hearing preparation for circle sentencing contributes to making the process more than just a different way of constructing a sentence. It enhances the capacity of the circle process to foster better relationships, promote moral growth, and advance the well-being of families and communities. Moving from an adversarial process dominated by professionals, to a consensual process that enables all to participate as equals, marks a significant shift in emphasis from merely constructing a sentence to improving relationships. This shift is substantially facilitated by comprehensive pre-hearing preparation.

In a community process what is more important than whether a consensus is reached on a sentence is the extent participation in the process transforms all participants by:

- developing a better understanding of themselves and each other;
- nurturing more positive attitudes about themselves and others;
- fostering an appreciation, often empathy, for the situation and problems of others; and
- generating respect for others with different values.

These transformations are essential to improve relationships and to establish constructive environments to sustain community justice initiatives. Improving relationships improves the potential for disputants to develop their own solutions.

If the process has not constructively changed the parties' initial attitudes, perceptions and relationships then the underlying conflict or causes of the conflict will persist. Changes in perceptions of others, permanent changes require more than simply reaching a settlement:

> She has always just been regarded as a thief – no one could see past her crimes – she too had begun to see herself as just that. It is quite amazing to me how differently all saw her after that long circle and sure enough how she now sees herself as different ... She is out there now in the community I'll tell you, playing a big role that's even making more changes happen, good things for her family, for all of us, the people she's working with too; you know (Mother of offender).

This offender and others who are caught in the vicious grip of substance abuse may reach a point in the circle when they are committed to change. However, if the process does not inject new self-images, new self-esteem and carry these changes over to the perspective of others, offenders will be severely pressed to persevere in their healing journey.

Moving difficult issues through the consensus-building process of circle sentencing in a manner that empowers all to participate can reshape the way people interact with others in their homes, neighbourhoods and workplaces. These cumulative benefits cannot be overlooked in assessing the value and importance of the consensus-based process. By processing conflict through adversarial procedures, the differences and negative attitudes about others can be entrenched; by focusing on narrowly defined legal results, the underlying causes of conflict are ignored and often exacerbated. By treating the sentence as the sole objective of the process, the potential in resolving conflict to precipitate constructive changes within the immediate environment and among all participants is often lost.

In contrast, community justice processes based on peacemaking, mediation and consensus-building possess the potential to do much more than simply construct a better sentence. These processes can change not just situations, but people themselves and thus society as a whole.[28] Unlike the formal justice system, community processes view the conflict surrounding crime as an invaluable opportunity for constructive change. If the community and formal justice partnership is working, crime can be an opportunity for improving the underlying circumstances, and for ensuring all is done that can be done for victims and for offenders to advance their best interests.

CONCLUSION

Successful community justice processes are a series of small successful steps. The hoped for results envisaged at the beginning often seem too daunting to even attempt, especially in a single leap, or at one hearing. Success in the circle, and beyond the circle, must begin at the earliest possible moment, with many small steps that move all participants toward change, towards 'real differences'. We have much to gain, much to learn from communities. Can the justice system be sufficiently astute and humble enough to share with and learn from communities in exploring the potential of a partnership? More so than justice agencies, communities come to the partnership with a much greater willingness to learn and explore what is possible and what justice agencies can offer. In this context, the admonition offered by Crown Attorney Rupert Ross warrants repeating:

> ... and so long as the government and the officials of the country continue to act as if the original peoples are the only ones in need of instruction and improvement, so long will suspicion and distrust persist.[29]

Justice officials must be open to *learn* from *all* communities and to share the responsibility of creating and maintaining the wellbeing of our communities. Equally, all citizens must recognise and take up their responsibilities for preventing and responding to conflict within their communities. Community justice processes, especially the preparatory stages of these processes, provide an invaluable opportunity for both professional justice and community representatives to begin to learn and appreciate what each can and must contribute.

---

28 Bush, R and Folger, J, above note 6, p 206.

29 Ross, R, *Dancing With a Ghost*, above note 21 *supra* (the same notion applies with equal force to justice officials in appreciating the input of all laity).

9 WATER DISPUTES IN ONTARIO: ENVIRONMENTAL DISPUTE RESOLUTION AND THE PUBLIC INTEREST

*DIANNE SAXE**

INTRODUCTION

This chapter examines the opportunities to use ADR in managing public and private disputes over water taking and drainage in Ontario, Canada. It describes the environmental and legal context for these disputes. The two key statutes, the Drainage Act and the Ontario Water Resources Act, present an almost complete contrast in philosophy and structure. A comparison between the two illustrates limits and opportunities for classic mediation, and for related processes that may go by the same name but have dramatically different dynamics.

THE ENVIRONMENTAL CONTEXT

Canada in general (and Ontario in particular) is well supplied with water. Snow is heavy, rains frequent. There are thousands of lakes and rivers, and groundwater is abundant. Nevertheless, there are hundreds of disputes a year over water, particularly in the Southern areas of the province where the population is concentrated.

One typical problem arises when a high volume water user, such as a fruit or vegetable grower dependent on irrigation, draws down the water supply that his neighbour depends on. During the hot months of mid-summer when surface watercourses are depleted, heavy water use by some may leave those downstream with only a muddy rivulet. When the neighbourhood depends on groundwater, increased pumping rates by one farmer can lower the water table below the bottom of his neighbours' wells, thus depriving them of water for irrigation, or even for drinking and bathing.

Disputes over water management also arise between very different users: quarry operations and their neighbours are a classic example. In Southern Ontario, surface deposits of high quality rock and aggregate have often been exhausted. The quarries which continue to operate are often digging below the water table. This requires them to 'dewater' the quarry, pumping out groundwater as fast as it flows in. Sometimes that is very fast: quarries of sand and gravel are often located on glacial eskers which contain significant aquifers. To dispose of the water, quarry operators pump it into nearby lakes, streams or sewers, thus creating a massive transfer of water from groundwater to the surface. The deeper

---

* Lawyer/mediator and environmental law specialist in private practice in Toronto.

the quarry digs, the more it depresses the water table and the more it may interfere with nearby wells. In theory, the diverted waters could provide a replacement water supply, but this rarely works in practice. Surface waters are much more susceptible to contamination than groundwater, and the homes and farms that depend on groundwater wells rarely have direct access to them.

Too much water can cause as much trouble as too little. Proper drainage is essential to the productivity of woodlots and fields, and to protect buildings and roads from flooding. Typically, water draining from one home or farm must flow over several of its neighbours before reaching a water course. Changes in the drainage, grading, or uses of upstream properties can have dramatic impacts on the volume and velocity of water reaching downstream properties, causing flooding or erosion. If the downstream property attempts to protect itself by damming or controlling the flow of water, heavy rains may backup and flood the upstream property. In both cases, a great deal of money may be at stake.

In unusually dry or wet years, these interests come into particularly sharp conflict. In addition, changes in the availability of water have important implications for local ecosystems. There is considerable dispute over who has the right and the responsibility to speak for these ecosystems, and over how their interests are to be balanced with human ones.

THE LEGAL FRAMEWORK

Water quantity is controlled under two major Ontario statutes, namely the Drainage Act and the Ontario Water Resources Act, and by a network of common law rights. These two statutes are very different in both philosophy and structure. The Drainage Act recognises that many landowners may be affected when one parcel of land is drained; each of the people so affected have rights. The Act focuses on cost assessment and collection; since money is involved, it recognises that disputes are likely. To deal with these disputes, the Act is replete with detail, including formal fact-finding by an engineer and procedures for appeal. Altogether, there are more than 125 different provisions.

In contrast, the Ontario Water Resources Act governs water-taking. It does not require the payment of money, and therefore scarcely seems to foresee the likelihood of disputes. Water-taking is governed by a single provision, which leaves all decision-making to the sole discretion of a civil servant known as the Director. However, disputes can and do arise between neighbouring water users, especially in dry years.

To understand the role that mediation can play in helping to resolve these disputes, it is essential to understand in more detail the contrasting schemes of the two statutes.

THE DRAINAGE ACT

The Drainage Act is a statute of key importance to rural dwellers, although almost unknown by urbanites. Its goals are:

- to facilitate land drainage and development, by allowing the objections of some landowners to be overridden;
- to fairly allocate the cost of drainage works;
- to offset the adverse impacts of drainage works through appropriate compensation;
- a more recent goal, to temper human desires for the economic benefits of drainage with some consideration of the importance of natural water courses and wetlands to the natural environment.[1]

Section 2 of the Act allows drainage questions to be resolved privately, by agreement, by anyone willing to pay for it. Two or more owners of land may enter a written agreement for the construction, financing and maintenance of any drainage works. The agreement must state the lands to be drained, the costs of the drainage works and what portion must be paid by each land owner. The agreement may then be registered against the title of those lands and stays in effect indefinitely. The Act makes no provision for resolving disputes which may arise in the course of time over the operation of the drainage works, nor how the agreement would be affected by subdivision of any of the lands, or changes in the volume of water.

The rest of the Act establishes detailed procedures to drain lands where not all the owners agree on what should be done or on how it should be paid for. These procedures are initiated by the landowner(s) who want(s) their land drained.[2] For small projects costing less than $7,500, a single landowner may requisition a drainage evaluation from his or her municipality. Larger projects are commenced by public petitions, or, in the case of drainage for agriculture or roads, by civil servants.

THE ENGINEER

Once a request for drainage is initiated, the first review is a technical one: can the lands be drained effectively, and what would it cost?[3] This review is

---

1   Originally adopted to help 'civilise' the wild lands of the province, it sets up an elaborate scheme for dividing the cost of draining land among the landowners who 'benefit' from it. Drafted at a time when 'wilderness' seemed both inexhaustible and unnecessary, the Act originally assumed that land drainage is always desirable, subject only to limitations of engineering and of cost. In recent years, it has been amended to require at least a cursory review of the environmental impacts of a proposed drainage project.

2   Parties who initiate a drainage request that does not ultimately proceed may be required to pay the costs thrown away.

3   For petitions that the municipality intends to proceed with, the municipal council must give notice of the petition to affected landowners, to neighbouring municipalities, and to local conservation authorities or the Ministry of Natural Resources. Each of these may demand an environmental appraisal, but only if they are willing to pay for it.

conducted by 'the engineer', a professional engineer or surveyor appointed by the municipality. It is the engineer's job to examine the site, meet with the landowners, and prepare a detailed report to the municipal council on the costs and benefits of the project.

The engineer has substantial powers and responsibilities. She/he may enter private property and plant stakes and benchmarks, and it is a serious offence to obstruct him/her. The engineer has the initial say in every detail of the drainage works, from where each hole or trench is to be dug to where the removed soil shall be put. Typically, it is the engineer who assesses the impact on the environment, landowners' claims to compensation, and the overall balance of costs and benefits of the project. It is also the engineer who assesses who should pay what part of the project cost.

The heavy emphasis placed upon the engineer in the Drainage Act reflects a time when society had greater faith in science and experts to resolve our problems. Today, this faith has been substantially eroded. An engineer or surveyor may be well equipped to measure the lands affected, to design drainage works, to predict the effect on water levels and to estimate their costs, but there is little in their training that assists them to balance the competing desires of a developer and a naturalist, to fairly allocate costs, or to help different parties to find common ground.

In fulfilling all of these tasks, the engineer does not work for the landowners concerned. Instead, she/he is engaged in a public duty on behalf of the municipality, and must report to the municipality everything that she/he learns. As the Act puts it:

> The engineer shall, to the best of the engineer's skill, knowledge, judgment and ability, honestly and faithfully, and without fear of, favour to or prejudice against any person, perform the duty assigned to the engineer in connection with any drainage works and make a true report thereon.[4]

The rest of the Act sets out a complex set of procedures for review of the engineer's report and of any decisions that the council makes as a result. Council decisions may be variously appealed to the 'court of revision', the 'referee', the specialised Ontario Drainage Tribunal, and/or the courts. Different aspects of a single dispute can be appealed to different bodies. Different parties have different rights of appeal at different stages in the process.

It is apparent from this elaborate structure of appeals that drainage questions have long been a fertile source of disputes. Drainage can have a major impact on the productivity and profitability of a farm, and on the comfort and convenience of its inhabitants. Drainage cases have been known both to cause and to feed on a variety of social and domestic tensions. Sometimes they split families and communities, and linger on, causing resentment, for many years. These divisions and resentments can be exacerbated by the statutory dispute resolution process, which can be both lengthy and costly.

---

4 Section 11.

In years of average weather, the government receives approximately 500 drainage complaints a year. Most are resolved informally but about 10% result in public hearings. The Drainage Review Board, which hears most of them, is an administrative tribunal originally set up to provide a simple, speedy and inexpensive alternative to the courts. Over the years, it has become more and more like a court and is no longer simple, speedy or cheap. There are now hundreds of drainage appeals each year.

For these very reasons, all interested parties have a great deal at stake when the engineer makes his/her report. It is not surprising that the engineers experience strong pressure from the parties to make the recommendations that one side or another would prefer. On technical issues, engineers have the advantage of specialised training with which to stand their ground. However, an engineering degree is of no particular assistance in resolving the social, domestic, and emotional questions which often permeate drainage cases.

As a result, many drainage cases just won't go away, even after a technological 'solution' has been found; the parties may continue to call the engineers, and remain unsatisfied, years after their report is made. Having heard much praise of mediation, the drainage engineers in Ontario requested that they be trained as mediators. The relevant government ministry (Agriculture, Food and Rural Affairs) eventually decided to fund two days of training.

Can 'the engineer' be a mediator?

Technically qualified mediators have obvious appeal in technical disputes, such as those relating to drainage.[5] A technically qualified mediator can quickly understand and assess technical issues, can cut through jargon, and can help the parties understand the options available to them. Many parties find it helpful for a competent neutral to give an authoritative evaluation of their respective positions, but do not wish, as in arbitration, to be bound to accept it. On the other hand, it takes more than a short training session to turn an engineer (or anyone else) into a mediator.

More fundamentally, an engineer who must find facts and make a public report to a decision-maker (the town council) cannot conduct a mediation in the classic sense. To understand this problem, the task and role of the engineer under the Drainage Act can be compared with that of a classic mediator in a private dispute.

---

5   However, these advantages are less decisive in mediation than they would be in arbitration. A technically qualified arbitrator of a complex case is likely to have a much quicker and surer understanding of the technical issues and of technical evidence, and can better distinguish the legitimate from the purported expert. On the other hand, an arbitrator whose primary qualifications are his or her technical expertise may be less skilled in those cases where emotions and the truthfulness of lay witnesses play a large role. Some technically expert arbitrators are also limited in their experience of complex legal issues.

In contrast, the mediator's primary role is to manage the negotiation process, not to decide the issues. Thus, skill in the management of the mediation process is relatively more important, and skill in understanding technical issues is relatively less important, than in arbitrations.

	CLASSIC MEDIATION	ENGINEER'S ROLE
Who are the parties?	The immediate parties determine themselves. The plaintiff has a claim against someone; the defendant is a person from whom a plaintiff wants something.	This is a contentious issue. The initial parties are those who request the drainage project, or whose land will be directly affected by it. However, the Act makes no provision for dealing with indirect or cumulative effects of drainage. It has also proved difficult to determine 'who speaks for the trees, fish, birds, future generations, etc?'
Who determines the issues to be resolved?	The parties define the issues to be determined, often in a mediation agreement. Any issue that the parties wish to address can be included in the mediation. The mediator may assist the parties to develop the terms of reference for the mediation.	The issues are determined, in part by the initial petition, in part by the council, and in part by the engineer, in the exercise of his/her technical judgment about the appropriate scope of the project. Additional (eg environmental) issues may be raised by neighbouring municipalities and/or conservation authorities.
Neutrality	The mediator must be neutral.	The engineer must be neutral.
Role of the neutral	The mediator controls the process, but not the result. He or she creates an opportunity for the parties to find common ground. The mediator is their helper in the process of talking to each other.	The engineer is a fact finder charged with recommending a solution to a public body. He or she has a statutory responsibility to use their best judgment, on the basis of all the facts known to them, to recommend a plan of action. Inevitably, this makes the engineer more of judge than a mediator.

	CLASSIC MEDIATION	ENGINEER'S ROLE
How is the neutral chosen?	The parties generally choose their neutral by mutual agreement. If they are unable to agree on a mediator, they may decide to allow a third party or service provider select a mediator for them.[6]	The engineer is selected by the municipality, which is often an important source of work for him/her. Thus, the engineer's first loyalty is to the municipality, not to the parties.
Who pays the neutral?	The parties pay the neutral directly, generally in equal shares; other arrangements may be agreed upon.	The municipality pays the engineer, but may recover the cost (as part of the overall project cost) from those requesting and/or benefiting from the drainage.
The role of the parties	To bargain with each other in good faith.	To persuade the engineer of the rightness of their cause.
Who makes the ultimate decision?	The parties make their own agreement. The mediator has no independent power to decide.	A municipal council[7] makes the ultimate decision, on the recommendation of the engineer. Various appellate tribunals may vary or overturn the council decision.
Termination of the proceedings	At the parties' discretion.	Up to the engineer and/or council.
Are the proceedings confidential?	Confidentiality is as agreed upon by the parties. Typically, everything which is said during the mediation is kept confidential, and the parties agree not to subpoena the mediator to give evidence of anything that occurred during the mediation.	Proceedings involving the engineer cannot be confidential. The engineer has a statutory and contractual duty to make a 'true report' to the municipal council, and cannot omit anything relevant from it. As well, appellate tribunals may wish to scrutinise everything that led to a decision they may later review.

6   There are some cases, such as those referred to mediation by a court-annexed system of semi-compulsory mediation, who are simply instructed to appear before a court-appointed mediator. However, the parties accept this lack of choice where the services thus provided are free (for example, the pilot project currently operating in the Ontario Court (General Division)); see the Practice Directions at OR.

7   In Canada, unlike other jurisdictions such as New Zealand, municipal boundaries do not coincide with watersheds. Thus, the municipality making the decision to drain may not contain the resources who will be most affected by the project. The Act deals with this to a limited extent by allowing a neighbouring municipality to demand an environmental report (which they must pay for) and to appeal the council's decision.

	CLASSIC MEDIATION	ENGINEER'S ROLE
Communication of the result	As chosen by the parties, but results are typically kept confidential.[8]	Must be reported to the municipal council as part of the engineer's report. The Act has no provision for the private settlement of a dispute, once a petition has been launched.
Consequences for a party who fails to participate	A party who refuses to participate is not bound by anything which occurs during or as a result of the mediation.	Municipality can still impose a result upon them, eg requiring them to submit to and/or pay for drainage works.
Effect on third parties	None. Non-parties are not bound by any agreement reached through the mediation.	No one can be forced to pay for drainage if they did not receive notice and an opportunity to comment on the project. However, the physical effects of each drainage project, and their cumulative effects, may have a greater or lesser effect on every human and non-human species in the watershed.
Consequences of failing to resolve the dispute	The dispute goes to (or continues in) litigation. The parties lose control of the ultimate decision in favour of lawyers, courts and judges. Fear of the long delays, high costs and unpredictability of litigation are often the most powerful inducements to a mediated agreement.	The municipal council still makes the ultimate decision. The parties (who never had complete control once the petition was launched), lose only the opportunity to make a united recommendation to council. The dispute becomes a political one. Prolonged council deliberations may not impose direct financial costs on the parties.

As this chart shows, the power relationships and internal dynamics that characterise a private mediation are very different from those that affect 'the engineer' faced with a dispute under the Drainage Act. Therefore, while

---

8   It sometimes happens that a mediated agreement is relevant to the claim of a third party in the same or other litigation. For example, if a plaintiff settles a claim with one defendant, the amount of the settlement may be deductible from the plaintiff's claim against another defendant. In such cases, the agreement must be disclosed to the third party, whether or not the parties to the mediation agree to keep it strictly confidential.

mediation–type skills (such as interest-based bargaining) could undoubtedly be useful to the engineers in meetings with members of the public, it would be misleading for them to describe what they do as 'mediation'.[9] If 'mediation' terminology were used, parties would have inaccurate expectations for the process. This might lead them to feel betrayed if it did not produce the results they want. The engineers themselves might become confused about their role, and, for example, might promise to keep information confidential. This could expose them to serious ethical and contractual problems when it came time to write their report to council.

PRIVATE v PUBLIC DISPUTES

The essential difference between a private mediation and the Drainage Act 'engineer's report' is that private mediations deal with private disputes; drainage engineers deal with disputes that are, in some senses, public. In a previous paper on environmental ADR,[10] I proposed that *private disputes* could be defined as those which, if not resolved, could result in a civil lawsuit between (and controlled by) two or more parties. Examples include: disputes between vendors and purchasers over the cost of cleanup of contaminated land; disputes between landlords and tenants; disputes between lenders and borrowers; and disputes between fuel companies and their customers.

In contrast, the key characteristic of a *public dispute* is that it affects the public interest. Therefore, the parties are generally not entitled to resolve it in complete privacy, and their own desires are not the only relevant factors. There may be large numbers of actual or potential parties. In addition, the 'public' is a necessary party. How the public is to be represented, and how its needs for notice and accountability can be met, are frequently critical issues in the use of ADR for public disputes. In general, these disputes have quite different characteristics:

PRIVATE DISPUTES	PUBLIC DISPUTES
The essential issue between the parties is a private one that affects no one else, eg, a private environmental dispute relates to responsibility for an environmental problem or its resolution, not to the degree of harm to the environment which should be allowed or continue.	The essential issue between the parties affects the public interest, eg a public environmental dispute relates to how a key public resource shall be used or protected.

---

9   For example, the parties might believe themselves entitled to control over the ultimate result, confidentiality, etc.

10   See Saxe, D, 'Environmental ADR', in Stitt, A (ed), *ADR Practice Manual,* 1995, Toronto: CCH.

PRIVATE DISPUTES	PUBLIC DISPUTES
The parties are legally entitled to compromise their dispute. That is, the parties own their dispute, and can resolve it as they see fit.	The parties do not have exclusive ownership of their dispute, precisely because of the public interest that is affected.
All of the parties can readily be identified. Generally, there is a limited number of parties. If not, there is a judicial procedure for allowing some parties to represent others (eg class actions).	There may be numerous unidentified or self-identified parties. Determining who are proper parties can be difficult and contentious, especially if there is a dispute about who represents the 'public interest', the 'environment', etc.
Government in its role as regulator or as prosecutor is not directly involved.	Government is involved, generally as an ultimate decision-maker who is not a party to the dispute and who is exercising a statutory power of decision, namely an administrative tribunal or regulator.
There is no legal requirement that the general public be consulted as to the resolution of the dispute.	The general public often has a right to be consulted or at least informed.
There is no legal requirement for a public hearing.	There may be a requirement for a public hearing.

Many characteristics of a public dispute cannot be readily accommodated in a classic private mediation:

- Mediation means that the parties bargain with each other. A regulator with a statutory power of decision will not, and perhaps cannot lawfully, make a bargain on how to exercise that power. It certainly cannot do so in private.
- In a public dispute, the ultimate decision-maker is usually unwilling to come to the table and treat the other parties as equals. Those who do come to the table must usually report back to someone.
- Parties are usually unwilling to make concessions without gaining something of value in exchange. In public disputes where the ultimate decision-maker is not at the table, all that can be obtained in exchange for a concession is an agreement to make a recommendation, which the ultimate decision maker may ignore. The parties therefore have less to offer each other, and a greater risk of giving up something without ultimately receiving something in return.
- The confidentiality which is generally essential in a mediation, (eg to permit safe disclosure of weakness, and exploration of possible solutions) is

incompatible with the public disclosure and consultation required of a decision on a matter of public interest.

- There is no obvious mechanism for public participation in a classic private mediation process.
- How can a mediation, which depends upon the consent of the parties, define who the parties should be?
- A mediation is not the legal equivalent of a public hearing.

Drainage disputes are often, at least to some extent, 'public' disputes. How, then, can ADR be best used to help resolve them?

MEDIATION BEFORE PETITION

Classic private mediation is possible at the earliest stages of a drainage project, before it legally becomes a 'public dispute'. That is, mediation could take place prior to invoking any of the statutory remedies under the Drainage Act. The goal of the mediation would be to finally resolve the dispute without government action, either through a mutual decision not to drain, or through a mutual agreement between directly affected landowners on what to drain and how to pay for it.

The Drainage Act provides for such agreements in s 2. These agreements do not require the approval of the municipality, nor a public engineer's report. No tax powers are used to enforce their funding, and the elaborate structure of the Drainage Act does not apply to them. Thus, the mediation itself could take place entirely outside the statutory framework and therefore would be a true private mediation.

Private mediation may also play a useful role in handling disputes that fall outside the Drainage Act. For example, the Drainage Act does not provide a mechanism for determining claims for compensation that arise *after* a drainage project has been completed. These must be resolved by common law claims in the civil courts. The best known case of this type is *Scarborough Golf and Country Club v City of Scarborough*.[11] At the time, Scarborough was a rapidly growing suburb of Toronto. As fields and woodlots were replaced by roads and subdivisions, rain water and snow melt ran off faster and with greater force. That, in turn, increased the erosion of local creek banks.[12] In this case, one of the creeks wound through a local golf course. The increased water volume and velocity caused so much erosion that it widened the stream and changed its course, seriously compromising some holes of the golf course. The golf course sued the City for allowing the creek to be altered in this way. Years later, after a very lengthy trial, it was awarded $3,076,146 plus pre-judgment interest and costs.

---

11 (1986) 55 OR (2d) 193.

12 This is a common and well-known consequence of 'development', and is typically dealt with 'channelising' the creeks. This increases their water-carrying capacity, although it greatly reduces their usefulness as aquatic habitat.

Private mediation of such disputes should have numerous advantages for the parties:

- *Control*: the parties themselves would determine the issues that they required resolved. The parties would retain control of the process, and could not be forced to accept any settlement without their consent. The mediator would owe no duties to any third parties. If the parties to the mediation agreed on the resolution to the dispute, the resolution would be final and binding and would not require the approval of any third party.

- *Choice of mediator*: the parties themselves would choose the mediator and pay for his or her services; thus they could reasonably demand and expect to receive rapid, responsive service.

- *Confidentiality*: the parties could keep the dispute, and even the fact that there was a dispute, strictly confidential.

- *Effectiveness*: because the mediation would take place early in the development of the dispute, a high success rate seems likely, thus achieving substantial savings for the parties to the dispute and for the regulatory agencies who would otherwise be drawn into it.[13]

In fact, private mediation of drainage disputes has rarely occurred, although there are dozens of mediators actively seeking environmental work. There are significant barriers to the employment of private mediators for such disputes, including:

- lack of awareness of mediation among the agricultural and rural community;

- substantial difficulties in locating competent mediators, especially in the absence of a clear accreditation process;

- lack of technical qualifications to understand the issues among general purpose mediators;

- lack of mediation qualifications among the drainage engineers who understand the technical issues;

- lack of appropriate physical facilities and

- fear of high, unpredictable costs.

ASSOCIATION-SPONSORED PRIVATE MEDIATION

One way to overcome these barriers may be to offer mediation under the aegis of a popular rural organisation such as the Ontario Federation of Agriculture or the Food and Vegetable Growers Association. Such associations could set up mediation

---

13 This assumption is based upon the high success rates of mediation in the automobile insurance and court-annexed ADR projects in Ontario, both of which usually take cases at an early stage. Both report achieving immediate settlements in 50% to 60% of the cases referred to them, usually in a single three hour session. Many other cases are resolved in the weeks following the mediation, building on the foundation established there. See Macfarlane, J, *Court-Based Mediation in Civil Cases: An Evaluation of the Ontario Court (General Division) ADR Centre*, 1995, Ontario: Ministry of the Attorney-General.

panels for the various regions of the province, consisting of experienced mediators with specialised training in drainage and hydrogeology.[14] Due to the substantial bargaining power of large associations, they should be able to negotiate attractive rates for the mediations on a fixed fee basis. A mediation program of this type would have the greatest likelihood of acceptance by the agricultural community.

Pamphlets distributed through association offices could advise the farming community of the availability of the service and its cost. The pamphlet could contain a simple mediation agreement, which could be dropped off or mailed together with the necessary cheque to the association. The association would take a small part of the fee and in exchange would make arrangements to obtain a mediator and an appropriate meeting space. With a sufficient roster, it ought to be possible to schedule a mediation within days or weeks. Urgent cases, such as an immediate shortfall of irrigation or drinking water, could be given particular priority.[15]

If the mediation is successful, the parties could consult a lawyer to prepare the formal agreement or could pay a further fee to the mediator or to the association to have such an agreement prepared for them. If the mediation is unsuccessful, the parties could request the mediator to prepare a report outlining the issues; this would help to clarify the dispute in any subsequent proceedings.[16]

MEDIATION BEFORE A PUBLIC HEARING

At the other end of the spectrum, some form of mediation could be made available as part of the proceedings of the Drainage Review Board.[17] Once filed with the Board, cases could be referred to a mediator at the option of any party or at the direction of the Board itself. If mediation has not been tried earlier in the dispute, it could well be useful at this stage.[18] In a sense, the goal of mediation is a return to the original objectives of the Drainage Review Board itself, namely to resolve disputes in a simple, inexpensive, expeditious manner, preferably without lawyers.

'Mediation' of public proceedings before administrative tribunals can undoubtedly be useful. I use the word 'mediation' here, as tribunals typically do, to refer to the effort, guided by a neutral, to assist the parties to agree. However, it would be more accurate to describe this process as 'facilitation'. A skilled

---

14   The actual task of recruiting and administering the panels could be contracted out to ADR service providers.

15   Very short time frames are also necessary to resolve disputes in the construction industry, and have been met consistently by construction mediators.

16   The parties would have to choose, perhaps in the mediation agreement, whether or not they wish this to take place. If they prefer, there will be no written record from the mediation; it would be as if it had never taken place.

17   Numerous administrative tribunals, notably the Environmental Assessment Board, have been examining opportunities for mediation to settle some matters and limit the scope of others.

18   If mediation has taken place at an early stage of the dispute, the parties should not be required to submit to it a second time. Seems unlikely that scarce resources would be efficiently utilised by being devoted to repeated rounds of mediation on the same dispute. If parties wish to try again, they always have the option to return to the original mediator, for an additional fee, by mutual consent.

facilitator, using interest–based bargaining, can help reduce the parties to bridge their differences, and to design solutions that can be recommended to the ultimate decision–maker. She/he can avoid some hearings and greatly shorten others, by helping each party to recognise and articulate its own underlying interests and to seek common ground with those of the other stakeholders. Misunderstandings are often resolved, and many questions answered, by the simple exchange of information. In many cases, mediation is the first face–to–face opportunity for the parties to seek common ground since the dispute arose.

However, 'mediation' at this stage is not the same as it would have been before the petition was issued. By the time a drainage dispute has reached the Board, it has generally become a public dispute. The ultimate decision–maker is the Board, not the parties themselves. The Board has an obligation to ensure that the public interest is protected, no matter what the parties prefer.[19] In this sense, the immediate parties no longer own their dispute, and no longer have unfettered right to settle. This is particularly the case where a tribunal must conclude its proceedings by issuing a permit.

The powers and responsibilities of a Board have both positive and negative effects upon the prospects for a mediated settlement. In terms of advantages, there is no difficulty in identifying the parties to the mediation and in getting them to take the dispute seriously: they are the parties to the dispute before the Board. Where mediation is a standard feature of an administrative proceeding, parties who are generally unfamiliar with mediation must give it serious consideration. In the notoriously conservative agricultural and legal communities, such 'compulsory' consideration is key to more general acceptance of mediation.

---

19   The Ontario Environmental Assessment Board provides a useful model here. This Board hears long, contested cases about the approval of projects with major environmental impacts such as landfills and forest clearcuts. In an effort to shorten its enormous hearings, it has developed the most experience of any Ontario tribunal with mediated or negotiated solutions in public disputes. It has adopted a policy to ensure that settlements by the parties are consistent with the public interest. Under this policy, the board will not accept settlement agreements at face value. The Board wants to ensure that the consultation and environmental assessment process has been appropriate and complete. There must have been a preliminary hearing, at which the parties were identified. All such parties must accept the agreement and must waive their right to a public hearing. At least one formal public meeting must have been held to ensure that other members of the public have had an opportunity to be heard.

The Board will also review the documentation to satisfy itself of the substantive merits of the settlement. Logical and traceable documentation must explain the rationale for the agreement. A mediator's report could provide much or all of the 'logical, traceable documentation' that the Board requires to satisfy itself that all party's interests have been heard and accommodated through a fair and reasonable process. Indeed, one of the objects of the mediation itself would be not only to reach agreement but also to prepare a mediation report that adequately describes the agreement and its rationale.

The Board wants proof that regulatory authorities, such as the Ministry of the Environment, agree that their requirements will be achieved by the proposed settlement. For this reason, the Board prefers that the Ministry actually participate in the negotiations and be a party to the settlement. If the regulatory authority is not a party to the agreement, the proponent must present evidence to the Board that all regulatory requirements will be achieved.

The Environment Appeal Board, which hears appeals from the Ministry of the Environment decisions, has taken this concern one step further. In order to protect the 'public interest', this Board asserts the right to prevent the parties from settling any matter before it, even if the result of the settlement would be to withdraw the appeal completely.

The parties do not have the burden of finding a mediator, of designing a mediation agreement or of determining the appropriate process. All of this is done for them by the tribunal. The very fact that a hearing is approaching changes the legal options of the parties. Under tribunal rules, they must shortly disclose their whole case to each other; this means they must be well-prepared and makes it less attractive to hold back information.

Cost is also a significant factor affecting parties' willingness to attempt mediation. Administrative tribunals have generally provided mediators to the parties free of charge, in order to save the much greater expense of a publicly funded hearing. The costs and uncertainty of a hearing also begin to come home to the parties once a hearing is approaching and they must pay their lawyer to prepare for it.

On the other hand, the actual negotiations in a tribunal-annexed mediation are much more difficult than in a private mediation. Bargaining is more difficult where the actual decision-maker (here, the panel of tribunal members assigned to the dispute) is not at the table. Parties are usually unwilling to make concessions without gaining something of value in exchange. In these mediations, all that can be obtained in exchange for a concession by one or more parties is an agreement to make a recommendation, which the ultimate decision-maker(s) may reject. The parties therefore have less to offer each other, and a greater risk of giving up something without ultimately receiving something in return.

In private mediations, confidentiality is often the key factor that allows the parties to agree. It is confidentiality which permits parties to safely explore areas of weakness, make conditional concessions and explore possible solutions. Board-annexed mediations can provide very limited confidentiality, for at least three reasons:

- the neutral is typically either a member of the decision-making tribunal, or an employee of that tribunal;[20]

- any mediated solution must be reported to the Board, which must be persuaded that it is in the public interest; and

- there are often one or more organisations as parties that cannot obtain authority to agree without making a full report to their members.

The close relationship between the neutral and the Board can make a 'mediation' no more than an introduction to the hearing. Nothing can be said to the 'neutral' in confidence; everything said or done by any party may be taken into account by the tribunal in its final decision. The behaviour of the parties at the 'mediation' may be reported to the decision-maker, who may let it affect their ultimate decision. Will a party that gives up too little in 'mediation' be branded by the tribunal as unreasonable? Will a party that offers too much in

---

20 For example, all 'mediations' at the Environmental Appeal Board are performed by a member of the Board. Although the panel assigned to the case is not present during the mediation, there is no assurance that the panel members will not discuss the case with the 'mediator'.

'mediation' encourage the tribunal to include its 'concession' in the final result, even if that party did not obtain the concession it was seeking in exchange?

Thus, a substantial tension is set up. The success of mediation typically depends upon its informality and confidentiality; the parties are free to be open with one another because what they say cannot be used against them. Typically, the parties are also powerfully driven by the opportunity to obtain a certain result now rather than hope for a more favourable but less certain result later on. Board requirements for transparency and for the ultimate right of decision powerfully undermine both of these motivations.

Moreover, cases reach the Drainage Review Board only after the dispute has festered for a long time and the parties have hardened their positions by moving through a series of earlier appeals. This could also have an adverse effect upon the likelihood that mediation would be useful at this stage in the dispute.

THE ONTARIO WATER RESOURCES ACT

Water taking permits

The Ontario Water Resources Act is a broad ranging statute first adopted in 1961. In contrast to the Drainage Act, the OWRA is almost completely lacking in procedures and relies heavily on the Director's discretion.

This Act is concerned primarily with protection of water quality, with the proper construction of sewage and water works, and with licensing of well drillers. However, it does have one section to protect water quantity. A 'permit to take water' is required for any system that takes more than 50,000 litres per day from ground or surface waters.[21]

There are two major exceptions:

- a grandfather clause, exempting wells or waterworks which were constructed prior to March 29, 1961 (when the Act first came into force) and which have not been altered since that time;

- a 'domestic uses' exemption for water taken by any person (other than a professional distributor of water) for ordinary household purposes or for watering of livestock, poultry, home gardens or lawns.[22]

Water taken for ordinary human household purposes, for the immediate watering of livestock or poultry, or for fire fighting are always exempt from control (s 34(4)). Other uses, although normally exempt, require permits when, in the opinion of an official known as the Director, they 'interfere with any public or private interest in any water'.

---

21 Section 34.

22 This exemption does not apply to irrigation of crops which are grown for sale.

Of all the permits issued by the Ministry of the Environment, this is the easiest to obtain or to renew. The permits are generally issued for five or 10 years and authorise removal of a specified volume of water without other conditions. There are no public hearings; water taking need not be reduced in dry years; the applicant need not give financial security; neighbours of the applicant are not even entitled to notice.

Ministry hydrogeologists do try to space out water-taking permits so that there will be enough water for all, by requiring, eg that applicants locate new wells near the centre of their property. However, this method becomes less successful as population density increases and properties are subdivided, or as water demands increase.[23]

On the other hand, a water-taking permit is theoretically the easiest environmental permit to alter or revoke. Surprisingly, the issuance, alteration or revocation of these permits is not subject to any appeal. No one is entitled to receive notice, and the Director is not expressly required to give reasons or even to have reasonable grounds.[24] In practice, it has been very rare for water-taking permits to be revoked.

MEDIATION OF PERMIT ISSUES

Water-taking permits, being allocations of a scarce and valuable public resource, are matters of public interest. Thus, if 'mediation' were to be used in water permit cases, it would have to address the complex issues of confidentiality, public participation, and delegation of decision-making power that are discussed in relation to the Drainage Act.

In fact, however, mediation of the process of granting or revoking water taking permits is unknown, and to date, regulators have shown no interest in trying it. Upon reflection, this is not surprising. The allocation of power between water user, regulator and neighbour is highly uneven: the neighbour has no legal status in the permit proceedings, and the regulator has the sole right to decide. As discussed below ('disputes between neighbours'), regulators are often interested in mediation between one neighbour and another, simply to make their own jobs easier. However, they are not interested in mediation between an applicant and themselves, because this entails a lessening of their own power as regulators.

Under the OWRA, the Director has unfettered discretion to issue, alter or revoke water taking permits. S/he can meet with an applicant or neighbour, discuss her concerns, and take those into account when making a decision; all of

---

23 For domestic requirements, water quantity competition is usually limited by the stringent setback rules applicable to private sewage systems. These rules limit the density of development outside municipally serviced areas, often to the chagrin of property owners. Septic system permit disputes can be appealed to and decided by an Environmental Appeal Tribunal. Therefore, active water taking disputes are often concentrated among high volume water users.

24 This clearly betrays the 1961 origin of this part of the statute and the fact that it has never been updated.

this reinforces the Director's power. In contrast, the concept of mediation, with its assumption that all parties have equal rights in making the ultimate decision, means that the Director must have substantive control with the other party, and give up procedural control to the mediator. These losses are not off-set by any gain for the regulator. Thus it is no surprise that regulators bridle at the suggestion that permit granting be mediated; they don't feel that they need a mediator to help them do their jobs.

DISPUTES BETWEEN NEIGHBOURS

When water disputes arise between neighbours, the Ontario Water Resources Act provides no mechanism to resolve them. Accordingly, aggrieved water users turn to the courts and seek common law remedies. The leading case over excessive water taking is *Pugliese v National Capital Commission*.[25] In that case, the National Capital Commission constructed a new sewer main in a residential area. In order to keep the excavation dry, they decided to lower the ground water table by more than 10 metres.[26] Contractors 'dewatered' the area by pumping out large volumes of groundwater, far exceeding 50,000 litres per day, for a year and a half, all without the benefit of an OWRA permit. This caused the ground under more than one hundred neighbouring houses to subside, causing damage estimated at $2,000,000.

The homeowners successfully sued the Commission for this damage. The courts ruled that every person[27] has a common law obligation to exercise their right to take water reasonably so as to avoid harming their neighbours. They also agreed that the statutory threshold of 50,000 litres per day (without a permit) was the presumptive measure of what was reasonable. However, it is noteworthy that, even in the 1970's, the courts took four years to resolve a single preliminary motion; it took much longer before the plaintiffs actually received money to repair their homes.

Could ADR be used to help manage disputes such as this? Once the *Pugliese* dispute had ripened into a full-scale lawsuit, it was framed as a private, common law action, and all that was at stake was money. Such actions are frequently resolved through normal private mediation, if neither party needs to set a precedent. In *Pugliese*, there would have been some challenges due to the large number of plaintiffs, but these same challenges arose in the court and can be overcome.

There might have been a much earlier opportunity to use mediation; during the construction project itself. If the neighbours had realised at that time that their houses were settling, and had brought their concerns to the City's attention, it might have been possible to change the system of dewatering and prevent serious damage to the homes.

---

25 (1978) 8 CELR 68 (SCC).

26 This was presumably cheaper than the alternative of using compressed air during tunnelling.

27 Including a Government authority.

Timely awareness may not occur where homes slowly subside, but everyone notices when their water runs out. This points to another opportunity for technically qualified mediators or facilitators: to resolve disputes between neighbouring water users. In dry years, when water demand is high, disputes over fair water use are urgent and cannot wait for the outcome of litigation. To date, government officials working for the Director have tried to resolve these disputes. Their technical skills are not in doubt, but they have often found it a difficult and frustrating task. Informal mediation or facilitation skills would help them to better understand and manage the human side of these conflicts.

However, like the engineer under the Drainage Act, the Director (and his/her subordinates) are not neutral facilitators of a process of negotiations. The Director can control the result. She or he has a mandate to protect water quantity, and the statutory power to issue, alter and revoke water permits. Thus, if neighbours cannot agree, the Director can promptly intervene and force a change. No one else can do so. Even if the neighbours do agree, the Director may override their decision in order to protect public and private interests in water, including those of wildlife. Confidentiality is limited, because government officials are accountable to the Director, to their Minister, to the public and to the courts for the way they exercise their statutory powers.

Officials with such powers should not be described as mediators; mediators, if desired, would have to work outside the regulatory structure. Therefore, attempts to better manage these disputes should focus on improving the conflict management skills of the technically qualified staff of the Director. If funds permit, this can be supplemented by a panel of independent mediators who will be available for private mediations on request.[28]

In summary, the minimalist legislative scheme for disputes over water taking, which relies on the broad discretion of a regulator and not on the rights of parties, dramatically reduces both opportunities to use mediation and regulators' interest in doing so. However, there is an opportunity to reduce disputes by providing mediation–like, conflict-resolution skills to the front line staff who deal with water–taking issues.

CONCLUSION

This comparison between the Drainage Act and the Ontario Water Resources Act illustrates the importance of calibrating dispute resolution processes to the legislative scheme, and to the allocation of powers and interests between the parties to the dispute and the proposed neutral.

---

28 Neither of these approaches help the regulators to balance human needs and desires with the water requirements of wildlife and ecosystems. Mediation is designed to find common ground between people who can come to the table and bargain; it is not well-adapted to protect the interests of those who cannot bargain.

The term 'mediation' is best reserved for private disputes where the mediator is truly an independent neutral, with no stake in the substantive outcome, owing no duties to outsiders, and able to maintain confidentiality. Related processes based on interest-based bargaining, which are often loosely referred to as mediation, can play a useful role in many processes of government, including the issuance of permits and appeals to administrative tribunals. However, in these cases, careful attention must be paid to the powers and duties of the 'mediator', and to ensure that the expectations of parties and 'mediators' are adjusted accordingly.

10 COMPLAINT-MEDIATION IN PROFESSIONS

LISA FELD and PETER A SIMM*

INTRODUCTION

A person who is dissatisfied with the services provided by a member of a regulated profession may sue for malpractice. Another possible course of action is to complain to the agency which is statutorily mandated to govern that profession in accordance with protecting the public interest (the 'professional agency'). Staff at the professional agency would then investigate the complaint. If the agency's Complaints Committee found that a formal disciplinary hearing is warranted, the matter would be referred for that purpose to the agency's Discipline Committee.

In this paper we employ the term 'complaint-mediation' to refer to the voluntary process of using an intermediary to bring together a complainant, the subject member of the profession (the 'practitioner'), *and* the professional agency as parties trying to reach an agreement that will resolve a complaint without resorting to formal (statutory) discipline processes. As discussed below, there are two basic forms of complaint-mediation.

Complaint-mediation is a successful application of mediation in a new arena. In the late 1980s, the Australian state of Victoria pioneered the use of mediation in resolving complaints against health professionals. Some American states have formally experimented with mediation in settling medical malpractice lawsuits, but Ontario appears to be the only jurisdiction in North America where mediation is routinely being used to resolve complaints against members of health professions in the context of professional discipline.[1]

The standard conception of mediation, where a neutral mediator serves to help the parties reach a settlement, may be more specifically termed 'neutral mediation'. In distinction, the term 'interested mediation' may be used to refer to a hybrid of conventional mediation and negotiation: the person facilitating

---

*   Respectively Partner, Stitt Feld Handy, Houston; and former Research Associate, Stitt Feld Handy, Houston. Lisa Feld, BA, LLB, and Peter A Simm, BComm, LLB, are both members of the Ontario Bar practising in Toronto. This paper is drawn from Feld, L and Simm, P, *Complaint-Mediation in Ontario's Self-Governing Professions*, 1995, p 212, Waterloo, Ontario: Fund for Dispute Resolution. The authors served, respectively, as Executive Director and as Associate Director of the Study on Complaint-Mediation, conducted under the auspices of the Program on Negotiation at Harvard Law School. The authors wish to thank Ms L Jane Plaxton of the Ontario Bar for her able assistance in summarising a portion of the Study for this paper.

1   In Ontario, there is authority in s 4 Statutory Powers Procedure Act for a professional agency to use ADR to attempt to resolve complaints, even if express authority is not contained in the agency's particular governing statute. This statutory authority is crucial, because acquiescence or agreement by a practitioner cannot in law confer jurisdiction on a professional agency's organ: *Harris v Law Society (Alta)* [1936] 1 DLR 401 at 413; [1936] SCR 88 (SCC); *Branigan v Yukon Medical Council (No 2)* (1986) 21 Admin LR 149 (YTSC).

the negotiations is neutral as between the other parties, but openly seeks to advance an identifiable, ostensibly altruistic interest. We have coined the expression interested complaint-mediation (ICM) for the application of interested mediation to the resolution of a complaint. Here, the professional agency's representative is neutral as between the complainant[2] and the practitioner, and focuses on helping them reach an agreement. But unlike a conventional mediator, the facilitator also acts as a party to the process by advancing a particular interest – in this context one which aims to be synonymous with protection of the 'public interest'.

What we have labelled neutral complaint-mediation (NCM) is the modified application of neutral mediation to the resolution of complaints which implicate the public interest. This process, which is the focus of our paper, differs from ICM in several important respects. NCM is conducted by a mediator who is not the professional agency's employee, and who is neutral as to the specific terms negotiated (ie is not seeking to advance any position relating to the public interest or, indeed, any position at all). The agency, as represented by an authorised staff person, is itself a full party in NCM, and as such seeks to ensure that any agreement reached serves and protects the public interest. Finally, the mediator in NCM would not be callable as a witness in any subsequent proceedings.

The medical profession, through its professional agency, the College of Physicians and Surgeons of Ontario (CPSO), was the first self-governing profession in Ontario to institute a complaint-mediation program. The CPSO's model of neutral complaint-mediation has yielded agreements resolving complaints without a formal disciplinary hearing in almost 85% of the cases where it has been attempted. NCM has also achieved an overwhelming rate of satisfaction from both physicians and complainants in cases where agreements have been reached. Since each such agreement has also been ratified by the CPSO's Discipline Committee, that professional agency must be taken to be 'satisfied' that the public interest was served and protected. There is only a single known instance of a physician not complying with a mediated agreement.

The CPSO's model of complaint-mediation has proven to be a viable process for resolving some complaints made against practitioners. However, certain cases, such as those involving allegations of incompetence, incapacity,[3] or sexual abuse, are recognised as not amenable to complaint-mediation because the public interest requires a formal hearing if the professional agency is seeking to revoke the practitioner's license. Complaint-mediation would also not be offered as an

---

2   The College of Physicians and Surgeons of Ontario uses ICM primarily to resolve complaints made by institutions or arising from investigations by its staff. In cases arising from complaints by individuals, neutral complaint-mediation (below) is ordinarily used. However, ICM has been successfully used to resolve some relatively simple complaints filed by individuals who had no emotional stake and no interest in any further involvement.

3   An isolated clinical error might subject a health professional to disciplinary sanctions if he is found to have failed to maintain the standard of practice of the profession, but would not ground a finding of 'incompetence' unless the error were so egregious that it demonstrates that he is unfit to continue to practise. 'Incapacity' proceedings, which relate to the temporary or permanent suspension of practitioners with health problems or addictions, technically are not part of the disciplinary process.

alternative to the formal disciplinary process in a case where there is no reasonable prospect that an agreement could be reached and enforced. The severity of an adverse clinical outcome does not bear on the appropriateness of offering complaint-mediation; however, our study found that an agreement is much less likely in a case where the complainant is not the same person as the patient, such as where the patient has died or is a child. A professional agency contemplating using any form of ADR (alternative dispute resolution) to resolve complaints should carefully formulate a screening protocol for selecting the cases in which ADR will be attempted. Our study offers a framework for establishing such a protocol.

When used appropriately, complaint-mediation has several significant advantages over formal disciplinary processes, as discussed below. The potential disadvantages of complaint-mediation can be greatly alleviated or eliminated with proper program design.

Although complaint-mediation does not render all formal disciplinary hearings obsolete, it is not in the public interest to rely exclusively on the standard complaints/discipline mechanisms (see below). Complaint-mediation can, and should, be harmonised to co-exist with formal disciplinary processes, as well as with other modes of ADR that a professional agency might use to resolve complaints. Some form of ADR may be appropriate at several different stages in the complaints/discipline process.

PROBLEMS WITH PRESENT PROFESSIONAL COMPLAINTS/DISCIPLINE PROCESSES

GENERAL

The annual reports of many professional agencies show that they share certain frustrations in dealing with complaints against practitioners. One recurring lament is the high cost of formal disciplinary hearings. Another common theme is that most complaints could have been avoided if the subject practitioners had exercised better communication skills.

Many professional agencies seem to approach each complaint with a 'do-everything' or 'do-nothing' philosophy. This situation arises where an agency misinterprets its statutory duties to mean that when a complaint comes in, the agency must either dismiss it *or* proceed to a formal hearing, with nothing between these two extremes. Not surprisingly, agencies which fall prey to this false dichotomy recognise that their complaint-handling processes leave many complainants unsatisfied.

Although the governing statutes of some professional agencies expressly provide for certain ADR processes, these provisions have atrophied from disuse and neglect. A prime example of this neglect is the failure by some professional agencies to utilise fee-mediation committees where they have been explicitly authorised by statute. One agency admitted that if a person complains about a practitioner's fees, the complainant is not informed that the agency (theoretically) offers a fee-mediation service: the agency believes that a complaint is never merely about fees, and therefore always warrants a fuller investigation.[4]

We observe that explicit statutory permission for a professional agency to attempt ADR to resolve certain complaints is demonstrably insufficient to ensure the actual introduction, use, or institutionalisation of any ADR process at the agency. Without political will within the agency – in its Complaints Committee, Discipline Committee, and General Council – mere statutory authority to use ADR is not enough to overcome institutional inertia.

PROBLEMS WITH THE FUNCTIONING OF COMPLAINTS/DISCIPLINE COMMITTEES

In many professional agencies, the Complaints Committee is often unsure as to what it can and cannot do with a complaint, other than dismissing it or referring it to the Discipline Committee for a formal hearing. It is a commonly expressed concern that the statutorily mandated protection of the public interest reflected in the discipline process should not have to translate into the automatic, total exclusion of the private interests of the complainant from the minds of the decision-makers in the context of a disciplinary proceeding.

Discipline Committees also suffer from a variety of problems, which include some committees still being run like 'old boys clubs', as well as the difficulties all committees have in dealing with very complex issues and legal arguments. Perpetual difficulties typically include making decisions in a timely manner, fashioning appropriate penalties, writing reasons that can withstand judicial scrutiny, and maintaining committee expertise in the face of turnover of committee membership.

RELUCTANCE OF COMPLAINANTS TO APPEAR AS WITNESSES

As in any formal proceedings that depend on independent oral evidence, professional agencies have a problem with reluctant witnesses at disciplinary hearings. This difficulty is especially pronounced with witnesses who reside outside the hearing's locale, practitioners who complain on behalf of clients, and practitioners who lodge a complaint on their own behalf against a colleague.

There is generally surprise, followed by reluctance, when complainants learn that a formal hearing, akin to a trial, will be held and that they will be testifying under oath and be subject to cross-examination. Very often, complainants misunderstand their role in the hearing procedure, which is that of witness and not as party. It is common for them to ask, on learning that they will be cross-examined, 'Why am I on trial? I didn't do anything wrong'. To avoid this

---

4   Another agency explained that although it now has the power to mediate enshrined in its governing legislation, the agency still was not entirely certain as to exactly how, or if, it would use it in the near future.

misunderstanding and to reassure the witness, prosecutors must carefully explain why a hearing is being held and why the complainant is a necessary witness.

DELAYS IN FORMAL PROCEEDINGS

Another common difficulty faced by professional agencies is that their complaints/discipline processes have substantial backlogs. Professional agencies in Ontario anticipate that this problem will continue to increase. Delays are inconvenient and extremely costly, adding to the financial burden of an already expensive hearing process. Systematic delays cause great frustration for the agency, the complainant, and the practitioner, and may cause personal hardship in the form of severe anxiety and stress. Frequently, the slowness of the formal process is partly blamed on adjournments and motions on procedural issues brought by defence lawyers, who may be involved at every step.

PROBLEMS WITH DEFENCE COUNSEL AND UNREPRESENTED MEMBERS

Professional agencies often 'blame' assiduous lawyers for some of the problems with the operation of the formal complaints/discipline processes. Conversely, some problems can be attributed to defence counsel who are not familiar with the tribunal's process or the relevant law, and even more severe problems can occur when a practitioner appears at a disciplinary hearing without counsel. Despite concerns that some agencies express about lawyers in the process, it is accepted policy that complaints and discipline matters are very serious and that the practitioner and the complainant deserve to have all the protections afforded by law.

LACK OF INFORMATION FOR MEMBERS

Practitioners often do not truly understand the workings or mandate of their professional agency.[5] Apparently some believe that the agency exists to represent the interest of practitioners, rather than to protect the public interest. This could explain why many practitioners are extremely defensive about complaints and consequently may provide inappropriate written responses[6] which can effectively compound the original allegations. The complainant ordinarily is given a copy of the practitioner's written response and is invited to provide further comments. Professional agencies commonly believe that if the initial written responses by practitioners more frequently contained an acknowledgment or apology, the number of cases referred to disciplinary

---

5   Confusion often arises because in many professions there is a voluntary organisation that may lobby or bargain on behalf of practitioners in addition to the body charged with regulating the profession. For example, the Ontario Medical Association is a non-statutory entity that purports to represent the interest of physicians in Ontario, while the CPSO is charged with regulating the province's medical doctors.

6   In Ontario, professions that are governed by the Regulated Health Professions Act, the professional agency's Registrar must give the practitioner notice of a complaint that has been filed, and inform him that he is entitled within 30 days to make a written submission to the agency's Complaints Committee.

hearings would diminish.[7] Indeed, we found that an overwhelming majority of complainants entering the CPSO's complaint-mediation program are seeking, among other things, acknowledgment by the physician of improper or inadequate medical care. A majority are also seeking acknowledgment of the harm suffered.

Generally, if practitioners better understood the workings of the complaints process, cases could possibly be dealt with more expeditiously and certainly less expensively. Professional agencies are not mandated to assume the role of defence counsel, but should take reasonable steps to ensure that the unrepresented practitioner understands his obligations and rights within the complaints/discipline process, and within any ADR process that might be offered.

PROFESSIONAL DISCIPLINE AND COMPLAINT-MEDIATION

THE CONCEPT OF PROFESSIONAL DISCIPLINE AND SELF-REGULATION

Professional regulation is comprised of the range of methods and processes used to bestow a license on a practitioner and to deal with a licensed practitioner who no longer is deserving of a license, or, whose behaviour merits active disapprobation. Professional discipline is an element of professional regulation. It addresses a variety of problems, such as where a practitioner has behaved inappropriately, performed negligently in a particular instance, or become incompetent. Discipline potentially threatens the practitioner's registration, without which she cannot legally practise.

McCarberg observes that 'few professionals relish the prospect of judging a peer.' As members of a self-governing profession, practitioners may see themselves as owing their wayward colleagues a realistic opportunity for rehabilitation, and so seek to offer them appropriate retraining and re-education. Since a practitioner's work involves judgment and intuition as well as technical knowledge and a particular skill-set, there is often no clear-cut, preferred method to approach a particular problem. This latitude makes it difficult to say with confidence whether a decision was inappropriate based on what was known at the time. McCarberg further notes that 'Peer pressure, and empathy with the accused, also inhibit speaking out against perceived errors or abuses in one's profession.'[8]

The existence of a formal system of discipline is presumed to have some deterrent effect in discouraging practitioners from becoming lax in their knowledge, skills, ethics, and practice patterns. Indeed, where a practitioner is found guilty of professional misconduct, there may be extended discussion of the

---

7   Such a letter might, of course, be introduced at a hearing in cross-examination.

8   McCarberg, PJ, 'Discipline of the Errant Health Professional', in Falk, DS, Weisfeld, N and McCarberg, PJ (eds), *To Assure Continuing Competence: A Report to the National Commission for Health Certifying Agencies*, 1981, p 100, Washington, DC: US Dept of Health and Human Services.

appropriate form of sanction out of the limited types traditionally available, given that loss of a license would effectively preclude the professional from earning a livelihood. Of course, the formal disciplinary process is not the only means of quality control in a profession. The potential for informal disapprobation by colleagues and clients has some deterrent effect. As well, there are a variety of other mechanisms that help ensure that professionals are competent, such as systematic peer review, audits, risk management, continuing education, information feedback, evaluation, and negligence litigation.[9]

The practitioner who comes to the attention of the discipline process is entitled to a host of legal protections. In the jargon of administrative law, these are collectively referred to as 'natural justice' or 'fairness,' and may be found in the common law and/or statutes and regulations. In recognition of the serious consequences that a disciplinary hearing may have for a professional, these safeguards include the right to: receive notice of the allegation; have the grounds of the hearing set forth explicitly so that they may be challenged; be aided by counsel; present evidence in one's own defence; cross-examine adverse witnesses and hear their testimony; be judged only by an impartial and unbiased panel; have a full and fair hearing; have the decision reviewed fairly; and face no punishment grossly disproportionate to the severity of the offence.

Unfortunately, these laudable and necessary protections frequently cause disciplinary actions to drag on and to entail huge expenditures of resources.[10] Because the consequences of an adverse finding may be so devastating for a professional, it is not uncommon for negative outcomes to be appealed (or for judicial review to be sought) on the grounds of some denial of natural justice.[11]

The modern conceptual framework for professional discipline has a prophylactic rather than a punitive focus: the purpose of discipline is not to punish the errant professional; rather, it is to protect the public from harm. We found that this prophylactic focus accords with the motivations of most complainants. McCarberg is representative of most modern thinking on professional discipline when she states:[12]

> [R]evocation of the right to practice is evidence of a failed attempt at rehabilitation of an errant health worker, so that license revocations should not be tallied with smug satisfaction as proof of success of a disciplinary program. ... [L]icense revocation should be the final step in a long process of efforts to update the knowledge and skills of a health worker. ... [T]he goal of discipline is not the destruction of incompetent individuals, but rather retraining or rehabilitating while it is still possible.

---

9   Rosenthal, MM, 'Medical Discipline in Cross-Cultural Perspective: The United States, Britain and Sweden', in Dingwall, R and Fenn, P (eds), *Quality and Regulation in Health Care: International Experiences*, 1992, Chapter 2, pp 27–50, London and New York: Routledge.

10 Personal communications with Linda Bohnen, barrister and solicitor, who was substantially responsible for drafting the Regulated Health Professions Act in Ontario.

11 Even though they may be acting with the utmost good faith, members of disciplinary panels generally have no legal training (though the panel may obtain impartial legal advice on procedural matters).

12 McCarberg, PJ above note 8, pp 114–15.

Revocation of a license is not without costs for society. The public loses the care of a professional, whose formal education was heavily subsidised by taxpayers. Obviously, the individual's livelihood and self-image will be severely damaged, and the accompanying stresses and dislocations may also harm his personal relationships. Yet, if the professional is incorrigible, then license revocation may be the only solution available that adequately protects the public interest.

SOURCES AND TYPES OF COMPLAINTS

There are generally four sources of complaints against members of a self-governing profession: clients, employers, insurance companies, and professional colleagues. Professional agencies typically perceive that an overwhelming proportion of complaints by clients relate to communication problems. In most cases referred to neutral complaint-mediation at the CPSO, a failure of communication or insensitivity by the physician was at the root of the complaint, but perceived professional/technical failure was also a widespread basis for complaints. We found that a complainant tends to have a richer and more complex view of his complaint than is perceived by the subject practitioner, even where the latter has participated in a successful mediation of the complaint.

Where clients pay directly for a professional's services (eg the fees of lawyers, architects, engineers, veterinarians, accountants, or funeral directors), or where there often is a full or partial recovery from a private insurance company (eg for the fees of optometrists, dentists, pharmacists, physiotherapists, registered massage therapists), the relevant professional agency finds that most complains relate to excessive billing. Many complaints also pertain to the practitioner's failure to issue a receipt for the purpose of obtaining insurance reimbursement.

Another major category of consumer complaints relates to the attitude of the practitioner, manifested in such unprofessional activities as rude behaviour in collecting fees, making inappropriate or rude remarks, or failing to adequately respect the patient's privacy.

Complaints also come from employers, insurance companies, colleagues, and ex-colleagues, and these allegations are often much more serious. Some employers (such as hospitals) have a mandatory statutory duty to inform the appropriate professional agency of improper or deficient conduct by professional staff. This is often how professional agencies learn about impaired professionals and those professionals who fail to meet the profession's standards of practice. Allegations of fraud and other serious (and possibility criminal) acts tend to come from the police, insurance companies, and ex-partners. For example, members of the architecture profession, rather than members of the public, tend to be the primary source of complaints to the Ontario Association of Architects about other practitioners' alleged copyright infringement, slanderous statements, or collusion on project-bidding.

A 'TYPICAL'[13] COMPLAINT AND COMPLAINTS PROCESS

The following is a hypothetical synopsis of a 'typical' complaint and subsequent process based on the law, policies and procedures of various self-regulating professions in 'Montario'.

The agency

The Board of Registered Pastry Chefs of Montario (the 'Board') is the professional agency responsible for licensing pastry chefs in the province. It was created under the Pastry Chefs Act as that profession's self-governing body. The Board has the statutory mandate to develop, establish, and maintain: standards of qualification for persons to receive and retain certificates of registration; programs and standards of practice to assure the quality of practice; standards of knowledge and skills and programs to promote continuing competence among the members; standards of professional ethics for the members; processes to assist individuals to exercise their rights to complain about professionals; and processes to determine allegations of professional misconduct.

The complaint

While enjoying brunch with her family three months ago at the Garden Roof Restaurant, the complainant, Ms Enid Eater, ordered and consumed a chocolate eclair. It caused her severe stomach pains for two weeks. She specifically recalls asking the waiter the exact ingredients of the eclair as she has certain allergic reactions to carob beans and oil. The waiter returned, explained he had spoken to the pastry chef, and assured Ms Eater that she should not have any problems with the eclair. When the eclair was brought to her, she assumed it was made with pure milk chocolate and pure whipped cream.

Within five minutes, she began to develop severe stomach cramps. Her family took her home immediately, where she was bedridden for two weeks, recovering from an allergic reaction to an edible oil product and carob flakes.

Ms Eater needed her daughter-in-law to help her with her housework while she was unwell. Ms Eater has vowed never to return to the Garden Roof again, especially after the telephone call she had with the manager. He curtly blamed her for not asking the waiter the proper questions and claimed no responsibility for her allergic reaction. Ms Eater was angry at the rude response, and decided that the proper authorities should know about the pastry chef's error and how it effected her.

---

13 The Board and the specific facts are, of course, fictitious.

The process

With the support of her family, Ms Eater called the Board and was invited to put her complaint in writing. The Board forwarded a copy of her written complaint to the pastry chef, Mr Daniel Danish, for his response. He was also asked to provide the Board with a copy of his records for that day.

Besides being a duly licensed pastry chef, Mr Danish is proprietor of the Garden Roof. He graduated from Choux University five years ago and was registered in Montario three years ago. This is the first complaint the Board has received about him. In his written response to the College, Mr Danish denied any responsibility for Ms Eater's problem. He recalled the conversation with the waiter as an inquiry as to whether someone with allergies could eat an eclair. Mr Danish took the inquiry to mean that the patron suffered from a lactose intolerance. Because he never uses milk-based products, he accordingly had declared that she would have no problem with the eclair.

Mr Danish also admitted that he failed to keep a full and proper record of his conversation with the waiter, but asserted that it was his usual practice to keep a full and proper record of such matters in his daily journal.

The Board's Registrar ordered staff to retain an expert pastry chef to investigate the complaint. A full inspection report revealed that the Garden Roof violated certain regulations with respect to the preparation and presentation of pastries.

If, after proceeding through the usual complaint process, the matter was to be referred to a formal discipline hearing, the prosecutor would draft a formal Notice of Hearing, interview all witnesses, and retain an expert witness to substantiate the allegations of professional misconduct (which would probably include 'failing to meet the standard of practice of the profession').

At the hearing, Ms Eater would not be a party, but might be called as a witness (in which event she would be subject to cross-examination). Mr Danish would be given the opportunity to present a full defence.

If Mr Danish were found guilty, counsel for the Board would make a recommendation regarding penalty, without consulting Ms Eater. Also, she would not participate in the penalty phase of a hearing. The Discipline Committee's choice of penalties would be limited to those provided by law (eg a reprimand, a fine, or suspension). Mr Danish could appeal the finding and penalty to a court.

CRITERIA FOR SELECTING ADR PROCESSES

Comparing mediation to judicial involvement in the resolution of public-interest disputes, Phillips and Piazza observe:[14]

---

14 Phillips, B and Piazza, AC, 'The Role of Mediation in Public Interest Disputes' (1983) 34 *Hastings LJ* 1231–44, at 1233–34.

By contrast, mediated negotiations allow public agencies to maintain their delegated role of administering policies set by the legislature; the agencies simply are given the opportunity to perform that role with the advantage of input from the most directly concerned sector of the public.

The introduction and institutionalisation of ADR in resolving complaints against professionals raises a number of questions. If an allegation is considered very serious, then a formal disciplinary hearing may be required. However, if the case meets the ADR screening criteria, an agency may well employ more than one model of ADR (our study presents six specific models, including NCM and ICM), with the applicable model depending on, among other things, the case's stage in the complaint-handling process; and whether the allegations were made by a public complainant, an institution, or by agency staff on the basis of an inspection.

In broader terms, the following considerations (in addition to transaction costs) should govern the choice of a dispute-resolution process:

- the extent to which a creative – rather than strictly monetary – result is possible or desirable;
- the value placed by the parties on their future relationship;
- the need for the parties to cooperate in implementing or complying with a solution;
- the parties' desire to be listened to, to participate actively in the process, and to retain control over the outcome;
- the need for finality, and thus the avoidance of appeals or other challenges to the result;
- the desirability of establishing a principle to govern the resolution of future disputes; and
- the parties' preference for an objective standard of what is a 'fair' result, versus their own private notions of fairness.

In addition, in selecting any alternative to a formal disciplinary process, an agency must ensure that the public interest is protected, and that the process conforms with the agency's statutory framework.

CAN COMPLAINT-MEDIATION STILL PROTECT THE PUBLIC INTEREST?

NEUTRAL COMPLAINT-MEDIATION (NCM) AT THE COLLEGE OF PHYSICIANS AND SURGEONS OF ONTARIO

The Statutory Powers Procedure Act ('SPPA') is the statute which governs most administrative hearings in Ontario. It contains a provision which, by necessary implication, provides the statutory authorisation for neutral complaint-mediation. Subsection 4(a) of the SPPA provides that proceedings otherwise requiring a hearing may be disposed of by agreement where the parties have waived such hearing. Accordingly, if the complainant, the practitioner, and the agency have agreed to attempt to resolve the complaint through mediation and the mediation then yields an agreement, the Discipline Committee need not hold a formal disciplinary hearing to dispose of the specified allegations of professional misconduct.[15]

The mediator will meet with the parties, separately or together, in person or by telephone. If an agreement is reached, the mediator drafts a memorandum of agreement that reflects consensual decisions reached. This is circulated to the parties for signing and then to the Discipline Committee for ratification (and the issuance of a consent order if a Notice of Hearing had been served). If the complaint is resolved, the case is closed (subject to the practitioner meeting her obligations under the agreement, as monitored by the professional agency).[16] If an agreement cannot be reached, the formal disciplinary process is automatically re-activated. Nothing that occurs in the mediation process is admissible as evidence at the disciplinary hearing, and no staffperson who takes part in the negotiations would be able to participate in any subsequent deliberation or decision of the Discipline Committee in respect of any matters that were subject of negotiations.

NCM may be attempted after a referral to the Discipline Committee from the Complaints Committee (but before a Notice of Hearing is drafted or prosecutor assigned). If the Complaints Committee decides that a complainant otherwise slated for a disciplinary hearing is amenable to mediation, the practitioner and the complainant are offered mediation as a voluntary alternative to the formal complaints/discipline process. If those parties give informed consent to try mediation, the agency retains a mediator, who reviews the case and contacts the parties. The professional agency would be represented in the negotiations by an authorised staffperson, and any agreement reached would have to be ratified by the Discipline Committee. The College of Physicians and Surgeons of Ontario describes the disclosure to potential mediation participants as follows:[17]

> Staff in the Professional Affairs Department familiarise themselves with the case, including any expert opinions, and relevant background material. They then call both the complainant and the physician to advise them of the referrals to both

---

15 If a patient sues a physician for medical malpractice, then an agreement between the patient and the physician can settle the lawsuit. But when a patient complains about a physician to the CPSO, an agreement just between the physician and patient cannot bring an end to the matter: *Shulman v College of Physicians & Surgeons (Ont)* (1980) 29 OR (2d) 40 (Div Ct). Note also that after the Complaints Committee has referred the matter to the Discipline Committee, then for purposes of s 4 Statutory Powers Procedure Act, the College and the physician are parties but the complainant is not a party: s 41 Health Professions Procedural Code. Once specified allegations of professional misconduct have been referred to the Discipline Committee, the agreement of the College and physician are necessary to resolve the matter without a hearing by the Discipline Committee; but agreement by the complainant is not legally required.

16 The CPSO's Professional Affairs Department monitors compliance and would report to the Executive Committee any breach by a physician of a ratified agreement.

17 CPSO, Professional Affairs Department, 'Alternative Dispute Resolution at the College', policy paper, 4pp, September 1994, p 2, Toronto: the College.

Discipline and ADR. Included in the discussion are the reasons behind the referral, the requirements the College would expect prior to resolution, and the option to continue to [a formal] discipline [hearing] and drop ADR at any point. If both parties are interested in exploring ADR, they receive a package of information, followed by an offer for meeting at their [respective] convenience for a further exploration of the options. Support persons or lawyers for both parties are welcome to attend.

NCM could be attempted earlier, before the matter is referred by the Complainants Committee. In this scenario, NCM would be conducted as part of the investigation within the power of the Complaints Committee. An authorised staff person of the Complaints Committee would represent the agency in the mediation, and that committee would have to ratify any agreement.

Regardless of its exact timing, the truly significant feature of the neutral compliant–mediation (NCM) model is the participation by the professional agency as a *party* in the mediation (compare interested complaint-mediation, below). Being present as a party at the bargaining table allows the professional agency to remain involved in the process, but without it having to 'take the heat' of keeping the negotiations always on track. A complainant's interest is not necessarily synonymous with the public interest in the case,[18] and so the agency can not rely on complainants to ensure that any agreements made are in the public interest. The public interest is voiced by the very entity statutorily entrusted with that task, without weakening the mediator's role as a neutral. Having the agency as a party also serves as a counterweight to minimise any power imbalances between the complainant and the practitioner in the mediation. Perhaps more important, however, the agency serves an extremely useful function as an informational resource, and so has substantive input into the terms of an agreement. For example, the agency is more knowledgeable about available courses and assessment and remedial programs than any complainant could reasonably be expected to be.

Of course not all complaints can be, or should be, resolved informally. Some issues will need adjudication due to the intractability of the dispute. Others should be aired in a formal hearing because of the high level of public or professional interest, or because protecting the public interest may entail that the practitioner's license be revoked. Each case should be carefully examined for such elements. Once it is tentatively decided that a case is appropriate for mediation, the consequences of mediation breaking down must be considered. Motivation to participate plays a large role in the success of any mediation, and the professional agency as well as the mediator must have a clear understanding of the motivations behind each party's participation. As well, the agency must generate substantive proposals for settlement, since mere information–sharing would only go so far in the successful resolution of complex clinical cases.

---

18 For example, a complainant may be seeking merely an apology from a professional while the public interest may require that the professional undergo an assessment of her clinical skills (and upgrading if needed) in an apparently problematic area of practice.

The terms of the complaint-mediation process are also important. The terms form the mediator's shield as well as the parties' charter of basic rights. Thus it is imperative to take some care in drafting the terms to ensure that they adequately protect the agency and mediator, as well as safeguard the rights of the complainant and the practitioner member. (See Appendix 'B' below for suggested terms for a neutral complaint-mediation process.)

Although no written guidelines for screening cases exist, an 'appropriate' case for mediation usually involves an isolated incident that does not warrant public sanctions, and that seems amenable to a less-formal process. Some types of cases arising from complaints against physicians, such as those relating to incompetence, incapacity or sexual abuse, are considered inherently unsuitable for mediation because the public interest requires a formal hearing. Also, if agency staff conclude there is a significant possibility that 'harmful' material, such as evidence of other possible acts of professional misconduct, might be disclosed or discovered in the course of the complaint-mediation process, the mediation option is not offered.

The formal disciplinary process will be reactivated immediately if either the practitioner or the complainant declines the invitation to try mediation, decides at any point to cease participating, or refuses to sign an agreement; or, if the Discipline Committee refuses to ratify a signed agreement (unless the Discipline Committee also directs that an attempt be made to return the matter to mediation, with a view to certain amendments of the memorandum of agreement). As well, the practitioner will automatically be subject to formal disciplinary proceedings if she reneges on an agreement ratified by the Discipline Committee. There has only been only one known instance of non-compliance with agreements reached in the CPSO's complaint-mediation program.

INTERESTED COMPLAINT-MEDIATION (ICM) AT THE COLLEGE OF PHYSICIANS AND SURGEONS OF ONTARIO

After the agency receives a written complaint, its staff, as functional delegates of the Complaints Committee, complete a preliminary investigation including the solicitation of a written response from the practitioner (which the complainant should then be invited to comment on or rebut). A trained staff person then facilitates the negotiation of a resolution to the complaint, being neutral as between the complainant and the practitioner, while openly seeking to advance the agency's conception of public interest. Interested complaint-mediation fits into the complaints and discipline framework as follows.

When the complaint is received, the matter falls within the Complaint Committee's power to 'investigate complaints'. The investigation of the complaint would include a determination of:

- whether the complaint is potentially amenable to mediation (ie determining whether it meets the criteria in the screening protocol);

- if so, whether the complainant and the member are willing to attempt to resolve the complaint through ICM to be conducted in accordance with the agency's 'Terms of Interested Complaint-Mediation';
- if so, whether an agreement-in-principle can be reached that is in the public interest; and
- if so, what that specific terms of the agreement would be.

If applicable, the latter two questions would be investigated by actually attempting ICM in accordance with the institutional protocol and the facilitator protocol. If the answer to any of first three questions is negative, then the matter will proceed as if mediation had not been available as an alternative means of resolving the complaint.

If an agreement-in-principle is reached and signed by all the parties, then staff would bring it before the Complaints Committee, together with all relevant records or documents, namely, the written complaint, the written response, the agreement-in-principle, etc. If the Complaints Committee does not consider that the agreement-in-principle is in the public interest, then it would direct that all or part of the matter be referred to the Discipline Committee. However, if the Complaints Committee believes that the agreement-in-principle is in the public interest, then it would advise the Registrar in writing that it proposes to ratify the agreement, and give its reasons therefor. The 'Terms of Interested Complaint-Mediation', signed by the complainant and the member prior to the mediation's commencement, would provide that each such party relinquishes his right to a hearing by any review or appeal tribunal in the event that the Complaints Committee proposes to ratify an agreement-in-principle signed by all parties.

SELECTING NCM OR ICM

ICM works well as a means of resolving a relatively fresh, unemotional complaint, if early investigations reveal that the parties, with the aid of some facilitated negotiation, would be able to reach an agreement. ICM is best suited for those cases when the agency is not strongly concerned by the practitioner's actions and conduct, such as where it is a first complaint, involves a minor incident, and the professional is willing to work with the complainant and respect the agency's role. When the agency only needs to facilitate an agreement and monitor compliance, ICM is a useful process. Complaints from institutions (such as hospitals) tend to be resolved by ICM.

NCM is usually reserved for those cases where extra expertise is required to conduct a more sophisticated work-up and mediation. In the cases where the agency personnel are not as comfortable negotiating with the parties, or when the practitioner or the complainant are 'difficult' or need extra attention, the use of an outside neutral can be extremely helpful. It is also useful to retain an impartial mediator for those situations where the agency will be seeking an undertaking from the practitioner to perform certain acts, and wants to be able to participate actively in the negotiations, unfettered by the responsibility of facilitating an agreement.

THE ADVANTAGES OF USING COMPLAINT-MEDIATION

Participation by all parties is voluntary throughout either form of the complaint-mediation process. Any party may, at any time, withdraw from the process, and automatically reactivate the formal disciplinary process. Ironically, ensuring that parties know that they have absolute freedom to leave a mediation can serve as one of the most powerful incentives to stay.

Because complaint-mediation is completely confidential and 'without prejudice', both the complainant and the practitioner have a real opportunity to tell their respective stories and disclose how the incident(s) affected them. Matters can be revealed, discussed, and examined in a private, informal setting without being subject to legalistic objections or cross-examination. The process is conducted in a controlled and professional atmosphere with great importance placed on the contribution of all participants. Since it is less formal than a disciplinary hearing, complaint-mediation is less intimidating to the complainant and practitioner. In addition, mediation sessions can be scheduled for any time or place, thereby minimising inconvenience to the individuals involved.

The process is non-adversarial, assessing neither blame nor penalty. It is geared to reaching agreements that are acceptable to the parties and will be carried out by the practitioner, whose compliance will be monitored by the professional agency. There have been no known instances of non-compliance in the CPSOs programme.

Complaint-mediation is substantially less expensive than a formal disciplinary hearing, approximately one-tenth of the latter's cost. This enables the professional agency to reallocate resources in order to deal better with complaints that are not amenable to ADR (such as the growing number of sexual abuse cases in the healthcare professions).

By resolving cases faster than the formal disciplinary process, complaint-mediation addresses a complainant's concerns and helps provide her with a sense of closure earlier. Correspondingly, the practitioner does not have the matter hanging over him pending the slow workings of the formal discipline process. Faster resolutions also mean that remedial action is taken more quickly; and the backlog of complaints may be reduced.

As a full participant in the complaint-mediation process, the complainant can obtain the psychological benefits that result from playing an active role throughout the process. This contrasts with the formal disciplinary process, where the complainant is statutorily marginised as a non-party. In complaint-mediation, the parties voluntarily agree to provisions which they have participated in creating, rather than being mere observers as a tribunal imposes a resolution.

Participation of the professional agency as a party in NCM and ICM, and then as a ratifier, ensures that the public interest is protected. The presence of the agency also serves as a neutral counterweight to minimise complainant/practitioner power imbalances. As well, the agency may be extremely useful as an informational resource.

Outcomes are *different* from those of a disciplinary hearing, but not inferior. Provided cases are appropriately screened, in many instances resolutions achieved through complaint-mediation are superior from a public-interest standpoint to those likely to result from the formal disciplinary process. If, at a hearing, the Discipline Committee finds that the professional agency has failed to discharge its heavy burden of proof, the committee lacks jurisdiction to take any action. The outcome of a mediation does not hinge on evidentiary or procedural questions or the battle of expert opinions. Instead, resolution of a complaint depends on formulating an agreement acceptable to all parties (including the complainant, whose interests would not be considered in a formal disciplinary hearing), and which is independently judged to be in the public interest.

Even where an allegation of professional misconduct is proven at a disciplinary hearing, the penalty imposed may have little rehabilitative or remedial effect, or it may have little meaning for the complainant. The outcome of the complaint-mediation process is, in contrast, specifically designed to address the complainant's interests and to provide remedial and rehabilitative measures appropriate to deal with any identified deficiencies in the professional's knowledge or skills. The complaint-mediation process facilitates creating solutions tailored to fit the case (such as apologies, acknowledgments, independent expert evaluation of skills or knowledge, undertakings to upgrade skills or retrain in a specific area of practice, monitoring and inspections by the professional agency, etc) rather than being restricted to a limited range of statutory penalties (revocation or suspension of license, fines, reprimands). Mediated resolutions thus not only serve to protect the public interest, but also reflect the complainant's interests. Lastly, the resolution of a complaint is truly final in that the terms of the memorandum of agreement are not subject to appeal (the parties having waived their right to appeal by agreeing to the Terms of Complaint-Mediation).

SAFEGUARDS AND CAVEATS

Without a screening protocol, the choice of cases for compliant-mediation will be somewhat arbitrary, and mediation may be attempted in inappropriate cases. At the CPSO, there are two levels of approval before the parties can even be offered mediation as an option. Staff can recommend that mediation should be attempted. However, an actual offer of mediation is only made if the Complaints Committee has decided it would be in the public interest to make that option available in this particular case. Complaint-mediation is made available only at the discretion of the professional agency, and is not demandable by the parties as a matter of right. This is likely to remain the case unless changed by specific statutory or regulatory amendments in Ontario.

One or more of the prospective parties might not consent to participate. In particular, the practitioner may be advised by a lawyer that s/he has no tangible incentive for participating unless a disciplinary hearing is the inevitable alternative. This could make it difficult to attempt ADR earlier in the complaints process, when the positions of the parties may be less ossified. However, defence counsel have generally recommended that the practitioner accept an invitation to attempt complaint-mediation.

If complaint-mediation is attempted but fails to yield an agreement, this effectively delays the formal discipline process. However, by-products of unsuccessful mediations, such as agreed statements of fact, have often been found to expedite the subsequent disciplinary hearings. It is also important to keep in mind that the CPSO's program has yielded agreements in almost 85% of the cases where NCM has been attempted.

The complainant is rarely represented by counsel in mediation, while the practitioner generally is. The mediator has no duty to assert or protect legal rights of any party. However, practitioners typically believe that the advice of counsel had no effect on their decisions during the mediation process.

Arguably, there is an inherent power imbalance between a practitioner and (former) client, but the mediator should help to redress this imbalance. Also, as mentioned above, the participation of the professional agency as an independent party provides a substantial, neutral counterbalance. Furthermore, an appreciation and understanding of the statutory and regulatory framework for the formal discipline process can help each party understand its best alternative to a negotiated agreement.

Once a practitioner has complied with all the terms of a ratified agreement, the professional agency would be prohibited from disclosing that the practitioner was involved in any type of disciplinary action. However, such information would be available in determining the appropriate penalty if the Disciplinary Committee subsequently found the practitioner guilty of professional misconduct in another matter.

If the programme lacks defined criteria for selecting mediators/facilitators, a protocol for procedures to be followed by mediators/facilitators, or a formal system for monitoring and evaluating mediators/facilitators, the quality of the mediation process may be unacceptably inconsistent and excessively dependent on the particular mediator assigned to the case. Accordingly, we strongly recommend that any professional agency intending to establish a complaint-mediation program ensure that all necessary protocols and systems are in place before implementing the program, and that all relevant personnel have received appropriate training.

The existence of the mediation option is not widely known in Ontario among the public or by members of regulated professions with ADR programs.

Professional agencies should consult with their stakeholders before instituting any ADR program, and should make continuing efforts to increase awareness and understanding of whatever such programs the agency does establish.

CONCLUSION

Two basic types of complaint-mediation were examined in this paper. In what we term 'neutral complaint-mediation' (NCM), the intermediary is a neutral person, a 'mediator' in the traditional sense, who is not an employee of the professional agency. However, in what we call 'interested complaint-mediation' (ICM), the intermediary, referred to here as a 'facilitator', is an employee of the professional agency. Although neutral as between the complainant and the professional, the facilitator seeks to advance the agency's conception of the public interest as applied to the particular dispute, and is therefore not a mediator in the conventional sense.

Where used appropriately, complaint-mediation can serve the public interest better than a formal disciplinary hearing by ensuring problems are addressed relatively quickly and by producing outcomes tailored to ensure that the deficiencies in skills or knowledge are remedied rather than simply punished. Since it is a substantially less expensive alternative to a formal disciplinary hearing, appropriate use of complaint-mediation allows the professional agency to reallocate resources to other aspects of its complaint/discipline process, such as dealing with sexual abuse complaints. Most important, complaint-mediation enables the agency to fulfil its statutory mandate of playing an active role in serving and protecting the public interest. In cases where the outcome of a disciplinary hearing cannot be predicted with certainty, complaint-mediation can enable the agency and the complainant to achieve an outcome that addresses their concerns rather than running the risk that no remedial action will be taken.

For a practitioner accused of professional misconduct, complaint-mediation gives her a chance to resolve the matter without the trauma of a formal disciplinary hearing and without bearing the attendant risk of an official conclusion that she violated a law or regulations. The practitioner also gains an opportunity to avoid the possibility of being subjected to penalties such as license suspension or revocation.

Complaint-mediation gives a complainant the chance to obtain a relatively fast and highly responsive resolution to her complaint. The practitioner generally shares this strong appreciation for timeliness. Unlike the formal disciplinary process, the complainant in a mediation enjoys the status of a full party. If the complainant refuses to sign an agreement, then the matter automatically reverts into the traditional complaints/discipline process. As well, complaint-mediation may provide the complainant with certain desired outcomes, such as an apology or an acknowledgment, not available from a formal disciplinary hearing. Finally, we found that there are important intangible outcomes of the NCM process of the College of Physicians & Surgeons of Ontario. Most physicians and complainants felt that the process enabled them to explain their own stories, including the venting of complainants' emotions; while a very large majority of those who reached agreements felt a personal sense of closure.

Used in appropriate cases, complaint-mediation has several significant advantages over formal disciplinary processes. Proper program design building on our *caveats* (above) can substantially reduce or eliminate potential disadvantages and abuses of the mediation process. Even at the time of concluding this chapter, the CPSO is again reviewing and restructuring its complaint-mediation policies and procedures and is now looking to integrate ADR into the entire agency. Building on the positive outcomes experienced by the CPSO, it seems likely that other agencies will be encouraged to test complaint-mediation, and other forms of dispute resolution techniques all along the investigation-complaints-discipline-compliance spectrum, to assist in fulfilling their dual role of guiding the practitioner and protecting the public interest.

APPENDIX A
SELECTED CASE SUMMARIES OF SUCCESSFULLY COMPLETED NEUTRAL COMPLAINT-MEDIATIONS

CASE SUMMARY I: CLINICAL STANDARDS

The complainant wrote a letter to the College of Physicians and Surgeons of Ontario ('CPSO') regarding the care and treatment he received from his orthopaedic surgeon. Following four arthroscopic examinations, the physician performed a Hauser procedure on the patient's left knee.

Over a three year period, the patient developed recurrent infections in the operative site. He continued to consult the physician with complaints of infection and swelling, with bruising on the kneecap and the back side of the leg, for which the doctor prescribed antibiotics. At this time, the complainant requested a referral to another orthopaedic surgeon for a second opinion.

Long-term oral antibiotics prescribed by the second physician failed to eradicate the infection, so saucerisation of the area was performed. The patient was symptom free for some time following the procedure, but he returned with further redness and swelling. Episodes of swelling or pain are treated as an exacerbation of the patient's chronic osteomyelitis and he is prescribed Cloxacillin.

The College wrote to the doctor on numerous occasions, but he failed to reply to these requests for a response to the complaint. The matter was presented to the CPSO's Complaints Committee without the benefit of the doctor's response. The Committee deferred the matter for an expert opinion. A duly qualified orthopaedic surgeon was asked to comment upon the care rendered by the physician. He found at least one deficiency, suggesting that a lateral reticular release should have been done prior to the Hauser procedure, however, the expert stated that he was hampered in providing a thorough report as he did not have access to the physician's clinical notes.

The Complaints Committee referred the doctor to the Discipline Committee with the allegations of failing to maintain the standard of practice with respect to the complainant, and for failing to respond to the college, as this clearly hindered the investigation and evaluation of the complaint. The Executive Committee subsequently referred this matter for mediation, and on 10 July 1992, the parties signed a memorandum of agreement that is summarised as follows:

- The physician regrets that the level of communication between him and his patient did not permit them to work out the patient's concerns directly between themselves, and will provide an apology to the patient.

- The physician has made himself aware of and now understands the patient's complaints concerning the treatment he received. The physician acknowledges that as a patient, the complainant was entitled to be listened to and to have his medical concerns taken seriously.

- The physician apologises to the College for his failure to respond to his patient's complaint promptly.

- The physician shall deliver to the College proof that he has attended the following continuing medical education programs concerning the diagnosis and treatment of osteomyelitis:

  (a) the joint meeting of the Canadian Orthopaedic Association, American Orthopaedic Association and British Orthopaedic Association; and

  (b) the meeting of the Ontario Orthopaedic Association, at which the subject of chronic osteomyelitis is being emphasised.

  The proof shall consist of a certificate of attendance, a stamp given by the course convenor or such other proof of attendance as is satisfactory to the college.

- The physician shall deliver to an associate registrar of the College, a written 'reflective' statement which will include a statement of that which he learned or became reacquainted with concerning the diagnosis and treatment of chronic osteomyelitis, and any other observations about the subject, as a result of attending the continuing medical education programs specified above.

CASE SUMMARY II: CLINICAL STANDARDS

A 57-year-old gentleman was feeling unwell with complaints of epigastric pain and gastroesophageal reflux that he thought was attributable to his hiatus hernia. He attended at the local emergency department and was seen by the physician on call. He described his symptoms, and explained that he had a hiatus hernia and had eaten a late dinner the night before. The physician ordered blood work, an electrocardiogram, and the patient was started on 30 cc's of Maalox. A second dosage of Maalox was ordered when he continued to complain of upper abdominal pain. The emergency room physician interpreted the ECG as normal. When the patient began to improve on Maalox, he was sent home with a prescription for ranitidine and advised to follow-up with his gastroenterologist.

Two months later, the patient returned to the emergency department for evaluation as he was experiencing shortness of breath. He was diagnosed with pulmonary edema. The ECG taken during his first visit to the emergency department was re-examined. It revealed a massive anteroseptal infarct with left anterior hemiblock, complete right bundle branch block with persistent ST segment elevation compatible with widespread aneurysm formation, as well as frequent VPBs on the end of the T wave. It was determined that a cardiologist had interpreted the ECG to be abnormal following the patient's first attendance. Because a referral had not been made to this specialist, the ECG and the report were filed in the patient's chart, following normal hospital procedure. He was admitted to the cardiac care unit and treated for his congestive heart failure. He was eventually released on medications with a diagnosis of coronary artery disease, congestive cardiomyopathy with widespread global hypokinesis, and left ventricular thrombus. As he had suffered severe and permanent myocardial damage, he was advised that he would not be able to return to work and was cautioned to avoid any physical exertion. Unfortunately, his cardiac condition continued to deteriorate until his death some months later.

The College was asked to inquire into the care and treatment received by the patient during his first visit to the emergency department. The Complaints Committee was assisted by the opinion of a peer who felt that the electrocardiogram performed during the first visit to hospital was clearly abnormal. A family physician practising in an emergency department should have the capability to recognise the abnormalities present in this case. Appropriate action based on the ECG would have been referral to a cardiologist for an immediate consultation or admission to a coronary care unit for further investigation. The Committee was also concerned that there was not any apparent method of ensuring follow-up of abnormal electrocardiograms at the hospital, making it particularly important that the ordering physician be able to identify significant abnormalities.

The Complaints Committee deferred this matter pending an attempt to resolve the complaint through mediation. The memorandum of agreement that was endorsed by all parties is summarised as follows:

- Without admitting the truth of the allegations made by the complainant in this matter, and without admitting professional misconduct, the physician agrees that his reading of the electrocardiogram may be seen as an error in judgment on his part.

- It is agreed that the complainant, on behalf of the family of the deceased, will write to the administrator of the hospital to outline the incidents and to suggest that they amend their emergency room procedures. Specifically, the complainant will suggest that the hospital institute a procedure whereby any discrepancy in the reading of an ECG between the emergency room physician and the internist/cardiologist on call will be reported immediately (within 24 hours) by the internist/cardiologist to the physician who was on emergency room duty at the time the patient was seen. It would then be the responsibility of the emergency room physician who had seen the patient to notify the patient of the discrepancy and to follow-up with appropriate care or referral. The complainant will provide a copy of this letter to the Ministry of Health and to the respondent.

- It is agreed that the physician will work with the College of Physicians and Surgeons to develop a remediation program regarding the interpretation of ECGs which will be acceptable to the Registrar of the College.

CASE SUMMARY III: CLINICAL STANDARDS/
COMMUNICATION

At 16 days post-delivery, an otherwise very alert and contented infant began to cry and would not stop, despite efforts by both parents. Following several hours of continuous crying, the parents took the infant to the emergency room, where she was examined by the physician on call. The physician reported that the infant was healthy; he advised the parents that they could take her home, where she continued to cry for several more hours.

Two days later, another crying spell began, and when she had not stopped by morning, she was taken to her family physician. Examination of all systems appeared normal, the physician prescribed Ovol drops, and instructed the parents to take the baby to the emergency room for further testing should the incessant crying recur. The baby began to cry again later that evening. She was taken to hospital, and examined by the emergency room physician who could find no serious underlying illness. The parents, whose first language is not English, insisted that all relevant tests and X-rays be performed, and in an attempt to relieve parental anxiety, the infant was referred to the paediatric service. The admitting intern found no obvious physical abnormalities and no evidence of infection, but it was felt that the mother may be having difficulties breastfeeding.

Shortly after admission, the infant developed a fever, and was transferred to a private room. Over the next two days, the baby continued to run a fever; however, the paediatrician's examination disclosed a normal fontanel, no evidence of infection in the ears, nose or throat, the chest was clear, and all test results were reported as normal. The health care team continued to focus on the mother's ability to breastfeed.

While assessing the mother's feeding technique during rounds the next day, the paediatrician examined the infant and found a dramatic change in her condition. Her symptoms immediately suggested meningitis with septicemia; she was taken to the treatment room, where oxygen was started and a lumbar puncture was performed. Purulent fluid was obtained and an intravenous was promptly started administering appropriate fluids and antibiotics. When the infant's vital signs stabilised, she was transferred to a tertiary care facility. Despite appropriate treatment, her illness rapidly progressed and the infant subsequently died.

The parents complained to the College with regard to the care afforded their infant daughter by the paediatrician. The Complaints Committee was aided by a peer paediatrician who was of the opinion that the physician had not ordered sufficient and necessary laboratory investigations. The peer believed consultation paediatricians should know neonates act as though they are immune-suppressed, and bacterial sepsis is therefore a serious worry in a neonate. In the peer's opinion, a health care team must be vigilant to this possibility; a suspicion of sepsis requires a full septic workup and appropriate IV antibiotics until cultures are returned negative. In this case, the peer felt the physician did not have the critical negative information required to disprove sepsis plus or minus meningitis.

The Complaints Committee referred the physician to the Alternative Dispute Resolution department, and an agreement was reached between the parties that is summarised as follows:

- All parties are of the opinion that the outcome of mediation should be a productive, positive and useful result. An educational forum is felt to be the context for responding to this intention, in the form of a learning experience open to all health care professionals at the hospital.

- Physicians, nurses, physiotherapists, occupational therapists, and emergency staff will be invited to the seminar. The parents will be invited, and intend to be in attendance at the seminar. The physician and the parents have all had input into the topics to be covered in the educational forum and agree it will include the following five points:

  (a) *Communication in general*: The emphasis should be placed on the health care team to listen to what the patient has to say, taking into account that the patient or family should not be blamed if there is a problem with language or communication.

  (b) *History of the child*: The health care team should be encouraged to consider and value information and opinions of parents with respect to their own child. Health care teams should listen to what the parents have to say notwithstanding the fact that the parents may be non-English speaking and/or come from a different culture.

  (c) *Ethnic minimisation*: The parents wish to stress that just because people look different or speak a different language, this does not mean that they have no ideas and no feelings. Too often ethnic groups feel marginalised in settings such as hospitals as they are perceived to be less intelligent because they cannot communicate well.

  (d) *Widespread approach*: The parents would like other hospitals to be informed that this kind of educational presentation can be a useful way to assist health care teams to deal with a wide variety of ethnic groups that come to hospitals seeking care and treatment.

  (e) *Grief support*: The seminar will stress that death could be dealt with better by health care professionals. Instead of offering rationalisations based on medical conditions (such as 'it's better the baby died because otherwise she could have been brain-damaged') or abandoning the parents at a time of great distress and grief, more sensitivity could be shown and more support given.

APPENDIX B
THE TERMS OF THE NEUTRAL
COMPLAINT-MEDIATION PROCESS

The mediator is responsible for distributing the terms to all three parties. Some mediators present the terms when first meeting with the complainant; others send out introductory letters covering the terms, with an explanation that once all parties are 'signed on,' the next step will be to arrange meetings. The prototype below is typical of the terms of mediation used to introduce and govern the conduct of the mediation process:

- *Party identification*: The parties to the mediation are the professional agency, Ms Client and the subject practitioner.

- *Mediation defined*: Mediation is a voluntary and informal process in which a mediator assists the parties to attempt to negotiate a settlement responsive to the parties' respective needs.

- *Role of mediator defined*: The mediator, (name), is an impartial and neutral third party who does not represent any party in the mediation. Her role is to assist the parties to negotiate a voluntary settlement of the issues arising out of the self-governing professional agency's investigation. The mediator is an independent contractor. She is not an employee of the professional agency nor in any way directly associated with it.

- *Effect of delay if no agreement*: Delay cannot be a grounds for dismissal. The mediation process shall be carried out as expeditiously as possible. The parties participating in the mediation process waive any right to move for a dismissal of the complaint based upon any delay attributable to the process.

- *'No-money' rule*: Monetary settlements shall not be discussed during the mediation, nor may they be incorporated into any memorandum of agreement. (Note: we recommend that this rule be relaxed to allow discussion of limited payments to charities, and reimbursement of the complainant's out-of-pocket expenses.)

- *The mediator may terminate the process*: The mediator may withdraw from the mediation process (ie terminate the mediation) if she reasonably believes that circumstance makes it impractical to continue.

- *Agreement not binding unless ratified by the Discipline Committee*: Any written agreement reached between the parties is not binding unless ratified by the professional agency's Discipline Committee.

- *Professional agency will monitor agreement's implementation*: The Executive Committee shall monitor the implementation of any memorandum of agreement to ensure that the public interest continues to be served and protected.

- *Publication of Agreement*: If the matter is voluntarily settled, the professional agency may publish a summary of the complaint and its disposition, disguising the names and any identifying fact. Any party may access this information no sooner than 30 days after the memorandum of agreement has been signed.

- *Confidentiality*: The mediation is a confidential process and the parties shall keep in confidence all communications and information forming part of this process, including the terms of any memorandum of agreement. The mediator shall not voluntarily disclose to anyone who is not a party anything said or done by anyone in the mediation, nor any materials submitted to the mediator, except:

  (a) to person(s) authorised to participate in the mediation on behalf of, or as an assistant to, a party;

  (b) for research or educational purposes, on an anonymous basis; or

  (c) where the information suggests an actual or potential threat to human life or safety.

- *Process is 'without prejudice'*: The parties may discuss the matter with the mediator individually or together. All discussions pertaining to the negotiation shall be on a 'without prejudice' basis. This means that if the matter cannot be settled, any disclosure made by any party will not be used against that party by anyone in any internal, legal, administrative, or other proceedings.

- *Limited uses of the Agreement by the professional body*: Where an agreement is reached, the professional agency shall not refer to this matter (as set out in a notice of hearing, letter of complaint or statutory investigation) except:

  (a) if the subject professional is found guilty by the Discipline Committee, and then only in regard to penalty;

  (b) in factual statements on certification generated by the professional agency, and then only until the terms set out in any memorandum of agreement are completed to the registrar's satisfaction;

  (c) if a party to the mediation breaches the confidentiality requirements; or

  (d) as otherwise specified in the memorandum of agreement.

- *Mediator's protection*: No party shall call the mediator as a witness for any purpose, whether during or after the mediation. No party shall seek access to any documents prepared for or delivered to the mediator in connection with the mediation, including any records or notes made by the mediator.

- *Parties' independent advice*: Parties are responsible for obtaining their own legal advice and/or representative. The professional agency shall determine the extent to which a person who is not a party may participate in the mediation on behalf of, or as an assistant to, a party. The mediator has no duty to assert or protect the legal rights of any party, to raise any issue not raised by the parties themselves, nor to determine who should participate in the mediation. The mediator also has no duty to ensure the enforceability or validity of any agreement reached.

11 MAKING COMMUNITY MEDIATION WORK

GORDON HUSK*

INTRODUCTION

With mediation being successfully used to address issues as diverse as youth gangs and international conflicts, it appears to offer hope in dealing with violence in a seemingly uncontrolled world. Paradoxically, even though mediation is part of the new wave of the future, it also offers a return to a past when neighbours looked after one another, and the world was a safer and surer place. However, as popular as it is becoming, all is not well with mediation. Even though consumers of mediation consistently show great satisfaction with it, community mediation programmes continue to be understaffed, insufficiently utilised, and even stagnant. Just what's going on with community mediation?

This paper's examination of community mediation is from a personal perspective. It will briefly review the history of mediation, and in particular, community mediation; name concerns; and then offer suggested ways forward. These insights come from over six years experience as co-ordinator of Community Mediation Services, a small non-profit project in Kitchener, Ontario, Canada.

COMMUNITY MEDIATION: A BRIEF HISTORY

Community mediation programmes originally emerged from concerns over a backlogged court system. Although there had been alternative dispute resolution (ADR) programmes for decades before the 1970s,[1] the more formal diversion programmes of the mid-seventies became the precursors of community mediation programmes. In 1969 a court-based diversion programme was established in Philadelphia (The four As) and in 1971 a similar programme was set up in Columbus, Ohio to deal with personal debtor/creditor disputes. The latter was one of the first to state that it wanted to solve 'interpersonal disputes'. By 1973, of the three federally funded 'Neighbourhood Justice Centres' in Atlanta, Los Angeles, and Kansas City, the LA programme was the most focused upon interpersonal disputes in the community. By 1976, the Community Boards programme of San Francisco was attempting '... the nation's first effort at systematically building a new justice model at the neighbourhood level'.[2]

---

* Co-ordinator, Community Mediation Services, Kitchener, Ontario.

1 Cook, RF, Roehl, JA and Sheppard, D, *Neighbourhood Justice Centers Field Test: Final Evaluation Report*, 1980, US Dept of Justice, National Institute of Justice, Office of Programme Evaluation.

2 Shonholtz, R, 'Neighbourhood Justice Systems: Work, Structure and Guiding Principles' (1984) 4 *Mediation Quarterly* 17.

The San Francisco programme was one of the first to be funded privately and more importantly, it was the first to attempt '... to penetrate target neighbourhoods in that city ...'. With only a 100 cases a year, it was considered ineffective compared to the court-based programmes. However, the Community Board's broader effort was directed at changing the approach to justice, promoting not an adjunct to the courts but an alternative justice system. From the dozen US court-based programmes operating in 1975, by 1985 there were over 182 US community mediation programmes.[3]

Although Canada's community mediation programmes also evolved from court-based programmes, they were from the outset more ideologically linked to alternatives to the retributive justice system, and often started by religious groups like the Mennonites. The Victim Offender Reconciliation Programme (VORP) began in Kitchener, Ontario in 1974 and its model was copied by later court-based programmes. By the late-seventies court-based mediation programmes existed in Halifax, Quebec City, Montreal, Winnipeg and Regina.[4]

In 1978, the first truly community (not court) based mediation programme in Canada, later known as Community Mediation Services (CMS), was established in Kitchener, Ontario. It was a sister programme to VORP and part of a larger Community Justice Initiatives programme. Shortly thereafter Toronto, Canada's most populous city, started its own programme under the auspices of the St Stephen's community resource centre, known as St Stephen's Conflict Resolution Service. Both programmes were based on the San Francisco model (above). In 1989, The Network[5] was born and became a national organisation of community mediation programmes and individuals across Canada. In 1996, there were more than a dozen community mediation programmes in Canada.

Mediation possibilities seem almost boundless, as new areas continually emerge (for example, separation/divorce, family, unions, municipalities, environmental, land development, schools, gangs, police). Yet the community mediation programmes seem stagnant, even considering their advantages over the costly, inefficient, time-consuming, and ineffective approach of the courts. Why?

THE ORIGINS OF COMMUNITY MEDIATION

The Kitchener Community Mediation Service (CMS) grew out of the VORP programme and gradually developed into the larger umbrella organisation, Community Justice Initiatives (CJI). To better understand CMS and its philosophical basis of 'restorative justice', it might be helpful to examine CJI's history and its founding principles more closely.

---

3   McGillis, D, *Community Dispute Resolution Programs and Public Policy*, 1988, Washington, DC: National Institute of Justice.

4   Perry, L, Lajeunesse, T and Woods, A, *Mediation Services: An Evaluation*, 1987, Manitoba Attorney General Research, Planning & Evaluation.

5   Network: Interaction for Conflict Resolution, The Dispute Resolution in Canada: A Survey of Activities and Services, 1995.

The Mennonite community in Ontario regularly places volunteers into various areas of concern such as the criminal justice system. In their effort to change the adversarial justice system, Mennonites draw on Old Testament principles (making shalom). In 1974 two young Mennonites, probation officer Mark Yantzi[6] and his friend Dave Worth,[7] suggested a radically different approach to a local Kitchener justice, Judge McConnell. What would happen if the youths before the courts were given the 'opportunity' to face their 22 victims and work out some sort of compensation? To their astonishment, the judge agreed to let them try. From the first tentative offender's knock on the surprised victim's door to the confident second knock with certified cheque in hand, there emerged the certainty that for all concerned, something positive and wonderful had happened in the process. One consequence was that justice was better seen to be done by the victims, the justice system, and even the offenders themselves. In this way the Victim Offender Reconciliation Programme was born, now known world-wide as VORP (among other names).

THE PHILOSOPHICAL UNDERPINNINGS OF CMS

The Victim Offender Reconciliation Programme is the quintessential restorative programme, bringing victims and offenders together in the presence of members of the community (volunteers). Simply put, VORP brings together the victims and offenders in the same room, with agreed upon ground rules (for example, courtesy and respect); clarifies the hurts and harms done; determines accountability; encourages apologies; offers ways to repair the harm done; seeks forgiveness from the victim; and essentially tries to return the parties to a relationship they 'should' have had (the ideal harmony envisioned in the peaceful kingdom). One necessity of this approach, of course, is that the parties are willing, ready, and able to come together, which in some cases require extensive time, years even, of self-healing and self-help. It is important to understand that this restorative approach does not require that the parties necessarily come directly together, but it is believed that some sort of meeting helps the healing process (for example, CJI has held meetings between a group of survivors of incest and unrelated incest perpetuators). The community mediation programme provides the opportunity to bring together those in conflict, regardless of court involvement. Another programme, the CJI Pre-Release mediation programme, offers those convicted of a crime a way to reconcile with significant others such as family members or an employer, an opportunity for becoming more connected and 'healed'.

---

6   Mark Yantzi personal communication, 1995.

7   Worth, D, 'VORP: A Look at the Past and Future', supplement to the *Community Justice Report*, CJI Newsletter, Kitchener, Ont, 1986.

Restorative justice stands in direct contrast to the present criminal justice system, the latter being based upon punishment and vengeance, the overuse of state intervention, and the removal of everyday citizens from justice process. The state, with its blunt instruments, and its narrow focus upon 'due process' and procedure, is unable to deal with the wide damage done in the community. When a crime is committed, our present criminal justice system appears unconcerned and uncaring about making matters right again. The usurpation of the justice process by the state began with Roman law. It is reflected in Henry I's declaration that crimes commited would be deemed to be commited against the palace/kingdom in 12th century.[8] By the late 19th century, there had been a dramatic increase in lawyers' involvement in criminal matters.

It is not surprising, therefore, that citizens feel that justice is out of touch. Justice has become equated with courts, time in prison and punishment. The compensation for suffering experienced is lost in the shuffle. Victims and offenders alike feel processed like meat, with their involvement almost tangential to the great court battle in a bewildering and overwhelming place. Lawyers and judges talk a strange language. They usually come from the dominant ruling minority of society (white and male), and often have little in common with the people whose lives are so affected by their decisions and processes. How could such a system hope to understand women defending themselves in abusive situations, or theft by the poor? Laws are made by those privileged, and usually against those who offer potential threat to the *status quo* (those without). Is it no accident that those mostly affected by this system are the powerless and marginalised in a society which doesn't really know them; hence, fears, and tries to control them.

Advocates of restorative justice argue that it is time to bring justice back to the people most directly affected by crime: victims, offenders, and the community. From a religious perspective, the Old Testament is held as a model.[9] This restorative approach to justice was the foundation upon which CMS was established, and requires radical changes to existing (retributive) justice systems. Figure 1 tries to summarise the differences between the restorative model of justice, and the retributive model of the adjudicative system.

---

8   In Context: A Quarterly of Humane Sustainable Culture, Bainbridge Island, Wa, Spring, No 38, 1994.
9   Zehr, H, *Changing Lenses: A new focus for crime and justice*, 1980, Scottsdale, PA: Herald Press.

Figure 1

RETRIBUTIVE SYSTEM	RESTORATIVE SYSTEM
• sees crime controlled by lawyers directed to the system's needs	• sees healing controlled by the participants themselves directed to people's needs, defined by themselves
• participants' rights	• participants' needs
• solution imposed by third party	• participant solutions
• emphasises due process	• emphasises holistic approach
• narrow range of deliberation	• deeper understanding
• (information) focusing on facts	• focusing on feelings/concerns/ solutions
• aims for punishment	
• guilt/blame	• aims for accountability
• built on hierarchy	• understanding
	• built on egalitarianism

The original victim offender reconciliation model was so well received, that newly graduated Mennonite student Dean Peachey and others helped adapt the programme to be offered to the community before conflicts went to court. They would bring together neighbours to discuss grievances such as shared driveways, uncut hedges, and barking dogs. They reasoned that they could promote a better justice in the community by having neighbours come together with trained volunteers. Thus Community Mediation Services began in 1978.

MOVING TO A CASE DEVELOPMENT MODEL

By 1989, 95% of the co-ordinator's time at CMS was being spent on handling disputes outside a formal mediation process, from complainant phone intakes, to spending inordinate time trying to convince the respondent to come 'to the table'. Of the 18 volunteers listed then, about nine were active, and waiting for calls to mediate. The CMS advisory committee considered these problems, re-assessed the purposes of the programme, and decided that the mission of CMS was 'to help the parties resolve their own disputes', a subtle but radical shift towards a self-help model (and away from the predominate view in the community mediation model). Conflict resolution, not mediation, would be the primary focus of the service, despite its name. CMS would now try to help parties resolve their own disputes with as little interference as possible. This change to the 'case development model' required more focus upon the pre-mediation phase, not so much as perquisite for mediation (which it would also be), but sometimes as an *alternative* to mediation. This contact time with the disputants could be used to help them better resolve their problems. The volunteer position of case manager was created to oversee the process: assign the 'case developers'; appoint volunteer mediators; set up any subsequent mediation; collect statistics; and follow-up after the case was closed. The case developers would hold individual face-to-face meetings with the disputants, during which they would help define the problem; review the history of the problem; and brainstorm about untried approaches. If the situation had deteriorated badly, or if the disputants were unable (or unwilling) to try to resolve the problem themselves, then mediation would be suggested, even encouraged. Regardless, the trained volunteers were to use their own skills in helping the parties work it out together. The volunteer mediators were usually different individuals than the case developers. The mediators would be debriefed by the case developers and/or case manager, often with a written summary from the case developer. This change in approach bought volunteers into greater contact with clientele, challenged them more, and started to take the heavy focus off mediation, although this was still the primary tool of conflict resolution.

CMS AND VOLUNTEERS

In a restorative approach to conflict resolution, the extensive use of volunteers is more than a way to cut costs. Volunteers represent the community in helping those harmed, and those harming, along with significant others. They are not necessarily experts, nor should they be significantly different from those whom they serve. Trained in the principles of restorative justice, they will apply this approach to other community members. Furthermore, they will explain this philosophy to those they contact, both those with whom they 'work' as clients, and also their family, friends, and workers. Volunteers are a critical part of the programme. The role of the staff in this model is to 'keep the wheels greased', so that the volunteers can get the work done; staff are not there to be the front line workers. It was no accident that CMS case work done by volunteers shifted from about 20% in 1989, to 85% in 1994, the volunteer base moving from just 18 to over 100.

CMS volunteers are trained in communications, mediation, and conflict resolution generally. As the case development model evolved it aimed to 'train' clients how to fight fairly with one another; how to approach one another in a way that enabled a win/win solution(s) to be found. If need be, the volunteers would be the ones who facilitated an explicit process (story telling, exchange, transition, and agreement), and the parties would come out understanding one another better. There would be a moving towards a healthier community, one which was more understanding, more tolerant, more able to deal with conflict, and which might even welcome conflict as a way of them moving forward, and growing together.

PROBLEMS

Like other community programmes, by the late 1980s and early 1990s, CMS was experiencing stagnation of referrals and outcome data, particularly in relation to mediations. The problems being experienced by CMS could be broadly classified as internal, external, and systemic (including the challenge of mediation to predominant values about conflict resolution). These problems are generally not unique to CMS. From my interactions with other mediation programmes, they seem general to community mediation programmes.

INTERNAL PROBLEMS

Stagnation in the referral base

In the early 1990s, the number of referrals first grew dramatically (probably due to a more explicit tracking of all requests) but then flattened out to about 240 per year with approximately 110 being 'assigned' to volunteers, of which about 30 cases annually went to mediation. Although other mediation programmes also experience low referral numbers, they usually assert that:

- most people don't know about the programme; and
- it would be used more extensively if it were better promoted and known.

But how does one increase referral base with limited funds and overdrawn resources? Programmes like CMS are judged by quantity, and with relatively few people coming to mediations, funders inevitably question the programme's value to the whole community. Even though the programmes may be free, quick and relatively efficient, people just aren't using them.

Lack of focus

Community mediation programmes often believe, like many new social service programmes, that they are the 'be-all-and-end-all' to cure all society's ills. It is hard for a struggling new programme not to accept everything that is remotely related to its mission. Since conflict is a broad field, everything is accepted and processed as best it can, even at the expense of the programme itself. Consequently, complex multi-party cases, which demand much more independent analysis and preparation, are sometimes taken on and dealt with, to the detriment of the clientele, the programme, and the people directly involved with the programme (staff and volunteers). Failure can cause serious damage to a programme's reputation and disillusionment for the staff and volunteers. Furthermore, it can negatively affect funding.

Possible extra income is also seductive. Anything that can buoy up a meagre income is enticing. For example, when it is proposed that the programme should be expanded to include (for example) school mediation, limited programme resources may be devoted to trying to promote, develop, and operate such a new endeavour. A programme proceeding without clear direction or process leaves itself open to not only wandering aimlessly, but to any whim or prospect, potentially disastrous to its existence as a programme devoted to community mediation.

Programme sloppiness

Continuously changing staff and volunteers requires systematic procedures, for example set criteria for when mediation is and is not appropriate (including screening procedures), data collection and client follow-up. But such procedures require time, meetings, drafts, discussions, and especially thoughtfulness, which is far removed from the romantic notions of bringing feuding parties together. The outcome of poor preparation can be disasterous, for example prematurely bringing together unprepared people. Whether they should be brought together at all requires careful forethought and some guidelines.

Programmes rush fairly new mediators to intervene in cases which sometimes they (and sometimes the programme) are not ready to handle. Without clear directions about the concerns such cases involve, and the inherent dangers, such cases contain the seeds of destruction.

Lack of ethical guidelines

Linked to reflection and consistent procedures is the need for ethical guidelines. After 18 years, CMS still has few clear directions for staff and volunteers. Only three years ago, we developed a confidentiality form. We still need clear guidelines for matters such as appropriateness of cases for mediation; terminating a mediation; agreement acceptability; appropriate data acquisition; and destruction of information.

Volunteerism

With poor funding, community mediation programmes use volunteers extensively. Regardless of the philosophical importance of volunteerism to programmes like CMS (above), volunteer processing can be sporadic and inefficient, and quality control leaves much to be desired. Sometimes untrained and unready volunteers are brought too quickly into conflicts because of programme needs and impulse. Even before training, and more so afterwards, most volunteers are gratefully accepted by the agency. Thus they are only reluctantly questioned about their behaviours. Because letting go a volunteer is very difficult for an agency busy trying to recruit new volunteers, responding to complaints about a volunteer is also difficult.

Staff turnover

My six years as co-ordinator at CMS have seen at least three different job descriptions, the position moved from two days, to two and a half days to five days to three days, four different VORP co-ordinators and four executive directors of the agency. Under stressful conditions, including little guaranteed security, accompanied disillusionment, internal strife, and burn-out, relatively small return and little room for advancement, staff turnover becomes the norm. With another new person, often not all that familiar with the mediation programme, comes more instability and discontinuity, exacerbating the other problems already described above.

Being part of a larger agency

One way some community mediation programmes have survived is to join a larger organisation or an established institution. The programme may gain economic security, but adds other demands and procedures, as well as losing its critical autonomy. For example, the Kansas City Neighbourhood Justice Centre, housed in City Hall, experienced frustration with the red tape required to give an honourarium to its volunteers.[10] Even an umbrella not-for-profit agency can demonstrate not only a lack of understanding of the mediation programme and its operations, but also a lack of desire to understand a programme which may be a small, relatively insignificant operation among many. Agency policies more attuned to larger programmes may even run counter to the ethos of a community mediation programme. Programme changes can be painfully slow and frustrating to implement, slowed down by internal requirements and policy developments which may have little relevance. Competing with other, better funded, programmes also causes petty jealousies which can undermine a community mediation programme. On the other hand, if the mediation programme should develop a successful venture, the larger agency may take too much interest in it. For example, a successful new training programme by a community mediation programme may be seen by its agency as a potential 'cash cow', and as a consequence the programme may have to struggle with the agency to keep the training (and its income) in perspective with the overall goals of the mediation programme.

EXTERNAL PROBLEMS

Although internal problems affect programme delivery, they are generally within the control of the programme. External problems are farther outside its control, and can be far more devastating.

---

10   Cook *et al*, above note 1.

Funding

All the community mediation programmes I am aware of experience difficulty finding funding. Having small grants from many sources means having to please many masters, each with different reporting demands. For example, one funder required that CMS do a cost-benefit analysis, a very complicated, time consuming task, well beyond the reach of the presently underfunded programme. Small projects can continuously be under the fiscal microscope. Matters are not helped when, operating under pressures of time, the funders only gain at best surface understanding of the programme. Making different reports to many funding sources can be time consuming and resource demanding. Compare this to other projects funded by a single government department or a central agency (such as the United Way), with one report to make, and usually a consistent contact person who understands the programme and may even advocate for it. In addition, annual grants mean the possibility of drastic changes every year. This insecurity undermines planning and development, demanded by the funders.

Sporadic innovative sources, such as the Ontario Government's three year Fund for Dispute Resolution, all too quickly get caught up in political fray. Funders may openly praise the mediation process, but when it comes to the financial crunch they don't fund them sufficiently. There is a vicious circle in which funding is needed to develop and promote the programme in order to gain stability to gain public confidence, resulting in more use with which to attract further funding.

Turf

New programmes often have to make room for themselves in the social service landscape. Even though they may be adding a new service to the community, in one way or another they may be treading on another established service's perceived domain. This perceived, if not actual, threat is not taken kindly, and the obvious response is not to make referrals to the new programme.[11] Even an established programme like CMS only received 14% of its referrals from social agencies in 1992. If the popularity of a mediation approach increases, local social service agencies often begin to develop their own mediation type programmes (for example, parent-teen mediation) even though a programme like CMS may already have expertise, knowledge, and resources.

---

11   See above note 1.

Cost benefit

Court-based mediation programmes definitely save the courts resources and time,[12] if not necessarily on a calculated cost per case basis.[13] Meanwhile, community mediation programmes have had more difficulty proving their economic worth. For example, it appears to be quicker and more convenient for landlords to use courts to evict undesirable tenants than to use mediation.[14] In 1993 CMS calculated the cost of cases resolved via the case development method to be $1,290 and mediated cases $1,890. This is not inexpensive. The question then becomes, are the overall benefits of mediation worth these monetary costs for resolved cases?

SYSTEMIC CRITICISMS OF THE MEDIATION PROCESS

Mediator neutrality is touted as being at the heart of the mediation process. But are mediators really neutral? They bring to the table their own values about the justice system, what justice means, the roles of men and women, the use of punishment, and what fairness means. Some mediators are quick to give their own opinions and solutions. Criticisms of mediator partiality and bias will inevitably undermine community mediation programmes.

Mediator approaches are quite diverse. Some emphasise successful outcome (the agreement) while others focus heavily upon relationships, spending more time in the 'exchange phase' and sometimes blurring the line between mediation and counselling. Meanwhile, the participants are generally compliant and naive to what the mediator is doing. Mediators more concerned with getting an agreement can easily override less assertive disputants and obtain 'agreements' in a more open and adversarial process.

Within the mediation session itself, those not verbally quick can find themselves at a severe disadvantage, since mediation emphasises the spoken word. Decisions about what topics are to be covered in the session, although theoretically in the domain of the participants, are often laid out by the mediators who then usually choose the order. With a complicated array of topics to cover, it is unusual to cover them all, and the session is often concluded with unresolved matters.

Feminist critics of mediation are concerned that mediation may not only put women at a disadvantage in bargaining with men generally, but could actually lead to harm. In response to domestic violence charges, for instance, women are sometimes encouraged to come to the table unsupported, to voice their feelings

---

12   Stevens, C, Valente Jr, E, and Mace, RR, *Mediation of Interpersonal Disputes: An Evaluation of North Carolina's Programmes*, 1992, Institute of Government, Univ of NC at Chapel Hill.

13   Cook *et al*, above note 1; Eldridge, C, personal communication, 1993.

14   Macfarlane, J, *Final Report of the Landlord/Tenant Dispute Resolution Project*, Ontario Ministry of Housing, 1994.

and concerns in front of their abusive partner, with personal safety allegedly provided by witnesses and the ground rules of the mediation process. Afterwards, though, they are at the mercy of their partners who may not be too pleased with what has been voiced.

Other critics have suggested that as a free service, there is a danger that community mediation will become the option for those of less means,[15] who cannot afford expensive lawyers, and other costly means of promoting their cause. If mediation were to become an overwhelmingly 'successful' alternative to the courts, it could eventually lead to a two-tiered justice system or a 'second class justice', with the poor being shunted to the local mediation programme while the rich use the courts.

CHANGING VALUES

Mediation may be seen as part of a long-term strategy to change society, a new way of making justice, moving away from the punitive and retributive justice model towards a more holistic and restorative approach. In this new paradigm, people involved in a harmful situation (regardless of its criminality) would come to know what happened, how it has affected others, and how things might be best righted again. Cultures and societies do not change their values overnight, however, and we often cling to processes familiar to us rather than change. The experience of community mediation has demonstrated that some of the current dominant values of our mainstream North American society are antithetical to promoting mediation.

- *Individualism.* The individualism of Western culture, particularly in North America, leads to a belief that we are not responsible to our neighbourhoods to work out local disputes. We prefer to wall ourselves off from our neighbours rather than engage them in the kind of collective decision-making required for mediation to proceed.

- *My rights are more important than your rights.* A corollary of individualism is that each party in a dispute is likely to believe that he or she is the one most wronged, the true victim whose rights have been trampled. This leads to battles of competing rights which make it difficult for each party to compromise in a mediation session.

- *There has to be a winner (and a loser).* Our adversarial justice system and our competitive society have led us to expect that disputes must produce just one winner, and that the 'winner takes all'. We are taught that the only way not to become a loser is to defeat our opponents. This interferes with a willingness to enter mediation, which disavows the notion of one total victor.

- *Justice means punishment/the stick works better than the carrot.* Our society has developed a justice system which defines many ways of injuring others in

---

15   Cook *et al*, above note 1.

conflict as crimes against the state, and focuses on punishing those involved. This process excludes helping the parties to find ways to repair the damage that was done and to avoid doing more harm in the future. When parties in a neighbourhood dispute feel injured, they may believe that in order for justice to be done they must punish the other rather than seek mutually beneficial solutions. If we continue to believe that only harsh treatment makes people change, mediation will not appear to be the answer.

- *Reliance on authorities and experts to solve problems.* In our scientific and technological world, we are encouraged to refer problems to those with more knowledge, expertise, and power. We call those people 'experts' and defer to them, often paying high fees for their services. Police and lawyers may thus be called on to deal with disputes, because these professions are more clearly representative of expert 'authority' than are mediators, and also because the disputants need not develop their own solutions.

- *You get what you pay for.* Community mediation is often offered free by volunteer mediators, both to make it accessible and to avoid further tension over who will pay. Low cost, however, is often interpreted as indicating lesser quality, harming the credibility of mediation services.

- *The myth of equality before the law.* We want to believe that the courts will protect our rights, despite evidence that they continue to discriminate against the disadvantaged. Those with few resources may prefer the courts out of fear that mediators have insufficient authority to safeguard their rights, even though those with more resources can afford higher legal fees to boost their own chances of victory in an adversarial system.

- *Conflict avoidance.* Instead of recognising that living together makes conflict inevitable, we often vainly hope conflict will disappear if ignored ('least said, soonest mended'). We are sometimes reluctant to involve an outside mediator because conflict (as opposed to a legal dispute over 'rights') is seen as shameful.

WAYS FORWARD

In reviewing the preceding section, the future of community mediation seems gloomy. Is its success tied to the arrival of a more enlightened society? Ironically, mediation may be one of the significant change agents. Community mediation has momentum on its side. There are many participants interested in more than just its survival, but also its promotion and expansion. Even at a subsistence level, community mediation programmes are steadily expanding knowledge and promotion of mediation.

In relation to the problems identified in this paper, the internal ones present less difficulty to resolve than the external and systemic, since they are more readily under the control of those working in community mediation programmes. The external problems, however, especially the value-laden ones, are the real challenges: deeply ingrained and highly resistant to change, especially in the short-term.

The final section will suggest some ways forward. It is not intended as a definitive statement of strategy, but rather a starting point for those interested in making a better service and one that will become more common in our communities.

INTERNAL INITIATIVES

Overcome stagnation through promotion and liaison

The general criticism of the non-profit sector that well-meaning, but business-naive people are running programmes inefficiently (characterised, for example, by poor marketing strategies) may have some truth to it. However, in reality the bottom lines for profit and non-profit organisations are usually quite different (making a profit vs building a more caring society). Nevertheless, profit and non-profit sectors would benefit from more dialogue and less rhetoric. Taking a lesson from mediation practice, there should be more reaching for common interests between the two sectors.

We need to analyse the causes of stagnation in mediation services before doing something about it. It seems that a major difficulty for community mediation programmes is obtaining sufficient referrals. This problem is often caused by potential clients either not knowing about the service or being steered away from the service (for some of the value-related reasons described above). Making a mediation service better known to the potential referral sources, such as the police or courts, would undoubtedly help. Court-based programmes have shown that improvements in referrals can be made through maintaining a good relationship with the referral source; using media, especially TV, to promote the programme; and promoting mediation generally.

Making the service better known to the public is by no means the only issue here, as demonstrated by the now defunct, but well advertised project in Windsor, Ontario in the early 1980s.[16] Mediation has to become part of our evolving culture and one means of achieving this is through television and other media exposure. This means a conscious effort, which requires the investment of time and resources.

Balance expansion with planning

A community mediation programme may initially improve its image by becoming involved in every local dispute, but this is expensive in resource terms.

---

16 *The Windsor-Essex Mediation Centre: History and Pilot Project Evaluation*, 1984, Ottawa: Canadian Bar Foundation.

Programmes need to develop, but with careful consideration of new demands, assessment of the true costs (resources, staff, etc) and especially any potential damage to the existing programme. At a meeting of a similar agency to my own, when an enthusiastic staff member suggested more international involvement, he was promptly asked 'What will you be dropping to find the time needed to meet this new venture?' This critical question puts a whole new light upon expansion, forcing staff and board members to assess the many costs of new areas. If, after due consideration, the programme is willing to pursue a new direction, the expansion should be time and resource limited, with a specified period for evaluation, and with some formal body, for example an advisory committee, overseeing the initiative (see also below).

Reducing programme sloppiness: systematic procedures and ethical guidelines

To its credit, CMS has tried to deal with its own sloppiness by creating an advisory committee, composed of practitioners, active volunteers, and front-line staff. This offered reflection, and direction, far closer to the action than the agency board. Nevertheless, first hand experience has taught me that the demands of an under-funded programme inevitably leads to some sloppiness; fine-tuning requires sufficient time and resources. Programme procedures often evolve unsystematically, precipitated by an informal and hasty evaluation of a crisis as it arose. Time and resources, as precious as they are, must be allocated for an adequate assessment of policies and procedures. An invaluable resource to help in such matters for strapped programmes is an appropriately gifted volunteer (or volunteers).

Besides the development of procedure and policies for operations, ethical guidelines need to be developed and practised as soon as possible. The logical first place for development and review of such guidelines is an oversight group like the advisory committee. Regional organisations could also be beneficial in this area, since policies are not likely to vary considerably. Developing regional guidelines (as opposed to rules) would allow each individual programme more flexibility for interpretation and would also be supported by a regional network for resolving novel problems or 'greywear'.

Systematic procedures can also be enhanced by pooling the resources and knowledge of other community mediation programmes. Through regular meetings, common standards and guidelines could be developed. Newer programmes would gain considerably by using tried and true operation guidelines, learned from the experience of others. Regular regional meetings would probably lead to development, review, and evaluation of procedures. Furthermore, such meetings would help maintain consistent procedures, especially vulnerable in times of personal change. We have found our own one-day regional meetings to be most helpful in learning about funding sources of other local programmes, formal and informal evaluations, and so on. Such important regional ventures need the help of larger network national groups (this particular coalition failed because there was insufficient spare time and energy to sustain it). Unless small community mediation groups like CMS find the time to become more proactive with such networks, however, we will probably continue to receive minimal attention and support.

Unfocused: have a small, focused working committee

CMS's fuzziness was reduced considerably with the establishment of an advisory committee, which then proceeded to review the mission statement and programme objectives. Besides the programme staff now having meaningful guidelines against which to test the operations, the advisory committee provided a forum to ask the hard questions about direction and methodology. Having a group of front-line practitioners assessing the programme helped bridge the inevitable gap between policy and practice. Setting realistic programme goals for the upcoming year (inspired by a visit to the San Francisco programme) further focused us for a year. An advisory committee can not only examine and set goals, but also build the morale of all concerned, especially important in light of other difficulties the programme may be experiencing.

Although the director's position is critical to keep the programme going, his or her responsibilities need to be spread. In effect, a well functioning oversight committee may be more important to the programme's consistency and stability than the co-ordinator *per se*.

Volunteers

Volunteers are more than cost-saving measures for ideologically based community mediation programmes like CMS. However, having volunteers as the heart of the programme is easier said than done. All too easily volunteers are taken for granted and considered (unpaid) staff, without the protection and respect afforded salaried staff. When major crises occur or major decisions are needed, volunteers seem less important and are more easily dismissed or forgotten.

However, volunteers do more than provide free service to the agency. They can be important barometers of policy shifts and changes. As such they should be part of agency decision-making. CMS's use of volunteers on the advisory committee has provided the agency with good direction (although it would probably be inappropriate to include all direct service volunteers on the board of directors, as one US community mediation programme does). However, a board composed of 50% service volunteers ensures that the agency's policies do not become too far removed from its service. When policy (talking) becomes inconsistent with service and administration (walking), the programme is in trouble.[17] This further indicates the overall need for reflection to consider concerns such as standards, ethical guidelines and procedures.

Coping with turnover

Staff turnover will undoubtedly continue to be a difficulty for community mediation programmes as long as there is unstable funding, and relatively low pay. A programme might be better overall maintaining a well paid part-time position than a poorly paid full-time position. Turnover can also be less problematic if there is a consistent and energetic advisory board/committee, close to the operations, which sees itself as responsible for maintaining a good programme. Drawing upon the volunteer base for new staff members also provides continuity, bearing in mind the need for 'new blood' from time to time. A clear understanding of the co-ordinator's role, to co-ordinate rather than be overly involved in direct service which is primarily the responsibility of volunteers, has helped CMS through many staff changes. One benefit of staff change is the opportunity for a different direction, allowing a programme to reconsider its goals and objectives, and then match these with a new person.

Working with court-based programmes

Court-based programmes have an important role to play in the survival of community mediation programmes. The dominant (adversarial) criminal justice system will undoubtedly continue to support such non-threatening services as VORP. By contrast, funding more radical, community based programmes such as community mediation is less likely. Court-based mediation programmes appear less likely to directly challenge the present paradigm (that is, the classic retributive model) then community mediation programmes which are more likely to actively promote a paradigm shift away from punitive or retributive justice.

However, there are also ways in which court and community programmes need one other, one to maintain financial security, the other to maintain ideological security. This probably encouraged the joining of Mediation Services in Winnipeg, Manitoba, the largest (and most successful) victim-offender programme in Canada, with the local community mediation programme. A court-based programme gains in this union by being associated with a community mediation programme, using an approach to the mediation of conflict which can be more radical, rendering the court programme freer to try different approaches, and enabling it to be better attuned to the real neighbourhood community. Association with the community mediation service also allows the court-based programme to seek non-system funding, for example, from service clubs. The community mediation programme benefits

---

17   Marshall, E, *Transforming the Way We Work; The Power of the Collaborative Workplace*, 1995, New York: AMACON.

from such an association because it can keep the court-based programme aligned with its long-term goal of changing the justice system. The court based programme can also ensure a regular stream of referrals.

Evaluating the costs of being part of a larger agency/institution

The benefits for community mediation programmes of being part of larger agency or institution include shared resources, policy development, more personnel, and relative financial security. The costs mainly revolve around loss of independence and how that affects programming, in particular the added complexity of decision-making, and a reduced ability to make decisions quickly. An umbrella agency board can be further removed, and seemingly less aware of the developments and concerns of a much smaller community mediation programme, than a board devoted specifically to the programme. Cost-saving measures which a small programme could institute on its own become far more time-consuming and ponderous within a larger organisation, which might be listening to different drums.

In summary, a small community mediation programme should be cautious how integrated it becomes with other programmes, even similar mediation programmes, particularly within an agency which houses more diverse projects. The potential advantages and disadvantages for the community mediation programme should be evaluated at the outset.

EXTERNAL SOLUTIONS

Unlike internal problems, over which the programme has a measure of control, external problems are more daunting, much larger than one programme can hope to solve. The resolution of these problems require broad community changes. Furthermore, with outside influences having a more devastating effect on the programme, these problems require immediate action.

Creative proposals for funding

Community mediation programmes will not be self-sufficient in the foreseeable future. Significant numbers of people will just not use, let alone pay for, conflict resolution services, in the absence of drastic changes in public values. Unlike the system supported court-based programmes, community mediation programmes will continue to have to scrape for their meagre funding.

For the foreseeable future, community mediation will need subsidy, whether from governments, community resources, churches, or foundations. With all governments fiscally constrained, more creativity is required for funding mediation programmes. Creative funding proposals need to be promoted by those involved in community mediation. For example, in California, a court surtax on small claims courts directly funds community mediation programmes.

Although more distant government bodies are generally not interested in funding mediation programmes, local (municipal) governments often see the value in utilising a local organisation to handle difficult situations and for relatively little cost.

Amalgamation and consolidation

The Carver[18] model promotes the idea that the management of non-profit organisations should accept an overall responsibility to the community as a whole. They should make sure that their agencies are serving the community in the best way possible. Amongst other things, this means that agencies – including community mediation services – should not be duplicating and competing with similar services already available. Carver further encourages non-profit boards to meet together to discuss more co-operation. Furthermore, agency staff should be directed to work closer together, for example referring appropriate cases to each other. Funders are likely to discontinue funding duplicate services.

Changing values

Predominant community values influence the utilisation and hence the popularity of mediation. Simply put, mediation is tied to other predominant, yet contradictory values, some of which have been discussed above. For example, if punishment is the valued response to harm done in the community, then there is no reason for people to regard a healing type resolution as desirable. A healing approach does not meet the desired (read valued) end; even worse, the perpetrator can be seen to be 'getting away with it'. If mediation is to move into the mainstream of everyday community dispute processing, there has to be a change in dominant values of blame and punishment.

The daunting challenge before us is to demonstrate the value of mediation to our community. We must be patient, moving from smaller to larger circles of influence, looking for opportunities to demonstrate the power of mediation, and then letting the testimonials speak for themselves. In the meantime, a more comprehensive model of justice needs to be developed, going beyond the restorative model as we now know it. Some have argued that a better paradigm is that of 'transformative justice',[19] which is less hampered by the 're' words of restorative, reform, restitution, and which would be more encompassing and truly radicalising.

Community mediation programmes have a long road to travel before being too successful will have to be a worry. However, we are part of a changing world. We seem, as a society, to be slowly crawling forward: democracy is evolving, hierarchies are being questioned, grave inequalities are diminishing and

---

18   Carver, J, *Boards that Make a Difference: A New Design for Non-profit and Public Organisations*, 1990, San Francisco: Jossey-Bass.

19   Morris, R, 'Not Enough' (Spring 1995) *Mediation Quarterly*, Vol 12 No 3, San Francisco: Jossey-Bass.

alternative understandings of how we organise society are constantly evolving. Mediation processes have the potential to bring us closer rather than separating us, to enable us to see our commonalties rather than differences, to encourage us to listen and understand rather than talk, and to value the richness of experiences of others rather than our own limited experiences. In the end justice will be better served through a more direct meeting of one another in a safe place, where we can find out what went wrong and work out how we can move forward together again.

12 THE TRUSTED MEDIATOR: ETHICS AND INTERACTION IN MEDIATION

CATHERINE MORRIS★

THE NATURE OF DISCOURSE ON ETHICS IN MEDIATION

Mediators tend to consider ethics most intensely when they are in a dilemma. Where, then, can they turn for guidance? The usual and obvious answer is to look to codes of ethics created by respected mediation organisations. Both the literature and the agendas of dispute resolution organisations indicate that discussions about ethics are often framed by people preparing to set standards which they believe are needed as 'safe-practice' guidelines for practitioners, or to protect the public from unsavoury or unwise practitioners. Another setting for discussions about ethics is training. Ethics are often taught either as an addendum or in the form of handouts. Except in the presence of an actual dilemma, the topic of ethics in mediation usually takes a back seat in favour of discussions about dispute resolution qualifications, skills and models. The irony is that ethical principles are fundamental to every assumption of both dispute resolvers and disputants. Judgments of right and wrong, good and bad, are at the root of virtually every dispute and every dispute resolution process.

Looking back at my own mediation and arbitration experiences, there have been no disputes in which ethics were unimportant to the people involved. Parties are rarely concerned only with pragmatic issues. Ethics are almost always brought into the argument, often with the cliché: 'It's not the money, it's the principle of the thing.'

A NARROW APPROACH: THE EXCLUSIVE FOCUS ON THE MEDIATOR

In spite of the importance of ethics to virtually all disputants, discussions about mediation and ethics often focus exclusively on the mediator's role, especially on ethical dilemmas faced by the mediator[1] or on the need for and possible contents of mediator codes of ethics. In the mid-1980s many conflict resolution organisations began to promulgate codes of ethics for mediators. Literature and codes of ethics focus almost exclusively on the role of the mediator. Codes of ethics are considered in some depth later in this chapter.

★   Catherine Morris, BA, LLB, is the Executive Director of the Institute for Dispute Resolution, University of Victoria, British Columbia, Canada.

1   Society of Professionals in Dispute Resolution (SPIDR), *Making the Tough Calls*, 1991, Washington, DC: Society of Professionals in Dispute Resolution.

A BROADER APPROACH TO ETHICS IN MEDIATION: THE INTERACTION BETWEEN MEDIATOR AND PARTIES

To be practical, discussions of ethics need to recognise that when mediators are invited into a dispute, they are usually invited into a problem laden with ethical undertones. The parties come ready with positions and arguments, and they believe strongly that they are right and the other is wrong. The mediator brings independent values and opinions about the dispute and a process for managing or resolving it. The parties and the mediator may or may not share a common set of ethical assumptions. The problem of mediation is essentially one in which an independent third party, the mediator, is asked to work with parties experiencing ethical tension, to help them interact in a way that will produce at least relief, and ideally consensus or even reconciliation.

Even where conflicting parties are not using an ethical framework to accuse one another, ethical dilemmas are often involved. For example, a dispute concerning the siting of a waste land-fill may be framed in functional terms. When one looks at the perspectives of the parties, however, the elements involving environmental and other public concerns are often expressed in terms of ethics.

The definition of an ethical dilemma is a difficult choice between two or more options which make seemingly equal ethical demands (or which seem equally difficult to support). Disputants typically do not see the problem in this way; rather each is polarised toward the desirability of one option over the other. The mediator, perceiving the dispute as a whole, often sees that the problem initially presents itself as a dilemmic choice between two or more 'positions' or options for solution which, seen together, are (from the mediator's perspective) framed as both 'best' and 'worst' by the parties collectively.

The very introduction of a non-partisan third party, who is called upon to understand and maintain the trust of people who are contradicting one another, provides an opportunity to transform the nature of the ethical problem. The transformation occurs as the mediator interacts with the parties in ways that help them recognise that the problem is not most usefully described as a struggle between one party who is 'good or right' and the other who is 'bad or wrong.' Since both parties see themselves as 'right,' the problem can be reframed as a difficult jointly-held ethical dilemma in which both parties can participate to resolve, sometimes, perhaps, in ways that acknowledge that the very essence of an ethical dilemma is tension of making choices between two 'rights' or 'goods', or alternatively between 'the lesser of two evils.' The very fact that the parties have consented to the involvement of a mediator means that at some level they are capable of contemplating the possibility of a solution neither has thought of, based on a common ground of jointly discerned ethics or values that transcend what the parties can presently perceive. This transformative role becomes complicated as the mediator's own independent ethical perspectives interact, either implicitly or explicitly, with those of the parties.

302

GRAPPLING WITH ETHICS IN MEDIATION:
FOUR EXERCISES

While is it useful to see ethics in mediation as a dynamic issue involving active participation by parties and mediator, parties have opportunities to consider ethics in mediation only when they are involved in the mediation of a particular dispute. Mediators as vocational process leaders are in a better position to consider ethics in depth.

Mediators grappling with the problem of interaction with parties about ethical situations can be assisted by four exercises. First, as leaders of dispute resolution processes, mediators can develop understanding of their own general ethics and their values surrounding the purpose of mediation generally and the purpose of a particular mediation. This paper provides a sampling of values ascribed to mediation, as well as descriptions of general ethical theories with which it is hoped that mediators can begin the process of reflection about their own ethical values. Second, mediators can compare their ethical understandings with those of others engaged in the practice of mediation as well as critics of mediation. This can be done through critical analysis of codes of ethics and relevant literature. The second part of the paper provides an analysis of several codes of ethics by which mediators can be prompted toward their own reflections and discussions with other mediators. Codes of ethics from Canada, the United States and Britain are considered along with literature primarily from the United States and Canada. The basis of current codes of ethics and proposals is questioned: what are the assumptions behind them? To what degree are proposals relevant to diverse societies? Third, mediators can develop a framework by which to work through the individual dilemmas they face in their day–to–day work. An example of such a framework is articulated in the third part of this essay. Fourth, mediators can interact at a policy level with others engaged in leading dispute resolution processes. Comments are offered about ethical accountability and the meta–message of current trends by mediation organisations, coalitions of mediation organisations and government agencies to propose broad-based standards for ethical practice.

WHAT DOES IT MEAN TO BE 'ETHICAL'?

Groups of mediators often debate ethics without examining their implicit underlying assumptions. People may intuitively say about a particular practice: 'That's unprofessional and unethical' or even 'I don't know what they're doing, but it ain't mediation!' Statements like these are laden with implicit assumptions which spring from individual or group world views and associated beliefs and values.[2]

---

2   Bush, RAB and Folger, JP, *The Promise of Mediation: Responding to Conflict Through Empowerment and Recognition,* 1994, pp 229–59, San Francisco: Jossey-Bass.

A consideration of ethics in mediation needs to start with a broader discussion: what does it mean to be 'ethical?' Does it mean acting consistently with one's own principles, one's own ethical compass? If so, how does one know one's compass is accurate? Are there different (but equally valid) ethical compasses for different people in different contexts and cultures? Are there some universal ethical principles that can guide discussions about ethics? Should moral decisions be made by autonomous individuals? Or should they be made in the context of shared community values, rights and responsibilities?

Placing these questions into the framework of an actual mediation creates another question: who should be the ethical decision-maker? The mediator alone? Each party autonomously? Or does the invitation of a mediator into a dispute demand that the ethical decision-making process be shared among the disputants and the mediator?

DIVERSE VALUES AND GOALS OF MEDIATION

Policy on ethics in mediation practice depends on the goals established for mediation. The goals are always dependent on the social and ethical values that drive particular programmes or organisations. Bush[3] has pointed out that mediators' ethical dilemmas should be analysed according to the values served by the mediation process. Determining the ethical values underlying mediation is complicated by the existence of diverse and overlapping views within the field.

Choices of goals include the following:

- *party autonomy* and control over outcome. The process is seen as a means to strengthen the parties' capacity for resolving their own problems or developing their own agreements without dependency on external institutions or professionals,[4] or to provide opportunities for increased direct democracy;

- *party satisfaction*. The process and/or outcome satisfies party needs, cost and time efficiency, and the stability of business or other interests;

- *community solidarity*. Particular groups or communities are strengthened in the use of mediation processes to resolve problems themselves, or empowered to achieve greater social justice;[5]

---

3   Bush, RAB, 'Symposium: The Dilemmas of Mediation Practice: A Study of Ethical Dilemmas and Policy Implications' (1994) *Journal of Dispute Resolution* 1 at 1–55. First published as *The Dilemmas of Mediation Practice: A Study of Ethical Dilemmas and Policy Implications,* 1992, Washington, DC: National Institute for Dispute Resolution.

4   Bush, RAB, 'Defining Quality in Dispute Resolution: Taxonomies and Anti-Taxonomies of Quality Arguments' (1989) *Denver University Law Review* 66, pp 335–80 at 347–48.

5   Bush, 1989, see above note 4; Bush and Folger, 1994, see above note 2.

- *social justice.* Mediation processes and/or outcomes contribute to fairer apportionment of material wealth or power,[6] or prevention or reparation of harms;[7]

- *social order.* Social order is enhanced through the development of increased consensus or resolution of underlying conflicts, rather than mere settlement of manifest disputes;[8]

- *personal, group or societal transformation.* Mediation processes provide disputants and groups with opportunities for personal change and growth in social responsible ways.[9]

Mediation programmes and processes may attempt to serve one or a combination of these goals. Definitions of 'success' and standards of practice will differ depending on what goals are set. Dispute resolution programmes which strive for efficiency tend to offer short processes aimed at settlement. An example is the mandatory mediation programme of 'settlement conferences' in British Columbia in which judges act as mediators to assist parties to settle small claim cases before trial. The mediation process tends to last about thirty minutes and focuses on the issues identified in the small claim pleadings. Evaluation of this programme found it was successful in terms of saving court time (that is, successful in the sense of being efficient).[10] Other programmes may emphasise party autonomy, social justice or community empowerment. Often these are community-based mediation programmes which utilise community volunteers and co-mediation. These programmes may offer longer processes which define parties and issues as broadly as necessary to resolve issues.

In terms of ethical choices, judge-mediators may consider it quite appropriate to use recommendatory methods ('muscle mediation') during the short time they have available for settlement. In contrast, community mediators may make an

---

6   *Ibid.*

7   Gilman, EB and Gustafson, DL, 'Of VORPs, VOMPs, CDRPs and KSAOs: A Case for Competency-Based Qualifications in Victim Offender Mediation' in Morris, C and Pirie, A (eds), *Qualifications for Dispute Resolution: Perspectives on the Debate*, 1994, Victoria, BC: UVic Institute for Dispute Resolution, pp 89–106 at 97; Landau, B, 'Qualifications of Family Mediators: Listening to the Feminist Critique' in Morris, C and Pirie, A (eds), *Qualifications for Dispute Resolution: Perspectives on the Debate*, 1994, Victoria, BC: UVic Institute for Dispute Resolution, pp 27–49, at 35–37 and 46.

8   Bush, 1989, see above note 4, at 347–48; Bush and Folger, 1994, see above note 2, at 22–23. This goal has been criticised because of the possibility that mediation processes may maintain the pre-eminence of powerful elites by pacifying individual disputants and thereby depoliticising conflict and diverting attention from the need for collective action. (See, for example, Abel, RL, 'The Contradictions of Informal Justice' in Abel, RL (ed), *The Politics of Informal Justice*, 1982, pp 267–320, New York: Academic Press; Nader, L, 'Harmony Models and the Construction of Law' in Avruch, K, Black, P and Scimecca, J, *Conflict Resolution: Cross Cultural Perspectives*, 1991, Westport, Connecticut: Greenwood Press and Nader, L, 'Controlling Processes in the Practice of Law: Hierarchy and Pacification in the Movement to Re-Form Dispute Ideology' (1993) 1 Ohio State Journal on Dispute Resolution 9, pp 1–25).

9   Bush and Folger, 1994, see note 2, at 20–21; Bush, 1989, see above note 4.

10 Adams, P, Getz, C, Valley, J and Jani, S, *Evaluation of the Small Claims Programme*, Vol 1, 1992, Victoria, BC: Province of British Columbia, Ministry of Attorney General.

ethical choice to be non-interventionist by avoiding recommendations to the parties. They may consider that muscle mediation is unconscionable because of its infringement on party autonomy. Thus, value choices lead to definitions of success, which in turn determine policies concerning practice ethics.

Sometimes mediation programmes find themselves constrained by funders or sponsors whose values differ from the sponsors of the programmes. For example, sponsors of some mediation programmes may value social justice or community empowerment. Other sponsors, especially if they are governments, tend to provide funding on the basis of the efficiency goal of reducing court case loads. Efforts to satisfy funder evaluations which emphasise high case loads and low costs may lead to ethical squeezes for mediators and mediation programmes. Programmes which find themselves trying to serve two competing masters may find themselves in ethical tension.

Divorce mediators may value party autonomy, social justice or both. These goals, if seen to compete, may place mediators in ethical tension concerning whether to mediate (or terminate mediation) in cases where party choices differ from mediator conceptions of social justice. For example, in a (real life) divorce mediation, the couple refused all mediator suggestions (in caucus and in joint session) to seek a valuation of the couple's pension plans. They both insisted that they would each keep her or his own pension plan, and each refused to consider any other alternatives. The wife was vociferous in her refusal. Predictably, the husband's pension plan was vastly more valuable than that of the wife. The law in the particular jurisdiction provided that in the normal course they should divide both pension plans equally.

The mediator was ethically torn between her commitment to autonomous informed consent of the parties and her belief in equity and social justice. She saw this case not as an isolated one, but as a case-type which reflected problems of social justice. Belief in party autonomy might lead to an ethical choice of maintaining non-directiveness.[11] Belief in social justice might lead to an ethical choice to use 'empowerment' techniques directed toward the woman, or to persuade the parties toward one outcome or another either by direct suggestion or by insisting on accounting or legal advice, or by terminating mediation. Mid-range choices could lead the mediator to utilise 'reality testing' questions or other supposedly non-directive methods which can be seen as serving either as a persuasive tool (social justice) or as a method of ensuring informed consent (party autonomy).[12]

Values concerning the goals of mediation lead directly to policy choices concerning ethical behaviour. All the issues reflected in the scenarios cited above have been the subject of animated and sometimes controversial discussion among mediators. Bush suggests that codes of ethics need to articulate the values on

---

11 Bush, 1994, see above note 3, at 9–10.

12 See the discussion about a similar case in Grebe, SC, Irvin, K and Lang, M, 'A Model for Ethical Decision Making in Mediation.' (Winter 1989) *Mediation Quarterly* 7(2), pp 133–48, at 140–46.

which they are based. Increasingly, newer codes of ethics are doing this.[13] Overwhelmingly, the dominant underlying principle articulated (or implicit) in the codes is party self-determination.

Part of 'exercise one' (of the four exercises suggested in this chapter) involves reflection by mediators (or mediation programmes) on their own values concerning the purpose of mediation, and their own definition of 'success.' These values, purposes and definitions may vary depending on the context of the dispute. Values, purposes and definitions of success in a given case may also be determined through interaction with the parties. Another part of 'exercise one' is a consideration of one's more general assumptions about ethics, and reflection on some of the following issues.

PHILOSOPHICAL PROBLEMS IN A PLURALISTIC SOCIETY

In rapidly changing societies, one can not assume homogeneous ethical values among either disputants or mediators. Most countries are affected by increasing cultural diversity as a result of immigration as well as social change. This creates challenges for mediators in particular cases, as well as for mediation organisations creating codes of ethics.

LeBaron Duryea's research[14] demonstrated that people who immigrate to Canada do not necessarily share the perceptions of the dominant Canadian culture as to how disputes should be resolved. In particular, the individualistic approach to conflict evidenced in Western thinking is not mirrored by those from more collectivist cultures, including Aboriginal peoples in North America.[15] The image of a fishing net may better impart the kind of 'network conflict' reported by members of some immigrant groups in North America:

> Each person is like one of the knots in a large fishing net with its intricate interlacing of innumerable knots. Each person is tied to many others. When all of the knots are firmly tied, the net is in good working condition. If any one of the knots is too loose or too tight, the whole net is skewed. Each knot, each relationship, has an effect on the whole. If there is a tear, a gap, in the net, the net is not a working one ... Nets are to be checked frequently, knots cared for tenderly, and if tears do appear they must be repaired. [16]

---

13 Mediation UK, *Mediation UK Practice Standards*, 1993, Bristol: Mediation UK; Academy of Family Mediators (AFM), *Standards of Practice for Family and Divorce Mediation*, 1995, Article I, Lexington, MA: Academy of Family Mediators; American Arbitration Association (AAA), American Bar Association (ABA) and Society of Professionals in Dispute Resolution (SPIDR), *Model Standards of Conduct for Mediators*, 1995, Article I, Washington, DC: Society of Professionals in Dispute Resolution.

14 Duryea, Michelle LeBaron and Grundison, JB, *Conflict and Culture: Research in Five Communities in Vancouver, British Columbia*, 1993, Victoria, BC: UVic Institute for Dispute Resolution.

15 Monture-OKanee, PA, 'Alternative Dispute Resolution: A Bridge to Aboriginal Experience?' in Morris, C and Pirie, A (eds), *Qualifications for Dispute Resolution: Perspectives on the Debate*, 1994, Victoria, BC: UVic Institute for Dispute Resolution, pp 131–40 at 138–39. Price, RT, and Dunnigan, C, *Toward an Understanding of Aboriginal Peacemaking*, 1995, Victoria, BC: UVic Institute for Dispute Resolution, at 3.

16 Le Resche, DN, 'Procedural Justice of, by, and for American Ethnic Groups: A Comparison of Interpersonal Conflict Resolution Procedures Used by Korean-Americans and American Community Mediation Centres are Procedural Justice Theories', PhD dissertation, 1990, George Mason University, cited in Duryca and Grundison, 1993, see above note 14, at 205; Lederach, JP, 'Of Nets, Nails and Problems: The Folk Language of Conflict Resolution in a Central American Setting' in Avruch, K, Black, P and Scimecca, J (eds), *Conflict Resolution: Cross Cultural Perspectives*, 1991, Westport, Conn: Greenwood Press.

Similarly, the individualist approach to ethics dominant in Western societies is not reflected in the ethics of many non-Western societies, where ethical values may reflect loyalty to family, religious or cultural values.[17] Codes of ethics developed for mediators in the West implicitly incorporate dominant Western views of both conflict and ethics. In pluralistic societies, this unexamined approach to the framing of mediator ethics may not be realistic in the long-term.

Working across cultures: 'Empower or Imperial?'[18]

It is increasingly recognised that mediation must be culturally sensitive when practised in a multicultural society. In addition, more and more trainers are being asked to conduct training or facilitate the implementation of dispute resolution programmes internationally. Significant ethical issues are raised, including the issue of working with people whose cultural and ethical frameworks may differ from those of the mediator or trainer.

Ethical concerns are being raised as commentators become concerned about imposing dominant culture standards on minority groups, or in the case of international work, neo-colonialism in the form of exportation of dispute resolution processes based on Western values. Readers are directed to the valuable literature which points to these issues.[19]

WESTERN THEORIES OF ETHICS

Mediation codes of ethics developed in Western nations will inevitably reflect Western ethical traditions. However, the literature on mediation ethics demonstrates only cursory knowledge of the vast and continually growing body of literature on Western moral philosophy. Likely, this is because few people in the field of dispute resolution are trained in moral philosophy. The undeniable

---

17 Salem, PE, 'A Critique of Western Conflict Resolution from a Non-Western Perspective' (1993) *Negotiation Journal* 9, at 361–69.

18 This was the title of a workshop given by John Paul Lederach at Interaction '92, a conference on dispute resolution held in Winnipeg, Manitoba, 6–9 May 1992 ('Cross-cultural conflict resolution training' (Fall 1992) *Interaction* 4(3), at 9–10).

19 Augsburger, DW, *Conflict Mediation Across Cultures: Patterns and Pathways*, 1992, Louisville, Kentucky: Westminster/John Knox Press; Duryea, Michelle LeBaron, *Conflict and Culture: A Literature Review and Bibliography*, 1992, Victoria, BC: UVic Institute for Dispute Resolution; Duryea, Michelle LeBaron, *Conflict Analysis and Resolution as Education: Culturally Sensitive Processes for Conflict Resolution. Training Materials*, 1994a, Victoria, BC: UVic Institute for Dispute Resolution; Duryea, Michelle LeBaron, 'The Quest for Qualifications: A Quick Trip Without a Good Map', in Morris, C and Pirie, A (eds), *Qualifications for Dispute Resolution: Perspectives on the Debate*, 1994b, Victoria, BC: UVic Institute for Dispute Resolution, pp 109–29; Duryea and Grundison, 1993, see above note 14; Lederach, JP, *Mediation in North America: An Examination of the Profession's Cultural Premises*, 1986, Akron, Pa: Mennonite Central Committee; Lederach, JP, *Preparing for Peace: Conflict Transformation Across Cultures*, 1995, Syracuse, NY: Syracuse University Press; Lederach, JP, 'The Mediator's Cultural Assumptions' (1986b) *Conciliation Quarterly* 5, at 2–5; Lederach, 1991, see above note 16; Lederach, JP and Wehr, P, 'Mediating Conflict in Central America' (1991) *Journal of Peace Research* 28 (1) at 85–98; Wiggins CB, 'Exporting Process Technology: Transplanting Public Interest Mediation to Central Europe' (Spring 1993) *Mediation Quarterly* 10 (3), at 273–89; Wildau, ST, Moore, CW and Mayer, BS, 'Developing Democratic Decision-Making and Dispute Resolution Procedures Abroad' (Spring 1993) *Mediation Quarterly* 10 (3), at 303–20.

relevance of moral philosophy to the discussion on mediation and ethics provides opportunities for more in depth research and consideration which would provide valuable guidance for the field of dispute resolution. Cooks and Hale,[20] Gibson,[21] Grebe[22] and Williams[23] are among the few who have examined mediation from the perspective of moral philosophy. For individual mediators seeking to understand their own ethical underpinnings, this section briefly outlines a few of the dominant themes of Western ethics that may implicitly weave their way into discussions of mediation and ethics.

This paper does not discuss concepts of moral theory from non-Western sources. However, other disciplines are addressing ethical issues from a cross-cultural and cross-religious perspective, and their work would provide a useful topic for further research. As one example, John McConnell's book, *Mindful Mediation: A Handbook for Buddhist Peacemakers*[24] provides a useful outline of Buddhist ethics relevant to dispute resolution.

Universalism versus relativism

Universalism

One of the most important questions in ethics is whether ethics are 'universal'. That is, are there some principles of ethics that apply to all human beings regardless of culture or context? The literature on moral philosophy provides many complex discussions on what it means for an ethical maxim to be universal. Thomas Aquinas acknowledged Divine Law as the basis for morality. Others, such as Kant, founded universalism not on God, but on the application of reason. More recently, efforts have been made to find a more pluralistic universalism (see below, 'communicative ethics').

In mediation, the practical relevance of universalism might be experienced in a dispute over parental responsibilities after divorce where there is an issue involving religious education. Each parent struggles with the dilemma of what, if any, exposure to religious teaching is best for the children. One party may adopt a universalist approach to religious or cultural values. 'My religious values are right (universally right, whether you believe it or not) and it is important that my children be taught correctly.' The mediator can become embroiled in the

---

20 Cooks, LM and Hale, CL, 'The Construction of Ethics in Mediation' (Fall 1994) *Mediation Quarterly* 12(1), at 55–76.

21 Gibson, K, 'The Ethical Basis of Mediation: Why Mediators Need Philosophers' (Fall 1989) *Mediation Quarterly* 7(1) at 41–50.

22 Grebe, SC, 'Ethics and the Professional Family Mediator' (Winter 1992) *Mediation Quarterly* 10(2) at 155–65.

23 Williams, BB, 'Implications of Gilligan for Divorce Mediation: Speculative Applications' (Winter 1994) *Mediation Quarterly* 12 (2) at 101–15.

24 McConnell, JA, *Mindful Mediation: A Handbook for Buddhist Mediators*, 1995, Bangkok: Buddhist Research Institute and others. Distributed by Asia Books Co Ltd, telephone 662–391–2680. Coordinated by Foundation for Children publishing house, 1845/328 Soi Charaslarp, Sirindhorn Rd, Bangplud, Bangkok, Thailand, tel/fax 662–424–6404).

dilemma when her or his own sense of ethics is offended by choices that the parents are wishing to make, for example, if a particular parent's religious choice is one that the mediator feels will not be in the best interests of the children.

An obvious problem with universalism is that it is difficult to find any test to determine the universal 'rightness' of any maxim. This is not only a philosophical problem but also a practical one. Another problem with universalism is that conflict among two 'universal' principles can qualify universality. For example, if one accepts the universal value of two ethical maxims, keeping promises and looking after aged parents, which of the two principles should prevail when one is faced with the dilemma of either keeping a promise to be the key-note speaker at an important conference on human rights, or caring for one's suddenly sick mother? Essentially, ethical dilemmas are not choices between right and wrong, but between two equally compelling (or equally undesirable) alternatives.

Ethical relativism

Ethical 'relativism,' by contrast, provides that there are no universal ethical principles. What is wrong for one person may be right for another. This sort of ethical relativism is popularly accepted. People are often heard to say 'I live by my own standards' or 'You have your standards; they may be okay for you, but don't impose them on me.'

Relativism judges behaviour by prevailing standards. A Canadian example is the law relating to pornography which defines pornography by what is acceptable according to prevailing community standards. The factual problem in determining the community standard is that communities are not very homogeneous.

Serious ethicists find little to commend the idea that 'anything goes.' Relativist morals are considered to be justified only if they are accepted with informed consent, that is, the moral views are held with full awareness of natural and logical consequences of one's assent to the principle.

Discussions of both ethics and qualifications standards for mediators implicitly reflect a struggle with the issues presented by ethical relativism and universalism. In the above-cited example involving parental struggle over religious education, the relativist parent may answer 'your religion may be right for you, but it is also right for me to have no religion, and further, when we consider what is right for our children, it is equally valid for our children to be taught no religion. My views about what is right are just as valid as yours.'

Another example involves cases in which mediators wonder how to proceed where parties come from another culture or religious tradition which does not share egalitarian views concerning the role of women. To what extent should feminist mediators facilitate parties' goals which reflect the view that subordination of women is not only 'right', but that egalitarianism defies fundamental principles?

Ethical relativism does not provide an easy answer to this complex issue. Many Canadian immigrants report that they do not wish to adopt traditional patterns to the extent that they perpetuate male dominance.[25] They will not be content with policies which respect any and all kinds of traditional dispute resolution processes on cultural grounds.[26] The final report of LeBaron Duryea's research says:

> Immigrants to Canada report that the traditional means of resolving conflict they may have employed at home are no longer used because extended family structures are not intact, and their communities are less cohesive. Where traditional conflict resolution methods have been identified, the parties may not wish to use them, nor to participate in processes into which they have been incorporated, because the methods are often not compatible with Canadian practices and values. Examples include the traditional male, elder-driven processes used in some cultures.

> For conflicts where disputants choose not to involve courts, many report a sense of confusion, isolation and a vacuum of options. This is especially true for women and for youth of both sexes. Therefore, there is a need to find processes which will respect the values of disputants without importing features of processes they cannot now accept.[27]

This problem points to the difficulties inherent in versions of moral relativism which are based in the view that what is considered right in one culture is genuinely right in that culture, regardless of whether it is considered right or wrong in another culture. Moral relativism often places high value on self-determination, pointing out that ethnocentrism can blind us to appreciation of the value of other groups' ethical values and practices, and can also lead to inappropriate imposition of dominant moral values on non-dominant groups. For example, one of the major criticisms of Western development programmes is that they tend to promote Western notions of individual rights and democracy. This criticism is also made of United Nations initiatives to set universal standards for human rights; the United Nations is dominated by Western nations and thereby dominated by Western world views.[28]

Pluralism is not always considered relativistic. When considered carefully, moral pluralism often applies universal standards of mutual respect, self-determination and informed consent applicable to all people. In dispute resolution this 'universal' ethical principle might also be summarised as respect for the right of 'autonomous informed consent of all those involved or affected,' a familiar concept in the field of mediation.

---

25 Duryea and Grundison, 1993, see above note 14, at 48 and Lund, B, Morris, C, and Duryea, M LeBaron, in *Conflict and Culture: The Report of the Multiculturalism and Dispute Resolution Project*, 1994, Victoria, BC: UVic Institute for Dispute Resolution, at 4 and 33.

26 Duryea and Grundison, 1993, see above note 14, pp xix, 196.

27 Lund, Morris and Duryea, 1994, see above note 25, at 33.

28 Many citizens working within their own countries to alleviate severe endemic human rights abuses do not agree with the criticisms that promotion of human rights will lead to corrupt Western individualism and the destruction of non-Western societal values of collective and family responsibility.

Relativism offers no way to adjudicate moral disputes conclusively. The prevalence of relativistic views in North America may be one reason consensus-based approaches to dispute resolution are increasingly being sought to replace adjudicative dispute resolution methods in pluralistic societies.

Consequentialist versus deontological theories of ethics

Consequentialism or utilitarianism

A dominant theory of ethics is 'consequentialism', which includes utilitarianism. Consequentialism says that the ethical value of a choice is based on its outcome. Classical theories of utilitarianism, including the work of John Stuart Mill, argue that the 'greatest happiness for the greatest number' is the most desirable outcome. In utilitarian theory an action is good if it is useful for promoting pleasure. The good of minorities might have to be sacrificed to the good of the majority.

Utilitarian goals for mediation can be seen when success in mediation is defined by party satisfaction with mediation, and satisfaction by funders and governments with the effect of mediation systems on the speed and cost-efficiency of the court system. Evaluations of a number of mediation services have been conducted using these criteria of success.[29]

Utilitarianism might manifest itself in family mediation where one parent asserts a better claim to custodial rights of children on the basis of being able to provide a more affluent lifestyle or a private-school education. In workplace or public disputes, utilitarian ethics could surface in the assertion of a particular solution to a policy or budget problem on the grounds of public palatability, efficiency or expediency.

The concept of consequentialist or utilitarian ethics is a relatively new one in Western culture and is not acceptable in many other societies. Salem points out that Western conflict resolution 'relies heavily on the assumption that pain is bad and pleasure, or comfort, is good'.[30] He points out that utilitarianism was not at all accepted in 19th century Europe where

> it flew (and still flies today among other cultures) against the more original principle that *'good* is good and *bad* is bad,' where the first usages of good and bad in this phrase are defined in general moral or religious terms having nothing to do with (individual) pleasure or pain.

Salem further suggests that Western preoccupation in the field of conflict resolution with

---

29 Moore, B, Morris, C and Pirie, A, 'Introduction', in Morris, C (ed), *Resolving Community Disputes: An Annotated Bibliography About Community Justice Centres*, 1994, Victoria, BC: UVic Institute for Dispute Resolution, pp 1–14, at 6–7.

30 Salem, PE, 'A Critique of Western Conflict Resolution from a Non-Western Perspective' (1993) *Negotiation Journal* 9, at 361–90, at 364.

suffering generated by conflict rather than on the justice or morality of the cause may not strike resonant philosophical chords in other cultures. To the contrary, suffering itself in many cultures, including pre-modern Western culture, enjoys a fairly high valuation as a means for moral or spiritual purification or a necessary divinely-ordained component of life.

Deontological theories

In contrast to consequentialism, deontological theories hold that certain actions are inherently right, regardless of outcome. Some deontological views are based on the guiding principles of the Divine. Others, such as Kantian ethics, are based on principles understood through the application of reason rather than God. It has been said that mediator codes of ethics, being prescriptive in formulation, are deontological in nature.[31]

Rawls'[32] neo-Kantian egalitarian ethics currently appear to dominate the field of law. Lawyers, in turn, are dominant in the field of dispute resolution. Rawls' most famous contribution is an imaginative device in which one formulates an institutional arrangement which will benefit everyone impartially by imagining a social contract made in ignorance of one's personal situation ('the veil of ignorance'). The idea is that if you are ignorant of the social situation in which you might find yourself, you are more likely to act to set social policy that will be fair to you should you be in the position of less fortunate members of society.[33] One obvious criticism of Rawls is that the device of the veil of ignorance cannot possibly blot out one's cultural assumptions. Thus, it seems impossible for anyone to achieve the kind of neutral objectivity that the device is designed to provide. However, the idea that people, and in particular mediators, can and should achieve autonomous objective neutrality is pervasive in the field of dispute resolution. This will be discussed further in the section on impartiality and neutrality.

Autonomy, paternalism and interdependence

Autonomy

A dominant theme in the field of mediation is the concept of respect for party autonomy.[34] Informed autonomous consent is said by some to be the guiding principle of mediation. By definition, mediation is 'an informal process in which a third party helps others resolve a conflict or plan a transaction but does not (and ordinarily does not have the power to) impose a solution'.[35] To the extent that they retain authority and practical ability to decide the outcome, the parties are autonomous. Some say that party autonomy is so central to the philosophy of

---

31   Grebe, 1992, see above note 22, at 164.

32   Rawls, J, *The Theory of Justice,* 1971, Cambridge, Mass: Harvard University Press.

33   Raphael, DD, *Moral Philosophy,* 1981, London: Oxford University Press, at 72.

34   Bush, 1994, see above note 3.

35   LeBaron Duryea, 1992, see above note 19, at 6.

mediation that mandatory mediation schemes are an anathema to the philosophy of mediation, or even an oxymoron.

The principle of autonomy is carried through in discussions about mediation ethics, where the mediator faces choices as to how to proceed. In discussing the role of the mediator in making ethical choices, the mediator is generally considered responsible for his or her own choices and behaviour. In discussions of mediator ethics, rarely is the ethical decision considered as part of an interaction among the parties and between the mediator and the parties. Instead, the parties and the mediator are each considered as autonomous 'moral agents.' Autonomy and self–determination underlie most mediation codes of ethics.[36]

What does 'autonomy' mean? Boskey[37] sees autonomy as capacity to negotiate. He reframes the concept of mediator 'pressure' as 'encouragement':

> ... to my mind a party's autonomy is compromised only in cases where that party has lost the capacity to made the decision to walk away from the agreement. That capacity is not lost because of economic pressures or because of encouragement by the mediator to agree. It is lost when the party's basic ability to function as a negotiation has been compromised. In cases where that has occurred, it is the responsibility of the mediator to terminate the mediation process and advise the parties of their other alternatives for reaching a solution to their problems.

Matz,[38] in discussing the relationship between mediator pressure and party autonomy, says many authors present a picture of autonomy

> as a space that ought not to be touched, a kind of special ground that should be left alone or even enlarged. In this picture, inappropriate pressure is seen as touching of that which should not be touched, a violation. This is a static picture ... When I mediate ... I see a different picture: I see a party's autonomy as a large, three dimensional shape, malleable in part, rigid in part, and endowed with an internal structure and vitality. When pressure is applied, it may yield, resist, or push back. It may yield first and push back later; or it may push back first, and yield later. It is a dynamic picture.

While both Boskey's and Matz's statements reflect an individualistic approach, Matz's statement more explicitly acknowledges that the very nature of mediation is an interactive dynamism among the group composed of the parties and the mediator. Exclusive reliance on ideals of individual autonomy belie the very nature of group dynamics inherent in the process of mediation, which is better described in ways that acknowledge that dialogue within the mediation context is always set in a social and cultural context which is interactive, interdependent, and mutually influential.

---

36 Grebe, 1992, see above note 22, at 164.

37 Boskey, JB, 'The Proper Role of the Mediator: Rational Assessment, Not Pressure' (October 1994) *Negotiation Journal* 10(4), pp 367–72, at 372.

38 Matz, D, 'Mediation Pressure and Party Autonomy: Are They Consistent with Each Other?' (October 1994) *Negotiation Journal* 10(4), pp 359–65, at 363.

Paternalism

According to Grebe[39] paternalism is a considerable influence in the practice of family mediation. Paternalism presumes that some people are incapable of self-governance, for example infants, or those suffering permanent or temporary impairment. Grebe suggests that in family mediation, paternalism exists in discussions concerning mediation and abuse, where those who are or might be abused need special protection. She suggests:

> The principle of paternalism derives from male-dominated feudal society in Europe, where the lord had near-absolute authority over his vassals. In exchange for this authority, the lord was expected to protect his subjects in time of war.[40]

It should be noted that both utilitarian and Kantian ethics stand opposed to paternalism. John Stuart Mill said paternalism was justified only when harm could come to another. Immanuel Kant also rejected paternalism on basis of its lack of recognition and respect for others' moral autonomy.[41]

To the extent that paternalism can be found in formulations of mediation ethics, it may stand in contrast and opposition to principles of self-determination. On the subject of protecting less powerful or vulnerable parties, however, much of the thinking of mediators appears to counter paternalism. Boskey points out that many proponents of power-balancing are in fact primarily concerned with maintaining party autonomy and informed consent. Those who advocate mediator interventions to balance power or lead parties to agreement often believe that maintenance of party autonomy should be paramount and that 'an agreement that is functionally imposed on the parties by aggressive mediator intervention is fatally flawed.'[42]

Integrating ethics into a framework of interdependence

People in a variety of disciplines, including mediators and moral philosophers, are critically examining the dominance of Western concepts of individualistic self-determination as well as paternalism both from within and without. On this point it is useful to quote law professor Patricia A Monture-OKanee, a member of the Mohawk Nation living in Canada, who, in her essay critiquing alternative dispute resolution says:

> You have probably heard that the Mohawk word for law translates into English as the 'great law of peace'. This is not precisely true. The word actually literally translates to 'the way to live most nicely together.[43]

---

39 Grebe, 1992, see above note 22, at 162.

40 *Ibid*, at 163.

41 *Ibid,* at 163.

42 Boskey (1994), see above note 37, at 367–68.

43 Monture-OKanee, P, 'Alternative Dispute Resolution: A Bridge to Aboriginal Experience?' in Morris, C and Pirie, A (eds), *Qualifications for Dispute Resolution: Perspectives on the Debate*, 1994, Victoria BC: U Vic Institute for Dispute Resolution, pp 131–40, at 140.

Aboriginal commentators like Monture-OKanee are fair in their criticism that this principle has not been mirrored in relationships among Aboriginal and non-Aboriginal people in Canada, including the field of alternative dispute resolution. However, for those who believe concepts of interdependence to be foreign to Western thinking, it is important to note that the Hebrew concept of '*shalom*' provides an analogous concept which is at the root of the Western 'good neighbour' principle of reciprocal human concern and mutual responsibility. '*Shalom*' is the ideal in which the community of people lives together in harmony and wholeness which integrates both justice and peace.

The influence of Carol Gilligan

Carol Gilligan[44] is frequently cited in discussions about mediation and ethics. Gilligan has argued that dominant theories of moral development have ignored women's ethical perspectives. According to Gilligan, discussions on ethics (dominated by men) tend to be framed in terms of justice, rights and individual autonomy. Women's constructions of ethics in terms of relationship, care and responsibility have largely been ignored. Sociolinguist Deborah Tannen's work,[45] which studied the speech of men and women, appears to affirm that women 'speak and hear a language of connection, of intimacy, while men speak and hear a language of status and independence'. While Gilligan found that most people use the voices of both justice and care, they tend to prefer one to the other. Preference for one tends to lead to omission of the other in moral decision-making. Gilligan's writings suggest that both justice and care are needed in a complete ethical theory.

Williams[46] uses Gilligan's and Tannen's theories to suggest that mediators who are sensitive to the ethical language of both care and justice can assist parties to understand each other's moral language. Mediators can thus facilitate parties' development of solutions that reflect the perspectives of both justice and care, rights and responsibilities.

Communicative ethics

The idea of 'discourse ethics' or 'communicative ethics'[47] is beginning to find its way into the literature of mediation ethics.[48] This thinking is drawn from

44 Gilligan, C, *In a Different Voice: Psychological Theory and Women's Development*, 1982, Cambridge, Mass: Harvard University Press.

45 Tannen, D, *You Just Don't Understand: Women and Men in Conversation*, 1990, New York: William Morrow and Company, Inc at 42.

46 Williams, 'Implications of Gilligan for Divorce Mediation: Speculative Applications' (Winter 1994) *Mediation Quarterly* 12 (2), at 101–15.

47 Benhabib, S, *Situating the Self: Gender, Community and Postmodernism in Contemporary Ethics*, 1992, New York: Routledge, Chapman and Hall.

48 Cooks and Hale, 1994, see above note 20.

Habermas[49] who points out that the development of ethics is not simply a rational exercise, and cannot be isolated from social experiences that occur in community. 'Communicative ethics' is said to provide an escape from moral relativism by thinking of universalisability not in terms of principles that cannot be contradicted, but 'as a test of communicative agreement'.[50] Thus, universalism is not seen as a particular 'truth' that cannot be contested, but as a product of communicative agreement within a particular social context. The universal ethical norms are said to be 'moral respect and egalitarian reciprocity.'[51] This theory is said to be deontological in that it contains particular conceptions of what is 'right' but 'pluralistic and tolerant in that it promotes the coexistence of all ways of life compatible with the acceptance of a framework of universal rights and justice'.[52]

Applying a framework of communicative ethics to conflict, it is said that 'disagreements emerge when two people become enmeshed within divergent ethical stories'.[53] The mediator's job is 'to help the disputants coordinate their meanings: to assist in creating a story commensurate with each person's goals and to help each party make sense of the other person's story ... The mediator's objective is to restore a moral and ethical order ...'.[54]

Using the ethics of mutual respect, reciprocity and interdependence, the task of the mediator is to help the parties integrate their concepts of right and wrong into a new framework which acknowledges the interdependence of the parties and their affected communities, and integrates the legitimate needs of all those affected into an outcome which all can recognise as both peaceful and fair.

EVALUATING CODES OF ETHICS

If mediators discover their 'ethical home' by comparing their own beliefs to some of the major ethical theories, they will be in a more informed position to participate in discussions about mediation ethics. An informed perspective is needed to evaluate existing discussions about ethics and to evaluate actual codes of ethics, because of the concise and often unexplicated form in which codes of ethics are promulgated by mediation organisations.

To assist mediators in the second of the four exercises proposed in this paper, the following section outlines and discusses the main ethical issues considered important by mediation organisations and in the literature. The discussion includes a survey and thematic analysis of selected codes of ethics from the

---

49 Habermas, J, *Moral Consciousness and Communicative Action*, translated by Lenhardt, C and Nicholsen, SW, 1990, Cambridge, MA: MIT Press.

50 Benhabib, 1992, see above note 47.

51 *Ibid*, at 29.

52 *Ibid*, at 45–46.

53 Cooks and Hale, 1994, see above note 20, at 59.

54 *Ibid*, at 59.

United States, Canada and Britain. The section is organised into a discussion of neutrality and impartiality (which subsumes a number of other topics), confidentiality, and competency. Exhaustive study of all the possible ethical topics raised by mediation is not possible in this paper, and readers are referred in addition to the codes of ethics themselves.

THE ROLE OF CODES OF ETHICS

Bush[55] believes practice standards are required for mediators for public policy reasons in order to provide clear standards that are both internally consistent and practical. Others believe qualifications and program goals should be created primarily for the purposes of education.[56] Codes of ethics reflect the considered thinking of groups of mediators. As such they can be a barometer of existing ethical philosophy and practice. Therefore, a variety of codes of ethics should be studied by any serious student of mediation.

However, when one considers the problem of ethics in mediation, codes of ethics for mediators provide a rather narrow answer. First, codes of ethics typically provide a prescriptive list of dos and don'ts which rarely fit the particulars of an ethical quandary. Second, codes of ethics focus only on one dimension of the ethical problem, tending to treat the situation as though ethical problems in the dispute were the exclusive responsibility of the mediator to resolve alone and independently of the parties. Third, codes of ethics usually do not detail the ethical values on which they are founded, and one is usually left with bare lists of dos and don'ts with little explication of the reasons for the prescriptions. Fourth, codes of ethics, generally framed in concise documents, give the illusion that the organisations of mediators who created them have reached a unified consensus about mediation practice; in fact, there is a considerable diversity of values and goals among mediators. What follows is a discussion of the most important ethical themes discussed in codes of ethics and in other relevant literature.

'IMPARTIALITY' AND 'NEUTRALITY':
A CONFUSING DISCOURSE

Mediators are often referred to as 'neutrals'.[57] The terms 'neutrality' and impartiality' are deeply embedded in the discourse of ethics in mediation. However, significant challenges have been presented to the 'folklore'[58] of neutrality. Model attitudes and

---

55   Bush, 1994, see above note 3 and Bush RAB, 'A Reply to the Commentators on the Ethical Dilemmas Study' (1994) *Journal of Dispute Resolution* 1, at 87–91 (1994b).

56   Stamato, L, 'Easier Said Than Done: Resolving Ethical Dilemmas in Policy and Practice' (1994) *Journal of Dispute Resolution* 1, pp 81–86, at 82.

57   Society of Professionals in Dispute Resolution (SPIDR). *Qualifying Neutrals: The Basic Principles:* Report of the SPIDR Commission on Qualifications. Washington, DC: National Institute for Dispute Resolution, 1989.

58   Rifkin, J, Millen, J, and Cobb, S, 'Toward a New Discourse for Mediation: A Critique of Neutrality' (Winter 1991) *Mediation Quarterly* 9(2), pp 151–64 at 151.

behaviours of mediators described as 'impartial' or 'neutral', have been criticised as mythical, unethical, culturally biased, or impossible.

In reviewing literature and codes of ethics, it is a significant challenge to understand what authors mean by 'impartiality' or 'neutrality.' Most codes of ethics discuss impartiality, neutrality or both. The terms are not always defined. Existing definitions are inconsistent. Concepts are entangled. The result is considerable confusion.

The existing discourse on 'neutrality' and 'impartiality' is confusing because the terms have been defined in various and sometimes contradictory ways, reflecting the fact that they are intertwined linguistically, conceptually and practically. Impartiality and neutrality are variously defined or described as follows:

- 'Impartiality' or 'neutrality' are not defined, or the terms are used synonymously; and/or

- 'Impartiality' means unbiased, and fair to all parties equally;[59] and/or

- 'Impartiality' refers to an unbiased attitude and 'neutrality' refers to unbiased behaviour and relationships;[60] or

- 'Neutrality' is comprised of two contradictory concepts: impartiality and 'equidistance' between the parties;[61] or

---

59 Webster's dictionary defines 'impartial' as 'not partial or biased' and 'treating or affecting all equally'. It is synonymous with 'fair' which Webster's defines as 'marked by impartiality or honesty: free from self-interest, prejudice, or favouritism'.

60 Christopher Moore distinguishes 'impartiality' from 'neutrality': '*Impartiality* refers to the attitude of the intervenor and is an unbiased opinion or lack of preference in favour of one or more negotiators. *Neutrality*, on the other hand, refers to the behaviour or relationship between the intervenor and the disputants.' Moore, C, *The Mediation Process: Practical Strategies for Resolving Conflict*, 1986, San Francisco: Jossey-Bass. Moore suggests the attitude of impartiality will be reflected in the mediator's conduct. Moore counsels mediators to tell parties that they are 'impartial' meaning that they have 'no preconceived bias toward any one solution or toward one [party] over the other'. (Moore, 1986, 157). Since the Academy of Family Mediators has adopted Moore's definitions of impartiality and neutrality in its 1995 *Standards for Family and Divorce Mediation*, Article IV, A and B, it is important they be mentioned in this discussion. Moore's attempt to clarify the differences and connections between behaviour and attitude is useful. While Moore's definitions help readers to understand his uses of the terms, his definitions have not found their way into widespread use either among the public or among mediators.

61 An important discussion about 'neutrality' by Rifkin, Millen and Cobb has often been cited in mediation literature. Citing authors sometimes do not discuss Rifkin *et al's* ((1991), see above note 58, at 152–53) unique two-pronged definition of 'neutrality' which incorporates two concepts: 'impartiality' and 'equidistance.' 'Impartiality' refers to 'the ability of the mediator (interventionist) to maintain an unbiased relationship with the disputants.' According to Rifkin *et al*, this means the mediators 'make it clear that they are present simply to listen and not to influence the disputants' explication of the case' ((1991), at 154). Parties are given equal opportunities to speak. 'Equidistance,' they state, 'identifies the ability of the mediator to assist the disputants in expressing their 'side' of the case.' Thus, mediators will temporarily align themselves with parties to support each party. Equidistance involves actively supporting each party in a 'symmetrical' way. Rifkin *et al* (1991) see impartiality (as they define it) and symmetrical alignment with the parties ('equidistance') as fundamentally contradictory to one another. Empirical research (Cobb and Rifkin, 1991a, 1991b, see note 74, at 37; Fuller, RM, Kimsey, WD and McKinney, BC, 'Mediator Neutrality and Storytelling Order' (Winter 1992) *Mediation Quarterly* 10 (2), pp 187–92) has pointed out that mediators do, in fact, influence both process and outcome, by affecting the legitimacy of each party's point of view. They do this by determining the order of speaking, when to intervene, when to give the floor to another party, when to caucus and the order of caucusing, and how to respond and reframe parties' statements. Rifkin *et al* do not see this problem as one of deficiency of skill in balancing the two paradoxical roles. Rather, they see neutrality as 'a problematic discourse for the practice of mediation because it has proven to be inadequate to account for the dynamic process involved in mediation storytelling'(Rifkin *et al* (1991), at 159–60). While Rifkin *et al* have provided an extremely valuable critique of the myth that it is possible for mediators not be aligned with parties and not to influence outcomes, their use of the term 'neutrality' may be confusing to those who do not take the time to read their definition.

- 'neutrality' means non-intervention;[62] and/or
- 'impartiality' and 'neutrality' mean (or include) objectivity.[63]

Some of these ideas overlap and some are contradictory to one another.

Unburdening valuable concepts from the baggage of 'neutrality'

The various definitions and uses of the terms 'neutrality' and 'impartiality' have made these words less than useful. The concepts buried within these terms include at least the following: non-partisan fairness, the degree of mediator intervention, role limitation and objectivity. The following is an attempt to elucidate and critique each of these concepts.

Non-partisan fairness

Here the term 'non-partisan fairness' is used to refer to the general concept of fairness to all parties. Were it not for the confusing discourse, this concept could be termed 'impartiality'. The term 'impartial' is a worthy one, and it is unfortunate that its usefulness has been undermined through confusion between its meaning and the related but different meanings of 'neutrality'. *Mediation UK Practice Standards* refer to the concept of non-partisan fairness as 'impartiality' which they define as 'attending equally to the needs and interests of all parties with equal respect, without discrimination and without taking sides'.[64] These standards do not use the term 'neutrality', either synonymously with impartiality or independently. The standards contemplate a variety of mediation contexts including multi-party settings.

---

62   Yet another definition of 'neutrality' refers to non-intervention. Webster's dictionary suggests 'neutral' means 'not engaged on either side; not siding with or assisting either of two contending parties'. There are two shades of meaning here. One shade of meaning connotes fairness to all parties ('not siding'). The other shade of meaning connotes non-intervention ('not assisting'). This second meaning attached to 'neutrality' can be interpreted as 'a kind of passive objectivity – the idea of being inert, disengaged, colourless, bland and even impotent and powerless' (Scambler, CM, 'The Myth of Mediator Neutrality' (May, 1990) *Interaction*, Kitchener, ON: The Network: Interaction for Conflict Resolution, 2 (1), at 14.) Thus, the 'neutral' mediator has been described as 'a eunuch from Mars, totally powerless (and totally neutral)'. This colourful analogy attributed to Roger Fisher in 1981 (cited in Mediation Development Association of British Columbia (MDABC) *Brief on Standards and Ethics for Mediators Presented to the Attorney General of British Columbia*, 1989, Vancouver, BC: Mediation Development Association of British Columbia, at 27) introduces the concept of 'neutrality' as the extent to which a mediator deliberately intervenes to influence the process or outcome of mediation. It must be emphasised that in this definition of neutrality, neutrality is placed in contrast to interventionism (and would not necessarily mean aligning with both parties equally). This is different from Rifkin *et al's* concept of neutrality which incorporates interventionism (under the concept of 'equidistance'). Thus, the term 'neutrality' has two contradictory definitions.

63   The analogy of the 'eunuch from Mars' referred to above in note 62 points to yet another important conception of 'neutrality', that being a 'outsider' or stranger to the parties will prevent any suggestion of bias toward one party or the other. This conception of neutrality springs from the idea that it is possible to put aside biases and be autonomously objective. Rawlsian 'impartiality' also includes this concept, which is critiqued later in this chapter.

64   Mediation UK, 1993, see above note 13, Summary, Art 20.

A joint effort by the American Arbitration Association (AAA), the American Bar Association (ABA) and the Society of Professionals in Dispute Resolution (SPIDR) has produced *Model Standards of Conduct for Mediators*.[65] which defines 'impartiality' as evenhandedness and lack of 'prejudice based on the parties' personal characteristics, background or performance at the mediation.'

Perhaps the desired attitude and behaviour connoted by the term 'impartial' can be summed up as the quality of being principled enough to remain equally committed to the legitimate interests of all parties. Thus 'impartial' persons may be ones who

> by virtue of their virtue, their relationships with both sides, and their commitment to the way of peace, are counted sufficiently trustworthy and wise to qualify as mediators or arbiters in the community's disputes.[66]

It is abhorrent to eliminate the term 'impartial' from the vocabulary of mediation; however, for the sake of clarity, this concept will henceforth be referred to as 'non-partisan fairness' except where quotation makes use of the term 'impartial' necessary.

Inappropriate pecuniary or other self-interests

Codes of ethics universally condemn the idea of mediating in cases where the mediator has a pecuniary or any other kind of self-interest in a particular settlement outcome. The concept of incorruptibility is central to non-partisan fairness. This concept may be a universal ethical principle of mediation.

Partisan relationships

Bush[67] has pointed out that problems with maintaining non-partisan fairness can arise in several ways. Problems can occur prior to mediator selection as a result of perceived partisan relationships with one or the other parties or with those they are affiliated such as lawyers, associates or family members. Sometimes, disclosure of affiliations can resolve potential problems or perception to the satisfaction of the parties and the mediator.[68] Problems can also arise once a mediation is in progress, if actual or perceived partisan relationships are discovered or arise after mediation commences. This is more problematic, as it can cause delays or dissatisfaction if there is a perceived need to change mediators.

These kinds of problems can spring from relationships with referral sources or repeat clients, or from previous professional relationships such as legal or

---

65 AAA, ABA and SPIDR, 1995, see above note 13, Article II.

66 Gilman and Gustafson (1994), see above note 7, at 101.

67 Bush (1994), see above note 3, at 9–10.

68 It is important that these kinds of problem be resolved to the satisfaction of the mediator, since a mediator's experience means they may be able to foresee future problems with perceived or actual partisanship that the parties cannot see at the commencement of mediation.

counselling relationships.[69] Article 2 of Mediation UK[70] provides an explicit 'duty to reveal to parties any conflict which may exist between their responsibility to their employers or referring agencies and their responsibility to act impartially between the parties.' AAA, ABA and SPIDR[71] explicitly refers to conflicts of interest that can arise from pressure to settle cases:

> Potential conflicts of interest may arise between administrators of mediation programs and mediators and there may be strong pressures on the mediator to settle a particular case or cases. The mediator's commitment must be to the parties and the process. Pressure from outside of the mediation process should never influence the mediator to coerce parties to settle.

To the extent that previous relationships with parties may make the mediator corruptible, they interfere with non-partisan fairness. However, close relationships with all the parties may not be considered inappropriate in some settings. This is discussed further below (see 'objectivity' and 'insider-partials').

Other problems can arise during mediation when the mediator feels aligned with a party or finds one of the parties particularly reprehensible. No one is immune to feelings of more or less sympathy. The quality of having sufficient non-partisan fairness to be effective as a mediator may be part of the rather intangible 'mediator's mindset'[72] of being continuously able to avoid or suspend judgment, and maintain an attitude of unconditional facilitative service to all parties until mediation is concluded. This concept of non-partisan fairness may be a universal ethical concept in mediation. It is difficult to find a theory of mediation that does not hold the principle of non-partisan fairness to be foundational to the ethics of mediation, even in discussions of 'insider-partial' mediation in which the mediator must have and maintain the trust of all the parties (see also below).

Degree of mediator intervention

Mediator settlement strategies may differ 'according to their location along a continuum between two polar positions, neutrality and intervention.'[73] Both context and values determine how interventionist a mediator's strategy will be.

The degree to which mediators should intervene to influence the process or the outcome is one of the most important debates in the field of mediation. It is this discussion to which the research of Rifkin, Millen and Cobb, and Cobb and Rifkin,[74] have substantially contributed to challenge the notion that it is possible for mediators not to influence process and outcome.

---

69   See also below on 'role limitation', p 327.

70   Mediation UK, 1993, see above note 13.

71   AAA, ABA and SPIDR,1995, see above note 13, Article III.

72   Gustafson, 1994, see above note 7, at 103.

73   Bernard, SE, Folger, JP, Weingarten, HR and Zumeta, ZR, 'The Neutral Mediator: Value Dilemmas in Divorce Mediation' (1984) *Mediation Quarterly* 4, pp 61–74, at 62.

74   Rifkin *et al*, 1991, see above note 58. Cobb, S, and Rifkin, J, 'Neutrality as a Discursive Practice: The Construction and Transformation of Narratives in Community Mediation' in Silbey, S and Sarat, A (eds), 11 *Studies in Law, Politics and Society*, 1991a, Greenwich, Conn: JAI Press. Cobb, S, and Rifkin, J, 'Practice and Paradox: Deconstructing neutrality in mediation' (1991b) *Law & Social Inquiry* 16(1), at 35–62.

Codes of conduct for mediators tend to be either non-interventionist ('neutralist') or interventionist in philosophy. Family Mediation Canada's (FMC) *Code of Professional Conduct*[75] guides mediators to distinguish 'impartiality toward the participants' from 'neutrality on the issue of fairness.' Mediators are told to express their concern to parties if they think a proposed agreement is unfair. It also states that it is a mediator's duty to terminate mediation:

- when they are unable to eliminate 'manipulative or intimidating negotiating techniques'.[76]

- 'whenever continuation of the process is likely to harm or prejudice one or more the participants ...'[77]

- if they are not able to 'restrain parents from coming to arrangements that are perceived by the mediator not to be in the best interest of the children ...'[78]

- when parties appear to be making an agreement which the mediator thinks is unfair or unreasonable.[79]

(The first two provisions above refer to the process of mediation. The last two provisions refer to the outcome of mediation.)

New draft clauses now being considered by FMC[80] propose a less interventionist approach, suggesting a mediator duty 'to assist participants to reflect upon and to consider how their proposed arrangements realistically meet the needs and best interests of other affected persons especially vulnerable persons'. FMC[81] states mediation should be suspended if the parties are 'acting in bad faith ... or when the usefulness [of mediation] has been exhausted'. Interventionist strategies are maintained where process issues are concerned, but tempered where outcomes are concerned unless the mediator find an agreement 'unconscionable' in which cases the mediator should withdraw. FMC appears to be retaining a more interventionist approach compared to the standards of the Academy of Family Mediators' *Standards of Practice for Family and Divorce Mediation*, which are less interventionist.[82]

The Academy of Family Mediators (AFM) *Standards*[83] emphasise party self-determination, stating that 'decision making authority rests with the parties' and clarifying that the 'role of the mediator includes reducing the obstacles to communication, maximising the exploration of the alternatives, and addressing the needs of those it is agreed are involved or affected'. Further, AFM outlines

---

75   Family Mediation Canada, *Code of Professional Conduct*, 1986, Guelph, Ontario: Family Mediation Canada, Article 9:4.

76   *Ibid*, Article 10:4.

77   *Ibid*, Article 12:1.

78   *Ibid*, Article 8:2.

79   *Ibid*, Article 12:3.

80   Family Mediation Canada, *Code of Professional Conduct (Revised)*, 1996, Draft Article 8:2.

81   *Ibid*, Draft Article 13:1,2.

82   AFM, 1995, see above note 13.

83   *Ibid*, Article I.

the value principles on which mediation is based: 'fairness, privacy, self determination, and the best interest of all family members.' In comparing AFM's 1986 guidelines with its 1995 version, AFM has become substantially less interventionist in philosophy. Nevertheless, AFM's 1995 version retains a provision which suggests mediation be terminated if 'a reasonable agreement is unlikely'.[84]

A question for the individual mediator becomes 'what standard of reasonableness and fairness should be applied?' What does 'reasonable' or 'fair' mean, and who is the arbiter of reasonableness and fairness: the parties? The mediator? The law? Some other standard? The fairness of parties, mediators and the law can all be challenged, creating dilemmas for those who have universalistic ethical conceptions of 'fairness.' In a pluralistic society, there are significant ethical and practical problems in identifying universally acceptable ethical criteria for 'fairness.' A retreat to ethical relativism may be acceptable to those who are committed to party autonomy as their primary ethical value. However, critics of mediation who are primarily concerned with social justice are unsatisfied with answers that may disadvantage disempowered groups in society.

The extent to which mediators intervene to ensure outcome fairness depends largely on the context. Commercial mediators and community mediators tend to follow the example of labour mediators in taking a non-interventionist approach to the role of the mediator. Labour mediators act on the principle that parties should be free to do as they please, provided that they are fully informed as to their options.

While the FMC and AFM standards appear to be becoming less interventionist, some literature is advancing more interventionist approaches in family mediation especially in relation to woman abuse, with emphasis on developing methods of screening and safe termination of mediation. There is a growing suggestion among family mediators that the bargaining weakness of one of the parties, risks of woman or child abuse, and family power dynamics make neutrality on these issues inappropriate in family mediation.[85]

The *Mediation UK Practice Standards*[86] contemplate a variety of mediation contexts including multi-party settings. In terms of mediator intervention, the standards provide for party control of the content of the discussion and decisions on agreements.[87] These standards require mediators to ensure voluntary participation by parties, including a very useful acknowledgment that voluntariness:

---

84   *Ibid*, Article X.D.

85   Barsky, AE, 'Issues in the Termination of Mediation Due to Abuse' (1995) *Mediation Quarterly* 13, at 19–35; Ellis, D, 'Marital Conflict Mediation and Postseparation Wife Abuse' (1990) *Law and Inequality* 8(2), at 317–39; Fund for Dispute Resolution, *Report from the Toronto Forum on Woman Abuse and Mediation*, 1993, Waterloo, Ontario: Fund for Dispute Resolution; Landau, 1994, see above note 7; Ontario Association for Family Mediation (OAFM), *OAFM Policy on Abuse*, June 1994, Toronto: Ontario Association for Family Mediation.

86   Mediation UK, 1993, see above note 13.

87   *Ibid*, Summary, Article 6.

is a relative concept and it is unlikely that many people come to mediation entirely without pressure of some kind—whether internal feelings of obligation, pressure from their communities or families, referral by criminal justice agencies, or threat of legal action.[88]

The standards do not, however, define what 'voluntary' does mean.

Regarding intervention into process issues, the *Mediation UK Practice Standards* also provide that mediators maintain conditions that will exclude violence, threats, shouting and discriminatory or provocative language 'by adequate preparation and by temporary or permanent abandonment of the mediation if necessary.'[89] Regarding outcomes, mediators are told they should not 'seem to recommend' a particular settlement, but may suggest options.[90] Mediators are also urged to encourage independent legal advice and to voice concerns about an agreement that is 'unjust, deleterious to any party (involved or not involved in the mediation) and in any other way unsatisfactory'.[91] No criteria are developed to describe what is meant by 'unjust', 'deleterious' or 'unsatisfactory'. The *Mediation UK Practice Standards* mirror Canadian and US family mediation standards which provide for significant intervention on process issues with less intervention to influence outcomes.

The AAA, ABA and SPIDR *Model Standards of Conduct for Mediators* explicitly recognise self-determination as 'the fundamental principle of mediation' and that mediation relies upon the 'ability of the parties to reach a voluntary uncoerced agreement'.[92] The document contemplates a variety of mediation contexts. These guidelines are remarkably non–interventionist, merely cautioning against providing professional advice (but instead suggesting to recommend outside professional advice). The only directive for mediator withdrawal is to prevent mediation from 'being used to further illegal conduct, or if a party is unable to participate due to drug, alcohol, or other physical or mental incapacity'.[93] Interestingly, these standards are the only ones which explicitly caution mediators against permitting the behaviour 'to be guided by a desire for a high settlement rate.' This refers to mediators' temptation to coerce settlements in order to boost their reputation for effectiveness.[94]

Codes of ethics thus reflect a tension between party self-determination and mediator influence to avoid party exposure to harm, to prevent abuse of mediation, or to ensure fair outcomes. The concept of non–intervention is based on the Western preference for self-determination and autonomy, and ethical tensions concerning when and how much to intervene reflect this bias. Not all

---

88   *Ibid*, Detailed Statement, Article 5.

89   *Ibid*, Detailed Statement, Article 4.

90   *Ibid*, Detailed Statement, Article 6.

91   *Ibid*, Detailed Statement, Article 8.

92   AAA, ABA and SPIDR, 1995, see above note 13, Article I.

93   *Ibid*, Article VI.

94   *Ibid*, Article VI.

groups are so committed to individual autonomy. Many groups, particularly those with hierarchical collectivist backgrounds are comfortable with models of mediation that feature mediator recommendations or pressure, provided the mediator is respected and trusted by the parties.[95]

If the issue of degree of intervention is placed in the whole context of the philosophy of ethics, the reasons mediators use for exercising mediator influence seem to reflect utilitarian ethics. Both consequentialist and deontological ethical frameworks might lead to interventionist strategies, but for different reasons. For example, mediators who believe that the purpose of mediation is party satisfaction or high settlement rates (consequentialist ethics) may feel ethically constrained to use strong mediator influence by way of recommendations and suggestions to parties. On the other hand, the same consequentialist mediator may consider coercive tactics to be unethical if he or she considers that parties will not be satisfied with mediator pressure. Deontological theories of ethics may encourage mediators to intervene strongly to protect the interests of affected persons such as children, or to effect justice, even at the expense of party autonomy.

Mediators struggling with the ethics of how much to intervene in a particular case may find themselves acting according to three criteria: their own sense of the ethics involved in a conflict; the gravity of effects to the parties; and the degree to which they care about the outcome for the parties. Even those holding deontological ethical positions may also look to the possible consequences to determine the paramountcy of one intervention over another. To illustrate, a labour mediator may differ with the ethics of one or both parties concerning a wage clause in a collective agreement. Yet the labour mediator may not consider the issue of sufficient ethical importance to intervene to attempt to influence the outcome in such a way that the mediator's ethical preferences would prevail. The mediator may not consider that the consequences to the parties are sufficiently grave to warrant intruding her or his own sense of what would be right. By contrast, a family mediator faced with the prospect of harm to a party or a child as a result of a potential decision by disputing parties may feel ethically required to intervene in order to influence not only the process, but also the outcome. In some cases, particularly in situations of violence or extreme injustice, third parties may be sufficiently moved by the gravity of the situation that they will not wait to be invited but initiate and seek out opportunities to intervene, regardless of (or even because of) prior affiliations with the parties. This often occurs with diplomatic intervention into international conflict or internecine violence. In such situations, third parties may become clearly activist in their attempts to influence both the process and the outcome. An 'insider-partial' mediator (described in the next section) may be extremely interventionist, coaxing parties toward behaviour and outcomes which uphold the mutually held principles of the particular family, institution, religion or culture.

---

95   Duryea, 1992, see above note 19; Duryea, 1994, see above note 19, at 116 and also Duryea and Grundison, 1993, see above note 14.

To summarise, in deciding the method and degree of intervention, mediators may act from a variety, or even a combination, of ethical perspectives from consequentialist perspectives (that significant harm could occur to institutional, economic, national or other interests) to deontological perspectives (that 'right is right' and justice must be done no matter what the consequences).[96]

Role limitation

Ethical problems can occur when the parties need expert information, advice, counselling or advocacy. All of these roles can provide challenges to mediators, especially if mediation is conceived to be a process which fosters party self-determination. Where the goal of mediation is self-determination, it follows that mediators would tend to play a non-interventionist facilitative role rather than a directive one. Providing counselling or advice is also clearly inconsistent with a non-interventionist model of mediation.

Bush[97] describes this issue under the category of 'separating mediation from counselling and legal advice.' By using the term 'role limitation' Davis[98] expands Bush's classification to include distinguishing a variety of non-mediation roles other than legal and counselling.

Mediation UK[99] refers to this issue under the topic of 'impartiality' saying that mediators

should not act as such in cases where one party is a client in another professional role, such as advocate or counsellor. Mediators should at all times keep their role as mediator distinct from any other roles they might play in other situations.

The issue has been most discussed by counsellor-mediators working with families. Counsellor-mediators are often enjoined to exercise caution against confusing mediation and counselling. AFM[100] warns that a mediator 'may be compromised by social or professional relationships with one of the participants at any point time' and prohibits mediation

unless the prior relationship has been discussed, the role of the mediator made distinct from the earlier relationship, and the participants given the opportunity to freely choose to proceed.

---

96 The topic of power and its use and abuse in mediation is one of the many issues which require much more research and theory development within the field of dispute resolution. In spite of the importance of looking at ethics in mediation through the lens of power, the literature on ethics in mediation is largely silent on this topic. The exception is feminist critical literature on mediation which contains implicit ethical arguments concerning the ways power structures in society affect bargaining power of individuals in mediation. The field of mediation is beginning to address some practical issues raised by these critiques, mainly in the area of screening out of mediation those who may experience abuse or coercion during mediator-assisted negotiations. (See, for example, Fund for Dispute Resolution, 1993, see above note 85; Landau, 1994, see above note 7.) These works, however, tend to present the issues in terms of competency and qualifications rather than in terms of ethics.

97 Bush (1994), see above note 3.

98 Davis, AM, 'Ethics: No One Ever Said It Would Be Easy: Bush's Contribution to Mediation Practice' (1994) *Journal of Dispute Resolution* 1, pp 75–79, at 79.

99 Mediation UK, 1993, see above note 13, Article 2.

100 AFM, 1995, see above note 13, Article IV.C.

However, prior relationships, by themselves, do not proscribe the mediator's involvement unless she or he has provided previous legal or counselling services.

FMC[101] contains similar provisions, and refers not just to counselling, but to all 'prior involvements,' which could include any kind of professional or other relationship. FMC's new draft[102] refers to 'prior *professional* and personal involvement'.

Dworkin *et al*[103] suggest several reasons for clear differentiation of roles. First, alliances with one of the parties created in a prior professional relationship could lead to problems with maintaining non-partisan fairness. Second, professionals could inappropriately suggest multiple services for pecuniary gain. Dworkin suggests, however, that it may be appropriate for mediator to offer multiple services if the parties are not able to obtain needed services elsewhere, especially where there has been some time lapse which makes 'switching hats' more acceptable.[104] Third, mediation would be clearly contraindicated if the mediator had previously acted as an advocate for one party. This would be clearly incompatible with the role of mediator.[105] In spite of these cautions, there is a strong thread of self-determination philosophy in these guidelines. It is suggested that if parties have full information concerning prior relationships, and the differing roles of the mediator are clear, the parties should be able to choose.

A related question particularly applicable to counsellor-mediators is how much therapy should be incorporated in mediation. Benjamin and Irving[106] have developed a model of 'therapeutic family mediation' which, in a premediation stage they use 'a frankly therapeutic process but restricted to behavioural and attitudinal change sufficient to allow the parties to negotiate'.[107] There is a wide range of mediation practice including large doses of therapy. It is considered important that the purpose of therapy should be limited to helping the parties negotiate toward agreement.

Similar questions arise in mediation and facilitation of multiparty public disputes. It is said that mediators who are experts in the substantive issues involved in pubic disputes may inappropriately affect the non-partisan fairness of the process by providing expert information to the process or by pressing for particular solutions which they believe to be best.[108]

---

101 FMC, 1986, see above note 75, Article 8:5.

102 FMC, 1996, see above note 80, Draft Article 8:5.

103 Dworkin, J, Jacob, L and Scott, E, 'The Boundaries Between Mediation and Therapy: Ethical Dilemmas' (Winter 1991) *Mediation Quarterly* 9 (2), at 107–19.

104 *Ibid*, at 111.

105 *Ibid*, at 112.

106 Benjamin, M, and Irving, H, 'Toward a Feminist-Informed Model of Therapeutic Family Mediation' (1992) *Mediation Quarterly* 10(2), pp 129–53.

107 *Ibid* at 131.

108 Cormick, GW, 'How and When to Mediate Natural Resource Disputes'. Paper presented to the Institute on Resolution and Avoidance of Disputes, 23 March 1984. Denver, Colorado: Rocky Mountain Mineral Law Foundation, 1984. Diepeveen, B 'Substance Abuse: The Risks Involved' (Winter 1992–93) *Interaction* 4(4), at 5–6.

In codes of ethics, this issue is often referred to under the rubric 'conflict of interest'. AAA, ABA and SPIDR[109] define a conflict of interest as 'a dealing or relationship that might create an impression of possible bias' and holds mediators responsible for disclosure of conflicts. FMC[110] provides that mediators 'must avoid any activity that could create a conflict of interest'. Included in prohibited behaviour that 'that might impair their professional judgment or ... increase the risk of exploiting clients' is to mediate among 'close friends, relatives, colleagues/supervisors or students' or 'to engage in sexual intimacies with a participant in the mediation process'.

To summarise, there are two ethical issues involved in the question of role limitation. One ethical concern is the possibility that one party may benefit over another through a previous professional or social relationship. This affects the non-partisan fairness of the process. The other ethical issue is related to party self-determination and autonomy. Within a culture which values individual autonomy, it is considered unethical to infringe inappropriately on that autonomy. Infringement on party self-determination could occur through the giving of substantive professional advice by the mediator, especially if the advice is delivered in a manner that seems coercive. Also, there is a sense in which multiple professional or process roles for mediators could limit party self-determination by confusing the parties over the nature and purpose of the mediation process.

Objectivity: myth and reality

Western dispute resolution practice tends to aspire to the ideal of objectivity, the notion that the model mediator is autonomously objective as in Rawls's concept of the 'veil of ignorance'. This ideal mediator has an objective sense of fairness and is unaffected by the context or the parties. This ideal state of objectivity can be hampered merely by knowing one or both of the parties, which is said to present the mediator with a conflict of interest or at least an uncomfortable dynamic that should be avoided.

Within the idea that previous relationships and feelings of sympathy are undesirable, is the notion that the 'moral agent' is an autonomous individual who is capable of being 'objective' in the Rawlsian sense. This idea may be challenged by those from hierarchical collectivist societies whose ethics contemplate adherence to traditional ethical principles.[111] The possibility and desirability of autonomous objectivity might also be challenged by those whose ethical theories contemplate interdependent communities whose members have mutually reciprocal responsibilities.[112]

---

109 AAA, ABA and SPIDR, 1995, see above note 13, Article III.

110 FMC, 1986, see above note 75, Article 4:1.

111 See the section on 'universalism', 'utilitarianism' and 'insider-partials', at pp 309, 311, 330

112 See the sections above which refer to Gilligan and communicative ethics, at pp 308, 316.

In many Western settings it is considered highly desirable and sometimes even vital that the third party be an unknown outsider who cannot possibly be influenced by the context or the parties. Practices in North American jury selection are an example of this principle; the fair and objective decision of 'neutral' jurors should not be influenced except by carefully packaged information conveyed in controlled circumstances. This notion has been brought into practices surrounding the selection of mediators. As previously discussed, the idea that it is possible for a person to be objective has been strongly challenged on both philosophical and practical grounds. For example, labour mediators may deal with the same parties on more than one occasion. In British Columbia automobile insurance mediators are used by the Insurance Corporation of BC through whom virtually all motorists are insured. These mediators cannot possibly avoid knowing the parties in every case, and indeed, it has been said that working too much in such settings can 'pollute neutrality'.

Feminist critics of family mediation have questioned the possibility of unbiased, value-free neutrality. Mediators 'have been raised in a largely patriarchal social system in which gender roles have only recently been questioned, primarily by white, middle class North Americans'.[113] People who are enculturated within a given social system often consider the prevailing norms, however unfair, to be 'objective'.

This is one of the most potent critiques of mediator objectivity. Everybody has values and biases. It is not possible for mediators to park them at the door of the hearing-room. The ideal of autonomous objectivity does not recognise the fact that mediators are influenced far more than they may realise by the culture and social setting in which they live, and the political, social and power structures within which they operate.

The objective mediator who can set aside all prejudices may be an ideal for those whose ethical framework contemplates self-determination and autonomy. Objectivity may not be an ideal for others with a more collectivist approach to ethics. In either case, this 'objective' mediator is a mythical creature removed from the realities of interaction among human beings who live in communities.

Preference for 'insider-partials'

Research on cross-cultural issues in dispute resolution points out that not everyone prefers an 'outside-neutral'. Detached objectivity is not universally sought. People from some cultural groups prefer 'insider-partial' intervenors.[114] Insider-partials are intervenors who have strong and continuing affiliations with the parties, and who are known and trusted by all the parties.

---

113 Landau, 1994, see above note 7, at 33.

114 Lederach, JP, and Wehr, P, 'Mediating Conflict in Central America' (1991) *Journal of Peace Research* 28(1), pp 85–98, at 87. Lederach, 1991, see above note 16. Lederach, see further above note 19.

LeBaron Duryea[115] criticises current standards of practice that prescribe 'neutrality,' discussing, by way of example, the work of Honeyman and his associates in the Test Design Project outlined in Interim Guidelines for Selecting Mediators National Institute for Dispute Resolution.[116] Referring to the preference for insider-partials in some contexts, she states:

> Where this preference exists, the impartiality criteria ('asked objective questions' … 'conveyed neutral atmosphere') set out in the Honeyman standards have little relevance. Insider partials will bring a sophisticated understanding of the parties, the issues, and the broader context in which the issues are situated. They may also bring set ideas about the 'right' conduct for each party and what roles parties should adopt in order to mend the rift. Conveyance of a neutral atmosphere is not anywhere on the map for such an intervenor, nor should it be.[117]

Because of the diversity of needs and preferences in different contexts, it is important that standards of practice be specific to the context in which they will be used. Codes of ethics promulgated by influential mediation organisations which prescribe neutrality may inadvertently delegitimise practices which are common not only among minority ethnic or cultural groups, but also in some mainstream institutions. There are numerous examples of informal and formal insider mediation conducted within a variety of institutional settings from universities to churches. In such cases, a person within the institution who is known and trusted by both persons is sought out for advice, counsel and conciliation. These processes may be unremunerated and informal and may bear little resemblance to the model of face-to-face mediation frequently taught in North America.[118] It would be unfortunate if the practice of these informal processes were either explicitly or implicitly discouraged by the heightened awareness of the option of 'professional' mediation with its accompanying structures and codification of ethical standards of practice. It would be worse if these practices were implicitly or explicitly labelled 'unethical' by professional organisations whose ethical framework excludes other perspectives.

The *Mediation UK Practices Standards* provides that mediators should be aware of 'local and cultural differences that need to be taken into account.'[119] This useful provision refers to all mediation practices generally. Family Mediation Canada is

---

115 Duryea, Michelle LeBaron, 'The Quest for Qualifications: A Quick Trip Without a Good Map', in Morris, C and Pirie, A (eds), *Qualifications for Dispute Resolution: Perspectives on the Debate*, 1994b, Victoria, BC: UVic Institute for Dispute Resolution, pp 109–29.

116 National Institute for Dispute Resolution (NIDR), *Interim Guidelines for Selecting Mediators*, 1993, Washington, DC: National Institute for Dispute Resolution.

117 Duryea,1994b, see above note 115, at 116–17.

118 A frequently taught four-stage model includes: (1) pre-mediation assessment and introduction; (2) party narratives; (3) exploration of party interests; and (4) development of solutions and finalising agreements. Increasingly, training is emphasising flexible (but still largely staged) models which incorporate assessment, conflict analysis and process design at the outset; and the possibility of implementation and monitoring agreements afterward.

119 Mediation UK, 1993, see above note 13, Article 3.

considering these factors in the creation of its new draft code of ethics. While the other codes of ethics do not explicitly preclude insider–partial mediation, FMC's draft standards appear to be unique in explicitly acknowledging its possibility. However, this possibility is couched within the framework of a strong preference for 'outside neutrality'. The draft standard suggests that 'except where culturally appropriate mediators must be cautious about mediating disputes involving close friends, relatives, colleagues/supervisors or students'.[120] The intention appears to be that insider–partial mediation is to be considered as an exception, rather than as one of a number of possibilities within a diverse society.

In increasingly multicultural societies, discussions of ethics in mediation require more awareness of the culturally specific ethical biases that are inherent in all such discussions. Ethical stances are important, and they inevitably reflect the culture within which they are situated. Discussions about ethics are most useful, and more fair, when they are clearly understood and articulated for all members of society (not just members of the dominant culture) to see and evaluate.

CONFIDENTIALITY

Most codes of ethics reflect a strong commitment to confidentiality. It has been said that 'lack of confidentiality will deter disputants from using the mediation process ...'.[121] This is true for most cases of commercial mediation, in which the usual recourse upon lack of settlement is the courts. Most of the literature on confidentiality in mediation has centred on the legal principles which might or might not protect the confidentiality of the mediation process. Other literature discusses appropriate exceptions to confidentiality. The ethical underpinnings of the concept of confidentiality have not received much treatment in the literature.

Considerations of the appropriateness or inappropriateness of confidentiality is dependent on the specific context of mediation. The ethical issue appears to be quite simple: the mediation process and the process leader must be able to guarantee that it can keep whatever promises are made concerning confidentiality.

The purpose of confidentiality

Confidentiality of the mediation process is considered important to ensure that parties feel free to disclose all relevant information in mediation. If confidentiality could not be guaranteed, and mediators were called to give evidence in subsequent proceedings, there would be a strong deterrent to the use of mediation as a pre-trial settlement option. Another reason given is that compelling a mediator to give evidence could impugn the perceived or actual

---

120 FMC, 1996, see above note 80, Draft Article 4:1.

121 Pirie, A, 'The Lawyer as a Third Party Neutral: Promise and Problems', in Emond, DP (ed), *Commercial Dispute Resolution: Alternatives to Litigation*, 1989, Aurora ON: Canada Law Book, Inc, pp 27–54, at 47.

non-partisan fairness of the mediator by requiring her or him to provide opinions, for example, about whether the parties (or one of them) was bargaining in good faith.[122]

It is beyond the scope of this paper to discuss the law of confidentiality, which is specific to each jurisdiction. Generally speaking, the confidentiality of mediation has been respected by courts in North America in spite of the lack of specific legislation in many jurisdictions to provide for confidentiality of mediation.

Exceptions to confidentiality

While mediation appears to be assumed as a general principle, there are several exceptions, most of which require ethical deliberation on the part of the mediator. Some processes are deliberately 'open' in that the parties and the mediator intend at the outset that the mediator will be a competent and compellable witness in any subsequent court proceeding.

Compellability by a court

Unless there is guiding legislation in the particular jurisdiction, judges have considerable discretion about whether to compel testimony about a mediation process. In Canada, mediators can do a good deal to provide protection for themselves and their clients from surprises by making confidentiality provisions a matter of written agreement before entering into mediation. Also, draft settlement memoranda, documents and other letters can be marked 'privileged' and 'without prejudice' to enhance the chances that courts will respect the confidentiality of the process. Readers are advised to regularly update themselves concerning the law on mediation and confidentiality in their particular jurisdiction.

People in need of protection

Most jurisdictions provide a legal duty to inform the appropriate authorities where a person has grounds to believe a child is in need of protection. Many jurisdictions also provide a duty to warn where there is a threat of harm to any person, for example if in caucus a party threatens to harm another person. Law, however, is often ambiguous and usually provides insufficient guidance. A legal analysis is incomplete because the law does not provide an adequate ethical framework for the issues related to confidentiality. There may be a variety of circumstances in which maintaining confidential would be a breach of ethics either for personal reasons, or in the public interest. Codes of ethics provide only general guidance.

---

122 Gibson, K, 'Confidentiality in Mediation: A Moral Reassessment' (1992) *Journal of Dispute Resolution,* pp 25–66, at 44–48.

Mediators can create their own standards by agreement with the parties. Written agreements with the parties can provide, for example, that the mediator will report to the appropriate authorities any information arising out of the mediation process which gives her or him reasonable grounds to believe that a child or any other person may be in need of protection. Agreements can also make explicit what will happen to notes or any records, and outline other possible limits of confidentiality, such as the fact that courts may have the power to compel mediators to give evidence.

Caucusing

Another sensitive issue arises in caucusing with individual parties. Sometimes mediators hold all information confidential unless the parties authorise release. In other cases mediators may decline to guarantee that information shared in caucus will remain confidential. In still other cases mediators and parties together make decisions about the disposition of information shared in caucus during a preliminary 'process design' phase.

The decisions concerning what to do with information shared during caucusing is a sensitive one and depends almost entirely on the context. Valuable discussion on this issue is found in SPIDR's publication, *Making the Tough Calls*.[123] Mediators who prefer not to guarantee confidentiality during caucuses can make this a matter of discussion prior to mediation, or make it part of a written mediation agreement.

The need for public accountability

For public policy reasons, it may be undesirable for multi-party public policy disputes to be mediated confidentially. Public policy mediations usually include specific negotiations concerning how information conveyed during mediation is to be used. Some public policy mediations are open to the public and the press. Others are not. Useful sample clauses of 'ground rules' developed by parties for the purpose of round table negotiations may be found in the work of Carpenter and Kennedy.[124]

Implementing party promises of confidentiality

In most cases, parties agree to hold information obtained during mediation confidential. It becomes a difficult ethical issue when the mediator becomes aware during the course of mediation that one or both of the parties is sharing or

---

123 SPIDR, 1991, see above note 1.
124 Carpenter, SL and Kennedy, WJD, *Managing Public Disputes,* 1991, San Francisco: Jossey-Bass, at 111–15 and 123–24.

using information in contradiction to their agreement. Mediators may wish to discuss with clients, or make it part of their agreement, what the consequences will be if this occurs.

Most codes of ethics reflect the policy assumption that mediation will normally be confidential. FMC[125] implicitly assumes that mediation processes will be confidential and provides a list of exceptions to confidentiality including non-identifying information for research or education, written consent of the parties, court order, threat to a person's life or safety, and open mediation. AFM[126] is much more general, including provisions that a 'mediator shall foster the confidentiality of the process' and 'inform the parties ... of limitations on confidentiality' and 'circumstances under which mediators may be compelled to testify in court.' Mediation UK[127] explicitly provides for a 'strong presumption of confidentiality' with similar exceptions to those of FMC, AAA, ABA and SPIDR[128] simply state that the 'reasonable expectations of the parties with regard to confidentiality shall be met by the mediator', that the expectations depend on the circumstances, and that matters the parties expect to be confidential will not be revealed without the permission of the parties or unless 'required by law or other public policy'.

While demands of confidentiality pose significant practical tensions for mediators, its concepts are not as controversial as the issues surrounding 'impartiality' and 'neutrality'. Likely this is because of widespread acceptance that there are a variety of legitimate models concerning what and how information is to be shared, depending on the purpose of mediation, and often the preference of the parties. Thus, confidentiality may be as much a technical as an ethical issue.

The central ethical concern relating to confidentiality is one of trust. In order to trust a mediator or a mediation process, parties need to know what will or might happen to the often sensitive information that will be exchanged among the parties or with the mediator. Most codes of ethics reflect that the most important policy concerning confidentiality is informed consent by the parties. While practical issues may be complicated, the salient ethical issue is that of keeping promises made about the use of information produced by the mediation process.

COMPETENCE

Is there an essential difference between a consideration of ethics and competency standards? Is one subsumed in the other? Discussions on mediation and ethics do not distinguish clearly between ethical and technical issues in mediation. Bush's[129] very useful empirical study on mediator ethics has been criticised by

---

125 FMC, 1986, see above note 75, Article 7, 11.

126 AFM, 1995, see above note 13, Article VI.

127 Mediation UK, 1993, see above note 13, Article 2.

128 AAA, ABA and SPIDR, 1995, see above note 13, Article V.

129 Bush, 1994, see above note 3.

Stulberg[130] on the grounds that the study does not open up the dialogue about moral vs non-moral dilemmas. He points out that a dilemma about 'right' or 'wrong' is not necessarily an ethical question. A question about what is 'right' may be a non-ethical dilemma based on technical or prudential issues.

Moral versus non-moral dilemmas

Moral philosophers have differed on the question of whether there is an essential difference between morality and prudence. Some suggest that 'moral choices' are essential egoistic or based on self-interest.[131] However, Kantian ethics distinguish moral imperatives from prudential or technical imperatives.[132] An example of a prudential or technical imperative might be: 'If you want to preserve your perceived non-partisan fairness as a mediator, avoid asking closed questions or making suggestions as to outcome.' An example of a true ethical imperative might be: 'You ought to refuse to mediate cases where you think someone might be harmed by the process.' Thus, dilemmas may be moral or non-moral.

While the distinction between moral and non-moral issues is interesting, it may have limited practical relevance in day-to-day practice. When faced with a dilemma, mediators may not really care whether their dilemma is a 'moral' or a 'prudential' one. For practical purposes, a dilemma is a dilemma and the goal is to resolve it. Neat philosophical points aside, many codes of ethics suggest that continued competence is essential for ethical practice. This includes admonitions that mediators have adequate initial training and continuing education. It is difficult to criticise an ethical principle that mediators should not hold themselves out as competent when they are not. The ethical concern is with keeping promises: mediators should be able to deliver what they say they can deliver. Thus, there are two related problems: one is that competency is tied to the particular values and goals of mediation which are various and often ill-defined; the other problem is the practical one of determining what is 'competent' in a field which has only just begun to be systematically studied.

What skills and abilities lead to competency?

The question of what skills and abilities are essential for competent and ethical practice is currently a vexed question. A considerable literature has grown on this and the related debates about qualifications standards. These qualifications debates (and the related debate about professionalisation) have been discussed

---

130 Stulberg, JB, 'Bush on Mediator Dilemmas' (1994) *Journal of Dispute Resolution* 1, pp 57–69.

131 Raphael, DD, *Moral Philosophy*, 1981, London: Oxford University Press, at 18.

132 *Ibid*, at 55.

at length elsewhere.[133] It is broadly acknowledged that the field of dispute resolution is in its infancy, and it is not known with any certainty what practices are effective to resolve disputes. 'There is no clear foundation from whence qualifications can emerge.'[134]

---

133 Alfini, JJ, 'Trashing, Bashing and Hashing It Out: Is This the End of 'Good Mediation?' (1991) *Florida State University Law Review* 19, at 57–75; Birkhoff, J, 'SPIDR Research Committee Draft Report to the Qualifications Commission: Research on Mediation Qualifications' in *Qualifications Sourcebook Compendium*: Prepared for the 21st Annual SPIDR Conference, Pre-Conference Session, 21 October 1993, Washington, DC: Society of Professionals in Dispute Resolution, pp 143–52; Bush, 1989, see note 4; Davis, A,'Ensuring High Quality Mediation: The Issue of Credentialling' (1992) *Conciliation Quarterly* 11, at 2–13; Duryea, 1994b, see above note 19, Edelman, J, 'A Commentary on Family Mediation Standards' (1986) *Mediation Quarterly* 13, at 97–102; Edwards, C and Morris, C, 'Competence and the Role of Standards for Neutrals' in *Alternative Dispute Resolution Practice Manual*, 1995, North York, ON: CCH Canadian Limited, at 8591–8699; English, P, 'Report and Recommendations of Certification and Standards' (February 1994) *Resolve* 7, at 1 and 14–20; English, P, *The Standards and Certification Project*, 1993, Guelph, Ontario: Family Mediation Canada; Gilman and Gustafson, 1994, see above note 7; Hartfield, EF, 'Qualifications and Training Standards for Mediators of Environmental and Public Policy Disputes' (1988) *Seton Hall Legislative Journal* 12, at 109–24; Honeyman, C, 'Five Elements of Mediation' (1988) *Negotiation Journal* 4 (2), at 149–60; Honeyman, C, 'On Evaluating Mediators' (1990b) *Negotiation Journal* 6, at 23–35; Honeyman, C, 'The Common Core of Mediation' (1990a) *Mediation Quarterly* 8, at 73–82; Honeyman, C, Peterson, N and Russell, T, 'Developing Standards in Dispute Resolution'. Paper presented at Law and Society Association Annual Conference, May 1992, Philadelphia; Honeyman, C, Miezio, K and Houlihan, WC, *In the Mind's Eye? Consistency and Variation in Evaluating Mediators*, 1990, Cambridge, Massachusetts: Programme on Negotiation at Harvard Law School; Honoroff, B, Matz, D and O'Connor, D, 'Putting Mediation Skills to the Test' (January 1990) *Negotiation Journal* 6, at 37–46; Landau, 1994, see above note 7; Maida, PR, 'Why Qualifications?' in *Qualifications Sourcebook Compendium*: Prepared for the 21st Annual SPIDR Conference, Pre-Conference Session, 21 October 1993, Washington, DC: Society of Professionals in Dispute Resolution, at 40–45; MDABC, 1989, see above note 62; Maute, JL, 'Mediator Accountability: Responding to Fairness Concerns' (1990) *Journal of Dispute Resolution* 2, at 347–69; Maute, JL, 'Public Values and Private Justice: A Case for Mediator Accountability' (1991) *Georgetown Journal of Legal Ethics* 4, at 503–35; Morris, C and Pirie, A (eds), *Qualifications for Dispute Resolution: Perspectives on the Debate*, 1994, Victoria, BC: UVic Institute for Dispute Resolution; National Institute for Dispute Resolution (NIDR) *Interim Guidelines for Selecting Mediators*, 1993, Washington, DC: National Institute for Dispute Resolution; Picard, C, 'The Emergence of Mediation as a Profession' in Morris, C and Pirie, A (eds), *Qualifications for Dispute Resolution: Perspectives on the Debate*, 1994, Victoria, BC: UVic Institute for Dispute Resolution, pp 141–63; Pirie, A, 'Manufacturing Mediation: The Professionalisation of Informalism' in Morris, C and Pirie, A (eds), *Qualifications for Dispute Resolution: Perspectives on the Debate*, 1994, Victoria, BC: UVic Institute for Dispute Resolution, pp 165–91; Riskin, LL, 'Toward New Standards for the Neutral Lawyer in Mediation' (1984) *Arizona Law Review* 26, at 329–62; Rubin, JZ (ed), 'On the Process of Dispute Settlement' (October 1993) *Negotiation Journal* 9, New York: Plenum Press; Schirch-Elias, L, 'Public Dispute Intervenor Standards and Qualifications: Some Critical Questions' in Morris, C and Pirie, A (eds), *Qualifications for Dispute Resolution: Perspectives on the Debate*, 1994, Victoria, BC: UVic Institute for Dispute Resolution, pp 79–87; Scimecca, J, 'Conflict Resolution in the United States: The Emergence of a Profession?' in Avruch, K, Black, P and Scimecca, J (eds), *Conflict Resolution: Cross Cultural Perspectives*, 1991, Connecticut: Greenwood Press; Shaw, ML, 'Mediator Qualifications: Report of a Symposium on Critical Issues in Alternative Dispute Resolution' (1988) *Seton Hall Legislative Journal* 12, at 125-36; Society of Professionals in Dispute Resolution (SPIDR), *Environmental/Public Disputes Sector. Competencies for Mediators of Complex Public Disputes*, 1992, Washington DC: The Society of Professionals in Dispute Resolution; Society of Professionals in Dispute Resolution (SPIDR), *Qualifications Sourcebook Compendium*, 1993, Washington, DC: Society of Professionals in Dispute Resolution; Van Slyck, M, *Determining Sources of Mediator Effectiveness: Predisposition, Training and Experience*, 1993, Monograph Series, New York: Research Institute for Dispute Resolution.

134 Duryea (1994b), see above note 19, at 112.

There is considerable consensus that the skills and abilities needed for resolving disputes are largely dependent on the context of mediation. For example, the skills and knowledge required for mediation of a complex public policy dispute[135] significantly differ from the skills and knowledge required for family mediation (see, for example, Landau[136]). There are many powerful critiques from those who fear that women and other cultural minorities may experience further disempowerment in society with increased institutionalisation of currently available dispute resolution alternatives.[137] Skills and models that appear to be useful for members of the dominant culture in North America may not be suitable for those from minority ethnic or cultural groups.[138]

While links between competency and ethics have been drawn, it has been fairly asked: 'competent to do what?'[139] Different contexts, values and purposes for mediation may require different skills. While impassioned discussions assert understandings of what skills are required for mediations, intuitive claims to know what is 'ethical' or 'competent' are generally based on experience in the specific context for mediation in which these claims are made. Looking at the whole spectrum of mediation models, ethical injunctions to 'be competent' are difficult to interpret reliably in a field which is still a long way from understanding what specific behaviours of mediators are effective to resolve disputes.

---

135 Susskind, L, 'Environmental Mediation and the Accountability Problem' (Spring 1981) *Vermont Law Review* 6, at 1–47; Cormick, GW, 'How and When to Mediate Natural Resource Disputes', paper presented to the Institute on Resolution and Avoidance of Disputes, 23 March, 1984, Denver, Colorado: Rocky Mountain Mineral Law Foundation; Diepeveen, B, 'Substance Abuse: The Risks Involved' (Winter 1992–93) *Interaction* 4 (4) at 5–6; Duinker, PN and Wanlin, MA, 'Attributes of Consensus Facilitators: Lessons from Some Experiences with Natural Resources in Ontario', in Morris, C and Pirie, A (eds), *Qualifications for Dispute Resolution: Perspectives on the Debate*, 1994, Victoria, BC: UVic Institute for Dispute Resolution, pp 65–77; Schirch-Elias, 1994, see above note 133; SPIDR, 1992, see above note 133.

136 Landau, 1994, see above note 7.

137 Bailey, MJ, 'Unpacking the 'Rational Alternative': A Critical Review of Family Mediation Movement Claims' (1989) *Canadian Journal of Family Law* 8, at 61–94; Grillo, T, 'The Mediation Alternative: Process Dangers for Women' (1991) *Yale Law Journal* 100 (6), at 1545–610; Hart, B, 'Gentle Jeopardy: The Further Endangerment of Battered Women and Children in Custody Mediation' (1990) *Mediation Quarterly* 7 (4), at 317–30; Landau, 1994, see above note 7; Leitch, ML, 'The Politics of Compromise: A Feminist Perspective on Mediation' in Saposnek, D (ed), *Applying Family Therapy Perspectives to Mediation* (1986–87) *Mediation Quarterly* (14/15), at 163–75; Maute, 1990, 1991, see above note 133; Rifkin, J, 'Mediation From a Feminist Perspective: Promises and Problems' (1984) *Law & Inequity* 2, at 21–22; Shaffer, M, 'Divorce Mediation: A Feminist Perspective' (1988) *University of Toronto Faculty of Law Review* 46 (1), at 162–200.

138 Avruch, K, 'Introduction: Culture and Conflict Resolution' in Avruch, K, Black, P and Scimecca, J (eds), *Conflict Resolution: Cross Cultural Perspectives*, 1991, Westport, Connecticut: Greenwood Press; Avruch, K, and Black, P, 'Conflict Resolution in Intercultural Settings: Problems and Prospects' in Sandole, DJD and van der Merwe, H (eds), *Conflict Resolution Theory and Practice: Integration and Application*, 1993, New York: St Martin's Press, pp 131–45; Barnes, BE, 'Conflict Resolution Across Culture: A Hawaii Perspective and a Pacific Mediation Model' (Winter 1994) *Mediation Quarterly* 12(2), at 117–33; Duryea, 1992, 1994b, see above note 19, Duryea and Grundison, 1993, see above note 14; Hermann, M, Lafree, G, Rack C and West, MB, *An Empirical Study of the Effects of Race and Gender on Small Claims Adjudication and Mediation*, 1993, New Mexico: Institute of Public Law, University of New Mexico; Huber, M, 'Mediation Around the Medicine Wheel' (Summer 1993) *Mediation Quarterly* 10 (4), at 355–65; Lederach, 1986a, 1986b, 1991, 1995, see above notes 16 and 19; Monture OKanee, 1994, see above note 15; Salem, 1993, see above note 17.

139 Birkhoff, 1993, see above note 133.

A PRACTICAL FRAMEWORK FOR MAKING ETHICAL DECISIONS

No code of ethics can imagine and take into account every ethical dilemma. Not only that, but codes of ethics inevitably reflect particular biases which may not be shared by all mediators in all contexts. Prescriptive codes of ethics can also lead to widespread rote development of unexamined mediation practices. This is especially so if codes of ethics do not indicate the specific contexts in which they are intended to be used, or fail to acknowledge the values on which they are based. For these reasons, codes of ethics are incapable of providing a complete or universal guide for conduct. Conduct guidelines are most useful when they articulate the contemplated purpose for mediation[140] and their underlying ethical assumptions, leaving the detailed working out to mediators in practice. Organisations can assist with this by providing ethics committees whose function is to assist mediators with ethical concerns in a facilitative manner.

A PRACTICAL FRAMEWORK FOR CONSIDERING ETHICAL ISSUES IN MEDIATION

How can mediators work through practical tensions and dilemmas in their everyday practices? As a third exercise (of the four exercises suggested in this essay), mediators can develop a framework with which to understand their values surrounding mediation and apply them to specific situations. What follows is one suggested framework[141] which might be used, developed or modified by individual mediators, groups of mediation practitioners in a business or non-profit agency, boards of directors of mediation organisations considering developing standards, and, to the extent it is relevant, by policy makers considering the establishment of mediation legislation, regulations or programmes. All or parts of this framework could possibly also be used during mediation to help parties work through ethical dilemmas facing them, or facing the mediator as a result of their situation. As such it can be a tool for the development of 'communicative ethics' as described by Cooks and Hale.[142] While the framework suggests a step-by-step process, one can likely begin anywhere and move through or around the framework in ways that suit the particular issue.

---

140 Bush, 1994, see above note 3.

141 The work of Bush,1994, see above note 3; Barsky, AE, 'Issues in the Termination of Mediation Due to Abuse' (1995) *Mediation Quarterly* 13, at 19–35; Callahan, JC and Grassey, T, 'Appendix 2: Preparing Cases and Position Papers' in Callahan, JC (ed), *Ethical Issues in Professional Life*, 1988, New York: Oxford University Press, at 465–76; Cooks and Hale, 1994, see above note 20; Davis, 1994, see above note 98; and Grebe, 1989, see above note 12, is acknowledged as providing source material for this framework.

142 Cooks and Hale, 1994, see above note 20.

A Know yourself

1 Understand your general ethical values. A brief outline of several ethical theories can be found at pages 307–17. Many people growing up in the mainstream society in Canada have never considered the basic principles on which they base their lives, their ethical values or the assumptions which underlie them. Understanding your general ethical philosophy anchors important decisions, and assists you to discern the relevance and value of advice you are given.

- do you believe in some ethical principles which you consider to be universally applicable?
- do you believe that some ethics are culturally or individually relative?
- do you believe that ethics must be determined with each new situation? If so on what basis do you decide what is ethical in each situation?
- do you believe that 'doing right' is 'right' regardless of foreseen consequences?
- what do you tend to emphasise: justice or caring; rights or responsibilities?
- what is your attitude to those who hold ethical values different from your own?

Guidance can be found through cultural traditions, religious teachings and sacred literature, United Nations principles, mediation literature and codes of ethics.

2 Understand your (or your organisation's) values concerning the practice of mediation. What are the quality goals of mediation, and your definitions of success?

- party autonomy
- party satisfaction
- community solidarity
- social justice
- social order
- personal, group or societal transformation
- cost/efficiency
- settlement rates

These options are explained at pages 304-07.

3 How do these goals mesh with your general ethical beliefs?

4 What are your (your organisation's) views concerning the following nine topics.[143]

- keeping within the limits of competency;
- preserving 'impartiality' (quotations mine);

---

143 Bush, 1994, see above note 3, at 9–10.

- maintaining confidentiality;
- ensuring informed consent;
- preserving self-determination/maintaining non-directiveness;
- separating mediation from counselling and legal advice (also described as 'role limitation'[144]);
- avoiding party exposure to harm as a result of mediation;
- preventing party abuse of the mediation process;
- handling conflicts of interest.

5 Analyse a variety of codes of ethics and read relevant literature.

6 Compare your ethical understandings with those of others engaged in the practice of mediation.

B Understand the problem

7 Define the ethical problem in question.
- what are the issues?
- outline all the relevant facts, including facts that would support any of the possible courses of action.

8 Define the moral principles and values involved in the particular issue or dilemma (eg honesty, loyalty to family or friends, keeping promises).
- the dilemma is, by definition, a problem in which a choice must be made between two principles and it seems that one cannot do both.
- some dilemmas are not really dilemmas in that the 'right' choice seems clear; the problem is that the 'right' choice is not a palatable or easy choice.

9 Define the options.
- what are all the possible decisions that could be made?
- what are the possible consequences to everyone of each possible decision?
- how grave are the consequences?

C Consider how to involve the parties

10 To the extent possible, discuss the ethical problem with the parties.
- what is the parties' understanding of the ethical dimension of the problem?
- in what ways could the problem be jointly framed by the parties?
- what ideas do they have about how to resolve the dilemma?

---

144 Davis (1994), see above note 98, at 79.

D Make decisions

11 To the extent possible, involve the parties in making the decision.

12 Make a tentative decision, reflect on it, and modify as necessary.

13 Communicate and implement the decision.

14 If appropriate, consider drafting clauses in mediation agreements to prevent future problems of a similar nature.

ETHICAL ACCOUNTABILITY

The fourth exercise for mediators involves a consideration of their interaction at the policy level with other members of the mediation community. The ethical question becomes: to whom is one accountable for ethical practice in mediation?

The development of literature on ethics and the creation of codes of ethics has its roots in concern about consumer protection in the light of the increasing institutionalisation of consensual alternative dispute resolution processes. With increasing institutionalisation come demands by governments, consumers and practitioners themselves for qualifications, practice and ethical standards. While mediators must certainly be accountable to their clients for what they do in mediation, individual consumers may have difficulty in addressing ethical concerns with mediators. Organisations of mediators have tried to address these concerns largely through the ongoing development of codes of ethics which are used mainly for educational purposes.

While this paper has its focus on substantive ethical issues in mediation, the related issue of how best to effect ethical accountability and how to deal with complaints about mediators is equally interesting. While it is beyond the scope of this essay to elaborate on the topic of ethical accountability, some brief comments are offered and some key questions identified.

All mediation associations receive complaints from time to time about the conduct of mediators. Associations can create procedures for discussing complaints with members, attempt to facilitate suitable resolutions suitable to the situation, or even remove mediators from membership. However, associations are unable to enforce accountability procedures against non-members. Conflicts can also arise when a complaint is made against a mediator who is member of a mediation association as well as another professional association. Whose responsibility is it to seek accountability from the mediator? Should it be done by the other professional association to which the mediator belongs? Or should accountability be sought by the mediation association? Or should mediators be accountable to both?

Mediation programmes and services can develop methods of seeking accountability from their staff or roster members, but what if the quality of work of an entire programme becomes an issue? How may an entire dispute resolution programme be held accountable to the community? Are evaluations conducted by funding sources conduct sufficient to ensure the ethical practice of community mediation programmes?

It is concerns such as these that have led some to suggest licensure for mediators, an idea which has been dismissed by some dispute resolution organisations.[145] With virtually no lawsuits being filed against mediators and a lack of evidence that public harm is being caused by mediators, it is difficult to put forward an case for licensure. Many mediation associations provide for certification procedures (for example, the Academy of Family Mediators), or are in the process of developing certification procedures for mediators (for example, the Mediation Development Association of British Columbia) as another way to maintain accountability for ethical and competent mediation practice.

DEBATES OVER PROFESSIONALISATION

Development of certification and accountability procedures has raised fractious debates within the field of dispute resolution. This is largely an ethical debate at the policy level. The ethical debate also raises the possibility of mixed motivation on the part of mediators. In addition to a desire to protect consumers, there is within the field of dispute resolution a strong motivation to protect the reputation of mediation itself and to protect the development of the field from non–mediator driven legislation concerning standards and qualifications.[146] In addition, some fear that the drive towards professional codes of ethics is also fuelled by the desire of mediation organisations to define and control what is meant by 'mediation' and to define and control what practices are considered 'competent' or 'ethical.'[147] Some suspect that practitioners' demands for professional standards obscure an agenda of guild formation. Pirie suggests professionalisation may be more about power, market control, prestige, elitism and patriarchy than it is about specialised bodies of knowledge and commitment to service and the interests of society.[148]

Thus there are profound ethical questions surrounding the larger question of professionalisation as it is evidenced by the continued development of codes of ethics, certification procedures and accountability mechanisms by a number of growing organisations of mediators. While different in scope, these ethical

---

145 Mediation Development Association of British Columbia (MDABC). *Brief on Standards and Ethics for Mediators Presented to the Attorney General of British Columbia.* Vancouver, BC: Mediation Development Association of British Columbia, 1989. Society of Professionals in Dispute Resolution (SPIDR), *Ensuring Competence and Quality in Dispute Resolution Practice: Report No 2 of the SPIDR Commission on Qualifications*, April 1995, Washington, DC: Society of Professionals in Dispute Resolution.

146 See Davis, AM, 'Ensuring High Quality Mediation: The Issue of Credentialling' (1992) *Conciliation Quarterly* 11, 2–13. Gilman and Gustafson, 1994, see above note 7, at 92–95.

147 Gilman and Gustafson, 1994, see above note 7, at 92–95.

148 Pirie, A, 'Manufacturing Mediation: The Professionalisation of Informalism' in Morris, C and Pirie, A (eds), *Qualifications for Dispute Resolution: Perspectives on the Debate*, 1994, Victoria, BC: UVic Institute for Dispute Resolution, pp 165–91 at 185–86.

questions are similar in nature to the ethical questions which concern actual mediations. That is, to what extent should a growing 'profession' intervene to influence the definition of mediation or the practices of individual mediators? To what extent should the principle of individual autonomy prevail in mediator selection and mediation practice?[149] Is it possible to say that there are universal 'rights' and 'wrongs' in the ethics of mediation? To what extent should a 'profession' composed of powerful organisations of mediators decide what are the goals, values and ethics of mediation? If groups of 'professional' mediators should make such decisions, on which ethical theories of which religions and cultures should they base their thinking?

The current thinking of those moving inexorably toward professionalisation does not reflect a widespread recognition of the validity of these questions. Instead, there is steady development of ethical standards which promote North American dominant culture values of individual autonomy and objectivity, without acknowledgement of the diversity of cultures and practices in the field of dispute resolution.

IS THERE A SOLID WAY FORWARD?

The increasing demand for both practice standards and qualifications, together with the debate about professionalisation and the incipient nature of knowledge within the field, makes for a great deal of uncertainty about ethical or competency standards. Nevertheless, there is no argument against the principle that dispute resolution practice should be of high quality, both ethically and technically.[150] Is there a way to resolve the tensions and move forward on solid ground?

First, given the uncertainties, perhaps the tensions should not be resolved but maintained, in order to provide an environment conducive for both studying and grappling with the issues. The ethical tensions between motives of consumer protection and motives of professionalisation should be clarified and emphasised. Second, given the growing consensus that ideal mediation practices are specific to their own contexts, including cultural contexts, there should be active resistance of efforts which suggest that certain ethical and competency standards are an adequate template for mediators across sundry jurisdictions. Third, there should be resistance to efforts that involve organisations' adopting each other's standards, furthering a monopoly on standards which marginalises minority or alternative perspectives on dispute resolution. Finally, mediation standards should not be used not to develop a powerful profession; rather mediation should be acknowledged as describing a diverse variety of processes for consensual dispute resolution. Mediators should direct their energies instead

---

149 SPIDR, 1989, see above note 57; 1995, see above note 145.

150 Herrman, M, 'On Balance: Promoting Integrity Under Conflicted Mandates' (Winter 1993) *Mediation Quarterly* 11 (2), at 123–38.

toward reflective experimentation in building high quality processes that can support and develop a community ethic of social harmony and justice.

Policy makers within dispute resolution organisations and governments need to recognise the ethical dangers inherent in mixed motivation for the development of standards. Policy makers need to develop sound practices and, if necessary, methods of accountability which do not at the same time foster prestige-building and monopoly-seeking by opportunists who see mediation as an opportunity to be part of 'a growth industry.' Policy makers need to beware of moves toward an elite, exclusive, formalised profession. Instead policy makers should include in the discussion the perspectives of those who are committed to being part of a diverse yet mutually accountable community devoted to understanding, promoting and enhancing both the skills and ethics of peacemaking.[151]

CONCLUSION: THE TRUSTED MEDIATOR

This paper has raised a number of complex questions, starting out with the broad questions: What does it mean to be 'ethical' and how is this question to be answered in a multi-cultural society? Who makes (and who should make) ethical decisions in mediation and in the broader field of mediation?

OVERARCHING PRINCIPLES: ARE THERE ANY UNIVERSALS?

Are there any universal principles? Michelle LeBaron Duryea's research tried to draw together a cross-cultural list of qualities of trusted mediators. Her project revealed the importance of trust, credibility and legitimacy in selection of mediators. The factors that contribute to trust, legitimacy and credibility may vary from group to group.[152] The overarching principles Duryea located in her literature search on conflict resolution across cultures boil down to the universal needs for respect, caring, and procedural fairness. What these mean may vary within different contexts and cultures.[153]

The dominant dialogue in North America is located within a policy framework which values individualist self-determination and assumes the possibility of individual objectivity. This paper has challenged the value both of these concepts, especially in increasingly multicultural settings.

---

151 For some practical suggestions about how this might be accomplished, see Morris (1994), at 20–22; Edwards, C and Morris, C, 'Competence and the Role of Standards for Neutrals' in *Alternative Dispute Resolution Practice Manual*, 1995, North York, ON: CCH Canadian Limited, pp 8613–24; SPIDR, 1995, see above note 145.

152 Duryea, 1992, see above note 19; Duryea and Grundison, 1993, see above note 14; Lund *et al*, 1994, see above note 25, at 37–38.

153 Duryea, 1992, *ibid*; Lund *et al*, 1994, *ibid* at p 26.

In North American societies, the primary discourse on mediator ethics is largely couched in the terms of 'impartiality' and 'neutrality.' The concepts buried within the terms 'impartiality' and 'neutrality' point to culturally specific constructions of the overarching principles of respect, caring and procedural fairness. It is hoped the discussion in this paper shows that continued discourse focusing on these rich, but variously conceived terms may be confusing, and should be replaced by discussion of the concepts that underlie these terms.

ETHICS AND INTERACTION

Finally, the dominant discussion has its central focus on the role of the mediator to the exclusion of the role of parties in ethical considerations. Ethical tension is inevitable among parties and mediators who may not share similar values. This ethical tension is also evident among groups of mediators in which there is ethical diversity. The tension cannot be entirely resolved by suggesting that there are overarching universal principles of interdependence, mutual respect, caring, and procedural fairness which affect mediation. These terms represent concepts that may be both intangible and variously interpreted.

The concept 'communicative ethics' may be of assistance in steering through the conundrums and complexities. Rifkin *et al* have proposed the adoption of a new and different discourse for mediation in which the mediator's role is 'to facilitate the production of a coherent narrative' by managing the process of story telling. The mediator is acknowledged as 'an active participant in the construction of the narrative'. Using the discourse of storytelling,

> the end goal of mediation can be redescribed as the construction of agreements in a discourse that empowers both the disputant and the mediators; that is, allowing agreements to be constructed in the absence of the conflicting demands of neutrality.[154]

Cooks and Hale suggest similar principles for the discussion of ethics in mediation. They argue

> that recognition of the discursive construction of mediation should be at the centre of any attempt to define a set of ethics or, at the very least, central to the explication of the ethical dilemmas extant in mediation. The term *discursive construction* refers here to the interactions and communicative challenges that define and describe the process of mediation for the parties (disputants and mediators alike). These interactions and communicative challenges constitute the reality of the mediation process, at least for the participants, and thus define the ethical accomplishment of a mediation.[155]

The discussion of ethics in mediation can be enhanced by expanding it to include not only mediators, but also the parties. This recognises the dynamic nature of the interaction among parties and mediator during mediation, as well as the fact that

---

154 Rifkin *et al*, 1991, see above note 58, at 162.
155 Cooks and Hale, 1994, see above note 20, at 56.

the very presence of a mediator transforms the dispute from a dialogue among parties (a two-way dialogue in the case of two parties) to a three-way dialogue in which the mediator is not just a passive participant but an active and influential agent of change to the very nature of the dialogue. The very presence of the mediator transforms the discussion from a discussion polarised among the parties to a discussion which is reframed and re-constructed through the third parties' interventions (and choices concerning non-intervention). Since conflicts are often essentially polarised differences in ethical interpretations of past acts or proposed plans, the discussion in a mediation may often be in essence an ethical discussion. The mediator's role is that of an active participant in trying to facilitate the creation of a transcendent and coherent ethical framework within which to resolve the problem peacefully and fairly. It does need to be acknowledged, however, that this transcendent framework may not always be found, and that respect requires that people's deeply held ethical values cannot be compromised.

The most important point for discussions of ethics in mediation is the fact of human interdependence. Human beings are not isolated, independent, autonomous units, nor are they independent from the environment and other living things. They live in interdependent and interactive communities. It is increasingly obvious that the whole world community shares in this interdependence. Therefore, theories of ethics which emphasise individuals over community (and individual rights over responsibility to others) do not reflect either the realities or the necessities of human social interaction, mutual care and interdependence. The ethical imperative for the creation of ethical policy in mediation will not be to prescribe 'impartiality' or 'neutrality', but to ask relevant community leaders, policy makers, mediators and parties what qualities of a process and process leader engender trust and demonstrate respect, caring and fairness.

13 THE TRAINING OF POTENTIAL MEDIATORS

ALAN SHARP★

This chapter argues that potential mediators need first to be highly skilled negotiators and that training is necessary for the desirable level of skill to be developed. It considers first, why training is needed at all; and then the general nature of the training required including some general principles underlying the design of training in order to develop skills. It goes on to look at the particular aims of training in negotiation, its content and its method. Finally it considers the question of monitoring progress in skill development, both during training and subsequently.

THE NEED FOR TRAINING

Before considering what sort of training might be helpful to those invited to act, or offering their services, as mediators, it is useful first to consider why training should be needed at all. If we start from the principles of training in general, it is clear that in any field of activity, there is a need for training when someone's equipment in skills (rather than in ability) is not adequate for the task to be undertaken. This generally arises when a person is called on to face a task at a different level of difficulty, or because some change in the task to be undertaken leads to the need for new skills. The particular question with which we are concerned is whether the task of mediating is sufficiently *different* from what those who are likely to be called on to mediate have previously been doing, that it requires the development of new and additional skills.

Members of the legal profession – who are the focus of this paper – have much experience of trying to get disputes resolved, whether through negotiating on behalf of clients out of court or representing them during litigation. It might be argued that such experience should equip them well for mediating between two (or more) parties in order that a mutually acceptable agreement can be reached out of court; that is, that all the skills needed for mediating will already have been developed in the normal course of events.

However, while that experience is relevant and useful, there are good reasons why it should be regarded as insufficient. The task of advocating the case in court as the representative of one client, and therefore with a particular loyalty to that client, is quite different from facilitating agreement between two or more parties, where no greater loyalty is owed to one than to another. Negotiating on behalf of a client, while it calls for many skills necessary for the task of mediating,

---

★   Director, Coverdale Organisation Scandinavia.

is still different from acting as an independent to mediate an agreement between two or more parties. This is particularly so when a case is negotiated with the parties, and their representatives, having very firmly in mind that it will still go to litigation if no agreement is reached. In such circumstances, as discussed later, there is a tendency for the representatives to focus very largely, if not exclusively, on the rights of their own client and adopt a negotiating approach that would not be helpful to a potential mediator. While training in negotiation is an essential prerequisite for acting as a mediator, some further training in mediation itself is needed to supplement this.

THE NEED FOR MEDIATION TRAINING

In order to answer the question 'what sort of training and for what particular skills?', it is useful to look at how the need for mediation arises in the first place. Presumably it comes about because the parties to some difference or dispute find it impossible by themselves, for whatever reason, to reach a mutually acceptable agreement. The issue in dispute is also presumably one where no one party sees themselves as able to enforce their will (or, even if he/she does think that is possible, nevertheless prefers not to do so): that is, if progress towards resolving the dispute is to be made, the agreement of all parties is needed.

The least costly, quickest and most satisfactory method of resolving any dispute is of course for the parties themselves to reach a good negotiated outcome. However, situations often arise where the parties are unwilling to negotiate or have insufficient skills to do so successfully. If a third party is able, through skilful intervention, to facilitate a good negotiated outcome, one that is durable and based on a sound precedent, in all or most circumstances this should offer the next best alternative. Skilful intervention implies being able to identify specifically what is preventing the parties moving towards a possible agreement, diagnosing the underlying causes of these difficulties and of the parties' failure to reach agreement, developing approaches for tackling these causes, and planning and implementing ways of applying those approaches. In effect a third party has to provide those very skills that the parties have not been able to provide for themselves.

Unfortunately, too often the parties' first action is not to go to an independent third party but for each to employ an agent, invariably a legal representative, to act on their behalf. The latter's main aim will be to secure as favourable an outcome as possible for his/her own client, just as it would be if the case goes subsequently to litigation. Since the negotiation takes place in 'the shadow of the law,'[1] with each lawyer therefore likely to focus on what they see as their own party's 'rights' and the probability of a court finding in their side's favour, they may well fail to secure a negotiated settlement, even when it is possible, that

---

1   An expression originally coined by Muookin, R and Koruhauser, C, 'Bargaining in the Shadow of the Law: the Case of Divorce' (1979) 88 *Yale Law Journal 950.*

would have been preferable for the client to the subsequent judgment. In the UK, it is not uncommon for legal costs to exceed the amount awarded in judgment, even when a case is 'won'. Lord Justice Woolf, appointed by the Lord Chancellor in March 1995 to review the current rules and procedures of the civil courts in England and Wales, has suggested that anyone seeking the services of a lawyer should expect complete answers to these three questions: the prospects of success; the likely total cost; and the time the case will take. At present he or she is likely to get an answer only to the first question. In *Access to Justice – Interim report to the Lord Chancellor*, Lord Woolf noted:

> Many of those who make their living by conducting litigation accepted that they would not be able to afford their own services if they had the misfortune to be caught up in legal proceedings (Chapter 3 para 17).

and

> The problem of disproportionate cost occurs throughout the system. It is most acute in smaller cases where the costs of litigation, for one side alone, frequently equal or exceed the value of what is at issue (para 18).

By contrast, an independent third party has as a main aim to *effect* an agreed outcome, which is judged by each party to be better than any alternative open to them without the agreement of the other party or parties, including going to court. To a mediator it is usually litigation that is an alternative to a mediated or negotiated settlement, and none of the parties should have recourse to it unless they have a probability, realistically assessed, of securing a judgment more favourable to them than can be worked out through a negotiated or mediated settlement. Such an assessment should take into account the costs and time likely to be involved in litigation.

If mediation is to be carried out competently, it is important that only those who have been trained act as mediators. An unskilled negotiator will be an incompetent mediator, and an incompetent mediator will do no more than delay proceedings, leading to increased costs, and may even worsen the situation by causing the parties to harden even further in their positions. For that reason there is a strong argument in favour of some form of accreditation for mediators.

Important skills required by any mediator are those of a *highly skilled* negotiator. 'Highly skilled' because:

- one of the reasons a mediator's services are needed is that the parties and their representatives, where employed, have been unable to reach agreement; and
- assisting others to reach agreement requires a significantly higher order of skill than the parties possess themselves. 'Higher' because it requires an even deeper understanding of the necessary skills to get others to do something effectively, than it does to do it oneself. Thus the training a potential mediator needs is training in the skills of negotiation, supplemented by training in applying those same skills as an independent third party.

GENERAL PRINCIPLES OF TRAINING DESIGN

If training is necessary and if that training is to assist the development of skills relevant to negotiating and mediating effectively, it is useful to set out important general principles which provide the basis for training design. These are applicable whether the particular skills are those of leadership, teamwork, co-operating with others, negotiating with others or mediating between others.

The first important principle to keep in mind when designing training is that helping people develop skills is different from providing them with knowledge or information. Skill development is concerned with the application of knowledge, not just its acquisition. It is concerned with learning to *do something* more effectively in practice, not with knowing about something or even with knowing how to do it in theory. At the end of a training experience it is important that people go away better able to do something, not merely able to describe it.

An implication of this is that training in negotiation and mediation can only be effective if it provides ample opportunity to practice. Just as you cannot learn to swim or ride a bicycle or drive a car skilfully without repeated efforts of trying to do so, you cannot learn to negotiate or mediate just by listening to lectures. A further implication is that any training experience needs to be of adequate length to provide for sufficient practice. While one may be able to provide information about key ideas and principles in a few hours, experience suggests that three to five days is a minimum for people to try those ideas out in order to gain a proper understanding of what it means to apply them, and to begin to do so. It is unrealistic to attempt to design a course in negotiation that is any shorter than this, and to it needs to be added further time exploring how to apply the same skills as a mediator.

A second important principle relevant to skill development is that the development of real and lasting skill only takes place with experience over time in actual situations, as opposed to the simulated situations which have to be used during a training course. Much can and needs to be done to help to establish a sound base during a training experience, but the important further development takes place afterwards. That means that, above all, people should leave a training course better able to learn from their own experience so they do keep on learning and developing increased skills.

A third principle is that whether one is concerned to work better with others, to negotiate agreement with others or to mediate agreement between others, learning to do so involves going through repeated cycles of preparing, doing and reviewing. In more detail this implies:

- observing what is happening and how it is happening;
- diagnosing or interpreting what is observed;
- identifying what needs doing in general terms in the light of the diagnosis;
- planning in detail how to do it;
- implementing the plans and observing the effects (and hence into a new 'cycle').

Using this general 'systematic approach'[2] for tackling anything forms the basis for learning, regardless of the particular skills someone needs to develop. Any training design needs to ensure that participants get into the habit of following such a cycle. By doing so they will both learn during the training, and will keep on doing so afterwards.

THE AIMS AND CONTENT OF TRAINING IN NEGOTIATION SKILLS

When we turn to consideration of the specific aims that negotiation training must be designed to meet, it is useful first to identify why many people, even with much experience of trying to resolve disputes, experience great difficulty in doing so effectively.

Some directly observable symptoms are:

- The parties themselves focus on arguing about their respective 'rights', what they will or will not accept in the way of resolution, and/or become so angry or upset with each other that they cannot discuss the issue sensibly.

- The parties place the matter in the hands of their respective legal advisers thus

  o effectively removing themselves for the present from further direct negotiation, and

  o setting an expectation that the case will 'go to court' unless an out-of-court settlement is reached.

  Therefore any negotiations take place in what has been described as 'the shadow of the law', with a consequent emphasis on the 'rights' of the respective parties.

- Assuming that the lawyers each believe that their own client has some 'right' on his/her side, they are each likely to focus in any negotiation on presenting their own client's position as favourably as possible (just as they would do in any subsequent litigation).

- This makes it difficult for the lawyers to negotiate any agreement that lies outside the positions now taken up, which are almost certainly incompatible or else presumably the parties would not still be in dispute. As a result when, as in the great majority of cases, settlement is reached before going to court, it tends to be very late, even 'at the courtroom doors'. This may well be after considerable costs in legal fees to the clients and often to the dissatisfaction of one or even both clients, who only agree because of the further costs of continuing and not because they see the agreement as meeting their interests well.

---

2   For a more detailed description of this approach, see Babington Smith, B and Sharp, A, *Manager and Team Development*, 1990, p 13, Butterworth Heinemann.

- If either after, or preferably before, going to separate lawyers, the parties do go to a third party to mediate, problems may still ensue. If the mediator is untrained he or she may focus initially on trying to get them to clarify their positions, in the hope that one or both can be persuaded to make some concession. The risks of locking them into those positions are obvious. The more I am invited to clarify my position, the more I am likely to convince myself that it, or something very close to it, is the only 'right' and just solution.

If we look for some underlying causes of these particular symptoms, possible diagnoses are as follows:

- One immediate cause is the widespread belief that negotiation is about working out your own side's 'position', focusing on presenting your strengths as favourably as possible, marshalling arguments in favour of your position and attacking the other side's position; and then trying to persuade, bargain with or even threaten the other party in order to get as close as possible to the achievement of your position. That is, you will concede as little as possible while extracting the maximum possible from the other side.

- One reason for this belief may be the fact that much conventional education is concerned with what have been called 'closed' problems,[3] where there is sufficient data available to solve them; that is, a known solution exists and what we have to do is to find it. This conventional approach encourages us to want to treat every situation in this way. The effect on a negotiator is to lead him or her to work out a desired outcome based solely on his/her information and perceptions, without taking any account of those of the other party, and usually without any dialogue with them.

- Unfortunately the basic education of lawyers does little to discourage this widespread belief. Working in the adversarial system of the courts, with its 'winning' or 'losing' judgments, almost certainly further encourages it.

- Thus as a result of both education and experience very many lawyers have what has been described as a 'positional bargaining'[4] approach to any negotiation in which they become involved. In addition, without appropriate training they are likely to carry this into the way they mediate.

It is obvious that the broad aims of negotiation training must be to enable participants to improve their skills so that they are better able to arrive at and to facilitate better negotiated outcomes. It should also leave them better able to keep refining those skills in the future. When we take into account the commonly observed symptoms and underlying causes of ineffective negotiating set out above, some more specific aims for training would include the following:

---

3   See *Manager and Team Development*, see above note 2, p 355.

4   For a description and critique of this approach, see Fisher, R, Ury, W and Patton, B, *Getting to Yes – Negotiating Agreement without Giving In*, 2nd edn, 1991, Penguin.

- To increase participants' awareness of:
  - the way people negotiate and its effect on the results achieved
  - their own negotiating behaviour and the implicit working assumptions that underlie it
  - different approaches to negotiating, their advantages and disadvantages.

All those attending a training course will already have experience of negotiating, some of them a considerable amount. Above all, training needs to provide them with the opportunity of stepping back and taking a fresh look at how they, and others, negotiate. It is very difficult to improve the way anything is done without an awareness of how it is being done at present. Therefore training must encourage participants to observe how they negotiate as a basis for working out and testing ways of improving.

- To offer some useful concepts for thinking about negotiation:
  - a framework of key elements to assist the diagnosis of difficulties
  - a general orderly approach to preparation
  - some common vocabulary or language for discussing the process of negotiating.

As participants observe their own and others' efforts, they usually find it helpful to have ways of organising their thinking in preparation before negotiating, in diagnosing what is happening during a negotiation and in review afterwards.

- To draw attention to common underlying causes of difficulty and success in negotiating and to offer some 'rules of thumb' and some 'tools' for overcoming the difficulties and extending the successes. There is probably no 'best' way to negotiate in all circumstances but experience drawn from a wide range of different settings, countries and cultures suggests some helpful guidelines.[5] Every negotiator will want to develop his/her own 'rules of thumb' and 'tools' with increasing experience. However it can be helpful to be introduced to some that others have found useful.

- To provide opportunities for participants to:
  - practise preparing, negotiating and reviewing
  - observe how they negotiate and compare observations with each other
  - bridge the gap between theory and practice, between what people say they know to be sound in theory or in principle and what they do in practice.

If participants are to go on learning from their own experience after a training course, they need to be encouraged to develop the habit of doing so in a self-conscious manner during the course.

---

5   See generally the work of the Harvard Negotiation Project at Harvard Law School; and *Getting to Yes*, above note 4.

If a course is successful in pursuing these aims, by the end participants should be better able to:

- vary their approach to negotiating according to the situation
- prepare for negotiations in an orderly and thorough way
- diagnose what is happening during a negotiation and work out how to tackle any obstacles to reaching a good agreement
- continue to learn from their own experience of negotiating.

Obviously the aims of any one training programme dictate its content, but typically a training workshop needs to cover the following areas:

- the negotiation process, its aims and its means
- the distinction between substantive issues, procedural issues and issues related to how the parties are interacting. In considering any negotiation we can look at the content (what it is about), the methods or procedures the parties are following (how they are trying to tackle the issues), and the interaction between them (how they are dealing with or behaving towards each other)
- how to judge 'success', what constitutes a 'good' outcome
- the key elements of effective negotiation
- different approaches to negotiation, advantages and disadvantages, when and how to use them
- how to prepare for a negotiation, individually, with a client and as part of a team
- how to manage the face to face discussions
- how to put oneself in the other side's shoes
- issues of perception, emotion and communication
- common causes of difficulty and 'rules of thumb' for avoiding or overcoming them
- how to negotiate as an agent or through an agent and managing dealings with clients.

TRAINING METHODOLOGY

Since a major part of the training time needs to be spent in practising negotiating, this raises the need for 'activities' or simulations to act as the necessary vehicles for this practice. Typically 'cases' are used, with written information provided for each party, so that participants negotiate in the light of the information they are given. The cases are not 'case studies' in the sense that they contain important 'lessons' or information to be conveyed to participants via their content, although the way they are written may tend to raise particular issues when they are negotiated; their importance is as vehicles for practising and studying the process of negotiating. After each exercise, participants need to compare observations with those with whom they have negotiated, and subsequently with the rest of the participants on the course. These reviews are used by the training faculty both to encourage the identification of useful 'lessons' by the participants themselves and, where relevant, to provide short inputs on useful ideas, concepts, methods.

With the exception of providing such short inputs, the job of the training faculty is to coach and facilitate, particularly during review sessions, to encourage the testing of ideas or theories, and to elaborate, illustrate and demonstrate points as appropriate. In short the main emphasis of their contribution is on assisting the learning of participants and coaching for increased skill, rather than on 'teaching' theory.

Negotiation exercises and cases can be drawn from many different contexts, legal to personal to business and international, and involve negotiating one-to-one, in teams or through agents. Experience shows there is benefit in some of the exercises being drawn from contexts that differ from those of the participants' usual work, since this can assist focus on the process of negotiating as opposed to the substantive issues involved in a particular case.

MONITORING PROGRESS DURING TRAINING AND SUBSEQUENTLY

Since training is concerned with helping participants to modify their behaviour and to develop increased skill, it is important that trainers look for signs that trainees are, for example:

- observant, distinguishing between issues of substance, procedural issues, issues of interaction between the parties, identifying specific successes and difficulties in the way negotiations are conducted
- purposive, focusing on what needs to be achieved in the future and underlying interests
- able to diagnose or interpret underlying causes of successes and difficulties
- able to propose general approaches for tackling causes of difficulties and for extending causes of successes
- able to develop ways of trying out those approaches
- actually trying out both 'lessons' drawn from earlier negotiations and the ideas, concepts and tools introduced by the training staff.

While some development in skill should be observable during a training programme, as pointed out earlier, significant improvement can only come about over time and with repeated experience. The implication is that training needs to be followed up afterwards by reviewing with participants their efforts to apply 'lessons' they derived from their training and encouraging them in their efforts to build on experience. For a period after training such reviews between trainers and participants are useful not only in monitoring whether the trainees are actually trying to apply 'lessons', but also in helping them to keep on learning.

Anyone going through this kind of training in negotiation skills should find it much easier to act effectively as a mediator. The great majority of lawyers will not be able to do so without such training. The reason for this is clear. The prime concern of a mediator is to facilitate a good outcome, not to arbitrate between the parties. Ideally this is best done by coaching the parties to arrive at an outcome themselves, on the grounds that in general people are more committed to implementing agreements they have negotiated themselves than in ones presented to them. Coaching others to negotiate effectively requires the skill to demonstrate the necessary behaviour oneself. Hence the need for training in negotiation.

However something more is required for a mediator to be effective. While the ability to demonstrate basic mediation skills is essential, in negotiation these are applied at a personal operating level. Helping someone else to develop those same skills can be seen as applying them at a higher level. Being purposive oneself involves asking oneself the right questions and clarifying one's own thinking. Helping someone else to be purposive involves asking questions of them in an effective way and assisting them to clarify their own thinking. Similarly, negotiating well requires the application of the skills of observing and listening, of interpreting and diagnosing, of proposing, of planning and implementing. Mediating involves steering, guiding and coaching *others* to apply those same skills. A mediator tries to encourage the parties to behave in ways he or she would if negotiating as either of them. For this reason further training in mediation itself, in applying the same basic skills and facilitating good negotiated outcomes, but as a third party, is also important. This is the subject of the next chapter.

Suggested further reading

Manager and Team Development by Bernard Babington Smith and Alan Sharp (Butterworth Heinemann, 1990) includes fuller description of ideas and principles underlying the development of skills in general.

Getting To Yes – Negotiating Agreement Without Giving In by Roger Fisher, William Ury and Bruce Patton (2nd edn, Viking Penguin, 1991) is particularly important for its description of a method of 'principled negotiation' and its benefits compared with 'positional bargaining'.

International Mediation: A Working Guide – Ideas for the Practitioner by Roger Fisher with the help of William Ury (1978 obtainable from The Program on Negotiation Clearinghouse at Harvard Law School) is intended 'to stimulate a mediator looking for some ways to loosen up a conflict situation or move it forward'. It contains useful ways of categorising and diagnosing negotiating problems as well as ideas for tackling them.

Clearinghouse Catalog from The Program on Negotiation Clearinghouse, 518 Pound Hall, Harvard Law School, Cambridge MA 02138, USA, contains details of teaching materials on negotiation and dispute resolution available from the Clearinghouse, including a large number of cases and exercises.

14 MEDIATION: THE TRAINING COMPONENT

JANINE HIGGINS*

WHY MEDIATION TRAINING IS NECESSARY

Mediation can be magical. There are times where parties who have seemingly been at war can come to an understanding of the other's position and develop mutually satisfactory solutions to their dispute.

Yet, other times, parties leave mediation unfulfilled, sometimes feeling they have been coerced, sometimes that they have wasted their time. Practitioners in jurisdictions where mediation is mandated sometimes say mediation is merely a procedural hurdle that does not increase the likelihood of settlement.

What differentiates these mediations?

In large part, the difference is the mediator. My thesis is that the mediator's training can significantly affect the outcome of and client satisfaction with the mediation process. The elements of training that make mediation most effective are as follows:

- the use of a model or structure for the mediation process;
- teaching communication skills to facilitate effective communication;
- teaching mediator interventions to facilitate the parties' shift from positions to interests;
- providing extensive opportunities to practice the model and the skills and receive feedback;
- providing a supportive learning environment where participants are willing to take risks and try new skills.

KEY SUCCESS FACTORS FOR EFFECTIVE MEDIATION

Let us consider what makes mediation work most effectively. Some of the mediator's 'tools' are fairly obvious and would be used naturally by most people who are interested in mediation. These include:

- mediator listening;
- analysing risk ('if you don't settle, what are your chances of winning? How much will it cost you to proceed?');
- compromise ('why don't you two meet halfway?');
- mediator creativity ('perhaps you could try this?');

---

* Mediator and trainer in private practice in London, Ontario.

- meeting with each party separately in turn, to separate bickering parties and to suggest shifts in position in a way that permits face saving ('caucus').

Mediation which employs these tools only will produce a resolution more frequently or sooner in the process than if no mediation were used. However, mediators who use only these instinctual tools will not be nearly as successful as those who use other, less instinctual, interventions and communications techniques.

Furthermore, the level of client satisfaction will not be as high if only the above methods are used. Rather than creating a solution themselves, clients may have been cajoled or worse, pressured into accepting a compromise. Compromises reached in resignation or under pressure do not tend to mend fences or promote the mutual understanding which can be one of the sources of client satisfaction in mediation.

Finally, the above methods do not promote optimal solutions. They may produce a settlement that ends litigation but nonetheless fails to meet the parties' needs in a truly satisfactory way, and in many cases a better solution could be found for both parties. In addition to reduced levels of party satisfaction, this may lead to a reduced level of compliance with the settlement terms, especially if more is required of a party than an immediate payment of money.

The elements of successful mediation that do not come naturally to would-be mediators, but which can make a significant difference in the outcome of a mediation, are as follows:

- the parties invent their own solution to the problem;
- solutions are not discussed until the issue in dispute is fully explored;
- the parties feel heard and understood with the result that their ears become open to hearing the other party's viewpoint and their minds become open to logic;
- there is a shift during the mediation from the parties' positions (the demands or proposed solutions they come in with) to the parties' interests (their needs, concerns, hopes and desires); and
- psychological factors and procedural complaints are considered, not just the substantive issues.

Before turning to the training methods that produce these results, let us consider each of these elements further to see why they make a difference, and why mediators need training before they will include these elements in their mediations.

The parties invent their own solution to the problem

Would-be mediators, generally people who are interested in problem solving, are often very good themselves at designing solutions to problems. It is baffling to them when disputants resist these well-crafted solutions. It does not come naturally to take the longer route and go with the parties' solution, especially if it is not the one which seems best to the mediator.

The parties' involvement with determining the outcome increases the likelihood that they will reach settlement since most people are more likely to accept their own ideas than someone else's. An additional benefit is that people are more inclined to support and work towards the implementation of a solution they thought of. Ideally, both parties have actively shaped the final resolution.

Solutions are not discussed until the issue in dispute is fully explored

This is a difficult shift for most people enrolled in mediation courses, especially if their background is oriented to action, decision and advice. Frequently these individuals want to get to solutions immediately. However, acceptable and optimal solutions are best created after the parties have sufficient 'building blocks' to create an acceptable and optimal resolution. The building blocks most critical to creating 'win/win' resolutions are the underlying interests of both parties, the needs, fears and aspirations that motivate each of them and which will need to be satisfied to some degree. New information which allows a party to construct potential settlement options or to re-evaluate their case can also provide building blocks. Objective criteria against which to measure possible solutions also constitute building blocks for resolution since they facilitate face-saving shifts in viewpoint that can be defended to others.

If these building blocks are not discovered, impasse is often the result. Even if there is resolution, it may be a grudging resolution that is barely acceptable to both parties: that is, one similar to the conclusion produced by a court.

People feel heard and understood so that their ears become open to the other party's viewpoint and their minds open to logic

The mediator's job is to ensure that each party explains what is important to them and why. Parties in disputes usually feel contradicted, not heard. When people do not feel heard they tend to repeat themselves, as the old song goes, 'second verse, same as the first; a little bit louder and a little bit worse'. This behaviour can be unreasonable and even irrational. In many mediations, once one party (often the feistiest, most difficult one) truly feels heard, he or she will sit back and listen and really understand the other's viewpoint, think logically and analytically, and even be ready to accommodate the other's needs. People who feel they have been genuinely understood will also be more open to discussions with the mediator or their lawyer about their options and to consider risk analysis of their alternatives.

Taking steps to ensure that someone feels heard is not, however, the natural instinct of most would-be mediators; in fact quite the opposite. When someone is being illogical or unreasonable, the natural reaction of most people is to point out the flaws in the speaker's position, and to carefully outline a more logical approach. They worry that acknowledging the speaker's strongly felt statements will signal agreement and cement the person even more firmly in the unreasonable position. Alternatively, they may feel that restating what has been said is redundant since the speaker's meaning was clear.

It is not obvious to most of us that we will be more successful in convincing another if we acknowledge their feelings or viewpoints first. Failing to use this tool can lead to impasse where a key to settlement is the risk and cost of litigation, but where the party who should be persuaded is not open to persuasion because he or she has not felt heard.

Shift from the parties' positions to their interests

Effective mediation sessions move from the parties' positions (the demands or proposed solutions they come in with) to the parties' interests. Instead of arguing who is right, the focus is on the parties' respective needs and priorities so that win/win solutions can be crafted. Focusing on rights usually generates win/lose options which the 'loser' tends to reject.

Unfortunately, training in debate and exposure to academic discussion tends to make would-be mediators focus on positions, either attacking or defending them. Attacking and defending positions tends to polarise parties. Shifting the discussion to interests, on the other hand, helps to bring them together or at least to increase the number of possible options for resolution.

Training in law or an adjudication background often means that potential mediators instinctively focus on rights not interests. Rights are usually argued from a positional viewpoint in the sense that parties' preferred solutions are supported by legal argument about their rights. However, when the parties' needs or interests are brought into the open, the opportunities for meeting both parties' needs increase exponentially.

The mediator's difficulty is that people are sometimes reluctant to reveal motivating factors since to do so seems weak to them. However, the reason people cling tenaciously to positions is because the positions satisfy their interests; they meet their unstated needs. Failing to understand this leads the would-be mediator to deal with the issues in the way the parties present them rather than looking behind the parties' words for the underlying interests. Training in the theory of interest-based negotiation is helpful to mediators in highlighting the need to shift off positions to interests. However, simply understanding the need for the shift does not in itself provide the would-be mediator with the tools to facilitate this shift.

Examine psychological factors and procedural complaints as well as substantive issues

Disputants rarely reveal the procedural or psychological issues which are driving the conflict, but getting to these factors often means the difference between a successful and an unsuccessful mediation. These underlying factors may seem too 'personal' or off-topic to potential mediators and are therefore avoided, to the peril of the mediation process.

Training in law and other fact-based disciplines usually includes training in 'relevancy'. Keeping the parties' discussion to what is relevant to the substantive issues frequently does not get to the nub of the problem. In mediation, avoiding the tough issues (which may be procedural and/or psychological issues) is often an indication that impasse will result.

MEDIATOR TRAINING

This section discusses what are the ingredients of a mediation training program. These ingredients fall into three main categories: firstly, the mediation model, or how to structure the discussion; secondly, what I sometimes refer to as 'the mediator's toolbox', including the communication skills and interventions that facilitate the most productive discussion; and thirdly, elements of a training programme that allow participants to develop a new paradigm for approaching conflict and conflict resolution.

The mediation model

The number of stages in an effective mediation process or model is somewhat arbitrary since the various stages of the process could easily be grouped in many different ways. In my own training sessions, I teach a four-stage model.

Stage one is the mediator's introduction of the process to the parties. The mediator tries to set a collaborative tone, make sure everyone is introduced, describe the mediator's role, describe the roles of the parties (that is, if possible, to arrive at their own resolution with which they are both satisfied), discuss confidentiality, confirm that the people attending have authority to settle (and if not clarify whether the mediation should proceed), set out guidelines for communication, and get the mediation contract signed.

Stage two is the time for the parties to make opening statements and for the mediator to propose an agenda for the discussions and obtain agreement on the agenda.

Stage three is the heart of the mediation. This is the stage in which the building blocks for resolution are revealed to the parties and the barriers to resolution are removed.

The mediator's most difficult task in stage three is to discover the parties' underlying interests. This facilitates each party clarifying what needs and aspirations they would like met through the resolution to the conflict, and more importantly helps each understand what needs and aspirations of the other party must be satisfied or partly satisfied in order to make a resolution satisfactory to them. In addition, stage three facilitates the sharing of information that may be needed by the parties to assess their risk, to consider what is reasonable and to create options.

Along the way, the mediator also attempts to remove barriers to resolution. One technique is to clarify assumptions. Another is to shift the discussion from the general to the specific in order that more precise problem-solving can occur. Additionally, the mediator clarifies misunderstandings about the meaning of key words. The mediator can also encourage the parties to 'park' areas of disagreement and move on to another point.

Another element that can be included in stage three is the use of objective criteria. If it is possible for the parties to agree on standards that are derived from sources other than themselves, they can justify a shift in their positions to others outside the mediation and also save face within the mediation.

Stage four is comprised of two main elements. The first is the generation of multiple options and the second is finalising the agreement. The purpose of developing multiple options is that the parties are more likely to be able to find a resolution that satisfies both of them from a long list of options than they are from a short list (comprised simply of 'my way' and 'your way'). Additionally, developing a list of options frequently sparks creativity so that a more optimal solution may be created by someone after hearing several possibilities.

From the list of multiple options, the mediator works with the parties to consider which options meet their interests and are realistic. The mediator again works from the general to the specific and asks who, what, when, where, and how questions to ensure that the agreement is clear. Depending on who is present at the mediation, either the parties' lawyers or the mediator will write up the agreement and ask the parties to sign it.

Mediators should not be slavishly devoted to adherence to this or any other model. They need to be open to considering adjustments to meet the needs of particular individuals and situations. However, to learn mediation without any model at all is akin to being at sea with various means of propulsion but with no charts to follow; one may or may not end up where one wants to go.

Furthermore, in my view one of the strengths of this model of mediation is that it postpones a discussion of solutions until the issues are fully explored. Negotiations often fail because each side wants to hear the other's bottom line. Unfortunately, when parties hear offers without an understanding of the interests the offers satisfy, or the information on which the offers are based, they can be insulted rather than satisfied. Tensions may be heightened by the transmission of offers before thorough exploration of the issues.

The mediator's toolbox of skills

In addition to understanding a process to follow, would-be mediators must also have a range of tools at their disposal to ensure that the discussion throughout the process is a productive one.

Mediators need a thorough grounding in communication skills. For example, it is important to understand the elements of non-verbal communication. Such an understanding allows the mediator to pick up non-verbal cues from disputants which can be critical in some mediations. The mediator also learns how to ensure that his or her own non-verbal communication is helpful.

Active listening skills are also vital to mediators. Mediators need to train themselves to be accurate listeners. Through paraphrasing and summarising, they can give disputants comfort in the process and encourage more openness by assuring speakers they have been accurately heard. Paraphrasing and summarising key points made by one party also helps the *other* party accurately understands what is being said.

Empathy plays an important role in mediation as well. Mediations can be blocked by unacknowledged emotion. When a mediator effectively uses empathy to acknowledge a party's strong feeling, the intervention can facilitate the party moving past an emotional block towards better listening and, ultimately, problem-solving.

It is also important that mediators understand how to frame questions. The goal in mediation is to elicit information and interests. In normal conversation and in many professional settings, closed questions (those that can be answered by 'yes' or 'no') are by far the most common way of eliciting information. Unfortunately, closed questions have two problems in mediation. The first is that they limit the area of inquiry to what is in the mediator's mind.

> Example: Q: 'Does the contract contain a provision about this situation?'
>
> A: 'No.'

Asking the question in an open manner may yield more helpful responses.

> Example: Q: 'In your view, what criteria should guide the resolution of this issue?'
>
> A: 'Well the contract doesn't mention it specifically, but I think the way we've done business in the past sets a precedent. Additionally, insurance disputes face similar issues and the way insurance companies deal with them is ...'

The second difficulty with closed questions in mediation is that they frequently imply a judgment by the speaker, a problem where the mediator is trying to ensure neutrality. Continuing with the example above, the question, 'Does the contract support your suggested approach?' may suggest to the listener that the mediator thinks that if the contract does not support the approach, the approach is invalid. A further problem is that the listener may give the answer the mediator wants or appears to want, rather than a more accurate shading on their viewpoint, or the facts.

Mediators should also use questions to shift parties from positions to their underlying interests. Therefore, the content of open questions is also important. Questions that ask about concerns, hopes, fears, value, importance, impact are more effective than more vaguely worded open questions like 'what is your viewpoint on ...?' In addition, questions about expectations and assumptions can facilitate the removal of negotiation barriers caused by misunderstandings about motive or procedural elements to disputes. Questions are not the only tool used to shift from positions to interests. Paraphrasing, reframing and probing are also important in this transition.

In addition, questions and other tools are needed to move the discussion from the general to the specific. Mediators need to learn how to probe.

> Example: 'What does "custody" mean to you?' or
>
> 'You mentioned that you would like a fair process. What would a fair process look like to you?'

Other tools, besides questions, also help in probing. These tools include the use of silence perhaps accompanied by an expectant look, minimal encouragers to say more such as 'go on' or 'yes ...'. Paraphrasing key comments also prompts many speakers to give more specific information or an example or to reveal the motivation for the statement, thus revealing an interest.

Mediators must also learn to reframe negative statements made by parties. Reframing is the art of making the speaker's words more hearable to the other party or more productive for the process, all without being inaccurate. Parties resent having the mediator mis-state what they said and put it forward in a way that is inaccurate and seems to be what the mediator wishes they said. However, the mediator can put a negative statement into a positive frame and still be accurate.

> Example: 'It's unfair that you made the decision without even consulting me.'
>
> Reframed: 'You would like to be sure the decision-making process is fair and to be consulted before decisions are made.'

The former statement might be perceived as an attack that required a defensive response. The reframed statement is less likely to provoke a defensive response. The best reframes include the parties' interests. The speaker's interests in the above reframed statement were fairness and being consulted.

Mediators need to understand how to recognise and then deal with resistance shown by the parties. In addition, an understanding of how anger affects negotiations and how to manage the process when anger becomes an element is important in many mediations. Tears can also be present in mediation and would-be mediators need to know when to ignore tears, when to stop the process and when to continue moving on.

Another important tool for the mediator is caucus, or separate meetings with individual parties. This can be a very helpful intervention. The mediator needs to understand when to use caucus, how to introduce caucus, what to say and what not to say in caucus, and to have developed a protocol for confidentiality in caucus.

Finally, mediators need to develop techniques and tools to ensure that they always maintain their neutrality. There is nothing so precious to the mediator as neutrality, yet would-be mediators frequently do things the parties perceive as non-neutral. For example, mediators sometimes use the language of one party to frame the issues for the agenda, or begin a caucus by asking a party to respond to what the other just told the mediator in caucus, or make eye contact with one party more than the other. The mediator needs a solid understanding of ways in which neutrality is safeguarded. The concept of neutrality must be stressed throughout training sessions since it should pervade every element of mediation.

Facilitating a 'paradigm shift'

Collaborative problem-solving methods are new to many participants in mediation courses. Participants frequently experience a shift in their personal approach to conflict and conflict resolution. Mediation training should include elements that facilitate this shift. Examples of these elements include lectures on the principles of collaborative or win/win problem-solving, stories of unexpected but clearly optimal solutions arrived at through an interest-based approach, and the use of games or exercises.

Playing the role of a disputant in a role play can trigger an 'aha' moment for some participants. When they experience the way in which sound mediation techniques facilitate collaborative problem-solving, the value of using these techniques becomes apparent. It is not uncommon for a person playing the role of the disputant to express some surprise about how effective the process is, even though when they started in the role they were determined to defend their original position.

Demonstrations can also facilitate this paradigm shift. Where course participants observe a mock mediation, they frequently wonder how the conflict as presented can be resolved and come to a slow realisation that an approach quite different from their usual approach to negotiation is slowly moving parties in conflict towards resolution. A course that does not include a demonstration of an effective mediation runs the risk that participants in their own role plays will be unskilled and the role players will not feel that the mediation process is effective. The longer the course and the more coached role play time, the less likely this will be a problem.

Another element that must be included in training designed to facilitate this paradigm shift is ethics. If we have a new way of approaching the resolution of conflicts in a largely unregulated industry or profession, inculcating ethical standards in future mediators is very important.

MEDIATION TRAINING METHODS

'Say, show, practice' is the principle which should guide mediation training. Brief seminars almost invariably concentrate on the 'say' element. The lecture portion, what the trainer says, gives the participants a theoretical understanding of the issues. This provides a critical underpinning to the training, but in itself is completely insufficient.

Some concepts in mediation are not obvious, especially since participants have to un-learn some of their previous professional training. The lecture component can assist participants to grasp this element and, as mentioned above, the show or practice components can deepen one's understanding of new concepts. However, perhaps the most important reason for including the show and practice component is that the hardest part of learning to mediate is not getting the ideas into one's head, but getting what has been successfully understood by one's brain to come out of one's mouth. Of course, it is what comes out of the mouth (or, just as importantly, what doesn't come out of the mouth) that makes or breaks a mediation.

The feature lacking in much mediation training, especially short courses, is 'practice'. I have been a participant in many short mediation courses. I have also been a mediation trainer and coach. My observation is that almost no one is beginning to mediate effectively before their fifth day of training, even with practice built into each day. Without practice, I would question whether any mastery of the process will be achieved. Could one learn to drive by reading a thorough manual and observing someone else drive?

A learning curve looks something like this:

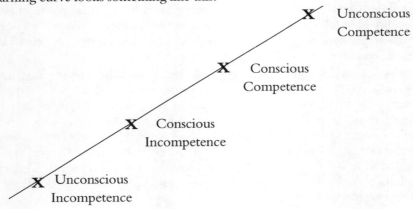

Would-be mediators want to be on the far right of this curve. While it is unlikely that training alone will produce that result, it should produce those who are consciously competent. However, without significant practice, cours? participants do not achieve that skill level. Unlearning old habits is incredibly difficult. Without practice and feedback, it is nearly impossible.

Learning on the job, in actual mediations conducted following training, does not guarantee that trainees will solidify the new skills they heard about during training. If trainees do not get their new skills to 'come out of their mouth' during training, then under the pressure that a real mediation brings they will likely fall back on their old ways of doing things. The result will be that their mediations will tend to include only the obvious elements of mediation and not those elements which must be learned. More impasses can then be expected.

The single most important feature of training, therefore, is practice, enough practice to solidify new habits so they can be repeated under pressure. Doing something over and over 'the wrong way' is not helpful, so the practice I refer to is role play or other exercises under the watchful eye of a coach who is skilled in mediation. Through re-enforcement of what worked well and constructive comments on what could be changed, participants' mediating techniques are shaped.

Coaches should have the same broad philosophical approach to mediation as the trainer since it is very confusing to participants if the coach is somehow undermining the trainer's work. At the same time, it is also helpful for participants to be exposed to different coaches so they see variations in style, again re-enforcing that there is no single correct way to mediate.

DESIRED LEARNING OUTCOMES

In order to make mediation as effective as possible, by the end of their training would-be mediators should have a thorough grounding in and an ability to effectively utilise the following:

- a process or model they can use to facilitate the resolution of disputes;
- communication skills which ensure that the parties feel heard and understood, in order that they can get on the 'logic track';
- an understanding of what fuels conflicts, including psychological or procedural factors and mistaken assumptions;
- a range of methods for eliciting and recognising the parties' underlying interests (as compared to their positions);
- listening skills including how to listen without judging, how to make the parties feel understood, how to acknowledge without agreeing (being empathic and neutral at the same time), and how to listen accurately;
- appropriate questioning skills;
- an understanding of ethical considerations.

Mediation training is vital for all would-be mediators to ensure that the full potential of mediation is achieved. Mediation training should provide participants with the skills set out above through a combination of lectures, demonstrations and, most important of all, guided practice.

15 MEDIATION FUTURES

Professor *KARL MACKIE**

Mediation practice over the last 10–20 years has grown like a silent revolution across the globe. Its presence is now felt in influencing the agenda of public legal systems, commercial disputes, family, neighbourhood and environmental conflict resolution, not to mention a resurgence of its role in international diplomacy in the Middle East, Bosnia and Northern Ireland.

For those of us involved in the 'mediation movement' (I am careful about using this phrase now after a City lawyer friend chided me for its quasi-religious overtones) the journey has been fascinating and challenging. There is undoubtedly much further to go to realise the potential of the 'sleeping giant' of the dispute resolution spectrum. Views on this potential differ amongst mediators, from those who are content with work to sharpen it as a pragmatic tool of legal practice, to those who sense a capacity to effect a social transformation in society's coping mechanisms for social conflict. Also, the future of mediation will be driven by deeper social agendas than that of mediators, but such is the pace and interlinked character of change in modern society, that one has to accept that the 'mediation project' will flow in unpredictable ways. My outline of mediation futures therefore is less one of crystal ball gazing and overarching schemes, than of 'airing' some important themes and suggesting possible outcomes or actions on these themes. I hope this will help stimulate not only debate and reflection amongst users, but also point to opportunities for developing future practice in the field.

BACK TO THE FUTURE

It is intriguing how little has been written on the topic of the history of mediation. This is all the more remarkable given the emergence of mediation as a social phenomenon within the last 20 years, expressed across a rich variety of settings, including international conflicts, family, community, schools, labour relations, victim-offender, consumer small claims, civil litigation, environmental conflicts and commercial disputes.[1]

Mediation is a 'recent' phenomenon primarily in the sense of the explicitness of its promotion and practice by enthusiasts in the separate sectors. In other senses of course, mediation is centuries old. However the confluence of the various tributaries of action has created the effect of a river-swell, the 'mediation movement', that has changed and is changing the structure of the 'grievances,

---

*   Chief Executive, CEDR; Professor in ADR, University of Birmingham, England.
1   See Mackie, K, *A Handbook of Dispute Resolution: ADR in Action*, 1991, London: Routledge.

negotiations, disputes and justice' landscape, as well as leading to a reappraisal of its own strengths, vulnerabilities and, as some might say, dangerous undercurrents.

The fact that many of these tributaries do appear to have separate sources confirms that mediation is more than a passing phenomenon. It suggests that what we are witnessing (or participating in) stems from a deeper social impulse to fill a 'gap' in society's needs and carries the potential of radically transforming our institutions of, and attitudes to, conflict management. In the corporate or commercial sector, for example, one can point to the rapid transformation of business practices and the ensuing need for dispute resolution techniques that are fast, flexible and customer oriented rather than the rigid, producer-driven systems of traditional litigation.

The 'magic' of mediation works on at least two levels, first in its ability to transform individual cases, and second as an expression of potential for social transformation. The former domain is now better charted than it once was while the latter remains a more elusive and often unrecognised or unspoken aspect of the development of mediation practice.

The excitement of mediation futures is a compelling topic but I therefore start it with a plea to historical scholars to help us chart our roots better. Even to chart the recent social history of mediation, and the factors which drove the leaders of the field in various sectors, would extend the richness of our sense of mediation as a practice and profession. At least one commentator has also articulated three 'epochs' within the emergence of mediation practice: the 'first church' phase of missionaries promoting the field; the 'pilot project' phase of legal/social experimentation; and more recently the 'institutionalised practice' phase where mediation flows into the mainstream of legal and social practices.

MODELS OF MEDIATION PRACTICE

The growth of mediation as a practice is likely to intensify the search to define mediation and to articulate the various models and practices that exist under the label of mediation. This search will be influenced by the emerging claims of mediation practitioners to be regarded as a social group justifying resource allocation and recognition as a 'profession', as well as by the differing historical roots of different areas of mediation practice. The difficulty is exacerbated by the limited theoretical underpinning of mediation practice, 'all very well in practice but where's the theory?'[2] One can oversimplify the differences but there is a sense that family and community mediation tend to reflect origins in counselling, social welfare, communication or pacifist traditions. This 'model' of mediation, one might call it 'purist', stresses the facilitative role of the mediator both in theory and in associated language. Mediators 'facilitate communications', 'empower parties', and 'transform conflict'. Sometimes this emphasis extends into shared assumptions

---

2   See Fuller, L, 'Mediation – its Forms and Functions' (1971) *Southern California Law Review* 44, at 305.

on the effective tactics of the mediator, with stress on joint meeting rather than shuttle diplomacy, on 'managing anger' rather than 'doing the deal'.

By contrast, labour conciliation/mediation and mediation associated with corporate disputes and civil litigation tend to reflect a more 'pragmatic' rather than a purist approach. Indeed even the theoretical 'discipline' associated with mediation of corporate disputes and civil litigation, (not labour mediation however which has longer historical roots in 'conciliation'), is described differently. ADR (Alternative Dispute Resolution) is often used as the generic term in this area rather than 'mediation'. The irony within this is that the most commonly used and fastest growing ADR approach in civil litigation as well as in corporate/commercial disputes is mediation, despite earlier US stress on the 'mini-trial'.

Mediation literature in the corporate/litigation context tends to talk of the role of mediation in helping parties 'save time and costs' rather than 'transform conflict', and enabling parties to 'control the outcome' rather than of 'empowerment'. 'Getting to a deal' or 'settlement of actions' is the prized target in this domain, although sometimes ADR is also promoted for its capacity to achieve 'creative outcomes' or assist 'continuing business relationships'. This divergence from a purist model of mediation is further compounded by differing interests fuelling the growth of ADR; lawyers seeking to avoid loss of litigation business or seeking a new career in an associated area, judges and politicians seeking to curtail the growth of court costs and claims.

The ultimate divergence from the purist model of mediation is found in the growth of 'evaluative mediation' as a differing emphasis from 'facilitative mediation' (sometimes described as 'rights-based' as opposed to 'interest-based' mediation). In evaluative mediation, the mediator may give the parties a view on the merits of the case if it went to trial (or more generally on the rights or fairness of the claims). This capacity to give an opinion is more formalised in ADR techniques such as 'rent-a-judge', early neutral evaluation, the 'mini-trial'. While there is limited data on this, some commentary suggests that US and Australian mediation practice has increasingly shifted towards an evaluative mediation approach in relation to court-annexed mediation, despite early stress on the power of facilitative mediation.

This divergence of mediation sectors, in their historical roots and nature as well as in their social contexts of practice, often leads to a sense of unease between the differing sectors. It may lead ultimately, as in previous eras of counselling and therapy, to a clash of 'models' or a sense of 'betrayal' of roots. Such a development would also no doubt spring in part from the need for different sectors to carve out a slice of the social resources cake (including business and professional resources) that may be available as mediation grows in credibility.

I would not want to overdo the potential for conflict in the field. The growth of the various sectors also offers greater opportunities for cross-fertilisation of ideas and practice to the greater benefit of all. The tensions between the contexts and models of practice are, however, likely to be reflected in academic scholarship that further refines the distinctions rather than synthesises the practice.

I would suggest therefore that the future of mediation will gain most if mediators live by their own counsel. Rather than taking 'positions' on different models of mediation practice, mediators need to recognise the richness within mediation practice and the potential to call on a variety of approaches, tools and techniques according to what is most uniquely appropriate for the parties, the context of dispute, and the mediator.

The touchstone of the conflict between differing models of mediation tends to rest on the notion of 'evaluation', and is well demonstrated in recent debates over the terms of a code of conduct being drawn up by the Society of Professionals in Dispute Resolution.[3] Evaluation, however, is not itself a simple concept. Certainly there may be a clear element of evaluation in a mediator putting forward a professional view of the merits of a case. However, arguably evaluation is also present whenever mediators choose (or not) to put forward questions reflecting what they regard as important issues, or when they attempt to assist parties move from 'positions' to broader 'interests' agendas. And if both parties choose to seek an evaluation from a mediator with expertise to give it, is this not consistent with party control or empowerment?

The tensions between the models of mediation and within the definition of evaluation lead to frequent confusion amongst researchers, practitioners and users. A recent example landed on my desk in the form of a request for mediators for a court pilot scheme. The request contained the injunction that the pilot scheme would be based on a 'facilitative' model of mediation practice, but that only lawyer-mediators (ie those with legal, evaluative expertise) should be nominated if both parties were unrepresented.

Observing the development of debates within the growing field of mediation, I am reminded of reading many years ago a study on schools of psychotherapy. The researchers reached the conclusion that while the therapists' dialogue and rhetoric differed according to their 'school', the practice of the therapists with their patients varied very little. Studies of practising mediators prominent in different fields in the USA led Deborah Kolb and her associates to a similar conclusion.[4] They went on to suggest as I have done that future theory in the field should avoid starting from pure theoretical models, but should rather focus on the complexity and richness of existing pragmatic practice. Judging mediation 'effectiveness' in terms of simple bipolar constructs such as 'evaluative' and 'facilitative' can underestimate both the richness and the reality of much mediation practice. For example, mediators can be evaluative in relation to party 'interests' as much as to party rights. Similarly it is inappropriate to appraise the

---

3   SPIDR, *Model Standards of Conduct for Mediators,* 1995, Washington: SPIDR.

4   Kolb, D *et al, When Talk Works: Profiles of Mediators,* 1994, San Francisco: Jossey-Bass; for a contrasting approach promoting a 'school' of mediation, see Bush, RA, and Folger, JP, *The Promise of Mediation: Responding to Conflict through Empowerment and Recognition,* 1994, San Francisco: Jossey-Bass.

role of the mediator in consensus-building in an environmental dispute by the same yardstick as that of a mediator in a commercial case where the parties are engaged in bargaining in the shadow of the court.

Regardless of how the debate develops on evaluation and on contrasting models of mediation, the involvement of more practitioners in this field will assuredly mean enrichment of knowledge of mediation practice. This will occur not only because of the insights increasingly springing from research and from reflective practitioners, but also as mediation draws on the development of understandings from related fields, law, counselling, negotiating theory, group and personal dynamics. While there is a need to avoid oversimplification of the facilitation-evaluation (or settlement/empowerment) debate, undoubtedly a research agenda for the future should help to tease out the assumptions that mediators (and parties) bring to the process and begin to delineate the ways such differences impact on case management and outcomes. The aim of mediation trainers should be to grow more skilful in assisting would-be mediators draw on a wide range of strategic tools.

ACCESS TO JUSTICE

A major factor underlying the growth of mediation practice has been establishing a linkage into existing 'institutional' systems, pre-eminently court procedures. Mediation is also however extending its reach into government practice and the practice of regulatory authorities, tribunals and Ombudsmen. The process has gone furthest in the USA with widespread court-annexed mediation or arbitration (both binding and non-binding) schemes.[5] Other jurisdictions, including Australia, Canada, and the UK, have followed with more limited experimentation.

The growth of such schemes has proved a meeting point for the articulation of inherent tensions within mediation practice, and of the nature of mediation as a 'profession'. These issues include (in addition to the contest of 'models' described earlier) the role of lawyers versus non-lawyers; regulation and ethics; selection and training; fee-based versus *pro bono*; meeting criteria of client needs or system efficiency; interest-based outcomes versus rights-based outcomes.

Equally such debates feed back into debates on the role of the state and of court systems in ensuring cost-effective access to justice. The managers and funders of the system tend to give greatest weight to the potential for mediation to reduce the costs and delays that are afflicting judicial systems globally; proponents of mediation tend to emphasise the capacity of mediation to 'enrich' the quality of civil justice procedures and outcomes. Perhaps more often such schemes are propelled, as most human behaviour, by apparently mixed motives. In any case

---

5   See CPR Institute for Dispute Resolution, Civil ADR: *Elements of Program Design*, 1992, New York: CPR.

each side seems only too pleased to have the opportunity to justify the case for reform by inclusion of the others' rhetoric.

The growth of mediation has coincided with (and contributed to a sense of) an emergent global 'crisis' of public resources for judicial systems. This crisis has allowed state and judicial systems to welcome ADR experimentation alongside other attempts at reform of litigation practice, usually by way of case management and closer management of public funding of access to justice. Case management and budget management initiatives have in turn provided a practical base for further extending court-annexed mediation schemes.

Despite the fragmented, *ad hoc* and at times 'amateurish' annexation of mediation practice to court systems one should not underestimate its potential significance. Not only have varying streams of mediation begun to flow together. Adding this momentum to the slow-moving, grand old river of the justice system, creates a potential which is as yet unpredictable but could be the basis for a profound transformation of 21st century legal systems. Indeed parallels have been drawn between the growth of ADR as a juristic phenomenon and the growth of Equity in the common law system in England.[6]

In part this potential may be realised by the impact of mediation theory and practice on the thinking of lawyers and the judiciary. In part the impact is expressed in the formal reform of court practices to incorporate court-annexed procedures, personnel and outcomes. On a more profound level, ADR practices are leading to a rethink of conceptions of justice and of the role of the courts. The ultimate expression of this is the notion of 'the multi-door courthouse',[7] where court staff introduce claimants or potential claimants to one of a series of doors deemed 'appropriate dispute resolution' for the case in question. In the process, concepts of 'justice' become transformed in a way that jurists and legal academics have yet to grapple with, and moving beyond the legal formalism of procedural descriptions of how a mediation works.

The future stable structures to emerge from this period of innovation and experimentation are uncertain. Partly this is because it is a period when most participants are still finding their feet with the new processes; partly it is the problem of finding adequate channels of interaction between the emergent informal mechanisms and profession and established structures; partly it is a problem of the evaluation and measurement of the outcomes (cost-savings or quality) of the new procedures compared to older procedures – which themselves have often had little evaluation or measurement – to provide effective comparison criteria.

Despite these difficulties, it is certain both that we are witnessing a remarkable global manifestation of a rethinking of litigation practice, and that further

---

6   David, J, 'Alternative Dispute Resolution: What is it?', 1986, conference paper, Canberra, AADRA.

7   Goldberg, S, Sander, E and Rogers, N, *Dispute Resolution*, 2nd edn, 1992, Boston: Little Brown.

experimentation, with all its promise alongside inelegance and failures, is likely to be the norm into the 21st century. While greatest experimentation is at present evident in the common law systems,[8] it is also likely that mediation will impact on the less adversarial civil law systems of Europe,[9] and will re-awaken and merge with traditional consensual approaches in Asian legal systems.

PROFESSIONALISATION AND INDUSTRY STRUCTURE IN MEDIATION

There can be little doubt of the growth of mediation as a professional concern for many individuals. Harder to predict will be the forms within which this emergent profession is regulated by way of ethical codes, training, and state regulation. There is a point in the growth of professions where there is an increase in attempts by practitioners to stake their proprietorial claims to the uncharted territory they have helped colonise. This tendency is reinforced as professional activities begin to integrate, overlap or be sold to the public at large, or to public institutions such as the judicial system, when concerns about standards and quality become manifest. Despite a certain sense of sociological inevitability around such developments, two features complicate the mediation professional horizon – the nature of mediation and the 'industry structure' of mediation practice.

Mediation is a service offered to parties in dispute, to assist them to transform their conflict and to reach an agreement on how they do this. It is thus inherently a more difficult 'sale' than most professional services requiring at least two persons to commit to a service at a time when they are inherently disposed to be critical or mistrustful. Frequently the 'purchasers' making the decision are more than two individuals – friends and family in the background of family or community disputes, professional or business advisers in the case of litigation or commercial disputes. For the service provider, there are therefore high costs in helping the process get started, in selling it, and in sustaining it.

It could be argued therefore that in a free market for mediation services, there is limited opportunity to exploit even individual consumers. The main justification for regulation of mediation therefore reduces to more special case arguments: where agreements may affect third parties (particularly children); where easy entry into the market (as in court-referred schemes) may confuse potential users as to the 'properly qualified' service providers; where unrepresented individuals might have unjust agreements imposed on them by non-expert evaluative

---

8   For a recent review in England, see Legal Action Group, Smith, R (ed), *Achieving Civil Justice: Appropriate Dispute Resolution for the 1990s*, 1996, London: LAG.

9   See Mackie, K, *The Use of Commercial Mediation in Europe* in WIPO Conference Proceedings on Mediation, 1996, Geneva: World Intellectual Property Organisation.

mediators or by mediators happy to ignore major imbalances of power between the parties in brokering 'unfair' deals.

A more specific manifestation of the professionalisation agenda comes in the 'turf wars' between existing professions to lay claim to mediation practice. Most evident in the family mediation sector, the struggle arises from a sense of threat to existing domains of control and generally takes the form of a contest between the legal profession and non-lawyers. At a general level, the 'mediation movement' has undoubtedly helped establish the principle that mediation skills are not the exclusive preserve of any one profession. However, equally effective in most jurisdictions has been the legal profession's capacity to recover ground and absorb mediation practice into the lawyer's professional tool kit for disputes, particularly disputes associated with, or part of, litigation actions.

A review of prospects on the professionalisation of mediation is also complicated by the absence of significant research or scholarship on the 'industry structure' of mediation, on the number and nature of mediators, on the range of modes of practice delivery, on the funding and business form of services. This question is further complicated by the issues addressed earlier in this paper: the variety of sectors of practice; the uncertainty of how mediation will link into court actions or be absorbed by the legal profession. At one extreme are the self-help, voluntary schemes that work with community disputes, at the other the major private ADR firms serving the US corporate sectors. A range of private consultancies, professional firm specialists and non-profit institutions populate the area between these two extremes.

For reasons outlined earlier, the initial 'market' for mediation as a new technology is not an easy one to establish. Mediation at a societal level therefore tends initially to be propelled by voluntary groups, by academics, by foundations and non-profit institutions and state-funded pilots (the 'mix' varying between jurisdictions). US practice tends to confirm that beyond this stage there is scope for full-time commercial mediation practice to be sustainable by mediation firms and professionals, although this is less pronounced to date outside the scale of the US system.

From the perspective of one who has watched this field develop in the UK (from an alternative model of a non-profit institution), the capacity of mediation to attract enthusiasts because of both its 'human' challenge and its income potential makes it a fascinating area for research and development. The industry structure of mediation practice justifies as much future research attention as does the content of practice, but seems unlikely to receive it given the narrower research interests of socio-legal scholars or other professionals attracted to mediation.

MEDIATION AND SOCIAL TRANSFORMATION

Greatest interest in mediation has been expressed in relation to 'legal' and individual disputes. Given the prominence of 'dispute resolution' within the practice of lawyering, this is not surprising. Nor is it surprising, given the ideological traditions of legal practice, that this interest is expressed less in terms of social change than in terms of procedural pragmatism or legal formalism. However, this may conceal the potential of mediation to have a greater impact on social mores and social institutions.

Even within the limited framework of discourse on mediation as a procedure, training and scholarship sometimes neglect the wider aspects of mediation practice. Most emphasis is given to the 'mediation meeting'. Yet the effectiveness of a mediation is determined by the processes and organisations which 'bring the parties to the table' and ensure an initial 'settlement momentum', as well as by the skills and qualities of mediators and of parties and their advisers. Significant within this is the role of mediation advocates and institutions in attracting wider social credibility to the mediation process. This is gradually ensuring a change of mindset in the practice of lawyers, judges and other social groups. At a broader social level, it is conceivable that we are witnessing the early stages of a global rethinking on the management of social conflicts, which will ultimately transform the nature of, or mechanisms for, national and international dispute resolution and management. The flexibility of mediation surely opens up such a prospect given sufficient commitment and persistence by its advocates. The range of sectors now being touched by early mediation efforts reinforces such a 'post-pragmatist' notion of the mediation movement.

The models and structure of the mediation practice of the future, the development and professionalisation of the various fields of mediation, the linkage between mediation practice and social institutions delivering justice, all of these will remain compelling topics for those of us working in the field. The future is nearly always different from what most of the experts predict, but perhaps the encouraging aspect for mediators is that the very core of our practice encourages us in the belief that while the future may be unpredictable, it is certainly negotiable.

INDEX

AAA, ABA, SPIDR. *Model
Standards of Conduct for Members*, 321, 325, 329

Academy of Family Mediators.
*Standards of Practice for Family
and Divorce Mediation*, 323–24

ACAS, .170

Access to justice. *See also* Woolf, Lord. *Access to
Justice*
alternative dispute resolution,	376
case management,	376
courts,	375–76
government,	375
litigation,	376
United States,	375

Accountability
complaints,	342
confidentiality,	334
ethics,	334, 342–45
mediators,	342–45
professionalisation,	343
standards,	344

Alternative dispute resolution
access to justice,	376
building and construction disputes,	146–53
Canada,	87–127
community mediation,	281
complaint-mediation in professions,	255–56, 262–63, 268, 270, 272
growth,	373
labour relations,	87–127
United States,	378
water disputes,	233, 243, 250

Arbitration
building and construction disputes,	144–45, 151
ICC,	151
labour relations alternative dispute resolution,	88, 104, 106 112, 113
Romans,	145
UNCITRAL,	151
United Kingdom,	145

Australia
building and construction disputes,	154

community and neighbourhood
disputes mediation,	169, 197
complaint-mediation in professions,	253
evaluative mediation,	373
family mediation,	54
personal injury mediation,	27, 33–34
Victoria,	253

Autonomy, 313–15

Bias, 318–32, 346

Building and construction disputes, 129–57
alternative dispute resolutions,	146–53
arbitration,	144–45, 151
Australia,	154
Canada,	155
case study,	8–11
causes,	139–43
civil rights,	9, 10
conferences,	144
construction industry,	
definition,	129–30
operation and organisation,	135–38
structure,	131–32
contract,	8–9, 143–45
demand,	130–31
design and build,	137
dispute resolution advisor,	148
Dispute Review Boards,	147
economic features,	130–31
employees,	132–33
employers,	151
European Union,	133–34
Finland,	155
foreseeability,	9
Germany,	155
good faith,	142
Hong Kong,	147, 148, 149, 155
India,	155
information,	142
insurance,	151–52
Ireland,	155
Japan,	156
legal profession,	152
litigation,	8–11
management,	138
mediation,	11–15, 129–57
mini-trials,	148
negotiations,	139, 141–42, 147, 151